European Monographs in Social Psychology

Understanding attitudes to the European Community

T0381616

European Monographs in Social Psychology

Executive Editors:
J. RICHARD EISER and KLAUS R. SCHERER
Sponsored by the European Association of Experimental Social Psychology

This series, first published by Academic Press (who will continue to distribute the numbered volumes), appeared under the joint imprint of Cambridge University Press and the Maison des Sciences de l'Homme in 1985 as an amalgamation of the Academic Press series and the European Studies in Social Psychology, published by Cambridge and the Maison in collaboration with the Laboratoire Européen de Psychologie Sociale of the Maison.

The original aims of the two series still very much apply today: to provide a forum for the best European research in different fields of social psychology and to foster the interchange of ideas between different developments and different traditions. The Executive Editors also expect that it will have an important role to play as a European forum for international work.

Other titles in this series:

Unemployment: its social psychological effects by Peter Kelvin and Joanna E. Jarrett.
National characteristics by Dean Peabody
Levels of explanation in social psychology by Willem Doise
Experiencing emotion: a cross-cultural study edited by Klaus R. Scherer, Harald G. Wallbott and Angela B. Summerfield

Understanding attitudes to the European Community

A social-psychological study
in four member states

Miles Hewstone

Department of Psychology,
University of Bristol

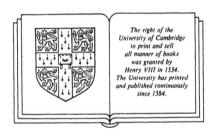

The right of the
University of Cambridge
to print and sell
all manner of books
was granted by
Henry VIII in 1534.
The University has printed
and published continuously
since 1584.

Cambridge University Press

Cambridge

London   New York   New Rochelle

Melbourne   Sydney

Editions de la Maison des Sciences de l'Homme

Paris

CAMBRIDGE UNIVERSITY PRESS
Cambridge, New York, Melbourne, Madrid, Cape Town, Singapore,
São Paulo, Delhi, Dubai, Tokyo, Mexico City

Cambridge University Press
The Edinburgh Building, Cambridge CB2 8RU, UK

Published in the United States of America by Cambridge University Press, New York

www.cambridge.org
Information on this title: www.cambridge.org/9780521154956

© Maison des Science de l'Homme and Cambridge University Press 1986

First published 1986
First paperback edition 2010

A catalogue record for this publication is available from the British Library

Library of Congress Cataloguing in Publication Data

Hewstine, Miles.
Understanding attitudes to the European Community
(European monographs in social pychology)
Includes index.
1. European communities - Public opinion.
2. European Economic Community - Publis opinion.
3. Public opinion - European Economic Community
countries. I. Title. II. Series.
JN15.H44 1986 341.24′2 86-6149

ISBN 978-0-521-32165-5 Hardback
ISBN 978-0-521-15945-6 Paperback

TO MY PARENTS
who showed me Europe

and

TO THE MEMORY OF JOS JASPARS (1934–1985)
who taught me research methods

I don't like it. I don't like it. When you open that Pandora's box, you will find it full of Trojan horses.

(Ernest Bevin on plans for European unity)

Am Rhein, da wächst ein süffiger Wein –
der darf aber nicht nach England hinein –
   Buy British!
In Wien gibt es herrliche Torten und Kuchen,
die haben in Schweden
nichts zu suchen –
   Köp svenska varor!
In Italien verfaulen die Apfelsinen –
laßt die deutsche Landwirtschaft verdienen!
   Deutsche, kauft deutsche Zitronen!
Und auf jedem Quadratkilometer Raum
träumt einer seinen völkischen Traum.
Und leise flüstert der Wind durch die Bäume...
   Räume sind Schäume.

(From *Europa* by *Kurt Tucholsky, 1932*)

Contents

x   *Contents*

List of Tables

List of illustrations

Foreword

by Ronald Inglehart

This study provides a new perspective on public attitudes toward the European Community. The author, Miles Hewstone, develops a penetrating analysis of mass orientations toward a set of institutions that play an increasingly important role in western European politics but, as this study demonstrates, remain almost incredibly little known among the general public, more than three decades after their inception. Bringing a social psychologist's insights to bear on this problem, Hewstone integrates his work with a well-balanced account of previous research and then goes beyond it to provide an interpretation of how members of the French, Italian, German and British publics perceive the European institutions; this account is clearer and more complete than anything previously available.

Hewstone's study comes at a time when the entry of Spain and Portugal has expanded membership in the European Community to twelve nations – and raises the question whether the Community can successfully integrate the publics of these two new member nations into seeing things from a common European perspective; or whether the European consensus that seemed to be emerging in the 1960s is doomed to be submerged beneath the claims of a multiplicity of narrow national interests.

The question is a pointed one because it is clear that the Community has been markedly more successful in developing a European perspective among the publics of the six nations that formed the European Coal and Steel Community in 1952, and then the Common Market in 1958, than among the publics of the four nations that joined them in the 1970s. This contrast between the relatively solid pro-Europeanism of the publics of the original six, and the much more divided state of attitudes among the publics of the four new members cannot be attributed simply to some aspect of national character, such as an inherent insularity on the part of the British. Quite the contrary, time-series evidence indicates that, in the early 1950s, the British (together with the West Germans) were markedly *more* favourable to European unification than were the Italians or French. The rift in attitudes that opened up between Britain and Europe only emerged later. It appeared after a number of years of generally positive common experience within the European Community had led to the development in France and Italy of a pro-European consensus so broad that it included even the electorates of the Communist parties, who had originally been extremely suspicious of European integration; while in Britain, on the other hand, years of absence from the European experience – initially, by choice, but later as the result of two Gaullist vetoes – had led to the emergence of a very divergent outlook. When Britain entered the European Community in 1973, her public was about evenly divided on whether membership was a wise choice. The subsequent years of economic difficulty and an understandable perception that the Common Agricultural Policy placed inequitable burdens on her, have not dispelled rather widespread feelings that membership in the Community is not beneficial to Britain – though there has been a gradual development of a diffuse affective attachment to the European idea, to such an extent that in 1985, 68 percent of the British public were favourable to European unification (as compared with only 37 percent in 1973).

Among the other relatively new member nations, the Danes are about evenly divided about whether membership is a good thing, but tend to reject the goal of European unification. In striking contrast to the Danes, however, both the Irish and the Greek publics were, by 1985, overwhelmingly likely to perceive their country's membership as a good thing, and even more overwhelmingly favourable (though no more so than the British) to the goal of European unification.

Whether or not a new pro-European consensus will emerge in the enlarged 12-member European Community is an open question. It depends, in large measure, on whether the leaders of the European Community nations succeed in restoring a sense of progress to the Community through effective action on such measures as the proposal for a genuine role in decision-making for the European Parliament; the proposal for a move to majority rule; and progress toward political unification. If it continues to wallow in bureaucratic in-fighting, then a Community of 12 will probably be even more unwieldy than the expanded Community of the past decade.

The evidence of the past 25 years seems to show that publics *can* be won over to a European perspective under favourable conditions. The publics of the original six member nations are now solidly pro-European. Significant progress in this direction has taken place among the Irish and the Greek publics, but not among the Danes. The British remain a mixed case, emotionally favourable to European unification but divided in their pragmatic assessments. What will happen in Spain and Portugal remains to be seen.

It is readily conceivable that, given more favourable economic conditions than those that shaped the past decade, the development of a European identity would resume. But the process seems to reflect a complex interaction of economic, political and psychological factors. The present study by Miles Hewstone provides insights that will be valuable in assessing what is happening, and what is likely to happen.

Acknowledgements

As a social psychologist, relatively innocent of the world of political science, my fascination with the European Community has, at times, threatened to swamp me. I have, however, been helped by many people to whom I owe varying debts of gratitude.

Appropriately, for a study which has consumed so much of my time and spanned four countries, my list of acknowledgements is long and wide. It begins with those friends and colleagues across the European Community who helped in the preparation and collection of data: Carla Fiori and Augusto Palmonari (Universita' Degli Studi Di Bologna); Rupert Brown (University of Kent at Canterbury); Adrian Furnham (University College London); Louis Young (University of Bristol); Dieter Frey (Universität Kiel); Joanna Goodman (Universität Trier); Michael Diehl and Wolfgang Schön (Universität Tübingen); Geneviève and Henri Paicheler (Université de Paris) and Geneviève Vinsonneau (Université de Tours).

The open-ended responses were content-analysed by Claudia Hammer, Carla Fiori and Brunza Zani, while the whole series of statistical analyses was computed with infinite patience, care, skill and good humour by Helmut Schweiker. I also thank Hannelore Omasta who typed and re-typed the complete manuscript in her usual conscientious and cheerful manner, and those members of my family (my parents and brother-in-law) who, for two years, have been obliged to cut out and send me any newspaper articles concerning the Community. For their helpful comments on the manuscript, I thank Professor Dr G. Kaminski, Dr G. Winter, Klaus Jonas, Rolf Ulrich and Helmut Schweiker, again. The original manuscript has undergone a number of revisions, and I am grateful to the series editors, Dick Eiser and Jos Jaspars, for their critical and constructive comments, and to Penny Carter of C.U.P. for her support and patience. I record here with great sadness the tragic death of Jos Jaspars, who contributed so much to my graduate training and will be sorely missed as teacher, friend and colleague. His comments on this manuscript were as incisive and exact as ever, yet he was never able to see the final work appear.

This research was financed, in part, by a Grant for Research into European Integration from the Commission of the European Communities. It was my good fortune to have as my advisor in Brussels, Jacques-René Rabier, Special Counsellor to the Community with responsibility for the *Euro-Baromètre* series of public opinion surveys. His enthusiasm has been a source of support and encouragement.

This study was conceived, carried out and completed thanks to the generous funding of the Alexander von Humboldt-Stiftung, which awarded me a fellowship, with extension, to study in peace and great comfort at the Psychologisches Institut, Universität Tübingen. I am deeply grateful to Wolfgang Stroebe, my host Professor, for making my time in his institute so enjoyable and productive. He has made so many insightful and invaluable contributions at every stage of this research, that I could not possibly list them all here. I am especially grateful to him for so selflessly encouraging me to write this volume alone, and for taking such interest in the research from beginning to end. Finally, my loving thanks to Claudia who has lived with this book so patiently and has never ceased in her encouragement, in spite of my bad moods.

Notwithstanding the help received from all these people, I alone accept responsibility for the final work. The views expressed herein are my own and do not necessarily represent those of the Commission of the European Communities.

*   *   *

I am grateful to Times Newspapers Ltd for permission to quote from *The Times* the extracts on pp. 38–9, 110, 112, 186 and 197, which are © Times Newspapers Ltd. The following publications also generously permitted me to quote from them: *The Economist* (on p. 151), *The Guardian* (on p. 205), *The Guardian Weekly* (on p. 110) and *The Observer* (on pp. 109–10).

1 The idea of Europe: dream and reality

(L'Europe) C'est un mot dont les lettres essayent de se séparer les unes des autres pour survivre alors qu'elles feraient mieux de rester groupées pour former un mot dix fois plus solide.

(Anonymous French child)

1.1 The idea of Europe

The idea of Europe is old indeed. According to Duroselle (1957) the etymology of the word 'Europe' is uncertain: 'Does it derive from the Semitic *oreb* or *éreb*, which means "western", or from the Homeric epithet for Zeus, *the far-seeing* (*eurus*, "wide", and *ops*, "eye")?' (p. 11.) It is perhaps not inappropriate that, for the Greeks and later the Romans, the word Europe was associated first with 'myth' rather than 'science' (Hay, 1966). 'Europa' has two entries in *Lemprière's Classical Dictionary*. Europa was the daughter of Agenor, King of Phoenicia, and was seduced by Jupiter in the shape of a bull. She was, of course, also one of the three 'grand divisions' of the earth, 'superior to the others in the learning, power, and abilities of its inhabitants'.

These learned inhabitants have apparently long entertained the idea of European unity. Some authors argue that the Europe of the distant past was indeed more united than it is today. Friedrich (1969) claims that the Europe of the Middle Ages – centuries A.D. 800–1450 – was a 'rather close-knit cultural community' (p. 2), while Liska (1964) points out that Europe has twice been loosely united since the late Roman Empire; first in the 'Holy Roman Empire', and then in the 'Concert of Europe'. Further historical details are given in Voyenne's book, *Petite Histoire de l'idée Européenne* (see Duroselle, 1957), while some of the more important proposals for the effective organisation of the European political community were (according to Friedrich, 1969) those of Sully (Henry IV's minister, in 1610) and Immanuel Kant (his *On Eternal Peace*, 1795). This 'European Dream' has been shared by many thinkers and men of letters, including Dante, Rousseau, Victor Hugo, Saint-Simon,[1] Bentham and Garibaldi. It has been summarised by Barzini in the following passage:

> Europe should clearly evolve one common will, speak with one calm majestic voice, have a clear idea of its identity and goals, cultivate and defend its

economic prosperity, and pursue a single foreign policy in its own interest
(and the world's). It should therefore forget its trivial disputes and rivalries,
put its own house in order, set up authoritative common democratic
institutions, arrange its financial affairs according to more or less uniform
criteria, adopt one currency, and set up one redoubtable defence
establishment. (Barzini, 1983, p. 23)

The present work deals, however, not with history, but with the present and,
inevitably, the recent past. It is nonetheless concerned with the idea of
Europe, in the form of opinions and attitudes held by Europeans. Specifically,
it examines some of the determinants of pro-European attitudes and trends
in such views – the aim being to achieve an *understanding*, and not merely
a description, of attitudes to Europe. The purpose of this brief historical
introduction is to emphasise the continuity of the idea of Europe, an
understanding of which may set the reported findings in an appropriate
context. As van Zeeland (1957) has argued: 'Europe is a task at once
magnificent and necessary. The difficulties which lie on the way are in
proportion to the goal to be achieved.' (p. x.)

1.2 From the United States of Europe to the European Community

Notwithstanding the historical roots of the European Dream, it was only
after World War I that statesmen and politicians gave serious attention to
the idea of European unity. Count Coudenhove-Kalergi called for 'Pan-
European Union', Aristide Briand for 'European Federal Union' and, in
Zürich in September 1946, Winston Churchill gave his famous speech
calling for the establishment of a 'United States of Europe'.[2]

   The United States of Europe was the phantasy, the European Community
(also frequently referred to as the European Economic Community, E.E.C.,
or Common Market) was the reality. Built on the stepping-stones of the
European Coal and Steel Community in 1952 (see Swann, 1981) and given
momentum by the Messina declaration of 5 June, 1965 (the so-called
'relance européenne', see Willis, 1965), the European Community was the
design, principally, of Jean Monnet and Robert Schuman. The Treaty of
Rome, the basis of the Community, was signed, on 25 March, 1957, by
France, West Germany, Italy, Belgium, The Netherlands and Luxembourg
('The Six'). The Community has twice since been enlarged: in 1973 'The
Six' became 'The Nine' (with the accession of Ireland, Denmark and the
United Kingdom (U.K.)); and in 1979 'The Nine' welcomed Greece to form
'The Ten'. The establishment of the Community was 'the latest in a series
of steps designed to break down the bastions of European national separa-
tism'. (Lindberg, 1963, p. 3.)

   The general aim of the Rome Treaty is given in its Article 2: 'to promote throughout the Community a harmonious development of economic activities, a continuous and balanced expansion, an increased stability, an accelerated rise in standards of living...'. The more immediate objectives include the following (see Deniau, 1958; Kitzinger, 1962; Prag, 1967):

> the establishment of a customs union (elimination of customs
> duties between member states and the establishment of a
> common customs tariff for third countries);
> the 'four great freedoms' – free movement of persons, goods, services
> and capital;
> a Common Agricultural Policy and a Common Transport Policy;
> the creation of a European Social Fund.

Thus the Treaty provided for the creation of a common market between member countries, hence the often-used term 'Common Market', the economics of which are well explained by Swann (1981) and Harrod (1983). If the above objectives, now achievements, seem modest in comparison with the grandiose ideas of the past, the Community can nonetheless be seen as a 'daring experiment.' (Lindberg and Scheingold, 1970, p. 1.) It is worth noting that one opponent of the Common Market claimed that the Treaty of Rome brought with it the most far-reaching changes in the U.K. since Henry VIII broke with Rome![3]

The political factors which gave rise to the desire for European unity are not of direct concern here (see Spinelli, 1957, 1966), but it is generally acknowledged that prosperity and peace were the prime motivations. The wish for prosperity, natural enough, is emphasized by the economic underpinnings of the Community and has its roots in the free-trade tradition of Adam Smith. But the establishment of a customs union was always seen as partly political, this measure of economic integration preparing the ground for political unification. This primacy of politics was made clear in a famous remark of Walter Hallstein, first President of the E.E.C. Commission: 'We are not in business at all – we are in politics'.[4]

Despite these economic bases, the search for a durable peace was certainly an equally important impetus towards unity. For centuries the peace of Europe had been disturbed, most notably by the *Erbfeindschaft*, or hereditary enmity, of French and German peoples (see Willis, 1965).[5] Fear, says Barzini (1983), was *the* prime motivation. Fear of Russia's military might, fear of America's economic might, and the Europeans' fear of themselves. As Barzini says of these Europeans: 'They know anything might happen in Europe because everything has happened.' (p. 223.)

Views of the European Community that has been built are, of course, myriad. Is it 'little more at the present time than a fragile customs union, a mosaic of myopic, national, sacred egotisms badly harmonized'? (Barzini, *op. cit.*, p. 30.) Or is it 'the most successfully integrated international community that Europe, and perhaps the world has known'? (Willis, 1965, p. 327.) Whatever position one takes, the focus on the Community or Common Market, rather than that vague term 'Europe', can be readily justified 'for all its limitations, its despondency and consequent materialism, the common market remains the most important of all European institutions. The common market may be a dry and circumscribed kind of Europe, but it is so far the only really concrete step towards a unified Europe that we have.' (Sampson, 1968, p. 55.) In the following pages the public's verdict in four countries – W. Germany, Italy, France and the U.K. – will be examined. First, however, it may be useful to paint in some background for each nation. For social attitudes, such as those about the Community, do not exist or develop in a vacuum. They are generated, moulded and modified as a function of historical, political and economic forces. How the public's view has turned out will therefore probably be related to the way respective national governments have behaved towards the Community.

1.3 Acceptance of the European Community: W. Germany, Italy, France and the U.K.

Although the Community has passed in stages from The Six to The Ten, the focus of this work is 'The (big) Four'.[6] This decision is primarily pragmatic and financial, but can be justified on other grounds too.[7] These four countries are widely acknowledged to be the most important in determining the present and future course of European integration. Some indication of the 'power' of the four within the Community is given by their allowance of 81 seats each in the European Parliamentary Assembly. This represents a block of 324 out of 434 seats, which is almost enough to invoke article 144 of the Rome Treaty, whereby the Assembly (with a two-thirds majority) can pass a censure motion on the Commission. Perhaps because of the power and size of these four nations, they have served before as the basis of such research (e.g. Merritt and Puchala, 1968; Wildgen and Feld, 1976).

W. Germany

According to Noelle-Neumann (1980), Germans embraced the European idea as a refuge after the horrors of World War II. Europe was, she says, 'a compensation for their own lost national consciousness.' (p. 56.) It must also be said, that W. Germany *needed* the Community in order to be allowed to produce and rise again, regain national autonomy and utilise European markets for its goods. All this would help the nation to cast off pariah status. Public opinion polls in the immediate post-war period show that negative feelings towards the Germans (by Italians, French and British) overwhelmed in the 1950s (see Buchanan and Cantril, 1953; Merritt and Puchala, 1968).

The Community (first in the form of the European Coal and Steel Community) provided the German phoenix with the chance to rise from the ashes; the opportunity was grasped and utilised to the full.

Today W. Germany has become rich, strong, efficient, productive and scientifically advanced. This has led some Germans, annoyed because they think their country is forced to contribute too much to the Community coffers, to argue that W. Germany no longer needs the Community and could go it alone. Despite this view, there can be no question of governmental support. In this sense one would expect the German public to support the Community.

Italy

Italian enthusiasm for the Community today is following in the footsteps of Altiero Spinelli's *Movimento Federalista*, which wanted full political union established by means of a European Constituent Assembly (Coombes, 1970). Italian officials are known as fervent supporters of Europe and exerted themselves on behalf of the U.K.'s late membership bid.

Part of the reason the Italians are so sensitive about the Community is that their own governments change colour as often as a chameleon. According to Barzini, Italians have long been in search of 'a magical formula, a political panacea, or philosopher's stone, which would liberate them from the national nightmare and solve all problems overnight'. (1983, p. 182.) Italians, he continues, wanted a treatment for the 'persistent and probably incurable disease, the *ingovernabilita*.' (*op. cit.*, p. 192.) One should also note that Italy is a net beneficiary from the Community, while according to most sources none of the other three countries considered here can boast net gains.[8]

Barzini provides a compelling image of Italian support for Europe in terms of two fourteenth-century frescoes by Ambrogio Lorenzetti. '*Il Malgoverno*' (bad government) is filled with battles, ruins and desolation. '*Il Buongoverno*' (good government) shows industrious farmers, healthy cattle, ripe crops and happy faces. For many Italians, Barzini suggests, Europe was (and still is) the contemporary form of the ancient dream, '*Il Buongoverno*'.

France

Given the pioneering role of Monnet and Schuman, it goes without saying that France supported the Community from the beginning. Although it was not the only reason, the troublesome relationship with Germany was certainly a key factor, as was the desire to assume European leadership (Slater, 1983). If Germany needed the Community for its rehabilitation, then France needed the Community in order to control the Germany which had opposed France in all three European wars since 1870. Once again, Barzini has accurately expressed this delicate relationship: 'This is why France must now keep abreast of the Germans, keep them under surveillance, maintain the most intimate relations with them, and hold them in an embrace as close as a stranglehold.' (1983, p. 154.)

Despite their original and continuing advocacy of European unification, the French at a national level have sometimes deviated from the path of true Europeanism. Three occasions are notable. On 14 January, 1963, General de Gaulle blocked U.K. entry to the Community. Obviously his idea of a United Europe 'from the Atlantic to the Urals' did not go via the U.K. More spectacularly, perhaps, on 1 July 1965, France withdrew its government representatives from Brussels, leaving an 'empty chair' at the Council of Ministers for seven months (until January, 1966). Finally, in 1966 France postponed the day fixed by the Treaty of Rome when all decisions would be taken by simple majority, and no longer by unanimous vote. This was the famous 'Luxembourg compromise', which allowed for member states to protect their own national interests (see Holt, 1973). All these decisions, according to Barzini, are bound up with the need of French leaders 'to restore to their countrymen a feeling of pride and a sense of national mission'. (1983, p. 148.)

Despite the De Gaulle interlude (see Inglehart, 1970 *a,b,c*), which is a testimony to French independence, France has been generally supportive of Europe and has in François Mitterand a politician who appears to espouse the European ideal. That fact, coupled with Helmut Kohl's financial support for the Community, gives a remark of de Gaulle's a prophetic quality: 'The unification of Europe will be performed by France and Germany, France being the coachman and Germany the horse.'

The U.K.

It is hard to believe, looking just at contemporary events, that British statesmen played a constructive role in the 'founding' of Europe. But the European movement, out of which grew the Council of Europe, was influenced by Churchill, Bevin and other British politicians, and both Labour and Conservative governments encouraged integration. What distinguished the U.K. was, however, that: 'While paying lip-service to the lofty ideal of European unity, (Britain) has actually withheld collaboration when it was particularly needed and has obstructed progress towards European integration.' (Florinsky, 1955, p. 161.) This gave the British a reputation for 'selfishness and perfidy' (Florinsky, *op. cit.*, p. 159), hence the repeated accusation of 'la perfide Albion'.

The most notable example of holding back was, of course, from the original European Economic Community. Part of the explanation may lie in the U.K.'s (then) perceived influence and economic strength, as well as a reluctance to swop Commonwealth for Community. The U.K. was, however, not in favour of supra-nationalism and has always been particularly unwilling to relinquish sovereignty (Jowell and Hoinville, 1976a). It is often stated that for many Britons Europe began (and even still begins) at Calais; and many might even today agree with Nancy Mitford that 'abroad is unalterably bloody and foreigners are fiends'.

With a change of heart the U.K. applied for full membership under Macmillan in 1961 (see Lieber, 1970), and as Raymon Aron has written: 'Those who lost World War II, by joining together, forced the only European nation who felt really victorious in 1945 to a self-examination of historic proportions.' (1964, p. 57.) But it was not until 1973 that the U.K. became a full member, joining 'disastrously, too late, too expensively, at the wrong moment... reluctantly and somewhat squeamishly' (Barzini, 1983, p. 60), as some would have it. With its application the U.K. brought a range of problems ranging from kangaroo meat to cricket bats (Swann, 1981). The two thorniest, and closely related, issues, however, were, and still are – the Common Agricultural Policy (C.A.P.) and the U.K. contribution to the Community budget. In short, the U.K. has always felt that with 70% of the Community budget spent on agriculture, the slice of the cake from which she can gain is small. The 'budget problem' (still going strong since the Dublin summit of 1975) is equally complex, but comes down to the simple claim that the U.K. pays too much into the Community and gets too little out of it (see Harrod, 1983; Swann, 1981).

These problems reached something of a climax in 1975 with the first nationwide referendum in the history of the U.K. (Butler and Kitzinger, 1976; King, 1977). Should the U.K. stay in the Common Market? The public answered resoundingly: 17 million said 'yes', 8 million said 'no' (or 67.2% vs 32.8%, with a 65% turnout). Somewhat incredibly some opponents of the Community still insist that this was a 'clear but reluctant "yes"'. (See Peter Shore, *The Times*, 4 January, 1983.)

Although since 1975 the anti-E.E.C. line has really only been followed by the Labour Party, the opposition to the Community at the time united the strange bed-fellows of the Labour left and Conservative right. Thus while Labour opponents argued against a capitalist Europe (see Holland, 1980), Lord Selbourne (a Tory) felt sure that U.K. membership would 'be at the expense of sacrificing our imperial heritage.... The continental nations may be charming neighbours and good friends, but they are not to be preferred to our own kith and kin who owe allegiance to the Queen.' (Quoted by Jowell and Hoinville, 1976, pp. 9–10.) Such unusual political alignments and later changes of heart by prominent political figures have undoubtedly perplexed the electorate. The confused nature of Community membership as a partisan issue is revealed in a number of analyses by Himmelweit, Humphreys, Jaeger and Katz (1981), and Macfarlane (1981) is surely correct to describe the E.E.C. as a 'football in British politics'. (p. 151.)

Summing up the complex picture in the U.K., the British are clearly 'different'. But why? The answer must lie in a complex of historical, geographical and political factors (see Benoit, 1961; Robertson, 1959). Once again, Barzini has captured the point in eloquent terms: 'In a way Britain still sees itself as the sceptered isle cut from the Continent by divine will. If God had wanted to tie it to the rest of Europe, He would evidently not have dug the channel. Wasn't it therefore sinful and somewhat sacrilegious to attach Britain to the terra firma by treaties, tunnels, or bridges?' (1983, p. 59.)

From these brief sketches, the four countries in question should provide interesting contrasts and reveal to some extent the diversity of responses throughout the Community. On this basis one would expect exuberant attitudes in Italy; somewhat less positive, but supportive, attitudes in France and W. Germany; and both real support and real opposition in the U.K. The extent to which public opinion conforms to this pattern is dealt with in the following chapter, which begins with an analysis of the place of public opinion in the study of political integration.

2 Public opinion and European integration: a review and critique

> The European idea is empty, it has neither the transcendence of Messianic ideologies nor the immanence of concrete patriotism. It was created by intellectuals, and that fact accounts at once for its genuine appeal to the mind and its feeble echo in the heart.
>
> (Raymond Aron, 1954)

2.1 Integration theory and the place of public opinion

Puchala (1972) has compared the process of integration to an elephant, and researchers to blind men manipulating different parts of the body in an attempt to guess the shape of the whole animal. Ways of studying integration are certainly as diverse as befits an animal the size of an elephant and, as Harrison (1974) notes, integration is 'a process of political but also far-reaching, social transformation'. (p. 14.) This has resulted in very different studies of integration – in anthropology, political science, sociology, economics and law (see Hodges, 1972; Lindberg and Scheingold, 1971). The popularity of European integration as a topic of study is immediately apparent from the vast numbers of books on the topic. Their very titles indicate whether optimism ('Europe ascendant'),[1] pessimism ('Europe at sixes and sevens'; 'Uncommon market'; 'The impossible Europeans'),[2] reservation ('Integrated Europe?'; 'Europe's would-be polity'; 'A new Europe?')[3], or anxiety ('Can we save the Common Market?')[4] is the order of the day. Most approaches are, unfortunately, still multi- rather than inter-disciplinary. Furthermore, very different types of integration – political, economic, social, policy and attitudinal – form the basis of this research (see Nye, 1971). The present work, therefore, underlines its restricted bailiwick at the outset, concentrating on *attitudinal* evidence of integration.

Mathew (1980) argues that regional integration scholars have rather neglected mass attitudes, focussing instead on trans-national *institutions* and the economic and political *authorities* and *elites* which direct political cooperation. As Mathew points out, movement towards European political integration can be considered in three parts: the elite stage; informed public opinion; and mass acceptance. Theorists differ, however, as to whether the integrative process affects the average citizen and as to whether the views of the mass public affect the process of integration. These theorists fall into four broad categories – federalists, pluralists, functionalists and neo-functionalists (see Etzioni, 1965; Pentland, 1973) – the distinctions between which indicate relevant concerns for the present research.

The federalist approach can be identified with a legalistic perspective on sovereignty, and an emphasis on the transfer of formal power from national to supra-national bodies. The views of the public are only important for these theorists insofar as the success of integration is seen to depend on the elite's persuasion of the wider public. Limitations of this approach are shown by the move away from legalistic to more sociological conceptions of integration: 'The use of the term "federalism" to describe the process of unification has tended to give way in popularity to vaguer and more general expressions such as "integration" and "political unification"; the end product has been treated less as a fixed type of governmental structure and more as a sociological phenomenon, a "political community" or a "union".' (Coombes, 1970, p. 31.)

For pluralists, the development of a popular consensus towards the new institutions is a prerequisite for integration. This is most clearly seen in the work of K. Deutsch and colleagues. They describe integration as:

> the attainment, within a territory of a 'sense of community' and of institutions and practises strong enough and widespread enough to assure for a 'long' time, dependable expectations of 'peaceful change' among its populations. (Deutsch *et al.* 1957, p. 5)

Sense of community is further elaborated as:

> a matter of mutual sympathy and loyalties; of 'we-feeling', trust, and mutual consideration; of partial identification in terms of self-images and interests; of mutually successful predictions of behavior, and of cooperative action in accordance with it. (*op. cit.*, p. 36)

Similar interpretations of this notion of a 'sense of community' are also to be found in Easton (1965*a*, p. 332), Taylor (1972, p. 205) and Harrison (1974, p. 18).

Indices of integration, for Deutsch, include 'exchanges': the extent of trade, numbers of people crossing borders to work and study, cultural exchanges, political consultation, media consumption, and volume of mail between countries. Such communication flows are central to Deutsch's work, and he argues that a relatively high frequency of exchanges is conducive to a sense of mutual responsiveness and trust (provided the exchanges are seen as rewarding; see Inglehart and Rabier, 1982). Using such measures (as well as interviews with elites; analyses of public opinion data; and content-analyses of the press), Deutsch (1967) made the bold claim that structural integration in Europe had slowed since the mid-50s and reached a peak in 1957 (at which level it was higher than at any time since 1890). But integration had then come to a halt or levelled off since 1957–58. Deutsch therefore concluded that Europe of the future would remain a collection of nation states, not a supra-national entity:

> The ensemble of the present public moods would not be much help to statesmen who would lead their countries toward a greatly deepened union. Rather, they may facilitate general expressions of good will, combined with policies of temporizing, caution, national consolidation, and only gradual and sectoral advance toward somewhat greater European integration. Bolder steps towards substantially greater European unity would have to be 'sold to' mass opinion by the sustained and concerted efforts of leaders and elites.... (Deutsch, 1967, p. 251)

The pluralists' emphasis on social-psychological dimensions of integration is highly relevant to the reported research, but it focusses too deeply and narrowly on the emergence of a 'we-feeling' and on mutual identification among peoples. In addition, too much of the responsibility for measuring integration is placed on 'exchanges'. The present writer tends to agree with Mathew (1980), that it is doubtful whether the European countries will ever achieve the degree of integration basic to the pluralist view.

Functionalism, according to Shepherd (1975), derives from the work of Mitrany (1966). It emphasises the development of a social-psychological community and views ties of mutual affection, identity and loyalty as the building-blocks of integration. The aim of the functionalist approach is:

> to capitalize on the problems which all nations have in common. The hope of functionalists is, in other words, to work for cooperative solutions to social and economic problems and thus to root out the material causes of war and to promote the establishment of increasingly intensive patterns of social interaction across national boundaries. (Lindberg and Scheingold, 1970, pp. 6–7)

Integration is, then, primarily a cumulative process of learning by association (see Pentland, 1973). While this approach may serve to remind us of the importance of variables such as international travel and contact experiences, it is, as Mathew argues, rather too rational and cognitive. One should not rule out the possibility of an emotional attachment to the European idea (especially given the historical roots traced above). Finally, one wonders just how many of the citizens of Europe have a chance to engage in, or perceive themselves to be engaged in, 'task-oriented cooperative activities'; this approach therefore seems less than optimal for the study of attitudinal integration.

The neo-functionalist approach is the most recent trend in integation theory. Early proponents of this view are typified by Haas (1964, 1968).

Their definition of integration emphasises the development of supra-national institutions, and shifts in political loyalties are seen as the ultimate measure of integration, although this need not necessarily imply repudiation of one's national identity (see Haas, 1968, p. 14). Thus Haas defines integration as:

> the process whereby *political actors* in several distinct national settings are persuaded to shift their loyalties, expectations and political activities toward a new centre, whose institutions possess or demand jurisdiction over the pre-existing national states. (Haas, 1968, p. 16).

But who are these 'political actors'? For Haas, it is clear, they are political elites, because:

> It is as impracticable as it is unnecessary to have recourse to general public opinion surveys, or even to surveys of specifically interested groups.... It suffices to single out and define the political elites in the participating countries, to study their reactions to integration and to assess changes in attitude on their part. (*op. cit.*, p. 17.)

This unashamed, rather imperialistic, elite-centred view is justified by the statement that decisions are made 'over the opposition and usually over the indifference of the general membership'. (p. 17.)

More recent neo-functionalist work is not as cavalier in its excommunication of the mass public (e.g. Lindberg and Scheingold, 1970). More attention has been paid to mass political attitudes, using as a theoretical basis the work of Easton (1965) and, in particular, his view that, ultimately, the survival of a political community depends on the existence of *some* demonstrable support.

Inglehart (1967, 1970*a,b*, 1971, 1977) is the most central of the 'new neo-functionalists', and his view has developed in opposition to that of Deutsch. Inglehart (1967) disagreed that Europe in the 1970s would remain a collection of nation states. In contrast to Deutsch's claim that integration had halted since 1957–58, Inglehart's study of 5000 students in France, W. Germany, England and the Netherlands revealed that a fundamental change in values and attitudes was taking place among *young* citizens of western Europe; giving hope for the future, there was a greater sense of 'Europeanness' in the young (16–19 years) than the old (especially those over 55). Inglehart's (1977) study went further, reporting the emergence of a supra-national identity in the countries of 'The Six'.

Following Mathew (*op. cit.*), two aspects of neo-functionalist research are particularly noteworthy. First, the analytic rigour of the empirical research; and second, the concern to identify the determinants of integration. In this latter respect, Lindberg and Scheingold's (1970) distinction between affective (e.g. loyalty) and utilitarian (e.g. perceived benefits) support will be considered further in Section 2.7. below.

This taxonomy for the study of integration is somewhat problematic because of the considerable overlap between approaches (see Nye, 1971; Taylor, 1972). Nonetheless it highlights the contributions of the various perspectives from which any piece of research can borrow. Given the present focus on public attitudes, the new neo-functionalists do appear to be the most useful, although as a social psychologist, and not a political scientist, one should be wary of gauging the success of European integration in terms of shifts in citizens' loyalty. Shifting the loyalties of the British, or the French, away from nation states towards supra-national authorities would be a Herculean task. Moreover, given work on multiple loyalties (Guetzkow, 1955) and multiple social identities (Tajfel, 1974), it may be an idealistic aim for the European Community, where the presence of widespread attitudinal support might be more realistic.

In turning now to an analysis of public opinion and the European Community, it is worth recalling that the ultimate aim of the Community was, in the words of the preamble to the Rome Treaty, to establish 'an ever closer union among the European peoples'. Evidence of shared, positive attitudes towards Europe must therefore now be examined, although many commentators were, and still are, sceptical.

2.2 The common Man and public opinion

Friedrich (1959) argues that belief in the 'common Man' is the core of the democratic creed, with roots in the thought of Thomas Paine and Jeremy Bentham, as well as more modern writers such as Whitman, Emerson and Thoreau. The defence of the common Man stands in contrast to Carlyle's 'elites' and Nietsche's 'supermen'; it was Thomas Carlyle who said, 'popular opinion is the greatest lie in the world.' Friedrich's view is quite different; he justifies attention to the common Man with the view that: 'Thought and opinion of the "common man" are, where (his) community context is democratic, in the last analysis of decisive importance.' (1969, p. 20.)

It is, of course, the common Man, or common people, who provide us with public opinion. According to Davison (1968), the term public opinion was coined by Jacques Necker (Louis XVI's finance minister) at the time of the French Revolution, but its definition continues to pose problems. In an authoritative review, Childs (1959) contends that, one should study, not define, public opinion. However, based on Childs' (1965) later work discussing over 50 definitions Davison defines public opinion as: 'a collection of individual opinions on an issue of public interest... these opinions can exercise influence over individual behaviour, group behaviour, and govern-mental policy'. (1968, p. 188.) Oskamp (1977) defines public opinion simply as 'the shared opinions of large groups of people (sometimes called "publics")'. (p. 16.)

Despite the attention paid to public opinion in past and contemporary politics, views on its importance are still polarised. Negatively, Sir Robert Peel referred to: 'that great compound of folly, weakness, prejudice, wrong feeling, right feeling, obstinacy and newspaper paragraphs which is called public opinion'. (Cited in Lippmann, 1922, p. 197.) More positively, Davison (1968) has characterised public opinion as: 'an expression of opinion from the public that reaches the government and that the government finds prudent to heed'. (p. 192; see Key, 1961.) These very different views have generated an important debate which should be considered prior to a review of public opinion on European integration.

2.3 Opinion – public or elite?

For many newspaper readers, politicians and scholars the striking fact about public opinion polls, or their results, is the sheer magnitude of the data. Despite these vast numbers, Converse (1964) has posed the question of whether this attention to numbers is of any relevance in many political settings.

This question arises because Converse doubts that the political views of the mass public can be said to constitute belief systems, defined as 'a configuration of ideas and attitudes in which the elements are bound together by some form of constraint or functional interdependence'. (p. 207.) By constraint is meant, basically, correlation between items within a belief system. If an individual does possess an ideologically coherent belief system, then it should be possible to predict his or her attitudes on a number of issues, given an initial, specified attitude. A true belief system should also be stable over time, the core ideological elements not changing chaotically in the face of new information.

To measure degrees of constraint, Converse calculated the (tau–gamma) correlation coefficients between attitudinal responses on various domestic and foreign issues. He compared a cross-section of U.S. citizens (as would be used in an opinion poll sample) with an 'elite' sample of U.S. congressional candidates. While the elite group did reveal moderately high correlations between responses on clusters of domestic issues ($r = +0.53$), only low correlations were found for the national sample ($r = +0.23$). Converse concluded that major policy attitudes were only modestly correlated in mass American, and French (see Converse and Dupeux, 1962) publics. Mass attitudes were also rather unstable, in the absence of systematic external pressure to change, as indicated by low test–retest correlations. Converse therefore concluded that belief systems did not underlie the political thinking of the mass public, a viewpoint that has excited some debate (see Converse, 1970, 1974; Pierce and Rose, 1974*a*,*b*). Although Converse did not disclaim the existence of 'folk ideologies' (Converse, 1964*a*), he argued that the mass of people could not explain the *whys* involved in many of the constraints between idea-elements. Sears (1969) has drawn the similar conclusion that: 'few citizens organize their political ideas in an abstract ideological framework recognizable to sophisticated political thinkers'. (p. 332.) Kerlinger (1984) has more cautiously stated that the correlation between social beliefs and other variables increases with education (Bishop, 1976; Wray, 1979) so that correlations are higher in educated samples than in relatively uneducated samples. This does not mean, however, that the mass public has little or no underlying attitudinal structure (see Knitzer, 1978; Luttbeg, 1968).

To poll or not to poll – is that the question? No! Converse's belief that a 'continental shelf' (1964*a*, p. 255) divides the views of masses and elites does not lead him to outlaw polling altogether. His solution is more circumspect. Believing that no more than 10–15% of the public construe political issues in terms of general ideological dimensions, he concludes that research on political attitudes should concentrate on elites. This view is captured by Henessy's (1970) statement, that 'political attitudes are an elite phenomenon. Most people do not have political attitudes.' (p. 463.)

If the first, and major, reason claimed for eschewing the study of mass publics is their lack of ideological thinking, then the second reason is their lack of knowledge. Converse argues that differences in information held in a cross-section population are simply staggering (Converse, 1964*a*, p. 212). This lack of information is held to reach some kind of nadir precisely in the study of foreign affairs. Even Friedrich (1950), champion of the common Man, gives foreign affairs as an exception, because: 'decisions in this field are of a nature that removes them from the average man's grasp. When foreign policy calls for judgment of a complex situation, the common man recoils from it because of his lack of knowledge.' (p. 117–18.) Kriesberg (1949) uses the rich phrase 'dark areas of ignorance' to characterise public opinion about foreign policy, for all except the highest socio-economic strata. Other writers have attempted to classify the public in terms of (lack of) knowledge. Almond (1960, p. 138) refers to a 'general public', an 'attentive public' and an 'informed public'; while Sears (1969; see Erskine, 1962, 1963; Hyman and Sheatsley, 1954) distinguishes the 'chronic know-nothings', the 'informed layman' and the 'attentive public'. Knowledge is, of course, closely related to, perhaps cause *or* consequence of, interest in political affairs. Cantril (1965), in a major study of 'human concerns', reports that political matters are low on the list, and Sears concludes that politics represents a world to which most citizens are 'quite indifferent'. (1969, p. 324.)

A third justification for studying elites is, simply, their power. As Merritt (1967) acknowledges, they play a crucial role in a state's policy-making process, and they are largely responsible for recruiting tomorrow's elites. But who, then, are the elites? Merritt is aware that the term means many things to many people; he uses it to denote 'formal and informal decision-makers at a society's national level'. (p. 4.) According to Sears (1969), elites are those who 'actively participate in political life beyond mere voting'. (p. 437.) These definitions are still very broad and mask a great deal of variety in empirical studies using elites. In fact there are many elites, as many as there are issues. Hence Converse advocates the study of 'issue publics' because 'different controversies excite different people to the point of real opinion formation'. (1964, p. 246.)

The argument in favour of elites – based on considerations of consistent political thinking, knowledge and power – appears to be a convincing one. It should certainly awaken us to an inherent problem of public opinion polling noted some time ago by Asch: 'The danger of polling on matters about which there is little information and in which people are not interested is that the data will spuriously support the assumption that public opinion exists.' (1952, p. 550; *cf.*, Converse, 1964*b*.) Notwithstanding these critiques and warnings, political opinion polls have long been, and will doubtless continue to be, a part of the political scene (notwithstanding Bourdieu's, 1972, bold claim that, 'L'opinion publique n'existe pas'). Some of the reasons for maintaining an interest in, and the study of, *public* opinion are now examined.

2.4 In defence of public opinion

If Europe, like most nation states, is dominated by political elites, why bother to seek the public's view anyway? One answer, to cite Voltaire, is that: 'Opinion has caused more trouble on this little earth than plagues or earthquakes.' If Voltaire was right, then this argument is the ultimate justification. There are, however, various lines of support for the study of public opinion.

In contrast to the elite view discussed above, a 'mass participation' view has also been put forward. Thus Lane (1962) contends that ordinary people do have political ideologies, although they are less clearly articulated than those of the elites (see e.g. Billig, 1978). Supporting this view, Wilker and Milbrath (1970) argue that because many voters consistently endorse the same party, the political beliefs of the general public must be somewhat stable. This mass participation rationale for the study of public opinion has been eloquently stated by Merritt and Puchala:

> An understanding of international relations in our new era of mass
> political mobilization and participation requires not only knowledge of
> how government officials and foreign policy elites perceive and react, but

also and to an increasing extent information about how the 'man in the street' thinks about, feels about, and responds to foreign countries and international issues and events. This 'man in the street'... is politically relevant: He votes, he makes demands on his government, occasionally he even riots or revolts. He knows something and cares about foreign affairs. Increasingly, his moods, his anxieties, and his hopes and aspirations enter into the considerations and foreign policy choices of his political leaders. (Merritt and Puchala, 1968, p. vii)

Public opinion surveys also have a communicative value and, according to Etzioni, they originally enabled the middle class to find out what the poor felt 'in a more systematic fashion than by simply asking their maids'. (Etzioni, 1969, p. 573.) Arguably, polls yield a more accurate picture of what the public thinks than that obtained from newspapers and informal interviews. To quote Etzioni again: 'It seems reasonable to conclude that surveys make the elite more responsible to the public, not by increasing public influence *per se*, but by sampling a "public" that is closer to the real public, with its wants and desires, than were earlier conceptions.' (1969, p. 573.) This 'information yield', with regard to public attitudes about and reactions to particular policies, is also identified by Merritt (1968). In turn, polls are held to fulfill an educational function, whereby both respondents and readers of the results are stimulated to consider and discuss the issues raised (Oskamp, 1977). Public opinion may, therefore, jolt the alienated citizen into political activity and help to remove what Rabier has called: 'ce formidable obstacle au changement qu'est l'apathie des citoyens'. (1966, p. 37.)

Davison (1968) reports that the relationship between government and mass opinion receives attention in the work of both Plato and Aristotle, while Machiavelli certainly warned princes to take good note of the public's views:

I conclude, therefore, that when a prince has the goodwill of the people he should not worry about conspiracies; but when the people are hostile and regard him with hatred he should go in fear of everything and everyone. Well-organized states and wise princes have always taken great pains not to exasperate the nobles, and to satisfy the people and keep them content; this is one of the most important tasks a prince must undertake. (Machiavelli, 1514; 1961 edn, p. 105.)

One important reason for looking at public opinion is, then, that a viable political community should have popular legitimacy. It is an article of western democratic faith that the legitimacy of governments rests on the consent of the governed (Putnam, 1983), and that an informed populace is the bulwark of freedom (Oskamp, 1977). The absence of such legitimacy (and the accompanying sense of solidarity) tends to be seen as a threat to the existence of any community (Slater, 1983) and so the European

Community has always taken an interest in this sphere. Regarding public opinion and public policy, a 'will of the people' viewpoint (see Oskamp, *op. cit.*) holds that the decisions of political actors should coincide with their constituents' views. This position has its roots in Rousseau's notion of the 'general will' and, as some would argue, gives public opinion a direct influence on the formulation of new policy (Merritt, 1968). Even if the link between the public and the government is not quite this strong, public opinion would appear to play a not insignificant role simply by instigating discussion and public information programmes (Davison, 1968).

All these considerations help to explain why the results of public opinion polls are 'omnivorously read' (according to Crossman, 1973, p. 15, cited by Jowell and Hoinville, 1976*b*), even if they are treated with 'lordly disdain' (*ibid.*) when their predictions are wrong. But is public opinion passive or active, leading or following policy decisions? With regard to the European Community, Slater (1983) asks whether the mass public has remained largely indifferent to its institutional arrangements, or whether an eager public has pushed for European unification. As Slater notes, this latter view was held by Walter Hallstein (1972) who maintained that, 'the decisions that have been taken lag far behind public opinion in Europe'. (p. 30.) In this respect it is interesting to note the pioneering role of the 'European Movement' which grew outside of mainstream party politics (Coombes, 1970).

Public opinion may, then, be conceptualised as a 'leading' or a 'lagging' indicator (Putnam, 1983). In the former hypothesis, public opinion is the core of a 'bubble up' theory of political change, as captured in the remark by Hallstein. Public opinion as a lagging indicator, in contrast, suggests a 'trickle down' theory, with public opinion reflecting or following public decisions (but nevertheless still being, perhaps, important in itself as a source of wider support). Etzioni (1969) argues that the available data support a downward flow model, with various elites and interest groups moulding the public's view. For foreign policy matters, in particular, the public's influence on national decision-making is seen as slight (see Rokkan, 1960). Notwithstanding Etzioni's view, one should also note Putnam's third hypothesis, that public opinion is, in fact, irrelevant to institutional change (but, note, not irrelevant *per se*). This is, at the very least, a proposition which ought to be borne in mind, especially since the value of public opinion is not tied to the issue of leading or lagging indicators. In fact, the interpretation of public opinion surveys might be more useful, and less tentative, if a more limited role were ascribed to the views of the general public.

This kind of modest, reasoned argument has been advanced by some scholars, accepting that:

The institution or maintenance of a democratic system is not contingent in any immediate sense upon public opinion. In the long run, though, it may well be that democracy thrives only where people actively support it. (Sears, 1969, p. 414)

and:

If policy makers show a strong normative predisposition toward European unification, favourable public opinion is likely to legitimize for them pro-unification policy decisions, if inputs from other sources such as interest groups, political parties, and various interested ministeries are also basically positive. In the absence of such predisposition and less positive, or even negative, inputs, public opinion strongly supportive of European unity may be far from being influential and may even be ignored to a large degree. Nevertheless, public opinion remains significant from the domestic political perspective, because policy-supportive public opinion provides governmental and political leaders with some leverage for important forward linkages in both domestic and foreign policy issues of the future. (Feld, 1981, p. 80.)

As Inglehart (1970a) argues, public opinion survey data are relevant to the study of integration for two main reasons. They indicate, when considered longitudinally, the influence exerted by the public on the decisions taken by national governments; and they measure the effect of policy on mass attitudes. But the relevance of mass political attitudes is generally constrained by whether national decision-making is 'pluralistic' or 'monolithic' in structure. A further justification for examining the public's views about Europe is that the European Community *has* taken an interest in, and specified a role for, public opinion. As Slater (1983) puts it: 'the founders of the European Community were far-sighted enough to see that the long-term survival of the Community in a democratic age would depend on its finding legitimacy with the general public' (p. 72); although Slater also points out that mass publics were not involved in the decision-making process in any real way until the first direct elections to the European Parliament, in June 1979. Although Aron (1964) has noted that the future of European unification does not necessarily depend on public opinion, various figureheads of the Community have doffed their hats to the public. Robert Schuman (1976) himself said it was the duty of the European Parliament 'to interpret the views of the general public' (p. 57), while Roy Jenkins (1977 – at that time President of the European Commission) warned that the Community 'must never forget the need to carry the people of Europe with them'. (p. 33.)

Finally, of course, public opinion has undoubtedly had its influence on the development of European integration via nationwide referenda. Newspapers (e.g. *The Observer*, 19 June, 1983) are correct in writing of a 'public mandate to stay in Europe' when one considers that in 1972 referenda in five nation states (Ireland, Denmark, Norway, Switzerland and France) concerned the Community, while this was the case for the U.K. in 1975. On such occasions public opinion actually does influence a major political, and foreign policy, issue. In fact, Dalton and Duval (1981) argue that, in the U.K., shifts in public opinion are playing an increasingly important role in determining relations with the Community, because public support is used to justify negotiations over changes in the original Treaty. These authors also maintain that as the envisaged nature of European integration develops, so do the 'costs' incurred for the general public. At this point, active public support, not just 'permissive consensus' (see Lindberg and Scheingold, 1970) is required. With this acknowledgement of the power of the people, it is now appropriate to examine some of the empirical findings of public opinion polls on European integration.

2.5 European public opinion: early evidence

Earliest opinion polls concerning European integration date from the mid-1940s. They provide a vast and formidable array of data which is far beyond the purview of this work (but see, for example, Merritt and Puchala, 1968; Shepherd, 1975). As Noelle-Neumann has written: 'Future historians will be better informed about the general mood of how the people of Western Europe awaited the emergence of the European Community than they have been about any other era in which a new political community was taking shape.' (Noelle-Neumann, 1980, p. 53.) While the present work focusses primarily on the *Euro-baromètre* polls (see Section 2.6) and on the four largest countries of the Community, it may be useful first to draw attention to some of the findings, and sources, of earlier work (i.e. before 1974).

Polls throughout the 1950s and up until the emergence of the Community revealed a high level of support for European unification: an average of 76% in W. Germany; 59% in Italy; 56% in France; and 67% (note) in the U.K. (see Slater, 1983). The first simultaneous poll of 'The Six' took place in February/March of 1963 and appeared to find evidence for a real 'European public opinion' (see data reported in the *Journal of Common Market Studies*, 1963). Despite the broad support for European unification, however, little strong feeling, curiosity or interest was expressed. Themes of 'security', 'the pursuit of well-being' and 'progress' emerged, but knowledge of the economic objectives of the Community was fragmentary. As Aron (1964) has remarked, support for Europe was evident, but not ardent, 'while favouring European unity, public opinion is only faintly militant or impassioned about it'. (p. 45.)

Notwithstanding the time-span of polls, many early efforts were limited in scope. Writing of public opinion in 1966, Rabier was able to say, with some justification: 'Les matériaux sont rares et les analyses très insuffisantes.' (Rabier, 1966, p. 11.) With regard to the favourable attitude towards European unification, Rabier wrote:

> 'Même s'il nous est apparu comme relativement stable, voire en lente progression, une étude plus approfondie des résultats des sondages nous montre que ce *consensus* quasi général est encore assez superficiel, insuffisament motivé, nourri d'une information assez vague, et correspond à une sorte d'engouement collectif, tantôt teinté d'affectivité, tantôt plus ou moins rationalisé, plus qu'à une option politique consciente pouvant conduire les citoyens à rechercher une participation active. (Rabier, 1966, p. 19.)

Clearly, more work was needed.

Some very useful sources of earlier polls focus, understandably, on one country (e.g. Stoetzel, 1957). Thus Noelle-Neumann's chapter: 'Phantom Europe: thirty years of survey research on German attitudes towards European integration' (1980). Like Aron, quoted above, Noelle-Neumann noted high levels of support since 1947, and an overall view of stability, but no real commitment: 'There are no signs of real enthusiasm for the European idea, and people do not appear to be captivated by the historical moment.' (Noelle-Neumann, 1980, p. 55.)

Not surprisingly, several in-depth studies of British public opinion exist (e.g. Hedges, 1976; Holt, 1972; Säarlvik *et al.*, 1976; Spence, 1976; *Journal of Common Market Studies*, 1968). As Kitzinger remarked: 'One might almost say that never in the course of British history have so many had to answer so many questions on a single issue as they did on that of entry into the EEC.' (1973, p. 352.) These studies provide a fascinating picture, over many years, of a country which, to borrow the title of Jowell and Hoinville's (1976*b*) chapter, took 'an unconscionable time deciding'. As Rutherford (1981) reports, there were even polls at the time that the Macmillan government was rumoured to be considering application and in July, 1966 (perhaps on the crest of a World Cup Winner's wave) 71% said they would approve of entry. This figure, however, was never again as high. By 1967, when Wilson's re-elected government applied for membership, only 35% approved, while 44% disapproved (21% did not know). Rutherford comments: 'It seems to have been the first time that there was at least a simple majority against belonging to the Community. It was by no means the last.' (1981, pp. 9–10.)

One striking finding from these early studies, and one that has been relatively overlooked in the frenzy to count those 'for' and 'against', is the level of knowledge (or lack of it) revealed. A French poll in 1955 (cited by

Haas, 1968, p. 17) on the European Coal and Steel Community reported the following findings: 10% were able to identify the six member states: 2% were able to specify the powers of the E.C.S.C.; 26% were ignorant of the existence of the E.C.S.C.; and 70% were ignorant of the existence of the High Authority. Merritt and Puchala (1968) report that in May 1957, on the eve of the European Community's birth, 38% of W. German respondents, 35% of French respondents and 33% of Italians had never heard of the E.E.C. In a similar vein, Rabier (1972) reported that 36% of Community citizens could name the member states of the Common Market. This contrasted with 90% who could name the Prime Minister of their own country, and 64% who could name their own country's Foreign Minister. On the other hand, Rabier (1966) noted that in Belgium and France (1962 polls), more 16–24-year olds could name three Common Market countries, than could name three ministers of their respective national governments. These data remind us, before we consider the evidence from *Euro-baromètre* polls, that for many Europeans, Community affairs (even ten years after the Community was founded) were still 'dark areas of ignorance'. (See Kriesberg, 1949.)

2.6 European public opinion: *Euro-baromètre* 1974–84

Since April–May 1974 the European Commission has collected, analysed and published public opinion data throughout the European Community. These twice-yearly surveys were carried out from the beginning:

> in order to follow the trends in European public opinion with regard to Community activities, particularly the areas of most interest to the public. (*Euro-baromètre*, No. 1, 1974, p. 1.)

The name *Euro-baromètre* was chosen deliberately because:

> Just as a barometer can be used to measure the atmospheric pressure and thus give a short-range weather forecast, this *Euro-baromètre* can be used to observe, and to some extent forecast, public attitudes towards the most important current events connected directly or indirectly with the development of the European Community and the unification of Europe. (*ibid.*)

Euro-baromètre results are accorded prime attention here for a number of reasons. First, because the *same* (carefully translated) questions are posed simultaneously in all member countries of the Community. This yields rich comparative data. Second, key questions are repeated on several occasions, some in every single survey, which means that short- and long-term trends in public opinion can be charted. This acceptance of European integration as a *process* is firmly in line with one of the Community's founders, Jean Monnet, who once said: 'The Common Market is a process, not a product.'[5]

Walter Hallstein made the same point, albeit more colloquially: 'integration is like a bicycle; you either move on, or you fall off'.[6] Longitudinal data are important for another reason. Because Europe is still a 'would-be polity' (Lindberg and Scheingold, 1970), public opinion in Europe is not one, but now ten yo-yos oscillating at different times and frequencies. With national governments changing at different times and specific domestic issues waxing and waning in each country, it is sometimes impossible to attribute unequivocally small-scale changes in *Euro-baromètre* responses to specific factors. For this reason, the following review will, where possible, consider responses to relevant items based on several polls.

Results of the *Euro-baromètre* studies are broken down by the usual demographic criteria – age, sex, socio-economic status, and so on – and include many cross-tabulations between replies to different questions (as well as, occasionally, multivariate analyses). Since poll no. 5, special attention has been paid to the views of 'opinion leaders' (those who influence the opinions of others), in comparison with the general public (see Slater, 1983). The importance of these various classifications can be readily inspected in the published reports. They will not be considered here for the simple reason that their inclusion and discussion would then move public opinion from the background to the foreground of the present work.

What follows is a selection of *some* of the most relevant questions asked in the ten-year history of *Euro-baromètre*. These questions have been grouped, broadly, in accordance with a scheme suggested by Handley (1981), which proposed four different kinds of support for European integration:

> affective sentiment for European integration;
> support for Community membership;
> intensity of attachment to the European ideal; and
> saliency of the Community.

A fifth group of questions is also considered, which share a focus on the most 'public' of the Community's institutions, the European Parliament. While several political scientists consider responses to questions about the Parliament to be indicative of the four support levels mentioned, these items appear to the present author to belong in a separate category, if only in terms of topic.

The exact wording of key questions is quoted in the text below, while the wording of all items can be checked in the original source. Finally, before considering the selected findings, it is important to repeat the caveat carried in the published report of each poll: 'Readers are reminded that sample survey results are *estimations*, the degree of certainty and precision of which, everything being kept equal, rests upon the number of cases. With samples of about 1,000, it is generally admitted that a percentage difference of less than five per cent is below the acceptable level of confidence.' (*Euro-baromètre,* no. 20, 1983, p. A5.)

2.6.1 Affective support for European integration
One of the most important questions asked in these polls is the following: 'In general, are you for or against efforts being made to unify Western Europe? If for, are you very much for, or only to some extent? If against, are you only to some extent against, or very much against?' Because this question has been asked in so many surveys, the valuable longitudinal data are reported in Table 2.1. and presented graphically in Figure 2.1. The authors of *Euro-baromètre,* no. 15, accept that this item measures 'a sentiment as vague as it is diffuse' (p. 16), but this need not be seen as a disadvantage or limitation. This question appears to tap the contemporary vision of the 'idea of Europe', without tying answers to any specific political or economic institutions. The question could be said to measure, simply: 'a "system of beliefs", reflecting views about whether or not European unification – without any further definition or proviso – is worthwhile, possible, desirable or even necessary as a project (or ideal)'. (*Euro-baromètre,* no. 20, 1983, p. 48.)

Responses to this question reveal a vast level of broad popular support for a united Europe – not merely in the ten years considered here, but also dating back more than 30 years for similarly worded questions (see Inglehart, 1977, pp. 344–6). Over the ten years of interest here, support has been remarkably stable, especially in France and Italy. German support has declined somewhat, while British support has increased. The recent decline for all countries except France, in poll no. 21, is probably attributable to the failures of 'summits' (European Councils) in Athens (4–6 December, 1983) and Brussels (19–20 March, 1984).

The difference between the U.K. and the other three countries is clear from Figure 2.1. What is not clear, but is in Table 2.1., is the size of this difference. Responses 'for' unification have varied from 50–70% in the U.K.; this maximum of 70% is the approximate minimum in each other country. Similarly, the minimum of British responses 'against', 14%, is only just under the maximum ever reached in the other three countries (16% in W. Germany). Notwithstanding these differences, there *is* net support in the U.K. and, as Figure 2.1. shows, the gap is less than it was ten years ago. Thus, although the British may be negative about the Common Market (see below), they cannot accurately be described as non- or anti-European.

It has been suggested that even pro-Europeans may have become impatient and disillusioned with the steady, rather than speedy, progress towards a united Europe. Certainly, there is substantial support for speeding

Table 2.1 *General attitude to the unification of Europe (1975–84)*[1]

Euro-baromètre no.	Date of poll	W. Germany			France			Country Italy			U.K.		
		for	against	net[2]	for	against	net	for	against	net	for	against	net
3.	May 1975	77	3	74	78	5	73	77	3	74	50	22	28
4.	Oct.–Nov. 1975	74	5	69	77	4	73	77	4	73	51	23	28
10.	Nov. 1978	78	5	73	80	7	73	83	5	78	63	22	41
11.	Apr. 1979	82	7	75	72	10	62	87	4	83	61	20	41
12.	Oct. 1979	81	7	74	75	10	65	85	4	81	61	23	38
13.	Apr.–May 1980	80	7	73	75	11	64	83	5	78	59	26	33
14.	Oct.–Nov. 1980	79	9	70	69	11	58	81	7	74	63	22	41
15.	Mar.–May 1981	70	13	57	73	11	62	82	11	71	52	29	23
16.	Oct.–Nov. 1981	75	12	63	79	8	71	82	7	75	64	21	43
17.	Mar.–May 1982	78	10	68	78	10	68	79	7	72	56	31	25
18.	Oct. 1982	70	16	54	82	8	74	76	7	69	61	21	40
19.	Mar.–Apr. 1983	85	6	79	75	6	69	80	6	74	60	20	40
20.	Sept.–Nov. 1983	76	8	68	79	9	70	80	7	73	70	14	56
21.	Mar.–Apr. 1984	72	13	59	81	8	73	77	8	69	62	23	39

Notes:
[1] Source: *Euro-baromètre* 1975–84, Commission of the European Communities, Brussels. All figures are percentages.
[2] Net refers to the net difference of 'for'/'against' replies: 'very much for'/'to some extent for' and 'to some extent against'/'very much against' categories collapsed; 'don't know' replies excluded.

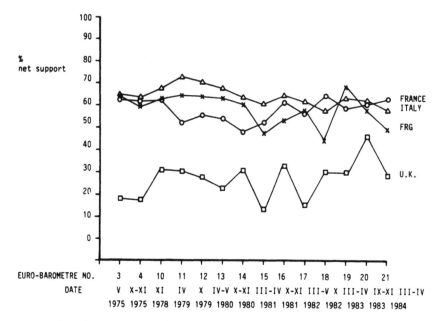

Fig. 2.1. Long-term trends in net support for European unification.

up movement towards the unification of Europe in W. Germany, France and Italy, but not in the U.K. (see, e.g. *Euro-baromètres*, nos. 4, 6, 7, 10 and 12). The results of poll no. 12 (1979) are typical, showing enthusiastic support in Italy (66%), less in W. Germany (43%) and France (35%), and lowest support of all in the U.K. (28%) for speeding up progress. Asked for their views on the future of the Community (*Euro-baromètre*, no. 9), respondents gave similar levels of support for a directly elected parliament plus an actual (European) government which would have the final say in some important areas (Italy, 57%; France 45%; W. Germany, 40%; U.K., 28%). It was only the British, showing that renowned concern for national sovereignty, who overall preferred that individual governments of member countries should have the final say. This question was asked in a similar form in 1982 (poll no. 17) and revealed that the supra-national option had lost ground in each country, with the W. Germans now also in favour of a national, not a European, government.

Summarising these data on affective support, the Italians are clearly out ahead, followed more cautiously by the French and the W. Germans. The British lag behind, but the picture is *not* as bleak as has sometimes been painted. As Rutherford has concluded:

> It is hard to spot a trend here because of the fluctuations, but it would be impossible to argue convincingly on the basis of the figures that British support for the unification of Europe has been falling off. It is just not as

Table 2.2 *General attitude to Community Membership (1974–84)*[1]

Euro-baromètre no.	Date of poll	W. Germany good	W. Germany bad	W. Germany net[2]	France good	France bad	France net	Country Italy good	Italy bad	Italy net	U.K.[3] good	U.K.[3] bad	U.K.[3] net
1.	Apr.–May 1974	59	8	51	68	5	63	77	5	72	33	39	−6
2.	Oct.–Nov. 1974	62	10	52	63	6	57	82	3	79	36	35	1
3.	May 1975	56	8	48	64	4	60	71	3	68	47	21	26
4.	Oct.–Nov. 1975	61	6	55	67	4	63	75	4	71	50	24	26
5.	May 1976	48	12	36	57	7	50	63	6	57	39	35	4
6.	Nov. 1976	57	5	52	52	7	45	68	5	63	39	34	5
7.	Apr.–May 1977	54	8	46	64	6	58	71	5	66	35	40	−5
8.	Oct.–Nov. 1977	59	7	52	57	9	48	70	5	65	35	37	−2
9.	May 1978	58	3	55	54	9	45	65	5	60	29	38	−9
10.	Nov. 1978	63	4	59	59	7	52	73	4	69	39	31	8
11.	Apr. 1979	66	5	61	56	8	48	78	2	76	33	34	−1
12.	Oct. 1979	64	3	61	58	6	52	75	2	73	29	41	−12
13.	Apr.–May 1980	65	5	60	51	9	42	74	3	71	23	49	−26
14.	Oct.–Nov. 1980	62	6	56	48	10	38	71	2	69	24	49	−25
15.	Mar.–Apr. 1981	49	9	40	50	11	39	73	5	68	24	48	−24
16.	Oct.–Nov. 1981	58	6	52	53	7	46	70	5	65	27	41	−14
17.	Mar.–May 1982	49	9	40	50	11	39	73	5	68	24	48	−24
18.	Oct. 1982	51	9	42	57	9	48	64	5	59	29	40	−11
19.	Mar.–Apr. 1983	61	5	56	53	7	46	70	4	66	28	36	−8
20.	Sept.–Nov. 1983	57	9	48	55	9	46	76	5	71	36	28	8
21.	Mar.–Apr. 1984	53	5	48	62	4	58	70	3	67	34	30	4

Notes:

[1] Source: *Euro-baromètre*, 1974–84, nos. 1–21, Commission of the European Communities, Brussels. All figures are percentages.

[2] Net refers to the net difference of 'good'/'bad' replies; 'neither good nor bad' and 'don't know' replies excluded.

[3] For the first time in *Euro-baromètre*, no. 3, results were from the U.K. (i.e. including Northern Ireland).

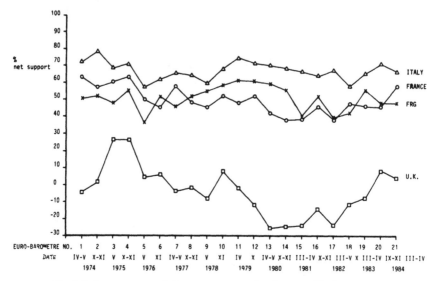

Fig. 2.2. Long-term trends in net support for the Common Market.

high as it is elsewhere. Those satisfied with the existing rate of progress have been consistently in the 40–50 per cent range. (Rutherford, 1981, p. 5.)

2.6.2 Support for Community membership

Support for Community membership has been measured by asking the following question in every poll: 'Generally speaking, do you think that (your Country's) membership of the European Community (Common Market) is a good thing, a bad thing, or neither good nor bad?' The longitudinal data are presented in Table 2.2. and Figure 2.2. Membership has consistently been favoured by the people of W. Germany, Italy and France, especially Italy, although support for this more specific form of European polity is not as high as that for the general idea of European unification. The correlation between the two variables +0.41 (see *Euro-baromètre*, no. 20, 1983).

Public opinion in the U.K. is, and always has been, less positive than in the other three countries. Once again, the magnitude of this difference is evident from the range of scores in each country. In W. Germany and France the number of 'bad' responses has rarely exceeded 10%, and never in Italy. In the U.K. the figure has never fallen below 20% and is now just under 30%. Net support for the Community reached its maximum in the U.K. in 1975, when at last 50% of responses were 'good'. This was, of course, the year of the referendum, which appears to have focussed minds on defence and security issues, thus leading to endorsement of continued membership.

Since that time net support in the U.K. has fallen quite steadily, leading Rutherford (1981) to suggest that: 'The Community may have ceased to be a minor irritant and become a major grievance.' (p. 16.) Despite this pessimistic view, support has climbed since early 1982 and the gap between 'The Three' and 'The One' is smaller than at any time since 1978. However, opinion in the U.K. is obviously much more capricious than in the other three countries, showing a remarkable range of scores (see Dalton and Duval, 1981, for a more detailed analysis and discussion of trends in British public opinion as a function of political events; and Inglehart and Rabier, 1978, for the relation between public opinion and economic indicators). This suggests that in Britain there is not yet any reliable reservoir of support (see Mathew, 1980; and Section 2.7., below).

In what respect is the Community seen as good or bad? This question was posed in 1977 (poll no. 6) and showed that the most positive effects perceived were in terms of the national economy (except in the U.K.). In all four countries more people considered the effect of the Community on consumer prices to be bad, rather than good (and especially in the U.K.). This would appear to justify a remark of Jo Grimond (former leader of the British Liberal Party) who once excoriated those who would put prices above all else: 'Is one of the great political decisions in history to be reduced to a question of 5% more or less on the tariff on canned peaches? It is as if at the reformation someone had said they were unable to make up their mind until they knew what price the monasteries were likely to fetch.' In the end, however, his anxieties were not warranted. Considering complaints about prices alongside net support, it seems that most voters will tolerate price rises in exchange for a boost to the national economy (see Lipsey, 1979). Indeed, in each of these countries except Italy, more people believe that their own country has benefited less, rather than more, than other Community members (*Euro-baromètre*, no. 10, 1979). As Kohler (1984) points out, this belief across all but one of the four countries 'runs counter to any logic' (p. 440), but it is nonetheless an important finding. This response was especially pointed in the U.K., where in 1982 (poll no. 18) 75% of respondents endorsed this view (compared with 45% in W. Germany, and 26% in both France and Italy). The U.K. is, in fact, the only country where a majority of those questioned (56%) felt that their country had *not* benefited from the Community. This response was given by only about 20% of respondents in each of the other countries, indicating once again the critical view of the British.

Subsequent analyses (see Dalton, 1980) have shown that asking whether the Common Market is a good or bad thing tends to prime positive responses. Asking whether it should be 'scrapped' has the opposite effect. Despite this tendency, responses to the more negatively worded item follow the same pattern (see *Euro-baromètres*, nos. 2, 4, 8, 15). The number of respondents who would 'regret' this development is lower than the number who say the Common Market is a 'good thing', but the Italians are still fairly consistently most, and the British least, supportive. In 1981 (poll no. 15) the percentage saying they would regret the demise of the Community was 50 in Italy, 42 in W. Germany, 34 in France and 21 in the U.K. More strikingly, and revealing the polarisation in British opinion, 46% of those questioned in the U.K. said they would be 'relieved' (compared with only 8% in W. Germany and France, and 4% in Italy) at this happening.

Asked to consult the crystal ball and judge the Community as it would be in ten or fifteen years time, the British are more positive. Only they show a marked increase in support (and decrease in opposition), although they still lag far behind the other three countries (see *Euro-baromètres*, nos. 8, 10, 11). Similarly, the British alone would vote against the Community in high numbers (50%) if they 'could start all over again'. (poll no. 6).

Commitment to the European Community also carries with it a willingness to work together and seek supra-national solutions to shared problems. But high numbers of the British (and only the British) consistently favour independent action by sovereign governments to concerted European action (see poll nos. 2, 3, 4). Even in 1975, the year of British decision, 40% still believed that their government 'should act independently of other countries in the best interests of the nation'; while only 47% supported the hardly radical proposal that 'the nine countries of the European Community should take joint action, but each government should have the final say on internal issues'. Most clearly, the British did not give their support to the suggested election of a European Parliament and Government (only 9% vs 30% in W. Germany, 38% in France and 46% in Italy).

One factor which would seem a reasonable predictor of support for Community membership is that the Community should be seen to function effectively. Several polls (see nos. 8, 10, 15–20) have asked: 'In your opinion, over the last 12 months has the understanding between the countries of the European Community (Common Market) in general increased, decreased or stayed about the same?' Responses were positive when this question was first asked (especially in 1978; see poll no. 10), but the halcyon days are now past. There has been a sharp drop in the number of people who feel that understanding has increased. Such that, in 1984 (poll no. 20) nearly twice as many respondents *in each country* felt that understanding had decreased, as felt that it had increased in the preceding 12 months. This is a worrying trend for the Community, because this item appears to have an influence on attitudes towards the Common Market (see *Euro-baromètre*, no. 18).

Summarising the data on support, levels of satisfaction with the Community are still high in France, W. Germany and especially Italy, but not in the U.K. Moreover, this negative view in the U.K. is systematically related to items concerning perceived benefits, dissolution of the Community, and a European government. The British even prefer a different, and more restricted, name for the Community. Most Britons choose the term 'Common Market' (33%), which is favoured by very few in the other countries (see also CRAM, 1985). The 'continental Europeans' use more expansive terms like the 'European Community', the 'European Economic Community' and 'Europe of the Ten' (see *Euro-baromètre*, no. 21, for an analysis which shows that this is more than a linguistic difference). The British are, however, more optimistic about the future; but with respondents in all four countries pessimistic about trends in understanding, the Community must pay heed to the possibility of reduced support in the coming years.

2.6.3 Intensity of attachment to the European ideal
Some hold the view that public feelings about the Community do not run deep and that responses in a poll may carry little commitment: 'Up to the present, the subject of "Europe" has not held any potential of risk; no courage has been required to profess one view or another; the subject has not been controversial; it had no partisan contours.' (Noelle-Neumann, 1980, p. 53.) Acknowledging this point, this section considers a number of questions which have pushed respondents a little further (testing more with a thermometer than a barometer) on their views about European integration.

On several occasions (see *Euro-baromètres*, nos. 6, 8, 10, 15) the following question has been posed: 'If one of the countries of the Common Market (European Community) finds itself in major economic difficulties, do you feel that the other countries, including (your own), should help it or not?' As the compilers of *Euro-baromètre* are aware, this item contains an element of 'facile generosity' (poll no. 8, p. 87), but it may nonetheless prove a useful measure of solidarity, a readiness to help others in difficulty. It was, after all, one of the basic aims of the Community to strengthen the feeling of solidarity between the peoples of its member states. Once again, the Italians show the highest levels of solidarity, with about 90% feeling that one should help (compared with around 70% in the other three countries). Italy is, however, one of the poorer countries of the Community, hence the Italians are rarely asked to help others financially. The Italians are also well aware that Community assistance works in their favour. In *Euro-baromètre*, no. 11, 73% of the Italians acknowledged that Community solidarity had worked to the benefit of their country (compared with 42%, 39% and 29% in the U.K., W. Germany and France, respectively).

Endorsing Community solidarity is one thing; paying for it oneself is another, as shown by responses to the following question: 'Are you, personally, prepared or not to make some personal sacrifice, for example paying a little more taxes [sic], to help another country in the European Community experiencing economic difficulties?' (see poll nos. 3, 4, 10). Responses in 1979 (no. 10) show the now-expected pattern of Italian support (64% are prepared to help) some way ahead of the other three (France, 37%; U.K., 35%; W. Germany, 26%). If the W. Germans are less than forthcoming, one should perhaps note that they are the ones who mostly pay out! But three years later in 1982 (poll no. 18), the Italian support has declined to 48% (France, 31%; W. Germany, 30%; U.K., 22%). The numbers now unwilling to make a sacrifice have risen steeply in the U.K. (71%) and France (59%), with many W. Germans (48%) and Italians (38%) giving similar responses. Evidently, taking Southern Italy as the poorest and Hamburg as the richest regions of the Community, one should not yet expect the W. German taxpayer to pay for the Sicilian farmer (Tsoukalis, 1983).

The importance of *trust* in political communities, as a measure of commitment going beyond mere friendliness, has been emphasised in the work of Deutsch (1952; Deutsch *et al.*, 1957). Such trust is seen as growing from increasing exchanges – trade, diplomatic, educational and so on – and leading to a readiness to engage in political activities (Almond and Verba, 1963). As one would expect, trust in one's own people is generally high, although lower in Italy (see *Euro-baromètre*, no. 14). More important for the Community is trust in the peoples of other member states. The W. Germans, French and British are judged 'very trustworthy' overall, but the ancient rivalries between the U.K. and France reappear in rather low levels of mutual trust. Comparing data over time (1970–80), the levels of increased trust are generally impressive (with the exception of France–U.K.). Perhaps most supportive of the European idea is the very high level of trust confided in the W. Germans, notably by the French. As Inglehart and Rabier (1982) have written, in a more thorough analysis of trust between nations: 'The Franco-German hostility that persisted for generations and was still manifest in the 1950s, has been overcome (p. 21)... the impact on trust of even such a gigantic historical event as World War II, can be undone.' (p. 23.) Trust in other nations is not, of course, a direct judgement on the European Community. However, if people attribute some or all responsibility for this increase in trust to the Community, then such subjective perceptions may be closely related to overall views of the political entity itself.

Asked to name the greatest obstacle to European unity, some would give national pride. Barzini (1983) begins the final chapter of his book with the following passage: 'What, then, are the obscure forces preventing the coagulation of Western Europe into a solid whole.... One, of course, is most evident. It is the apparently ineradicable survival of sensitive national prides.; (p. 257.) Whether Barzini is right, that pride hinders integration, is a moot point; but he is certainly right that it survives. Responses in 1982 and 1983 (*Euro-baromètres*, nos. 17 and 19) revealed that large numbers in each country were 'very proud' or fairly proud' of their nationality. The British, basking in bellicose post-Falklands glory, were most proud and the W. Germans, some way behind the others, were least proud (poll no. 17 figures for 'very proud': U.K., 57%; Italy, 40%; France, 36%, W. Germany, 17%). The W. Germans' responses would appear to bear the burden of history, about which more will be said in a later chapter. National pride is, then, whatever its impact on Community attitudes, alive and well.

Closely linked to pride is the idea of *identity* – how, in terms of what groupings, do people see and define themselves? This question has been posed as follows: 'Do you ever think of yourself as a citizen of Europe? Often, sometimes or never?' On both occasions when this question was asked (see poll nos. 17 and 19), responses followed a similar pattern. Few people often thought of themselves in these terms (though fewer, 8% in the U.K., than in France 21%, Italy 18%, or W. Germany 15%); large numbers of the W. Germans, French and Italians 'sometimes' felt like Europeans (49%, 37%, 36%; compared with 16% in the U.K.); and another large group (particularly large in the U.K., 74%) 'never' felt that way (Italy, 45%; France, 40%; W. Germany, 26%). These results give only limited support to the functionalist notion of a shift in public loyalties from national to supra-national institutions. The emergence of a cosmopolitan European identity within the Community, a European *Zusammengehörigkeitsgefühl* (to use a rarely justified German compound noun), cannot yet be hailed. If, as Emerson (1960) suggests, a nation can be defined as a body of people who *feel* they are a nation, then there is little support for the idea of a European nation in the psychological sense. The dragging of British feet comes as no great surprise; as Barzini has written:

> Still, today, when one asks a Briton, any Briton, pointblank, 'Are you European?' the answer is always, 'European? Did you say European? Er, er' – a long thoughtful pause in which all other continents are mentally evoked and regretfully discarded – 'Yes, of course, I'm European.' This admission is pronounced without pride and with resignation. (Barzini, 1983, pp. 64–5)

According to Noelle-Neumann (1980) preparedness to go supra-national fades as soon as it becomes imaginable and phrased in everyday terms. The validity of this statement can be gauged by a recent 'mock' European referendum on various aspects of integration (see *Euro-baromètre*, no. 21). It can be seen here that Europeans reserve their enthusiasm for some, but not all, European projects. In all four countries, especially France and Italy, there is strong support for a European passport (Italy, 93%; France, 86%; W. Germany, 79%; U.K., 71%). But few citizens want to give up independent ambassadors in Washington or Moscow, and even fewer want to send one 'European team' to the next Olympic games (Italy, 37%; France, 35%; W. Germany, 18%; U.K., 12%).

In sum, intensity of attachment to the European ideal is highly item-specific. The founders of the Community would be heartened by the professed willingness to help out others, encouraged by the impatience for a European passport, and delighted by the overall trend towards increased trust for other Europeans. However, they would also be disappointed by the reluctance of respondents to make personal sacrifices, to renounce national pride, and to embrace European citizenship. Once again the Italians emerge as most pro-European, forging an alliance of Latin sisters with the French; then come the W. Germans, followed at a safe and cautious distance by the British. The issue of differing response styles in each country will be dealt with below (see Chapter 5). However, it can be said here that the possibility of an acquiescent or enthusiastic response style, across all items, by the Italians, in particular, appears unlikely, simply because the Italians are *not* always the extreme responders. They consistently report that they are *less* happy or satisfied with life (*Euro-baromètres*, nos. 17, 18 and 20) than do the other three groups. As Ignazio Silone once wrote: 'There are no sadder people than those gay Italians.'[8] They appear to be genuinely enthusiastic about the European Community, not exultant *per se*.

2.6.4 Saliency of the European Community

This section considers the salience, or psychological importance, of the Community for its citizens, as measured by interest and information level. Public interest in Community affairs has been investigated with the following question: 'Are you personally very interested, a little interested, or not at all in the problems of the European Community (the Common Market)?' (see *Euro-baromètres*, nos. 3, 4, 10, 13, 17). The British were originally the most interested (poll no. 3, 1975: percentages answering 'very interested': U.K., 35%; France, 27%; W. Germany 26%; Italy, 24%) presumably because the issue became so highly politicised and publicly debated in the U.K. In recent polls, however, the Italians appear slightly the most interested, although the proportion of 'very interested' responses is about 20% in each country. Interest is higher among those with higher education and higher incomes, and among men than women.

If interest in Community affairs is rather low, exposure to the media is high. Italians follow the news primarily on television ('every day': Italy,

70%; U.K., 58%; France, 57%; W. Germany, 56%; poll no. 13), while citizens of the other three countries also read the daily newspapers ('every day': U.K., 57%; W. Germany, 44%; France, 31%; Italy, 27%). But what do all these assiduous viewers and readers learn? Apparently, very little, although quite high numbers judge themselves to be sufficiently well-informed (W. Germany, 39%; France, 29%; Italy, 21%; U.K., 18%; poll no. 17). Asked to demonstrate this knowledge (in a European Commission poll in 1973), by giving the names of new members of the Community and the former member states, respondents had great difficulty. With a maximum score of 9, 'high' knowledge (7–9) was demonstrated by a respectable 62% in W. Germany, but by relatively few respondents in the other three countries (France, 36%; U.K., 34%; Italy, 28%). 'Low knowledge' (0–3) characterised only 11% of W. Germans, but 41% of Italians, 31% of the French and 27% of the British (see Mathew, 1980, p. 167).

These data on saliency provide a more modest picture of the Community's place in the mind, as opposed to the heart, of its citizens. Except in W. Germany, where a reasonable level of knowledge is demonstrated by many people, only about 30% of the sample in each country can claim high interest in or knowledge about Community affairs.

2.6.5 The European Parliament

The European Parliament can be seen as the most supra-national and democratic of the Community's institutions, as well as the one closest to the citizens. Public opinion concerning the Parliament is dealt with in many polls, but especially in Euro-baromètres, nos. 10, 11, 12, 20 and 21.

Are people in favour of a directly elected European Parliament? Results in a series of polls (nos. 3, 4, 5, 6, 7, 9, 10 and 11) reveal strong backing for this institution. Attitudes 'for' easily outnumber attitudes 'against' and are highest in Italy (85%) and lowest in the U.K. (61%; W. Germany, 80%; France, 71%; poll no. 11). If this question is rather general, respondents in one poll (no. 12, 1979) were asked more specifically to indicate which, from a pre-arranged list, were their greatest hopes and fears concerning the Parliament. The principal hope in each of the four countries was that the Parliament would make member countries work together to face the economic crisis; the principal fear, was that there would be 'a lot of talk which in the end won't change things very much'. However, a substantial number of British respondents (30%) also voiced the fear that the Parliament would 'encroach on the powers of the national parliament', a possibility which aroused little concern in the other three countries.

Somewhat qualifying the generally pro-European attitudes, a high pro-portion in each country expect Members of the European Parliament (MEPs) representing their country to 'support the interests of (your country) all the time whether or not they are good for Europe as a whole'. The results are consistent over polls (see *Euro-baromètres*, nos. 9, 10, 12, 21), the most recent figures being for 1983 (U.K., 54%; Italy, 44%; France, 40%; W. Germany, 39%). However, the majority in France, Italy and W. Germany think that their MEP should 'support things that are good for Europe as a whole, even if they are not always good for (your country) at the time' (France, 48%; Italy, 45%; W. Germany, 43%; U.K., 33%).

Coinciding with direct elections to the Parliament, other items have examined awareness of the Parliament, voting intention and interest in election results. Public awareness is low (see *Euro-baromètres*, nos. 10, 11, 12). In December 1979, four months after the first direct elections, the percentage having heard something about the Parliament was surprisingly far short of 100 (W. Germany, 77%; France, 67%; Italy, 66%; U.K., 55%), and in every country there was a vast gulf between those having heard something and those who could recall what it was. As Inglehart and Rabier (1980) concluded: 'To a quite astonishing degree, the publics of given countries were not aware of the elections.' (p. 30.)

Voting intentions have been ascertained in a number of polls (see nos. 10, 20, 21) and actual turn-out is closely related to the number of respondents claiming they would 'certainly' vote. Looking at the 1984 data (*Euro-baromètre*, no. 21), the Italians and French (76% and 73%, respectively) appear far more motivated and interested than the Germans and the British (37% and 36% respectively).[9] Surprisingly, in view of these differences between countries, the numbers of respondents who say they are 'very interested' in the election results are quite similar and around 30% in each nation (see poll nos. 10, 11).

This final set of public opinion results reveals no great well of support for items relating to the European Parliament. Although seen by some politicians and commentators as Europe's 'jewel in the crown', it is appropriate to note that the word 'assembly' is more accurate than parliament, it being a deliberative, not legislative, body. As Slater (1983) points out, elections to the European Parliament neither directly nor indirectly determine the formation of governments; Reif (1984; Reif and Schmitt, 1980) has termed them 'second-order elections'. This impotence may be reflected in the voters' low levels of awareness, interest in election results and voting intentions, notwithstanding broad support for a European Parliamentary Assembly (see Blumler and Fox, 1982; Kohler, 1984; Rabier, in press). It is only the Italians and the French, following a familiar pattern, who are highly motivated to turn out and vote. The general trend, as observed by Hrbek and Wessels (1984) is that, 'less and less citizens in the European Community know and care about "their" European Parliament' (p. 21), although the very idea of the Parliament was bound up with the aim of generating interest, participation and knowledge.

2.6.6 Summary

Public opinion in, and about, Europe is obviously not a static phenomenon. Rather, there are fluctuations which sometimes hide important trends. Despite this flux, the *Euro-baromètre* series provides clear evidence for the existence of a European public opinion. This is seen in the broad consensus on several issues – most importantly, the unification of Europe, and support for Community membership – and in the consistency both between items in the same poll, and between the same items in different polls. Notwithstanding this evidence for both consistency and consensus, we should not forget that the public is human (Lipsey, 1979). It sometimes avoids the difficult issue, tolerates inconsistency and reveals a confused view of politics. However, opinion polls about Europe do have a role to play and have now achieved a permanent place on the political stage. As Lipsey remarked: 'Opinion polls are like oracles. They take a bit of interpreting; the answers they come up with are frequently disquieting; but they have an awkward habit of being right.' (1979, p. 12.)

If support for the Community is tangible, it must be kept in perspective. As revealed in *Euro-baromètre* no. 17, the unification of Europe is not a particularly important hope for the future; it is seen as much less important than, for example, scientific and technical developments. Similarly, a reduced role in the world for western Europe does not evoke cross-national insomnia; far more important a fear is the rise in crime and terrorism. As was seen above, support for Europe may be evident and stable, but Europe and the Community are not psychologically salient (see Handley, 1981). Overall, respondents are characterised neither by enthusiasm (except in Italy), nor by hostility. As Putnam (1981) has remarked, public opinion is less pro-European than the integrationists might like, but not as hostile as they may fear.

The authors of *Euro-baromètre* no. 17, report that favourable attitudes towards the Community are spread widely across all strata of Italian society, and are more resistant than elsewhere to disillusion and misgivings. The Italians are not only enthusiastic now, but impatient for acceleration towards a united Europe. Domestic governmental problems are probably relevant here, convincing Italians that a united Europe is the solution for them. French opinion is also strongly in favour, 'for all its reputation of being devious, Gaullist, nationalistic, obstreperous or whatever'. (Rutherford, 1981, p. 2.) The W. Germans can still be counted on for support, but it is neither ecstatic nor unqualified. Noelle-Neumann (1980) refers to the W. Germans' 'noncommital benevolence toward the construction of a united Western Europe without any signs of real enthusiasm for the European idea'. (p. 99.) In contrast, according to her data, the demand for W. German reunification is perceived as much more important, and is experienced as 'a deeply felt national concern'. (*op. cit.*, p. 102.)

The British deserve, or require, a new paragraph. They do support the loose notion of European unification, but they appear unsure or unconvinced that the Common Market (as they like to call it) is the best means of bringing it about. The '*Observer*' newspaper (19 June, 1983), noting that the European Community had not been an issue in the British general election of 1983, suggested that Community membership may have 'crossed that barrier of British conservatism beyond which things that were previously suspect are finally accepted as inevitable'. Given the slimmest of margins for net Community support in early 1984, it might take a brave man to give unqualified assent to that view. The British are *not* anti-European, but they are *not* pro-Community; their responses to so many of the above questions show how concerned they still are with matters of national sovereignty, and how reluctant they are to give any real, lasting commitment to the Community. This is certainly not an original conclusion, merely an echo, based on the latest findings, of views such as the following:

> The British public clearly did not see themselves as Europeans in the sense in which the inhabitants of the (other three) member states (considered here) did, and at no time displayed any strong desire to participate in the European integration movement. (Macfarlane, 1981, p. 144)

> The polls suggest that the British people remain to be convinced that membership of the European Community is part of their natural way of life. (Rutherford, 1981, p. 21)

> The preparations, the events, and the results of the European election showed that, after more than five years' membership of the EEC, the United Kingdom is not a European country like the others.[10] (Bibes, Menudier, de la Serre and Smouts, 1980, p. 65)

If these four countries show such wide variations in support, who are the real Europeans, and *how many* are they in number? Summarising the very latest data at this time (poll no. 21, May, 1984), the authors of *Euro-baromètre* conclude, from their multi-dimensional analysis, that about 33% of their total number of respondents (drawn from all ten Community countries) could be described as the 'hard core' of 'pro-Europeans'; at the other extreme, a minority of 15% could be described as anti-Europeans. The 33% represent a kind of pillar of hope for the Community, which can be related to the comment of a recent newspaper article:

> It is no good expecting a European 'pillar' simply to rise from the earth of its own accord. It would have to be built laboriously out of many stones,

such as European defence and foreign policy cooperation, that are still very rough-hewn, to say nothing of some, such as an industrial policy, an energy policy, and a transport policy, that have not yet been cut at all. (David Watt, writing in *The Times*, 30 March, 1984)

One stone that has been cut, but must be continuously polished (like the precious stone it is) is public opinion. For it is those with favourable attitudes who participate in the Community and exercise their right to vote in direct elections (see Blumler and Fox, 1982; Inglehart and Rabier, 1980). Given this importance of favourable attitudes, we must now move away from the *description* of public opinion to consider the more interesting question of what underlies overall favourable attitudes towards the Community.

2.7 Theoretical analyses of Community attitudes: the determinants of 'Europeanism'.[11]

The scientific contribution of opinion polls, or any other empirical method, is limited as long as data collection is undertaken in the absence of any theoretical orientation. Notwithstanding the often thoughtless generation of public opinion data for the mass media, it would be misleading to contend that there are no theories of attitudinal integration. This section considers some of the theoretical explanations for public opinion in Europe, focussing on the notions of support, value priorities and political skills.

In general terms, the determinants of positive attitudes towards Europe can be construed in terms of three broad categories (see Mathew, 1980):

(1)   individual psychological make-up – e.g. intelligence, personality;
(2)   social position – including age, occupation, income and education;
(3)   external influences – such as the impact of historical events, reference groups, political parties and international travel.

There is some indication from *Euro-baromètre* studies that support for the Community is higher among the better educated than the less well-educated (with social class as probable mediating variable), but the difference in support level according to both education and occupation is not great. If one divides the samples into well- and less well-educated, an absolute majority in both groups favours Community membership. There are also, for specific items and specific countries, differences attributable to age, regional variation and political affiliation.

These findings are all very well, and often indisputable. However, they are inappropriate for the present research for two main reasons. First, because students of similar age and educational level are used in the study reported below, the influence of age and education is 'controlled' out. Regional factors may well be at work, but this issue cannot be addressed

with our samples. Cross-national differences remain as the major demographic variable. A second reason for moving beyond broad demographic
variables is that they impart little information about the attitudinal structure
of pro-European views. Our question is: what social-psychological variables
appear to be related to positive attitudes towards the Community? This
question is answered, first, by considering in more detail the research of other
social scientists on the notions of *support, value orientations* and *political skills*.
Available analyses of the impact of these variables pave the way for the
present social-psychological analysis of Community attitudes.

Handley (1977) has suggested a more detailed analysis of Community
support based on the work of Easton (1965a,b). This begins with Easton's
distinction between 'supportive actions' (overt support) and 'supportive
attitudes' (covert support) and the justification for studying attitudes, not
actions, as we do here. According to Easton: 'In many cases, the ability to
detect accurately the existence of covert support, or supportive states of
mind, is far more important than its actual expression in overt behavior.'
(1965a, p. 161.) This is arguably the case with regard to the European
Community where, occasional revolting farmers excluded, people give verbal
indications of their support for the Community (or lack of it), rather than
taking to the streets. Following Easton, Handley suggests that there may be
several different types of support, such as support for the three basic levels
of a political system: the authorities, the regime and the political community.
These support levels are not necessarily correlated, for someone may well
support one level, but not necessarily other levels, of the system. Or, taking
this idea further, there may be support for one policy, but opposition to
another. If this is the case, then the impact of policy judgements on overall
attitudes will presumably depend on the importance, and value, attached
to the policy (see the expectancy-value analysis of attitudes discussed in
Chapters 3 and 5, below).

A further distinction made by Easton is that between 'specific' and
'diffuse' support. Specific support might be for a particular policy (e.g.
agriculture). Diffuse support has been conceived in a more general way:

> This forms a reservoir of favourable attitudes or good will that helps
> members to accept or tolerate outputs to which they are opposed or the
> effect of which they see as damaging to their wants. Except in the long
> run, diffuse support is independent of the effects of daily outputs. It
> consists of a reserve of support that enables a system to weather the
> many storms where outputs cannot be balanced off against inputs of
> demand. (Easton, 1965a, p. 273)

According to this view, diffuse support is a necessary underlying component
of favourable attitudes to the Community. In its absence, every little
dissatisfaction with the way the Community works will be transformed into

a major fluctuation in attitudinal support. From his own empirical analysis of Community attitudes, using *Euro-baromètre* data, Handley contends that there is evidence of a substantial 'diffuse affective orientation', without any clear idea as to why Community membership is good or bad.[12]

Lindberg and Scheingold (1970; see also Lindberg, 1966–67) also argue that the European Community functions smoothly because of the existence of a 'permissive consensus', or a general favourable orientation towards European integration. They propose, further, that support can be considered in terms of a matrix of 'levels of interaction' and 'basis of response'. Levels of interaction are 'identitive' and 'systemic'; the former refers to the perceived links among the peoples of the Community, and the latter refers to links between the public and the system. Basis of response is subdivided into two distinct sources, or types of attitude: utilitarian and affective support (see Easton, 1965a,b; Feld and Wildgen, 1976; Handley, 1975; Lindberg and Scheingold, 1970, pp. 38–45; Lipset, 1963; Pentland, 1973, p. 127).

Utilitarian support is more cognitive and related to perceptions of concrete gains and losses. Using the same reasoning as game theorists and equity theorists (see below), Lindberg and Scheingold see utilitarian support for European cooperation as based on the perception of larger pay-offs than would accrue from an independent, non-cooperative stance. While it is not necessary to embrace a learning-theory interpretation of the growth of utilitarian support, as do some functionalists and neo-functionalists, it seems a reasonable hypothesis that support will be determined, in part, by perceived gains and losses.

Inglehart and Rabier (1978) identified cross-national differences in utilitarian support between the various member states of the Community and also noted a decrease during the period 1973–77. Mathew (1980) reports that the general publics of the six original member states of the Community do express utilitarian support, but that this is not so for the three countries which joined later (excluding Greece; see also Inglehart, 1984). However, like Inglehart and Rabier (1978), Mathew uses as a measure the item asking whether Community membership is a good, or bad, thing. According to Mathew:

> a negative (bad thing) or positive (good thing) response denotes the
> respondents' feelings about whether their country has benefited or not
> from the existing Common Market relationship. (Mathew, 1980, p. 72)

This interpretation is difficult to sustain. The present writer can see nothing in the wording of the question to support this view. On the contrary, it appears entirely reasonable to conceive that many people who are currently *dissatisfied* with the Community, nonetheless answer that it (the only existing supra-national community that we have) is a good thing (in principle, perhaps). Mathew may simply be trying to make the item do too much work, and work for which it may not have been selected. It may also be noted that Handley (1981, pp. 348–9) uses the same item as a measure of affective support.

A more reliable point made by Mathew is that the Community is seen as a better thing for the nation's economy than for oneself (in terms of consumer prices):

> It is significant that the European Community is not seen as a major factor on a personal level, but, rather the general public tend to formulate attitudes based on the effects on their economy in general. The data suggest that supportive attitudes are perhaps rooted in a generalised awareness of the Community's effect on the national economy and not on personal experiences. (Mathew, 1980, p. 77)

This point, also made by Shepherd (1975), is backed up by an inspection of cross-tabulations and seems to contradict those functionalists and neo-functionalists who insist on a shift of support from national to supra-national entity. As Mathew explains, the supra-national entity is positively judged *because* it is good for the national entity, thus both sets of interests are compatible. In this sense, Shepherd (1975) explains that nationalists can favour Community membership, provided that integration does not end with unification, whereby national sovereignty is transferred (de Gaulle being a case in point).

Affective support is an emotional sentiment in response to the idea of European integration. It is related to the perceived legitimacy and popularity of, and loyalty to, the Community. As a measure of this kind of support, Mathew uses items concerning European unification, and the desire to speed it up or slow it down, support for European Political Union, Community policy in major areas, and support for the European Parliament. Evidence from this mixed bag of items is used to conclude that broad affective support is evident for past, present and future aspects of European integration, although there is still a gap between the new and old member states (as identified earlier by Inglehart, 1970b; Inglehart and Rabier, 1978). However, as with utilitarian support, these measures are not optimal, especially as straightforward support for the Common Market (good or bad thing) might be seen as an affective response. These reservations do not, however, contradict the view that the analysis of utilitarian and affective support dimensions is central to a full analysis of Community attitudes. The measure of affective support used by Inglehart and Rabier (1978) – helping out another member state in economic difficulties – seems a far better item. Using this question, Inglehart and Rabier reported, ' a surprisingly widespread willingness to share economic burdens in time of difficulties, and a certain readiness to place the interests of the Community as a whole above those of one's own nation'. (pp. 69–70.)

According to functionalists and neofunctionalists, utilitarian and affective support dimensions are not only interrelated, but are related in a temporal sequence: utilitarian support preceding affective support. The idea is that the perception of advantages, benefits or gains is a prerequisite for an investment of confidence and trust. Given the Community's main concern with economic integration, at least originally, Shepherd (1975) has proposed that support will be mainly utilitarian, 'with economic self-interest predominating over political self-interest; (p. 94). However, if Mathew's variables are accepted, there is evidence for both kinds of support.

The question of which kind of support emerges first is problematic and cannot be decisively answered here. Lindberg and Scheingold concluded that support for the Community was essentially, but not exclusively, utilitarian and that this is consistent with the idea of a 'cumulative logic of integration', whereby economic interests and successes pave the way for affective support. This conclusion was not, however, upheld by Shepherd (1975). Using more recent data, he reported strong utilitarian support and a clear demonstration of affective support for European identification; the former was not more marked than the latter. Considering Mathew's measures of utilitarian and affective support (e.g. support for Community membership, and support for European unification) one notes that 'affective' support is, and always has been, higher (see Figures 2.1. and 2.2., above). Either the temporal sequence is wrong, or the measures are not valid, or, perhaps, both. In view of present misgivings, the question should remain open. It seems at least prudent to consider that affective support may be 'independent of, rather than necessarily consequent upon, the satisfaction of utilitarian interests'. (Lodge, 1978, p. 240.) Alternatively, utilitarian and affective support may *not* be distinguishable. Wildgen and Feld (1976) attempted to develop measures of these variables by selecting ten items on an intuitive basis and then performing a factor analysis. Two factors did, indeed, emerge, although the authors state quite clearly that the factor analysis was computed with instruction 'to extract two (i.e. and only two) factors without regard to eigenvalues'. (p. 80.) This study cannot therefore be seen as a test of the empirical validity of the conceptual distinction. Wildgen and Feld are also reluctant to label their factors 'utilitarian' and 'affective'; they prefer to speak of 'institutional' and 'performance' factors. Given the methodology and results of this study, it would appear that the case for an empirical distinction between these two types of support has not yet been proven (see Chapter 6).

A rather different approach to the determinants of Europeanism has been taken by Inglehart. As noted above, his early work (Inglehart, 1967, 1970) found more pro-European views among the young than the old, although he neither argues, nor assumes, that youth is *always* more cosmopolitan. He ascribed this pro-European stance to their lack of direct experience of European war and to their socialisation in the post-war world of an increasingly cooperative Europe (see also Puchala, 1970). While it is accepted as almost axiomatic that the young are more pro-European, age differences no longer appear to be so large or so important (see Deheneffe, 1983; Mathew, 1980; but see Inglehart, 1970*b*). In more recent work, Inglehart (1977) has conceptualised the growth of support for Europe in terms of a 'silent revolution', reinforced by two processes of changing value priorities and political skills. Inglehart reported a strong relationship between certain value types, political skills and developing supra-national attitudes.

Regarding values, Inglehart proposes that 'the good life' in post-war western Europe has freed the public of worries about material well-being and physical security (a proposition based on Maslow's, 1954, theory of motivation). The new generation of Europe, 'post-Materialists', place greater emphasis on the quality, not the quantity, of life and are more favourable to European integration (Inglehart, 1971). By political skills, Inglehart referred to cognitive changes associated with a politically more sophisticated public. This sophistication, what Handley (1977) calls 'political empathy', is seen as a precondition for pro-European attitudes. It is the ability to perceive and identify with a political unit, a political situation, or relations with other groups of people, without which it would be meaningless to speak of support.

Inglehart uses the term 'cognitive mobilization' – 'the increasingly wide distribution of the political skills necessary to cope with an extensive political community' (1970*b*, p. 47) – and he contends that high levels of political awareness and skills in political communication provide the possibility of identifying with a supra-national political community. Thus he refers to it as a necessary, but not sufficient, condition for the development of support. Cognitively mobilised people are 'relatively likely to know about and discuss European politics and to view things from a European perspective'. (Inglehart and Rabier, 1978, p. 86.) Cognitive mobilisation is usually measured by responses to two questions, asking how frequently respondents discuss political matters, and whether they try to persuade others to share their views. Mathew (1980) has suggested that this variable should also be assessed with measures of level of public information and knowledge about the Community, hence the more extensive analysis of knowledge about the Community which is presented in the study reported below.

Inglehart has also related cognitive mobilisation to the emergence of a European identity (feeling like a European citizen) and considers cosmopolitan vs parochial identity (Lerner, 1958) as a predictor of Europeanism. As noted earlier, most students can be expected to be highly cognitively mobilised, thus this variable was not included in the present study. Inglehart (1984) himself has also reported that the linkage between cognitive mobilisation (and Post-Materialist values) and pro-European attitudes has declined, because the Community has been losing the support of opinion leaders. However, acknowledging Inglehart's discussion of identity, it will be of interest to relate stereotyping of one's own and other nationalities to pro-European attitudes.

These various determinants of Europeanism have been considered together in a thoughtful analysis by Mathew. Using data from a European Commission poll carried out in 1973, Mathew constructed a 'European Integration Support Index' (based on four questions dealing with Community membership – good/bad thing; for/against European Parliament; willingness to make a personal sacrifice to help the unification of Europe; and for/against the unification of Europe). This index served as the criterion variable in a multiple regression analysis with five predictor variables: cognitive mobilisation; changing value priorities; knowledge of and familiarity with the Community; public exposure to Community affairs; and geo-political (European) identity. The results of this analysis gave scant support to Inglehart's emphasis on cognitive mobilisation and values (but see Inglehart, 1970b, 1971; Inglehart and Rabier, 1978). Focussing on the four countries of interest for the present study (W. Germany, Italy, France and the U.K.), there was, as one might expect, a difference between the U.K. and the other three.[13] Examining the squared semipartial correlations, Mathew reports that most of the variance of the support index in the U.K. is due to sense of geo-political identity and knowledge of Community membership. In all three other countries, level of public information is the best predictor.

One wonders, however, just how important any of these variables are, because considering all countries together Mathew's five predictors account for only 12% of the variation in his index. In a further multiple regression analysis a dummy variable was added for late vs early membership of the Community ('The Six' vs 'The Three'). The percentage of variance explained then rose sharply to 28%, indicating that length of membership was the strongest predictor of support for European integration. Inglehart and Rabier (1978) also used a dummy variable to code date of entry into the Community, and this was by far the best predictor of Community support. As these authors noted, 'the sheer passage of time under common supranational institutions may tend to instil the habit of viewing things from a broader perspective than that of the nation-state'. (p. 78.)

This is an interesting finding, but one that leaves us with the rather unsatisfactory answer that the U.K., Ireland and Denmark are 'different'. Most vaguely inquisitive people would now want to know more. Does the answer lie in the seeds of time, realms of history or some mysterious notion of 'national character' (see Duijker and Frijda, 1960; Inkeles and Levinson, 1969)? Are the peoples of these three countries genetically non-European? Or, more constructively, what psychological reserves might the Italians, the French and the W. Germans (our interest, here, not lying with the Dutch, the Belgians and the Luxembourgeois) have built up in their 17 years of association, which could differentiate them so starkly from the 'new boys'? The problem is, that while Mathew identifies and discusses differences in various support levels between The Six and The Three, these items are then collapsed to form an index. If he had had one simple measure of overall attitude, then the various levels of support could themselves have seen service as predictors. In the analyses reported below, such an overall measure has been used, to which one can relate levels of different support and many other (possible) predictors; this ought to provide a more satisfactory answer to the question: what 'determines' Europeanism?

Despite the critical nature of this review, the present work has been given solid foundations to build on. Although some variables have not been included, such as cognitive mobilisation, and the nature of the prediction task has been changed (from predicting support, to using different kinds of support to predict overall attitude) these prior analyses have proved most useful. It must also be said that the present study (despite its own limitations, which are considered below) enjoyed the luxury of choosing its own variables for specified purposes. This was not the case in Mathew's analysis of survey data. Despite his careful attempt to justify choice of items, he was obliged to use someone else's items to answer his own questions. To that extent, his analysis of the determinants of Europeanism was hampered and constrained from the start.

2.8 Limitations of public opinion surveys

In spite of the vast data base and major importance of the *Euro-baromètre* studies, public opinion polling has some limitations as a technique in general, and as a measure of coherent political attitudes in particular. The elitist argument against polling *public* opinion has been dealt with above and will not be repeated. The issue here is less about *whom* to poll, than *how* to poll; for it concerns the wording, the range and interrelation of items, and the interpretation of polls.

At one level, public opinion surveys are limited because 'they have to operate with straightforward questions in order to get unequivocal answers which necessarily give only a simplified picture of a complex and differentiated reality'. (Kohler, 1984, p. 445.) While this is true, most people would probably argue that the constraint is justified, *if* large amounts of reliable and comparable data are generated. However, the value of the data is often curtailed not only by the simplicity of the questions, but by their ambiguity. A clear and classic example of the dangers inherent in a poorly worded poll was given by Cantril's (1944) analysis of 30 respondents who answered 'yes' to the question: 'Are you in favour of labour unions?' Further questioning revealed that eight people would enter a store being picketed; ten believed that most labour leaders were dishonest; 18 thought there should be more governmental control of unions; and 25 thought that labour unions with radical leadership should be prohibited (see Asch, 1952). Clear wording of items is therefore the basic prerequisite for a good poll, and different wording for questions intended to measure essentially the same thing – e.g. 'European Union', 'European Integration', 'United States of Europe' – may yield different results (see Noelle-Neumann, 1970).

While most items in the *Euro-baromètre* series are chosen with exemplary care, on occasions the meaning of an item, and hence a response, is ambiguous. An example is provided by the compilers of poll no. 11, regarding the following item:

> To choose your representative in the European Parliament, which of these are the most important in your choice? Their political party or their ideas about Europe? (*Euro-baromètre*, no. 11, 1979, p. 23)

Answers revealed a very strong, and hardly credible, tendency to say that ideas about Europe (as if most voters would even be aware of these) were most important. As the authors of the report state:

> It is virtually impossible to assess the significance of these results; many interviewees may well be giving a stereotyped answer showing an unconscious preference for the word 'European' rather than the word 'political'. (*op. cit.*, p. 23)

Another example, also from *Euro-baromètre*, is given by Rutherford (1981) and concerns the following item:

> Some people consider the Common Market as being a first step towards a closer union between the member states. Personally, do you yourself think the movement towards the unification of Europe should be speeded up, slowed down, or continued as it is at present? (Rutherford, 1981, p. 31)

Rutherford's misgivings justify quotation in full, because he makes a number of telling points about just one questionnaire item:

> The question should be examined closely before coming to any judgement about the answers. The second sentence does not necessarily follow logically from the first. It would be possible to be in favour of faster progress towards the unification of Europe without in any way approving

of the present organisation of the Common Market; such, presumably, is the position of some British pro-Marketeers. The phrase 'unification of Europe' is also undefined, which is possibly why it is used so often in the communiqués of European foreign ministers and heads of government. Finally, it is rather difficult to imagine that the majority at least of continental Europeans would be against the unification of Europe. One would hardly expect them to opt for its division. (*Op. cit.*, 1981, p. 3)

A more general aspect of wording is whether items are positively or negatively phrased. Oskamp (1977) says one should use both types of phrasing in order to avoid 'yea-saying', or always agreeing with the question. Relatedly, pollsters should, but do not always, obey the commandment, 'Thou shalt not prompt!' Many newspaper-sponsored polls unashamedly prompt respondents to give particular answers; needless to say, when this is so, the poll's results are quite worthless, except as a study of implicit social influence. In contrast to the present view, Bourdieu (1972) makes the radical suggestion that questions, rather than attempting neutrality, should be quite specific about the positions on an issue, in terms of which respondents should place themselves.

A final issue concerning wording is that of response format. Polls often restrict respondents to simple 'yes/no' answers to very complex problems, where a more reasoned answer would call for the qualifiers 'very', 'somewhat', 'quite' and so on. In their study of voting, Himmelweit *et al.* (1981) found that on several issues those voting for different political parties were *not* on opposite sides of the mid-point, but merely differed in degree of enthusiasm or dislike. A 3-point scale could not have detected this difference. In this regard, confidence in the findings of *Euro-baromètre* is increased by noting how many items allow for such differentiated responses.

Turning to the range of items in a poll, it is immediately obvious just how superficially the public has been, and is, polled on some of the great issues of our time. Roiser (1983) points out that opinion polls are often impoverished in scope, compared with marketing surveys. He quotes Jameson's (1981) criticism that: 'a survey on tinned peaches or suntan lotions will take 35–40 minutes, yet a widely publicised poll on re-alignment in British politics may take just four or five minutes'. (p. 14.) On the same issue, Himmelweit *et al.* (1981) propose that weak relationships obtained between attitudes, or between voting choice and attitudes, should not necessarily be attributed to an apathetic or politically unsophisticated public. Rather, the answer may lie in having questioned the respondent on an inappropriate or insufficient set of issues. One question per issue is the usual practice, but when wording is so crucial, and dubious, alterations in wording may bring out changes in response. The strategy adopted by Himmelweit *et al.*, asking several questions about key issues, appears a good solution, although one must obviously be aware that an exhausted or bored respondent will no longer give systematic and considered responses.

A further advantage of increasing the number of items in a poll is that the intercorrelations between different items (the *structure* of public opinion) can be analysed. This could be done by pollsters, when they do ask several questions, but as Himmelweit *et al.* observe, their approach is usually 'too facile' (*op. cit.*, p. 202). Most polls report results for each issue singly, although cross-tabulations are sometimes used to juxtapose two or three questions or issues. An encouraging trend in the *Euro-baromètre* series is the increasing use of indices of 'support', based on a set of responses, and of such techniques as multiple classification analysis (see poll no. 9) and multi-dimensional analysis (see poll. no. 21).

Even if a poll consists of carefully worded items on a range of issues, great care must be taken in the *interpretation* of results. Roiser (1983) gives two examples of mis- or over-interpretation. First, items are rarely chosen to imply a behavioural or conative component, although they are sometimes used as if this were the case. As was noted earlier, saying that the Common Market is a 'bad thing' does not imply any readiness to march on the Berlaymont building in Brussels or to contact one's Euro-M.P. Following Fishbein and Ajzen (1975), to know whether people would be prepared to do the latter, one would need an item which addressed this specific *behavioural intention*, rather than a general attitude. Second, as the authors of *Euro-baromètre* are careful to point out, a poll is not a referendum. In particular, it does not have the publicity and public interest of a referendum, and it does not carry with it the burden of responsibility. The British may never have been great supporters of the 'Common Market', but the referendum of 1975 provided a wonderful means of concentrating their minds on the gravity of the issue. It may not have converted agnostics, let alone heretics, but it did appear to convince people that 'it would be an exceedingly lonely world outside'. (Rutherford, 1981, p. 20.) Dalton and Duval (1981) also reveal that participation in a referendum is a major event, the significance and impact of which fade very slowly and are still revealed in respondents' attitudes months later.

A further problem in how to interpret responses, as in all questionnaire research, is that of socially desirable responses; or, put less politely, lying. A good example comes from a Gallup poll (reported in *The Economist*, 3 December, 1983) in which one Briton in eight claimed to be able to understand a French newspaper. With the British reputation for monolingualism, few would take this result at face value. A more subtle example of the same phenomenon appears, and is discussed, in the report of *Euro-baromètre* no. 12. Respondents were asked in October, 1979, whether they had voted in the June European election. In every single one of the ten member states, the percentage of people in the sample who 'recalled' voting was greater than the percentage of people in the country as a whole who did actually turn out to vote. This discrepancy was particularly large in the three new member states. It could be that the samples for this poll were simply not representative, but, rather, constituted a group of politically active and conscientious (i.e. voting) people. A less tortuous explanation is that respondents declined to present themselves to an interviewer in a negative light, by admitting to not having voted; they simply fabricated. Given the possibility of such responses, it is advisable, even if rarely possible, to obtain some objective measures (e.g. knowledge of Community affairs), rather than relying totally on self-reports of questionable validity.

To conclude this long chapter on public opinion polls, no objection to polling *per se*, or to polling *public* opinion, is being stated. Far from wanting fewer polls, the remedy prescribed is more, but better and different, polls. In particular, we need to collect more data aligned to a theory, or theories, not data in search of a theory. Too many questions have been generated, responses analysed and results published in the absence of any general theories or hypotheses about *why* people might respond in particular ways. More detail is needed if we are really to learn more about how people understand the Community, what knowledge they have about it, and what attitudes they hold towards it and its many associated principles, policies and products. Macfarlane (1981) wrote about the U.K. and the Community that: 'If one thing *is* clear about the issue of British membership of the European Economic Community... it is that the majority of the British public were *not clear* what it was all about.' (p. 140.) The latter part of this remark is surely as true for the publics of the other member states. Before we can agree that 'Europeanism' is a 'new ideology' (Bacot-Decriaud and Plantin, 1982), a more thorough analysis of attitudes towards the Community is required. The theoretical framework for the present research, based on social-psychological ideas, is presented in the following chapter.

3 Towards a social-psychological analysis of 'Europeanism'

It would probably be more accurate to speak, not of the development of a social psychology of international relations, but of the development of approaches to the study of international behavior in which social-psychological concepts and methods play an integral part.

(H. C. Kelman, 1965)

That social psychologists have a contribution to make to the study of international relations and political behaviour has long been recognised (see Etzioni, 1969; Kelman, 1965b; Sears, 1969). For Kelman, a social psychology of international relations has two central supports, dealing with how individuals and groups: 'a) conceive of their own nation, other nations, and the international system, of the relationship between these systems, and of their own relationships to them' (1965a, p. 24) and 'b) interact – officially or unofficially, directly or symbolically – with other nations, their representatives, and their individual nationals'. (*Ibid.*) As Kelman notes, most studies concentrate on one type of analysis or the other, although he acknowledges that the two are obviously related.

It is the former focus on images, attitudes and opinions, rather than the latter processes of interaction, which characterises the present study. The aim is to show that a detailed, in-depth analysis of European attitudes, in terms of various social-psychological theories and constructs, can provide an improvement on what Etzioni has called 'straightforward, one-point-in-time, two-variable, "cross-tab" reports'. (1969, p. 573.)

The contribution of a social-psychological approach has recently been elegantly and convincingly demonstrated by Himmelweit *et al.* (1981). Their analysis of 'how voters decide' shows that political attitudes are sufficiently complex to be termed 'cognitive maps'; that they cannot be dismissed merely as elite phenomena; and that, in a fundamental way, they matter a great deal more than past vote in influencing the voting decision. Notable aspects of the analysis by Himmelweit *et al.* were the variety of political attitudes investigated, and the complexity of their underlying structure, as well as the multivariate analyses skilfully used to explore fully the implications of the data. The link between the Himmelweit *et al.* analysis of voting and

51

the present focus on the European Community is that both allocate a primary role to cognitive concepts, and centrally to attitudes.

The study of such social cognitions becomes relevant when it is acknowledged that this 'social knowledge', and not some 'pure' or 'objective' form of knowledge, guides the behaviour of ordinary people. Thus, for example, if the E.E.C. is cognitively represented in terms of the need for a unified Europe to prevent the occurrence of another war on this continent, then it is this belief that will most likely determine the votes of individual members of a society, as in a referendum. Indeed, it is somewhat ironic that the Community has been the subject of several nationwide referenda, while no detailed attempt has been made to ascertain what people think, feel and know about the Community, its policies and its effects. The reported research originated in response to these lacunae and, having criticised many opinion poll studies for their lack of, or impoverished, theory, it is now important to indicate some of the areas of social-psychological theory which bear on the reported research. These theories helped to determine what and how questions were asked of our respondents, and how the data were explained.

3.1 Social representations

In order to understand people's attitudes to the European Community, we must understand what they know and think about it. If someone believes that the aim of the Community was to erase unemployment from the face of Europe, then her judgement may be very negative. On the other hand, if someone believes the Community was founded to increase trade between member states, then a more positive overall evaluation should be found. A first aim of the research should therefore be an analysis of common-sense understanding of the Community (*cf.* Heider, 1958; Wegner and Vallacher, 1981), including people's ideas about the perceived goals and guiding principles of the Community. Common sense has been defined as, 'the source or system of those very general beliefs about the world which are universally and unquestioningly taken to be true in everyday life'. (Quinton, 1977.) While this definition may seem ambitiously broad or far too vague, it is useful in guiding us, first, away from specific judgements and, second, towards those 'very general beliefs'. But what is general or common sense will, of course, vary between groups, societies and cultures. Hence one should expect cross-national differences to emerge from an analysis of the images and metaphors used to talk about the Community.

Influenced by the work of Moscovici (1961–76), a number of social psychologists in Europe have begun to approach the study of common sense using the notion of *social representation*, a term which has its origin in

Durkheim's (1898) concept of *représentation collective*.[1] According to Lukes (1975), Durkheim started using the term in about 1897, to refer to characteristics of social thinking as distinct from individual thinking (later Moscovici, 1984, was even to refer to a 'thinking society'). From Durkheim's point of view, collective representations described a whole range of intellectual forms which included science, religion, myth and so on. According to Lukes, this sort of representation was collective in at least three senses: 'in its origins... in its reference or object... (and) in being common to the members of a society or group... Durkheim wanted to say both that *représentations collectives* are socially generated and that they refer to, and are in some sense "about", society'. (1975, p. 7.) Durkheim also emphasised that a collective representation was not reducible to individual representations – it constituted a social reality *sui generis*.

Moscovici (1961–76) chose to replace Durkheim's term *représentation collective* with his own *représentation sociale* in order to acknowledge his scientific ancestry, but also to make explicit his own conception of the way knowledge is represented in a society and shared by its members in the form of common-sense 'theories' about all aspects of life and society. He saw social representations as the subject matter of social psychology, not sociology, and approached them from a different angle.[2] In particular, his view of social representations was more dynamic than Durkheim's, and he saw them as created by individuals in interaction with each other. Moscovici (1984) speaks of a continual re-constitution of common sense as, for example, in the course of everyday conservations.

Having introduced a new term, Moscovici was presented with the problem of defining his intuitively appealing but deliberately vague notion:

> (social representations are) cognitive systems with a logic and language of their own.... They do not represent simply 'opinions about', 'images of' or 'attitudes towards' but 'theories' or 'branches of knowledge' in their own right, for the discovery and organization of reality.... (Moscovici, p. xii in his foreword to Herzlich, 1973)

> By social representations we mean a set of concepts, statements and explanations originating in daily life in the course of inter-individual communications. They are the equivalent, in our society, of the myths and belief systems in traditional societies; they might even be said to be the contemporary version of common sense. (Moscovici, 1981, p. 181)[3]

These definitions do, at least, convey in a broad sense what the study of social representations is about – the way in which individuals construct social reality and orient themselves towards it (Herzlich, 1973). This approach shares with others – e.g. Berger and Luckmann's (1967) 'social construction of reality' – the aim of building a theory of the origins of common sense

(Moscovici, 1984) and, moreover, is concerned with a socially *shared* reality that can influence individual behaviour (Jaspars and Fraser, 1984).

The two major functions of social representations are to establish an order for the individual, helping him or her to understand and master the social world, and to facilitate communication with other members of a community, on the basis of a shared conception of reality (Moscovici, 1973). More recently, Moscovici (1984) has referred to the two major roles of representations as conventional and prescriptive. Representations 'conventionalise' the objects, persons and events we encounter, locating them within a category. Representations are 'prescriptive' in the sense that they impose themselves on us, through tradition, and determine what we perceive and conceive.

As its name suggests, representation refers to a re-presentation, a mental reproduction of something else – a person, an object, an event, and so on (Jodelet, 1984). Yet, a representation is not merely a reproduction but, rather, a construction or transformation. It is this aspect of social representations that is underlined in the present work: the idea that the *transformation* of specialised knowledge (whether in science, economics or any domain) is a fundamental aspect of common sense. Moscovici (1976) argues, quite reasonably, that specialised knowledge will only influence daily life *if* it passes from specialists to society. A complete analysis of social representations involves the study of how knowledge is transformed and represented, and by what route(s). This may take the form of interviews with respondents, content-analysis of the mass media and comparisons between the specialised and secular domains. At the point where specialised knowledge becomes part of everyday life, it becomes the province of social psychology (Moscovici, *op. cit.*). The present work has not considered content-analysis of the mass media, nor the role of communication between individuals, but it does provide a content-analysis of unstructured responses to questions about the Community and can, to a limited extent, compare these social representations with the economic principles behind the European Community.

The aim of transformation is to render complex knowledge 'accessible to everyone' (Moscovici, 1984). As Farr and Moscovici (1984) write in the preface to their volume, the theory of social representations, 'explains how the strange and the unfamiliar become, in time, the familiar'. (ix–x). The two processes that generate social representations are 'anchoring' and 'objectifying' (Herzlich, 1972; Jodelet, 1984; Moscovici, 1984).

Anchoring refers to the integration of the represented object within the individual's pre-existing cognitive system (Jodelet, 1984, writes that a representation is never written on a *tabula rasa*). As its name implies, anchoring is a mechanism to anchor new ideas, to classify them within a familiar context or network of categories. Thus someone learning about the

European Community for the first time might assimilate it to ideas about N.A.T.O., the U.N. and other international organisations. Anchoring is, then, a matter of classifying and naming and Moscovici (1981) has written that, 'representation is basically a classifying and naming process, a method of establishing relations between categories and labels'. (p. 193.)

The process of objectifying turns something abstract into something almost concrete; what is in the mind is transferred into something which has an almost physical existence. In the case of something quite complex, like a scientific theory, one phase of objectifying would be to select key elements of the theory and then to form these into some nucleus. In particular, words are linked to images, thus objectifying 'gives material reality to an abstract entity'. (Flath and Moscovici, 1983, p. 593.) Two aspects of this process have recently been discussed by Moscovici and Hewstone (1983):

(1) The *personification* of knowledge and phenomena refers to the association of theories, sciences or ideas with an individual, designated by name, who becomes the symbol of that approach (e.g. Freud and psychoanalysis). Sears (1969) has discussed the 'centrality of personalities' and suggests that persons may be unusually simple stimuili, easily represented and memorised. Politics may also be so easily 'personalised' because political issues are too complex to be comfortably assimilated by the mass public, and because the media constantly reduce politics to the level of personalities (see Lane, 1959; Lazarsfeld, Berelson and Gaudet, 1948). One might, then, hypothesise that the public's picture of the European Community is centred on 'personalities' such as its founders or contemporary protagonists.

(2) The *figuration* of knowledge refers to the process by which common sense substitutes metaphors and images for complex notions. As a rule, the pictures come to prevail over the remote or abstract ideas. An obvious and relevant example is the use of colourful imagery to convey agricultural surpluses of the Community – milk and wine 'lakes', butter 'mountains' and so on. These images are certainly found in, indeed appear to originate from, the mass media. It will be interesting to see if they also predominate in the social representations of our respondents.

These processes of anchoring and objectifying help ordinary citizens to grasp complex ideas. Leyens (1982) refers to nuclear physics, biochemistry, sociology of knowledge and ethology as four scientific approaches which few ordinary citizens could define. However, many people do possess some notion or social representation of what these disciplines involve. Moscovici's (1961–76) book, *La psychanalyse: son image et son public* is still the classic illustration of such social representations. It consists of a systematic study (using attitudinal measures and content-analytic procedures) and explication of how ideas about psychoanalysis permeated through French society and became transformed into a social representation; how the scientific jargon was vulgarised and taken up by ordinary people (e.g. terms like 'complex'); and how Freud's ideas, once transformed, changed the way people viewed themselves, others and society itself.

In view of the vague outlines of a theory of social representations which have so far been painted, some researchers prefer to speak of an approach rather than a theory, or a heuristic notion rather than a concept (see Leyens, 1982; and the paper by Potter and Litton, 1985, commented on by Moscovici, 1985; Semin, 1985; and Hewstone, 1985). Nonetheless, the social representations approach appears to the present author to offer the promise of a rich and valuable study of common sense, and to go beyond the notions of attitude, opinion and stereotype, in spite of some similarities. The contribution of this approach can be seen already in the broad and complex issues tackled by empirical studies of social representations (see Farr and Moscovici, 1984).

The main reason why the notion of social representation is so important for the present study is that it invites a focus on knowledge or information. In introducing the term social representations, Moscovici (1961; 1976, p. 79) called for social psychologists to study the knowledge that individuals and groups possess, and use, concerning society, others, and the world in general; and to specify how this knowledge is organised. Level of information is a central dimension of social representations (see Herzlich, 1972) and differentiates between individuals as well as groups, classes or even whole societies. In his study of social representations of psychoanalysis Moscovici found no clear and simple relationship between knowledge and attitudes, but social representations can be seen as the bases of public opinion in any society and this relationship should be considered further.

Generally, whether social representations of the European Community exist at all is, of course, an empirical question. But it would be pessimistic to envisage no social-psychological residue after 25 years of European integration. In this respect, it is interesting to consider the written responses of some French schoolchildren to the statement: 'L'Europe pour moi c'est....'[4] The percentage of children mentioning the Common Market varied with age, reaching 12% for those aged 15–16 years, while the responses of many children evidenced some 'fall-out' from television, newspapers, adult conversation and so on: 'En Europe on n'a pas de petrole mais on a du lait'; 'l'Europe... C'est une immensité de pays gouvernées différement. Il y a toujours quelque chose qui ne vas pas.' It would seem reasonable, then, to believe that the existence of the Community has been accepted by European society, although the details of this social representation will have to be analysed below.

The study of people's understanding of the Community can also be approached from Katona's (1975) analysis of 'psychological economics'. Katona emphasises that psychological dimensions – people's *perceptions* of events, their motivations, attitudes and expectations, and their trust and confidence – do have a place in economic analysis and an influence on economic behaviour. He argues that psychological surveys of economic issues should include three broad sorts of responses: 'information about', 'attitudes towards' and 'expectations of'. There is also an interesting overlap, with the above work, in his aim to analyse people's *understanding* of economics and even to study the *theories* that people form with respect to economic institutions and ideas. Katona suggests that the most productive open question, if one seeks to find out about these 'theories', is a simple probe (after a question), asking: 'Why do you say so?' Thus, respondents can be asked to give reasons for their answers, with the aim of increasing our knowledge of their real level of information and understanding.

It is interesting, in view of this discussion of knowledge, to note Piet Dankert's (ex-President of the European Parliament) argument that the Community's 'negative (public) image is attributable in large measure to a *lack of knowledge* about the effects of Community policies'. (Dankert, 1983, p. 8, emphases added.) This view suggests at once a number of points. First, one should make more of an effort to study people's knowledge (and not just their opinions) about the Community (including its effects); second, one should investigate the relationship between knowledge about the Community and the valence (positive or negative) of attitudes towards it; third, if such a relationship is found, one could use the results of this enquiry to improve education about the actual workings and achievements of the Community. Knowledge may play a key role in the formation of attitudes. On the one hand, the less knowledgeable might form opinions about the Community on the basis of limited and perhaps biased information. On the other hand, a high level of knowledge might counteract negative news stories and provide for a more objective judgement.

Some kinds of knowledge – like social representations – are probably easily available and may be termed 'active'. They can therefore be tapped with open-ended questions, allowing the respondent freedom of expression. Other views – such as ratings of specific policies and effects – may be 'passive' and thus need to be measured with a structured format. The results of both approaches are reported below, in an attempt to provide a more complete analysis of how the Common Market is understood.

3.2 Attitudes

According to Kerlinger (1984), 'attitude' is one of the great concepts of contemporary social science. Allport (1954) has argued that because attitudes could refer to the dispositions of single individuals or to broad patterns of culture, the concept could link psychology and sociology. Certainly, the notion of attitude is central to social psychology and some early theorists virtually defined the discipline as the scientific study of attitudes (Bogardus, 1931; Folsom, 1931; Thomas and Znaniecki, 1918; see Ajzen and Fishbein, 1980). In a masterly historical essay on attitudes, Fleming (1967) has even suggested that we are in the age of 'attitude man', and that the attitude concept brought about a dramatic change in people's views of themselves and others. More recently, Oskamp (1977) has argued that the study of attitudes is an important part of social science research for four general reasons:

> attitude provides a short-hand term for people's 'thinking' about an issue or object;
>
> an attitude *may* be the cause of a person's behaviour;
>
> a general attitude *may* help to explain the consistency of a person's behaviour, because it underlies a variety of different actions;
>
> attitudes are important for their own sake (the relationship with behaviour is not the sole *raison d'être* of attitude, even if it is important; learning about people's social perceptions can be of interest and value in its own right).

Because of the centrality of attitudes in social-psychological research, there are many theories of attitude structure and some of these should be considered in this section (given that attitudinal judgements form a major part of the questionnaire used in the reported study). Thus the following sub-sections deal with questions of definition, functions of attitude and theories of attitude structure. Wary of the tendency for attitude theory to become top-heavy with conceptual elaboration (McGuire, 1969), the present discussion is not intended to be exhaustive, but is rather oriented towards the analysis of political attitudes, using Fishbein and Ajzen's (1975) expectancy-value theory.

3.2.1 Attitude definition
In an early discussion of attitudes in the history of social psychology, Allport wrote that: 'Attitudes determine for each individual what he will see and hear, what he will think and what he will do. To borrow a phrase from William James, they "engender meaning upon the world"; they draw lines about, and segregate, an otherwise chaotic environment; they are our methods for finding our way about in an ambiguous universe.' (1969, pp. 17–18.) Appealing as this broad approach may seem, attitude research required a more specific and constrained definition, of which many were put forward (see Greenwald, 1968; Shaw and Wright, 1967). As Fishbein and

Ajzen (1975) relate, attitude came to be described as, 'a learned predisposition to respond in a consistently favourable or unfavourable manner with respect to a given object'. (p. 6.) The three basic features of this definition can be considered more closely. Few people would disagree with the statement that attitudes are learned, but as Fishbein and Ajzen point out, this view is difficult to confront. For example, what kinds of past experience should be considered relevant? Because attitudes are defined as predispositions to respond, and not as behaviour *per se*, they are not directly observable and must be inferred from observed consistency in behaviour. Thus an attitude has the status of a hypothetical construct and an intervening variable (*cf.* MacCorquordale and Meehl, 1948). It should also be noted that, because behaviour is defined in terms of overall evaluation, knowledge of a person's attitude does not predict any specific behaviour. Finally, Fishbein and Ajzen consider the term response consistency and find it ambiguous. Most attitude measures rely on 'evaluative consistency' (based on multiple behaviours at different points in time), but the specificity of measurement for disposition and response may not be closely aligned (this has implications for the relationship between attitudes and behaviour which are discussed in Chapter 7).

Fishbein and Ajzen propose a definition of attitude that specifies only the essential characteristics of the concept which must be assessed in order to obtain a valid measure of attitude. They view the major characteristic of attitude as its evaluative or affective nature and suggest that: 'attitude may be conceptualised as the amount of affect for or against some object... "attitude" should be measured by a procedure which locates the subject on a bipolar affective or evaluative dimension vis-à-vis a given object'. (1975, p. 11.) This definition is consistent with that of other scholars who have considered attitude to be simply the categorisation of an object along an evaluative dimension (see Fishbein, 1963; Jones and Gerard, 1967; Thurstone, 1931, 1946).

Having defined attitude, it is now appropriate to conclude this preamble by considering briefly its relation to concepts such as knowledge, value and opinion (see McGuire, 1969). Obviously, attitudes are considerably narrower, albeit more clearly defined, than social representations. Whereas social representations have been seen as a means of examining social knowledge, McGuire (1969) distinguishes attitudes from knowledge. He points out that, when asked, people can express an attitude on matters about which they have never previously thought (*cf.* Hartley, 1946). For present purposes, attitudes can be distinguished from values by regarding values as components of attitudes (as will become clear in the discussion of expectancy-value theories). Finally, some scholars have argued for a distinction between the terms attitude and opinion. McGuire (1969) has described the situation as 'names in search of a distinction, rather than a distinction in search of a terminology'. (p. 152.) Generally, having seen the trends in public opinion polling towards multi-point response scales, reverse-worded items and so on, we might agree with Asch's (1952) solution to the problem: 'Polling is attitude measurement plus sampling.' (p. 545.) Nonetheless, for conceptual clarity, the term attitude, as opposed to opinion, will be used throughout this work when referring to the present study. This decision is taken to emphasise the differences between large-scale, representative polling of rather superficial items and the present attempt to investigate the structure of a wide variety of attitudinal judgements, using a relatively small and *un*representative sample.[5]

Having defined attitude, and clarified some of its qualities, we can now turn to a consideration of the functions served by attitudes.

3.2.2 *The functions of attitudes*

Based on the work of Katz (1960; Katz and Stotland, 1959) and Smith (Smith, Bruner and White, 1956), McGuire (1969) has distinguished four functions served by attitudes:

(a) *A utilitarian (adaptive) function.* This function sees attitudes as useful in helping people reach their goals; people develop favourable attitudes towards objects that are rewarding and unfavourable attitudes towards objects that are unrewarding. For example, someone might favour the European community because it was seen to bring prosperity to his country. The utility of an attitude may sometimes reside in its social adjustment value (Smith *et al.*, 1956) – e.g. one adopts an attitude that is consistent with the view held by friends – rather than its actual instrumentality to goal attainment (e.g. one might not even know which outcomes were associated with the Community).

(b) *An economy (knowledge) function.* An attitude fulfilling this function should provide a picture that is meaningful and understandable to the particular individual holding the attitude (Oskamp, 1977). In this sense attitudes provide a context for new information, helping the individual to interpret new information in terms of 'categories of convenience'. According to McGuire (1969), this attitudinal function was proposed by Lippmann (1922) who suggested that public opinion consists of an economical simplification of the complex world. This cognitive economy function may tend to reduce change in attitudes (which is sometimes dysfunctional), but is obviously useful in giving stability to a whole belief system.

(c) *An expressive (self-realising) function.* This function denotes that taking a stand on issues helps to establish a person's self-identity. Attitudes give expression to our central values and self-concept.

(c) *Ego-defensive function.* This function recognises that attitudes may serve more to protect the insecure person from inner conflicts, than to deal with the characteristics of an attitude object.

Functional theories of attitude not only draw attention to the needs satisfied by attitudes, but also have implications for attitude change. Thus Katz (1960) maintains that we must know which psychological function of an attitude is important before we can predict what conditions are likely to engender change of attitudes. The functional approach holds, broadly, that when changed conditions make the old attitude no longer functional (e.g. new knowledge changes the utility of the attitude), then the attitude will change. Notwithstanding the possible contribution of a functional approach to attitude change, little work has been done in this area. It is, however, interesting to note Eagly and Chaiken's (1984) conclusion (to a recent review of cognitive theories of persuasion) that researchers might consider adopting a more functional approach.

There are also criticisms of the functional approach (e.g. Six, 1980). As with any taxonomy, McGuire's list of four functions can surely be extended, as could the relationship between the different functions. It should also be noted that while many attitudes seem to serve primarily one function, others may serve several, even all four, functions. The number of functions served may be related to the salience and centrality of the attitude in question (see Perry *et al.*, 1976). A more general criticism could be aimed at functionalism itself, which can appear vacuous if it claims that all attitudes held fulfil specified functions (see Hewstone, 1983). Certainly, contemporary attitude theories have devoted more time and attention to matters of structure than to matters of function (as seen by the relative lengths of this and the following section). However, attitude theorists would do well to keep an eye on the possible functions served by social attitudes. With regard to the European Community, the 'utilitarian' and 'economy' functions would appear most relevant, and these are clearly not inconsistent with the expectancy-value approach adopted below.

3.2.3 The structure of attitudes

As Ostrom (1968) acknowledges, attitudes possess the basic characteristics required of a theoretical construct: that of having multiple antecedents and of affecting multiple responses. Although there have been many discrete contributions to attitude theory, these can be conveniently organised into identifiable categories (e.g. learning theory; cognitive consistency theory; attribution theory; see Fishbein 1967; Fishbein and Ajzen, 1975; McGuire, 1969, Oskamp, 1977). It is this concern with theory which most distinguishes the social-psychological study of attitudes from studies of public opinion. The promise of such theories – to be examined in this volume – is to go beyond the description of attitudes to discover and provide an explanation for the structure of attitudes (see Kerlinger, 1984).

Cognitive consistency theories

The criterial attribute of cognitive consistency theories is the principle that people strive to maintain consistency among their beliefs, attitudes and behaviours (for reviews see Abelson *et al.*, 1968; Fishbein and Ajzen, 1975, chapter 2; Kiesler, Collins and Miller, 1969). Awareness of one's own inconsistency is viewed as psychologically uncomfortable, hence individuals are motivated to avoid inconsistency. This general approach has been particularly influential in the area of attitude change (Insko, 1967); if an individual receives new information which is inconsistent with his or her previous viewpoints, or if attention is drawn to inconsistencies, then attitude change should result. It should, however, be emphasised that the tendency assumed is not towards a strictly logical consistency, but rather a 'psycho-logic' (Abelson and Rosenberg, 1958), according a role to both value and emotion. As Oskamp (1977) puts its, consistency theories allow for such 'illogical' ways of maintaining consistency as denying the truth of new information which contradicts a person's present viewpoint, or searching for information to bolster present attitudes in the face of challenging new information (Abelson, 1959).

The origin of consistency theories can, in large part, be traced to Heider's (1946, 1958) balance theory, a very general model for representing a perceiver's cognitions. Heider (1983) traces the idea of a balance hypothesis to Spinoza's *Ethics* and relates how he, 'began to think in terms of a general tendency to prefer orderly and consistent arrangements of attitudes and unitlike connections to those that are less orderly and that can less easily be perceived as units'. (Heider, 1983, p. 151.) It was, according to Ostrom (1968), Heider's analysis of 'sentiments' and 'degree of belongingness' that had the greatest influence on subsequent attitude theory and research. Sentiment is the positive or negative evaluation (liking or disliking) the perceiver makes of some cognitively represented object; and relations between cognitive elements may also be perceived as positive or negative. Belongingness is the 'unit formation' existing between the cognitive representation of two elements; this can again be positive or negative.

The dynamic element of Heider's formulation is the need or motive to maintain balanced and harmonious relations between cognitive elements (Heider, 1958, p. 210). In Heider's symbolic $p-o-x$ notation: person, p, tries to keep her sentiments regarding another person, o, consistent with their mutual liking for an object, x. Heider's work characterised the relations between cognitive elements as balanced or unbalanced. In the case of balance, relationships are in a harmony, with no cognitive stress towards

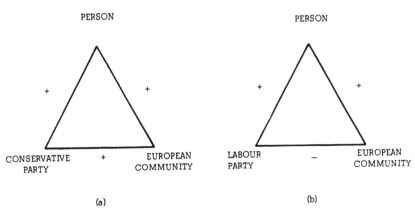

Fig. 3.1. Illustration of balanced and unbalanced cognitive structures.

change (if a balanced state does not exist, then forces toward such a state will arise). Consider, for example, an individual who identifies with the Conservative Party in the U.K., is in favour of the European community, and is aware that the Conservative Party is in favour of the European Community. This cognitive system could be represented in Heiderian terms as a *p–o–x* triad (see Figure 3.1(*a*)).

In contrast, an unbalanced relationship produces psychological tension in the perceiver which will motivate change in the perceived relationships. For example, an individual who is in favour of the European Community, but identifies with the British Labour Party, and is aware that the Party lacks support for the Community. This cognitive system could also be represented as a *p–o–x* triad (see Figure 3.1(*b*)). Heider viewed triadic systems as balanced when they have an odd number of positive relationships (either one or three); otherwise they are unbalanced. As Figure 3.1. shows, the system in the former example is balanced (all three relationships are positive), and in the latter example, unbalanced (only two relationships are positive).

Heider based his work on the assumption that one must understand an individual's cognitive representation of the environment (how he or she *sees* it) in order to understand the operation of attitudes and their relation to behaviour. Certainly, the notion of cognitive consistency has had great impact on theorising about the structure of attitudes and, as Fishbein and Ajzen note, 'balance theory is rich in its implications'. (1975, p. 35.) However, it also has certain limitations. For example, relations of both liking and unit formation are only conceived as dichotomous variables (each with only two possible values), yet the real world is obviously not that simple. However, Heider's conception does make relations conceptually easier and may even mirror people's behaviour in thinking and choosing first at a global level, at least in some situations (see Crockett, 1982). There have also been quantitative extensions of Heider's work – notably Cartwright and Harary's (1956) use of graph theory and Abelson and Rosenberg's (1958) use of matrix algebra – to generalise from 3-element systems to n-element structures (see also Osgood and Tannenbaum, 1955; Phillips, 1967).

A particularly interesting extension and revision of Heider's work is that of Rosenberg and Abelson (1960; Rosenberg, 1960), emphasising consistency in the relationship between the cognitive and affective elements of an attitude. Whenever these two components are inconsistent, Rosenberg argues, a homeostatic process will operate to restore consistency. This attitude structure approach postulates the existence of mutual, causal relations between cognitive elements. Research has shown that a change in either the cognitive or affective component can produce a change in the other component (see Carlson, 1956; Rosenberg, 1960), with changes assumed to be in the direction of increased consistency within the entire attitude structure. Other researchers have also provided evidence for Rosenberg's assertion that individuals tend to have consistent attitude structures (e.g. Fishbein, 1963; Insko, Blake, Cialdini and Mulaik, 1970).

Another variant of cognitive consistency theory is Festinger's (1957) theory of cognitive dissonance, which continues to stimulate research (see Cooper and Fazio, 1984). There are obvious parallels between the notions of imbalance and dissonance as psychologically uncomfortable states motivating attitude change. Cognitive dissonance theory, however, focusses on inconsistency between attitudes and behaviour, whereas previous approaches had concentrated on balance among cognitive elements, or affective-cognitive consistency. Dissonance theory was really innovative in emphasising that attitude change often results *from* a person's behaviour, rather than causing that behaviour. This would lead to the suggestion that the best way to change attitudes to the Community would be, first, to change people's behaviour (e.g. increase voting turn-out in European elections). Bem's (1972) self-perception theory went even further in questioning the importance of attitudes. For him, the key issue was whether people even know their own attitudes prior to inferring them *after* they have engaged in behaviour. Arguing from a radical behaviourist position, Bem conceived of an attitude as 'nothing but' a person's self-description of a like or dislike. In other words: 'I voted for the Common Market in the national referendum, therefore I (must) like the Common Market', as opposed to the usual view of things, whereby people's views or attitudes are seen to determine their actions. Viewed from this perspective, attitudes might be seen as 'mere epiphenomena', explanations given after-the-fact of behaviour, but not internalised (Fazio and Zanna, 1981).

Considering cognitive consistency theories together, one must agree with van der Pligt and Eiser (1983) that they are 'gross over-simplifications' of objective reality. They have, nonetheless, had a lasting impact on social psychological theories of attitude structure, including the expectancy-value approach which is espoused in this work. However, perhaps a major problem for consistency theories – as applied to political attitudes – is that most citizens seem to tolerate a great deal of inconsistency in their political views (see the work of Converse, 1964*a*, discussed in Chapter 2). Abelson (1968) explains this kind of inconsistency by proposing that much of our knowledge and attitudes exists in isolated 'opinion molecules', each of which contains only one or a few facts, feelilngs or sources of support. Unless used together, as in conversations, such contradictory beliefs may simply be unnoticed, remaining in 'logic-tight compartments', as Abelson called them.

The multi-component view of attitudes

Consistency is still central to the multi-component view of attitudes, although here it is intra-attitudinal consistency (between the various components of *one* attitude). The overlap between the two approaches is seen most clearly in Rosenberg's (1956) work on affective-cognitive consistency, which is obviously based on a multi-component view of attitudes.

The multi- or three-component view of attitudes is based on the conceptual distinction between thought, feeling and action. This trichotomy has an eminent philosophical tradition, which can be traced back via Herbert Spencer to Plato and Aristotle (see Allport, 1935), to Darwin and Sherrington (see Fleming, 1967), or even to the *Bhagavad Gita* (see McGuire, 1969). More recently, a number of theorists in social psychology have conceptualised attitudes in the framework of the cognition–affect–conation triad (e.g. Cartwright, 1949; Katz and Stotland, 1959; Smith, 1947). The cognitive component of an attitude (also called the perceptual, informational or stereotypic component) entails the ideas and beliefs that the attitude holder has about the attitude object. The affective component (also called the feeling or emotional component) deals with a person's feelings of liking or disliking for an attitude object. As the purely evaluative component, it has been viewed by some authors as the core of an attitude. The conative component (also called the action or behavioural component) of an attitude consists of the person's action tendencies towards the attitude object. Thus a person's attitude can be seen as a complex system made up of the person's *beliefs* about an object, *feelings* towards that object, and *action tendencies* with respect to the object (Ajzen and Fishbein, 1980).

The classic illustration of the three-component view of attitude is shown in Rosenberg and Hovland's (1960) schematic representation (see Figure 3.2). It should be noted that all responses to a stimulus object are mediated by the person's attitude towards that object. The different responses, however, are classified into three categories – cognitive, affective and

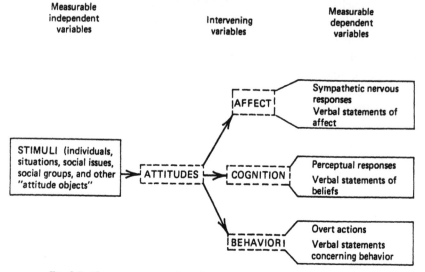

Fig. 3.2. Three-component view of attitude. (From M. J. Rosenberg and
C. I. Hovland, 'Cognitive, affective and behavioural components of attitudes', in
C. I. Hovland and M. J. Rosenberg (eds.), *Attitude organization and Change.* New
Haven, Conn.: Yale University Press, 1960.)

behavioural – each of which constitutes one component of an attitude.
This diagram also implies that all three components of an attitude must be
assessed for a complete description of an attitude.

A key validational issue for the multi-component view of attitude is the
question of how closely related the three components of an attitude actually
are. To be meaningful, correlations between the components should be
neither too high, nor too low, thus appearing separate, but not completely
unrelated. In fact, results indicate that the components are quite highly
intercorrelated (see McGuire, 1969). Ostrom (1969) attempted to obtain
independent measures of cognition, affect and conation with respect to the
church, and to examine the relations of these components to various overt
forms of religious behaviour. He reported that the three attitudinal
components were highly intercorrelated (correlations were of the order of
+0.70). Furthermore, the three components did not differ significantly in
their ability to predict behaviour; and taking all three components into
account did not improve behavioural prediction (but see Kothandapani,
1971, for some evidence regarding the discriminant validity of scales
measuring the three components). Although the multi-component view of
attitudes is favoured by some researchers (e.g. Krech, Crutchfield and
Ballachey, 1962), McGuire (1969) concluded that the three components had
proved to be so highly intercorrelated that the distinction was no longer
tenable.

An alternative viewpoint to the multi-component structure of attitudes (and one that builds on the classic trichotomy) is Fishbein and Ajzen's (1975) four-way distinction between beliefs, attitudes, behavioural intentions and behaviour itself. This view does not require a necessary connection between these concepts, but it does allow for a strong relationship under certain specified conditions. *Beliefs* represent a person's information about (but *not* evaluation of) an attitude object. A belief links an object to some attribute. For example, the belief: 'The European Community is a bureaucratic mess' links the object, the European Community, to the attribute 'bureaucratic mess'. People may differ in their *belief strength* with respect to any object–attribute association; that is, they may differ in terms of the perceived likelihood that the object has (or is associated with) the attribute in question. Thus Fishbein and Ajzen recommend that beliefs are measured by a procedure that places the respondent along a dimension of subjective probability involving an object and a related attribute. *Attitudes*, as noted earlier, are simply measures of affect on a bipolar scale. *Behavioural intention* is also indicated by the strength of the person's belief that he or she will perform the behaviour in question, and is measured on a scale of subjective probability (e.g.: 'It is extremely likely that I will vote'). Finally, *behaviour* refers to overt behavioural acts that are studied in their own right (as distinct from predispositions or intentions to behave; see Fishbein and Ajzen, 1975, pp. 11–13). These four conceptual distinctions are organised by Fishbein and Ajzen into a conceptual framework for the study of attitudes and behaviour. The following sections consider their approach alongside other expectancy-value theories, while the topics of attitude–behaviour relations and attitude change are left until Chapter 7.

3.2.4 Expectancy-value theories of attitude

Wahba and House's (1974) review of expectancy theories reveals that this approach has an impressive intellectual history. In fact, the expectancy models used in contemporary psychology have their origins in earlier models of choice behaviour in mathematical statistics and classical economics, dating from as early as the seventeenth century. Social psychologists using the expectancy-value principle to study attitudes are also building on well-established traditions in psychology itself, the principle having been central to studies of motivation (e.g. Atkinson, 1958; Lewin, 1938; Tolman, 1958), social learning theory (Rotter, 1954) and subjective expected utility models of decision-making (Becker and McClintock, 1967; Edwards, 1954).

Perhaps the best-known expectancy-value model is the subjective expected utility (SEU) model from behavioural decision theory (Edwards, 1954). According to this theory, people's behavioural choices are made by selecting that alternative which maximises subjective expected utility (i.e. the alter-

native which is seen as likely to lead to the most favourable outcomes).
The SEU of a given alternative is defined as:

$$SEU = \sum_{i=1}^{n} SP_iU_i \qquad (1)$$

where: *SEU* is the subjective expected utility associated with a given
alternative: SP_i is the subjective probability that performing the behaviour
will lead to consequence *i*; U_i is the subjective value or utility of consequence
i; and *n* is the number of relevant consequences. This approach to
behavioural choice is still widely used and has since been developed by
Beach and colleagues (Beach *et al.*, 1976; Holmstrom and Beach, 1973).

McGuire (1969) reports that early versions of expectancy-value (or
instrumentality-value) theory were applied to attitudes by Smith (1949;
Smith, Bruner and White, 1956), DiVesta (DiVesta and Merwin, 1960;
Woodruff and DiVesta, 1948) and Cartwright (1949). But the first published
presentation of an expectancy-value analysis of attitudes was due to Peak
(1955) and it was the 'Michigan School' that made most use of the approach
in the immediately following years (Carlson, 1956; Peak, 1958; Rosenberg,
1956, 1960; Zajonc, 1960).

Rosenberg's work has been cited earlier in relation to affective-cognitive
consistency. It was also particularly influential in forging a union between
cognitive consistency and expectancy-value approaches (Rosenberg, 1960,
1968), because he explored the implications of consistency between affect
(directly measured attitudes) and beliefs (defined in expectancy-value terms).
Rosenberg's model, formulated from a functionalist perspective (Smith *et al.*,
1956), argued that the more a given attitude object was *instrumental* in
obtaining positively valued goals (or consequences) and in blocking (or
preventing) negatively valued goals, the more favourable the person's
atittude towards the object would be. Thus attitudes are defined as some
combination of beliefs about an object either blocking or facilitating the
attainment of valued states or goals (Pagel and Davidson, 1984). Rosenberg
operationalised attitude as the algebraic sum of the products of (a) the value
importance of each value or goal associated with an object; and (b) the
instrumentality of the object for blocking or obtaining each value or goal.
The model can be expressed as follows:

$$A_O = \sum_{i=1}^{n} I_iV_i \qquad (2)$$

where: A_O is the attitude towards some object: I_i is the perceived instrumentality of A_O for leading to or blocking the attainment of a goal or
value *i*; V_i is the value importance of goal or value *i*; and *n* is the number
of goals or values.

In his study Rosenberg (1956) asked respondents to rate each of 35 values according to how much satisfaction it yielded him. Respondents were then asked to rate the attitude object (the Communist Party) according to whether it facilitated or blocked attaining each of the values. Each person's attitude was calculated according to equation (2). This 'summated means–end score', as McGuire (1969) calls it, correlated well with an independently obtained score of favourableness towards the attitude object. Thus the study showed that a person's evaluation of an object is strongly related to his or her expectations (beliefs) that the object furthers or hinders the attainment of valued goals. The link, via Rosenberg, between cognitive consistency theory and expectancy-value theory is explained by Insko *et al.* (1983). Since the multiplication in the instrumentality × value rule involves a corollary of balance theory's multiplicative rule (Cartwright and Harary, 1956), the fact that the sum of the results of such multiplication produced a number that correlated with attitude provides evidence for consistent affective-cognitive relations.

Although Rosenberg's work proved seminal for later developments in attitude theory (and, indeed, is still used: e.g. Chaiken and Baldwin, 1981; Fazio and Zanna, 1978; Pagel and Davidson, 1984) its place has largely been taken by Fishbein and Ajzen's (1975) expectancy-value theory of attitudes, which is now examined.

Fishbein and Ajzen's expectancy-value theory
As Eagly and Chaiken (1984) relate, it was Fishbein who took up the task of developing the expectancy-value approach as a general framework for understanding attitudes (e.g. Fishbein, 1963, 1967). Following the early work just reviewed, Fishbein envisaged the structure of attitudes as a composite of *value* (i.e. the evaluation of the goals or attributes related to the attitude object) and *expectancy* (i.e. the subjective probability that the attitude object is associated with, in favour of, or actually bringing about these goals or attributes). Fishbein proposed that attitudes are a function of beliefs about the attitude object and the evaluative aspect of these beliefs. To predict an attitude, the value and expectancy components associated with each attribute are multiplied together, and these products are summed. Thus overall attitude can be represented as a single algebraic quantity:

$$A_O = \sum_{i=1}^{n} b_i e_i \tag{3}$$

where: A_O is the attitude towards some object O; b_i is belief i about O (i.e., the subjective probability that O is related to attribute i); e_i is the evaluation of attribute i; and n is the number of beliefs.

It is clear from equation (3) that the evaluation of each attribute contributes to the overall attitude *in proportion to* the person's subjective probability that the object has the attribute in question. This model of the way information is integrated to form an attitude raises the interesting possibility that people holding *different* beliefs may have the *same* attitudes, because attitudes are based on the total set of the person's salient beliefs (see below) and the evaluations associated with those beliefs. If the same beliefs are held with different strength, or if evaluations of the attributes differ, attitudes will also be different. Conversely, if different beliefs are held with the same strength and they have identical values, then the same attitudes will result. As Fishbein and Ajzen (1975) point out, it therefore follows that knowledge of a person's attitude tells us little about the particular beliefs held by that person, or about how the attributes associated with the attitude object are evaluated.

Clearly, there is a basic similarity between the equations underlying the approaches of subjective expected utility, instrumentality-value, and expectancy-value, as a number of scholars have pointed out (e.g. Fishbein and Ajzen, 1975; Jaccard, 1981; Jaspars, 1973; Pagel and Davidson, 1984; Wahba and House, 1974). The SP_i (subjective probability), I_i (perceived instrumentality) and b_i (belief) components in equations (1), (2) and (3), respectively, are directly analogous; as are the U_i (utility), V_i (value) and e_i (evaluation) components, respectively. The models do, however, differ in their exact measurement procedures, as will now be discussed.

Let us consider how the expectancy-value approach could be applied to the study of attitudes towards the European Community. The first step, selection of items, is an important aspect of operationalising Fishbein and Ajzen's (1975) theory and they use the notion of *belief salience* to govern item selection. Although someone may hold a large number of beliefs about any given object, Fishbein and Ajzen (see also Ajzen and Fishbein, 1980) suggest that only a small number of beliefs can be attended to at a given time and these salient beliefs will be the immediate determinants of an individual's attitude. Citing research on attention span, apprehension and information-processing (e.g. Mandler, 1967; Miller, 1956), Fishbein and Azjen suggest that an individual's attitude towards an object is primarily determined by approximately 5–9 beliefs about the object. Fishbein and Ajzen emphasise that this figure of 5–9 beliefs is *not* absolute (given time and motivation someone might make use of more beliefs), but it is both theoretically-based and intuitively reasonable.

Typically, open-ended interviews are used to elicit such salient beliefs and Fishbein and Ajzen suggest that salient beliefs are those elicited first (see Fishbein, 1967; Kaplan and Fishbein, 1969). Referring to the work of Hull (1943), Fishbein (1967) based this approach on the learning theory idea that an individual's salient beliefs about an object constitute a 'habit–family hierarchy' in which the strength of the belief is a function of the stimulus–response association of the object and its attribute (i.e. salient beliefs will appear high in the hierarchy; Pagel and Davidson, 1984).

This approach to the elicitation of salient beliefs is, however, rather time-consuming, involving a free-response format and (potentially) a quite different set of beliefs for each respondent. In many situations it may therefore be desirable to have information about the salient beliefs in a given population (*modal salient beliefs*) which are the beliefs occurring with the highest frequency (Fishbein and Ajzen, 1975). Alternatively, as in the present study, beliefs may be chosen according to other criteria (e.g. beliefs based on the content of the Treaty of Rome) and held constant for all respondents, in order to maximise possibilities for comparisons between individuals and national samples. This is a completely justifiable procedure, because Fishbein and Ajzen say that their model 'is applicable to any set of beliefs, whether they are salient or non-salient, new or old'. (1975, p. 222.) Thus several studies have used a large number of beliefs (more than 20), and in one study no less than 54 (Smetana and Adler, 1981), which must be rated in terms of expectancy and value. However, van der Pligt and Eiser (1983) point out, quite correctly, that a sufficiently large number of expectancies and values (whose products serve as 'predictors') will, of course, always predict attitudes (the 'criterion') more or less accurately.

Once a set of beliefs has been chosen, the researcher must decide how to measure evaluations and beliefs for each respondent. The respondents are first asked to provide evaluations of the list of attributes (e.g. 'increasing trade', 'building peace', etc.), by rating each one on a 7-point good–bad scale. In keeping with their adopted definition of attitude (a person's location on a *bipolar* evaluative dimension), these ratings are scored -3 (bad) to $+3$ (good) (see Fishbein and Ajzen, 1975, chapter 3).

A second set of ratings, using the same items, measures the strength of each respondent's beliefs that the attitude object (e.g. the European Community) is associated with each of the attributes (e.g. 'increasing trade', 'building peace', etc.). Strictly speaking, if beliefs are to be regarded as subjective probabilities, then according to probability theory they must necessarily range from zero to one. Although Fishbein and Ajzen acknowledge this fact, they suggest, initially, that measures of belief strength can be obtained using 4-point scales ranging from 0 (improbable) to $+3$ (probable), because, 'our conceptual framework uses the notion of probability in a more general sense. For example, we do not assume that the beliefs about an object are mutually exclusive and exhaustive, and thus the probabilities are not expected to sum to 1.' (Fishbein and Ajzen, 1975, footnote on p. 61.) Later on in their book Fishbein and Ajzen actually recommend the use of 7-point scales with *bipolar* scoring in many practical applications of their approach.

This recommendation arises from the fact that, 'assumptions of symmetric probabilities and evaluations are not always warranted in psychological studies'. (p. 85.) For example, if 'aggression' were evaluated $+3$, 'pacifism' would not necessarily be evaluated -3. Fishbein and Ajzen suggest that one way to avoid at least some of the problems raised by this issue is to treat beliefs in a bipolar fashion (i.e. scored from $-$ to $+$, indicating a range from disbelief to belief or from 0 to $+$, implying a range from lack of belief to belief).

A large number of studies have used these bipolar operationalisations of the model's variables (see Ajzen and Fishbein, 1980; Fishbein and Ajzen, 1975, 1981). More recently, because belief components have been proposed as measures of subjective probability, there has been a return to unipolar scales of belief, scored 1–7 (Pagel and Davidson, 1984). Although in their most recent statement known to the author, Fishbein and Ajzen are quite explicit that the belief scale should be scored from -3 to $+3$, arguing that: 'This scoring system is essential for an expectancy-value model since it permits a disbelief that an object has a negative attribute to contribute positively to the overall attitude, i.e. $(-2) \times (-2) = +4$.' (Fishbein and Ajzen, 1981, p. 310, footnote 11.[6]) Using this approach, an attitude to the Community would be positive if it were seen as probably leading towards positively valued goals and probably *not* leading towards negatively valued goals. To the present author, this first assumption seems completely plausible, although the second assumption is dubious. For example, there seems no reason to assume that the European Community would be positively judged, simply because it was seen as *not* leading to a third world war.

Obviously, one way to resolve this scoring controversy is to examine the effects of scoring changes – do these make a difference? Pagel and Davidson (1984) suggest that the distinction may be of greater theoretical than practical significance, because Davidson and Jaccard (1979) report a correlation of $+0.93$ between $b_i e_i$ components based on bipolar vs unipolar scoring of beliefs. However, in their comparison of the Fishbein–Ajzen, Rosenberg, and Beach models, Pagel and Davidson reported that the Rosenberg model fared much worse than the other two, and that its instrumentality component was clearly the cause (p. 530). Significantly, the measure of instrumentality for Rosenberg's model was bipolar (-5 to $+5$), clearly distinguishing this model from both the Fishbein model (as scored by Pagel and Davidson) and that of Beach. The outcome of this rather technical debate is that scoring *can* make a difference, and that studies such as the present one should explore such possible effects. The potential impact of scoring procedures is, however, related to the combinatorial rule used to estimate overall attitude; this issue is now considered.

Fishbein and Ajzen (1975) propose their expectancy-value formulation as a model of information integration describing the way in which different beliefs (and the evaluations of associated attributes) are combined or integrated to arrive at an overall attitude. The model states explicitly that there is a multiplicative interaction between its two parameters (i.e. $A_O = \Sigma\, b_i e_i$) and that products are summed. These multiplicative and additive assumptions have led to some controversy (see Fishbein and Ajzen, 1975, chapter 6; Mitchell, 1974; Schmidt, 1973). Schmidt has pointed out that the fact of a specified computation rule implies that there should be *comparisons* between the adequacy of that (multiplicative) and other (e.g. additive, the most commonly considered alternative) rules. But few studies have actually compared the predictive validity of multiplicative and additive models (but see Insko *et al.*, 1970; Schmidt, 1973). Thus the present study includes a set of comparisons aimed at identifying the best form of the expectancy-value model for these data, including manipulations of scoring procedure (bipolar vs unipolar scoring for beliefs) and combinatorial rule (multiplication vs addition of the components). These issues, because so closely tied to the data, are best considered in detail below (see Chapter 5).

Some critical issues relating to the Fishbein–Ajzen model
In reading the many publications of Fishbein and Ajzen one cannot fail to be impressed by their contribution to the attitude literature. Their reinterpretation of other frameworks in the light of their own approach is particularly striking[7]. However, there have inevitably also been criticisms of this expectancy-value approach and these should be considered at this stage of the present work.

The first criticism (not specific to the expectancy-value approach) concerns whether an attitude is simply unidimensional, expressing the respondent's favourability/unfavourability towards the object in question. Some researchers have certainly taken this view (e.g. Osgood, Suci and Tannenbaum, 1957) and the Fishbein–Ajzen model of attitudes has followed the practice of combining many beliefs about an object and their evaluations into a single number representing the person's overall attitude (but see Bagozzi's, 1981, view that attitudes will more likely be multidimensional when the intricacy, ambiguity or salience of an attitude object is increased; see also Streufert and Streufert, 1978).

While the multi-component view of attitudes has been discussed above, an alternative criticism concerns the notion of attitude ambivalence.[8] A general characteristic of attitude scales is that respondents agree or disagree with items that indicate some degree of favourableness or unfavourableness towards the attitude object. In contrast to such a procedure which allows the respondent to make one and only one evaluative response to the attitude object, Kaplan (1972) suggests that the measurement of ambivalence gives the respondent the opportunity simultaneously to indicate both a favourable and an unfavourable attitude towards a given object.

Despite the appeal of a concept like ambivalence, it has received little research attention (but see Brown, 1965; Scott, 1969). Kaplan follows Scott's working definition of ambivalence: the greater, and the more equal, the opposing tendencies to view an attitude object both favourably and unfavourably, the higher the degree of ambivalence. This definition demands a special measurement technique and Kaplan has suggested a modification of the semantic differential technique, designed to separate out the positive and negative components inherent in any bipolar attitudinal response. Respondents are asked to focus, in turn, on purely positive or purely negative qualities of the attitude object, and these are measured on unipolar scales (see Section 3.9.2., below). According to Kaplan, this method produces three attitudinal components: first, the standard bipolar attitude (A); second, its positive or 'liking' component (A_p); and third, its negative or 'disliking' component (A_n). Kaplan reports good reliability components for A, A_p and A_n, and reveals that respondents are capable of treating their component judgements independently. Either component (A_p or A_n) seems capable of being the dominant determinant of overall attitude and knowledge of a person's responses to the two unipolar scales allows specification of his or her response to the bipolar scale. Of particular interest, however, a given bipolar response (e.g. $+2$) may be associated with very different unipolar responses (e.g., $+3$ and -1; or $+2$ and 0).

The idea that attitudes are sometimes ambivalent, containing relatively equal positive and negative components, seems quite likely for such a complex issue as the Common Market, where someone might favour agricultural policy, but criticise monetary policy, for example. Responses which differ widely, even swinging from positive to negative, as a function of these response scales might indicate the conditional nature of Community attitudes and perhaps have implications for attitude change via public information campaigns. It will be of interest to see whether focussing on positive, or negative, qualities alone will, in turn, result in positive *and* negative perceptions of the Community.

A number of more substantial criticisms of the Fishbein–Ajzen approach have recently been summarised by van der Pligt and Eiser (1983). To begin with, there are criticisms originating from the subjective expected utility model: the problem of deciding what outcomes to include in the equation, without including irrelevant outcomes or excluding relevant outcomes (Bagozzi, 1981); the fact that perceptions of values and probabilities are not independent (Sundstrom, DeVault and Peele, 1981) and that probability assessments tend to be poorly calibrated (Lichtenstein, Fischhoff and

Phillips, 1977); the need for ratio scales of subjective probabilities and evaluations (Schmidt, 1973); and the modest reliability of values of desired outcomes, and lack of cross-situational consistency (van der Pligt and Eiser, 1983).

The major thrust of van der Pligt and Eiser's criticism is more theoretically oriented and concerns what Wahba and House (1974) refer to as the 'rationality assumptions' underlying expectancy theory. As these authors explained, the essence of expectancy theory is *choice behaviour*, and most theories of choice were originally formulated as 'normative theories', validated in terms of what a rational person *should* or *would* do. Thus the formation of an expectancy-value attitude entails a number of relatively complex judgements and evaluations – a number of statements of belief and evaluation must be made and their products summed – and one must ask if such a model is not too complex for the average human being. Van der Pligt and Eiser (1983) raise important issues by considering this question in terms of *prediction* vs *description*. They acknowledge the contribution of an expectancy-value approach to applied research on decision-making, but argue that this applied focus has resulted in a primary concern with prediction, at the expense of considering the descriptive validity of the model. Research has assumed that individuals follow the rules incorporated in the expectancy-value model and van der Pligt and Eiser emphasise that while increasing the predictive validity of a model is important, it does not lead to improved understanding of the decision-making process.

These reservations about the descriptive validity of expectancy-value models are given substance by mounting evidence from cognitive and social psychology showing how restricted the normal individual's information-processing capacities are (*cf.* Fischhoff, Goitein and Shapira, 1982; Nisbett and Ross, 1980; Slovic, 1974).[9] Van der Pligt and Eiser conclude, that 'people could not use the decision model assumed by expectancy-value models even if they tried'. (p. 165.) Instead, these authors suggest that many everyday decisions and behaviours seem to be carried out fairly 'mindlessly', in the sense that individuals process information relatively automatically, and are characterised by much less cognitive activity than complex information-processing models assume (see also Palmerino, Langer and McGillis, 1983).[10]

Van der Pligt and Eiser (1983) suggest that the crucial question is *why* a person holds a particular attitude. As an alternative to the expectancy-value approach they suggest that a measure of perceived importance or salience could be more informative for the researcher in this respect, and would constitute a more realistic analysis of the decision-making process. They report that people pro- and anti- an attitude object tend to differ in their ratings of the *importance* of consequences (e.g. an opponent of the Community might see agricultural over-production as a much more important issue than would someone in favour of the Community). Correlations with overall attitude were, not surprisingly, much higher for more important, or salient, beliefs.

While van der Pligt and Eiser's alternative is appealing in terms of simplicity, Fishbein and Ajzen (1975) have reported that measures of perceived importance did not improve the prediction of attitudes, beyond the level of prediction achieved by the expectancy-value model. However, an appropriate comparison of these approaches should compare the predictive performance of the two approaches separately and until this has been done it is perhaps premature to discard the well-tried approach of Fishbein and Ajzen. Nonetheless, the idea of trying to tap salient beliefs without the trappings of an expectancy-value approach is an interesting one. It may, for example, be that attitudes towards the European Community are themselves determined by more general attitudes. A reasonable hypothesis is that people who support the Community (a supra-national entity involving closer rela- tions between nations) will also support positive, cooperative international relations in general. Thus Inglehart (1970a) concluded (from a study of over 3000 secondary school students in W. Germany, Holland, France and the U.K.), that 'Europeanness' tends to be associated with a broader inter- nationalism. A number of attitude scales with pre-tested reliability and validity can be found in this area (see Shaw and Wright, 1967). While several such scales are rather primitive anti-Communism scales, Helfant's (1967) 'Survey of Opinions and Beliefs about International Relations' was sufficiently short and straightforward to be included as a further measure of attitudes in the present study, and one that makes quite simple demands on respondents (see also the measures of 'utilitarian' and 'affective' support, discussed below).

Notwithstanding their criticism of expectancy-value models, van der Pligt and Eiser (1983) acknowledge that cognitive models do *not* have to mirror the thought processes they try to explain. Their argument is not so much with the use of such scales, as with those researchers who go the step further to claim that expectancy-value models not only predict, but also explain, decision processes (and they cite Ajzen and Fishbein, 1980). This point is fundamental and well taken. The present use of an expectancy-value approach could be termed a 'prediction is paramount' view; no assumptions are made about the intervening thought processes, and the reported results are considered only in relation to the model's predictive validity (a point discussed further in Chapter 5).

In sum, it may be considered doubtful that the expectancy-value model is descriptive of attitude formation for all (or even any) people, or attitude objects. Nonetheless, the extensive empirical research based on this approach does adequately reveal its applicability (in terms of prediction) in many applied settings. There are, as this section has tried to convey, some important controversies in this field of research. However, there still seems to the author an important contribution made by the essence of any expectancy-value approach: that in measuring attitudes it is not enough simply to know whether a set of statements is positively or negatively evaluated; one also needs to know if the attitude object is perceived to be bringing about, facilitating (or to be instrumental to) the achievement of the various goals or values. It is proposed that an interesting picture of attitudes towards the Community will emerge, when we learn not only that certain goals are valued, or not, but also whether the Community is seen (accurately or inaccurately) as probably bringing about these goals. Notwithstanding the criticisms of expectancy-value models, this approach to the study of attitudes does seem to embrace many alternative views. As McGuire (1969) has pointed out, the expectancy-value analysis rests on the utilitarian notion that attitudes dispose us towards objects that are instrumental in the achievement of our valued goals; this is consistent with the utilitarian function suggested by functional theorists. Rosenberg's (1956) classic analysis forges links between the expectancy-value approach and both affective-cognitive consistency, and the multi-component view of attitudes. Finally, the present use of an expectancy-value analysis is based on the wide and successful use of expectancy models in social science (see Feather, 1982) and especially in the social psychological study of attitudes (see Cialdini, Petty and Cacioppo, 1981; Eagly and Himmelfarb, 1978; Mitchell and Biglan, 1971).

3.3 Ethnocentrism: stereotypes, liking and national images

As Oskamp (1977) reports, authors from various disciplines have bridged the gap between international attitudes and international reality by using the term 'images' to describe the views, often distorted, of other peoples and countries (see Boulding, 1956; Jervis, 1970; Kelman, 1965a).[11] For Kelman, the term image refers to 'the organized representation of an object in an individual's cognitive system'. (p. 24.) This is taken to encompass past, present and future conceptions (after Boulding); for the present analysis this means the residue of historical events, contemporary politics and current affairs, and predictions or assumptions about the four nations and nationalities in question. Images may be simple or complex in detail, positive or negative in evaluation, but are always more or less structured. This does not imply that they are either clearly articulated or conscious, merely that component elements hang together in some way. Following Kelman, the term is selected primarily to place emphasis on the individual's definition of the object, be it a country or its people, rather than any assumption about how things really are 'out there'. To clarify the discussion here, the terms stereotype and image are used to convey perceptions of nationalities (i.e. people) and nations (i.e. countries) respectively.

The term *stereotype* was coined by Lippmann (1922) in making the distinction between 'the world outside and the pictures in our heads'. (p. 1.) Like attitude, stereotype is not only one of the oldest, but also one of the most frequently used, concepts in social psychology (Fishman, 1956). Allport's (1954–79) classic definition is still often cited: 'a stereotype is an exaggerated belief associated with a category. Its function is to justify (rationalize) our conduct in relation to that category.' (1979 edn, p. 191.) Stereotyping can be subdivided into three essential aspects:

(1)   Other individuals are categorised, usually on the basis of easily identifiable characteristics such as nationality, sex or ethnicity.

(2)   A set of traits is attributed to all (or most) of that category. Individuals belonging to the stereotyped group are assumed to be similar to each other, and different from other groups, on this set of traits.

(3)   The set of traits is attributed to any individual member of that category.

The essence of stereotyping is revealed in an amusing anecdote related by Barzini:

> At a party given a few years ago by the French consul-general in Stuttgart for a group of French businessmen, one of them noticed with alarm a ramrod-stiff gentleman with an Erich von Stroheim haircut, a supercilious expression, and a monocle. The businessman tugged at the sleeve of Professor Alfred Grosser (the celebrated bilingual academic authority on French–German relations in the rest of the world) and said in a stage-whisper, 'There they go again, they are back at their old trade, they cannot change.' Grosser was glad to reassure his nervous countryman. The bemonocled, ramrod-stiff, supercilious gentleman with the Erich von Stroheim haircut was the French consul-general himself, the host. (Barzini, 1983, pp. 96–7)

In other words, people see what they want to see, and often oversee what they wish to ignore. Following Sumner's (1906) writings on 'ethnocentrism' and the basic state of conflict between the 'we group' and 'other groups' – including the tendency he reported for people to prefer the characteristics, products and customs of their own group – attention in the stereotype literature has focussed on negative stereotypes held about other groups.

The status of stereotyping has been debated in the literature. To some, stereotypes are 'traditional nonsense' (Hayakawa, 1950); to others they contain a 'kernel of truth' and a 'well-deserved reputation' (Zawadski,

1948); still others accept stereotyping as a necessary time-saving evil (Bogardus, 1950). The point of focus here must be how stereotypes function and whether, for an analysis of European attitudes, they matter at all. Although stereotypes have been seen as inherently 'bad' or 'wrong' – because they are illogical in origin, resistant to contradictory information, morally wrong, and so on (see Brigham, 1971; Lippman, 1922; McCauley, Stitt and Segal, 1980) – Allport (1954) emphasised that categorical pre-judgement and erroneous generalisation were *natural and common* capacities of the human mind. They have also been found to develop at an early age. According to Lambert and Klineberg (1967, p. 184), six-year olds in various countries tended to think of all other nationality groups as dissimilar to themselves (see also Jahoda, 1963*a,b*; Piaget, 1961).

If stereotypes are important, then it must be because they function for individuals, groups and nations. Fishman (1956) listed the functions of rationalisation, self-justification and defence of loved-ones; he concluded that: 'stereotypes, not unlike folk proverbs, represent a unique combination of insight, projection, rationalization, and out-and-out self-gratification'. (p. 54.)

A more systematic view of the functions of stereotypes has been developed by Tajfel (1981) in terms of individual and collective functions served by stereotypes in intergroup relations. The two individual cognitive functions refer to simplifying or ordering the complex social world, and preserving an individual's system of values. The first of two major collective functions may be termed 'social explanatory' and refers to the creation and maintenance of group ideologies that justify and explain relations between groups, particularly reactions to and treatment of outgroup members. The second collective function is central to Tajfel's (1974, 1978) theory of social identity, which proposes that individuals strive for a positive view of themselves, in part by comparing their own group with others. To the extent that national groups assume importance for individuals in this sense, the aim of such inter-nation comparisons is to make one's own national group distinct, and positively so. Stereotypes, containing the content of beliefs about in- and out-groups, thus preserve, create or enhance the positively valued distinctiveness of the own group vis-à-vis other groups. Thus Tajfel's theory points to how stereotypes may interfere with the process of European integration, seen as the integration of the peoples of Europe, by explaining the behaviour of other nations and peoples in terms of 'national charac-teristics', and by maintaining national differences, rather than fusing to form a European nation.

Stereotypes have been accorded a place in the study of international relations because, it is believed, 'the stereotyped and prejudicial conceptions that national groups maintain with respect to each other often stand in the way of international understanding'. (Gilbert, 1951, p. 245.) Thus many studies have sought to provide a picture of how people from different nations see each other (e.g. Buchanan and Cantril, 1953; Karlins, Coffman and Walters, 1969; Katz and Braly, 1933; Klineberg, 1964). What these studies do *not* show is whether stereotypes 'lead to' or 'reflect' international relations. One would certainly expect the content of stereotypes to be modified by changes in international relations, and there is evidence to support this point (e.g. Seago, 1947; Sinha and Uphadyay, 1960). But stereotypes may then influence the development of subsequent relations, by anticipating their development and justifying their nature (see Doise, 1978). Restricting this analysis to international relations, the probable role of stereotypes is that outlined by Buchanan and Cantril: 'Stereotypes are less likely to govern the likes and dislikes between nations than to adapt themselves to the positive or negative relationship based on matters unrelated to images of the people concerned... they may follow and rationalize, rather than precede and determine, reaction to a certain nation.' (1953, pp. 56–7.) While this might appear to suggest only a passive role for stereotypes, it is nonetheless an important one. Consider, for example, the impact on stereotypes of the widely publicised wine, lamb and cod 'wars' which flare up from time to time between farmers, fishermen or lorry-drivers from different Community countries.

Despite the apparent wealth of evidence, some forms of methodology (e.g. the Katz–Braly adjective checklist) raise doubts about the validity of the responses obtained when researchers have tried to assess stereotypes. Respondents may simply have been forced to respond stereotypically (Eysenck and Crown, 1948; Gilbert, 1951) or may have recited the views they believed to be held by others. It is certainly not always clear whether traits in a stereotype would be personally endorsed by respondents, or whether they would be *used* in intergroup or international encounters (see Brigham, 1971).

The assessment procedure reported below cannot with certainty rule out the possibility that respondents answered with other people's stereotypes. However, by asking respondents to indicate what percentage of people in different countries can be described by the various traits, we at least have a measure of *how typical* various traits are. In the subsequent analytical procedure low scores are then given less weight than high scores. The methodology used also investigates both positive and negative stereotypes (see Allport, 1954), and stereotypes of one's own and other nationalities (see Vinacke, 1949). Triandis and Vassiliou (1967) refer to these in- and out-group perceptions as auto- and heterostereotypes respectively. Finally, the method of calculating a 'stereotyping score' adopts an individual measure. The distinction between 'group-shared' and 'private' stereotypes (see

Newcomb and Charters, 1950) gives researchers the possibility of adopting a measure compatible with the aims of their study. Because the present study is centred on individually held attitudes about the European Community, and correlates of such attitudes, an individual-based measure of stereotyping is appropriate (see McCauley and Stitt, 1978; McCauley, Stitt and Segal, 1980). The focus is, therefore, on the way individuals describe and evaluate 'foreigners', relative to the way they view their compatriots. However, because some previous research has shown respondents (especially students) to be reluctant to stereotype at all (Eysenck and Crown, 1948; Gilbert, 1951), a less contentious measure of 'liking' for members of one's own and other national groups can also be used to compute a score of nationalism, ingroup-favouritism, or ethnocentrism. Liking may not imply the same commitment as 'trust' (see earlier discussion) but it may help to differentiate respondents into those who are more or less positive, or negative, in their perception of foreigners.

Following research on people's 'images' of other countries, it seems that judgements of countries may be quite different from judgements of peoples (e.g.: 'I hate southern Italy, but the Italians are such friendly people'). It certainly seems possible that ratings of countries – e.g. their political and economic standing, their agricultural fecundity and so on – may have an impact on one's willingness to enter into or continue international cooperation. As everyone knows, the U.K.'s economic problems, Italy's political instability, France's communist influence and W. Germany's prosperity all receive their share of attention in the mass media. Whether ratings of countries along these dimensions are correlated with Community attitudes, or indeed with stereotypes, will be considered below.

National identity (whether as attachment to people and/or country) is obviously an important background characteristic of many people. We have come to expect certain uniformities within national groups and systematic differences between them due to differing cultural, social and political influences. It may be thought unlikely that such factors would influence overall attitudes to the Community, but that is a hypothesis to test empirically, rather than from the armchair. These measures of stereotypes, liking and images may, in any case, provide evidence for what Lindberg and Scheingold (1970) call 'identitive' support. This refers to a link with other people, not just political institutions. Thus a Frenchman might say that he likes and views positively the Italians, W. Germans and British, a judgement which might have some 'spin off' value in terms of support for the Community. Alternatively, such social-psychological judgements may be quite independent of Community attitudes, but may nonetheless be considered a useful reserve of support for the general idea of a united Europe.

3.4 Equity theory: perceived gains and losses of Community membership

Equity theory (see Adams, 1968, 1965; Anderson, 1976; Berkowitz and Walster, 1976; Blau, 1967; Homans, 1961; Walster, Berscheid and Walster, 1976; Walster, Walster and Berscheid, 1978) is concerned, broadly, with how people judge what is just, fair, deserved or equitable, and how these perceptions influence behaviour (Eiser, 1980). In social psychology equity has been defined as, 'a single rule that may be employed to determine what is a fair distribution of outcomes between interdependent actors'. (McClintock, Kramer and Keil, 1984, p. 185.) The theory deals, essentially, with the allocation of resources and, given the attention paid to dissatisfaction with allocation, might well have been called 'inequity theory'.

Part of the appeal of equity theory is that it seems to encompass a diversity of phenomena by means of four central propositions, designed to predict when individuals will perceive that they are justly treated and how they will react to perceived injustice:

> PROPOSITION I: Individuals will try to maximize their outcomes (where outcomes equal rewards minus costs).
>
> PROPOSITION IIA: Groups can maximize collective reward by evolving accepted systems for equitably apportioning resources among members. Thus, groups will evolve such systems of equity, and will attempt to induce members to accept and adhere to these systems. PROPOSITION IIB: Groups will generally reward members who treat others equitably, and generally punish (increase the costs for) members who treat others inequitably.
>
> PROPOSITION III: When individuals find themselves participating in inequitable relationships, they will become distressed. The more inequitable the relationship, the more distress individuals will feel.
>
> PROPOSITION IV: Individuals who discover they are in an inequitable relationship will attempt to eliminate their distress by restoring equity. The greater the inequity that exists, the more distress they will feel, and the harder they will try to restore equity. (Walster *et al.*, 1978, p. 6)

Without explicating these propositions in detail (see Walster *et al.*, 1976, 1978), the present work is primarily concerned with the extent to which individuals' 'distress' at perceived inequity may be related to their (lack of) attitudinal support for the Community. As proposition IV outlines, those who perceive a relationship to be inequitable will attempt to restore inequity, and one way this could be achieved is by withdrawing support for further payments to the Community (*cf.* the case of the United Kingdom).

A basis for any discussion of the theory is the question: What is an inequitable relationship? The simplest notion of equity is mere parity; for example, countries A and B receive the same *outcomes* from the European Community. But here no account is taken of the *inputs* contributed by each country. Thus Adams (1965), based on a reading of Aristotle's *Nichomachean Ethics*, proposed that a relationship will only be seen as equitable if, for all parties, the ratio of outcomes to inputs is equal:

$$\frac{O_A}{I_A} = \frac{O_B}{I_B}$$

where O_A denotes A's outcomes; O_B denotes B's outcomes; I_A denotes A's inputs; and I_B B's inputs. However, as Walster *et al.* (1976) point out, this formula is only adequate as long as all participants have inputs and outcomes that are entirely positive, or entirely negative. It is *not* suitable in social relations where inputs may be negative as well as positive.

Walster *et al.* (1978) suggest that a formal rule is needed, to convey what is meant by (in)equity, thus allowing the researcher to *calculate* whether a relationship is inequitable or not. They propose that an equitable relationship exists when the person scrutinising the relationship (i.e. the 'scrutineer') perceives that all participants are receiving equal *relative gains* from the relationship, i.e.:

$$\frac{(O_A - I_A)}{(/I_A/)k_A} = \frac{(O_B - I_B)}{(/I_B/)k_B}$$

where: I_A and I_B represent a scrutineer's perception of the inputs of persons A and B, respectively; $/I_A/$ and $/I_B/$ designate the *absolute value* of their inputs (i.e. the perceived value of their inputs, disregarding the sign; with the constraint that both $/I_A/$ and $/I_B/$ must be $\geqslant 1$); O_A and O_B represent the scrutineer's perception of the outcomes of persons A and B, respectively; the exponents k_A and k_B take on the value $+1$ or -1, depending on the sign of A's and B's gains (outcomes–inputs).

Notwithstanding the elegance and apparent simplicity of this approach, one must ask whether and if so how, equity theory can be applied to an issue such as perceptions of the European Community. Certainly Adams and Freedman (1976) have argued that equity theory has great relevance to 'economic, legal, interpersonal and intergroup relationships' (p. 55; see also Caddick, 1980), but to the author's knowledge the present application of the theory is the first of its kind. How, then, might one proceed?

Considered in terms of the European Community, inputs might be calculated or perceived primarily in terms of net budget contributions; outcomes might be considered in terms of gains via the Common Agricultural Policy, the Community Regional Fund, and the Social Fund. It is not, of course, proposed that individuals, our respondents, perceive matters in this complex way, nor that they are necessarily aware of the amounts of money which flow in and out of the Community coffers at various openings. However, the citizens of W. Germany and the U.K. in particular are fed a fairly unrelenting diet of 'gains vs losses' in the mass media. It is certainly a language they understand, and probably one in terms of which they have come to think. (Gunter's, 1985, content-analysis of television presentation of the EEC reports that explicit evaluation of the 'advantages and disadvantages' of membership is common).

Rather than ask anyone to estimate inputs to and outcomes from the Community for her own country, let alone the others, it is proposed to test a more general hypothesis: that those who perceive their own country to benefit least and/or to contribute most to the Community will have more negative attitudes than those who perceive other countries as minor beneficiaries or major benefactors. Asking separate questions about which member states contribute and benefit most or least (see Featherstone, 1981) is not, obviously, the same as a direct judgement of inequity (in terms of the ratio of inputs/outcomes). However, respondents who believe that their own country both contributes most *and* benefits least would appear to be conscious of a striking inequity. One can predict that such respondents will have more negative Community attitudes than those who believe only that their own country contributes most *or* benefits least; and these attitudes should be considerably more negative than those of people who perceive neither of the preceding conditions. Linked with questions of gain and loss are two further issues: whether the Community is seen as too big to be effective; and whether to stay in or leave the Community. Both questions are examined below.

One can also calculate perceived inequity in a manner analogous to the formula suggested by Walster *et al.* (1976, 1978). One simply calculates – for each of the four national groups of interests – the number of respondents who perceive that their own country (compared with the others) benefits most (or least) and contributes most (or least). One can then compare one's own country's ratio of 'benefits' to 'contributes' with the average of other countries, as perceived by their nationals. Such calculations, reported in Chapter 5, allow us to compare the perceptions of inequity in the four countries, and to see whether respondents are satisfied with the Community, or not.

Both types of equity theory analysis reported below acknowledge the emphasis of Walster *et al.* (1978), that ultimately 'equity is in the eye of the beholder'. (p. 15.) An individual's perception of how equitable a relationship is will depend on his or her assessment of the value and relevance of the various participants' inputs and outcomes; and participants often disagree with each other and with outside observers. Equity is, therefore, a matter of social psychology and not simply economics.

3.5 Utilitarian and affective support for Community membership

Also working from the general notion of equity, one can return to the political science idea of utilitarian support (Lindberg and Scheingold, 1970; see Section 2.7., above). As was noted, utilitarian support refers to concrete gains and losses. These are assessed in simple questions about who gains and contributes what, but it may be anticipated that some respondents will feel unhappy about making such critical judgements, given a lack of detailed economic knowledge. A section of closed-ended questions was therefore built into the questionnaire, dealing with both personal and national gain–loss from the Community (e.g. 'gains' from the C.A.P., or Regional Fund; 'losses' from national budget contributions and financial subsidies to other member states). This should give a clearer indication of the nature and extent of utilitarian support for the Community than has thus far been yielded from secondary analysis of survey data. Thus, here, we cannot claim that the notion of support is social psychological, but we can relate it to psychological variables and test its impact with more care.

Whereas utilitarian support is closely linked to notions of equity, affective support (also discussed above, see Section 2.7.) is a more emotional response to the idea of Europe. Although some scholars contend that utilitarian support precedes affective support, the present analysis neither makes, nor tests this assumption. It does, however, provide a set of questions dealing with more effective dimensions of support (e.g. solidarity, trust, confidence), the importance of which may place some constraints on the key role often ascribed to perceptions of equity and utilitarian support.

Finally, if utilitarian and/or affective support levels are sufficiently high, the functionalists' desired shift in public loyalties (from national to European institutions) might be observed. This issue could not be definitively resolved within the constraints of the adopted questionnaire, but an attempt was made to compare levels of confidence both in a national government's and the Community's handling of economic affairs.

3.6 The effects of personal contact and travel

Although Kelman (1965*a*) acknowledges the importance of the larger societal context in which any social interaction takes place, his definition of social psychology and his view of this discipline's impact on international relations centre on social interaction. The interactions between travellers in foreign countries and their hosts are seen, to some extent, as manifestations of the interactions between nations. Mathew (1980), discussing Kelman's work, has characterised this as a functionalist perspective, which proposes that individuals who experience cooperative international contacts may undergo both cognitive and affective attitude change which contributes to the broad aim of integration.

Contact, like the Lord, moves in mysterious ways which remain arcane to scholars because they usually decline, or are unable, to analyse the *process* of contact (see Hewstone and Brown, 1986). However, there are various ways in which contact has been conceived to work. For example, cooperative meetings may result in the perception that interests are shared, and that further goals and benefits could be shared (see Kelman, 1962). Contact may also render national stereotypes and images more positive, thus amounting to an attenuation, or even the disappearance, of ethnocentrism (to this end, correlations between the measures can be examined below). In this vein, Farquarson and Holt (1975), focussing on W. German–French relations specifically, view travel and associated contact as dispelling false (and negative) stereotypes. The idea of false stereotypes implies some measure of veridicality and is therefore questionable, but one can assess changes in the content and valence of sterotypes as a function of contact. Other variables, of course, also influence national images and Farquarson and Holt accept the primary role of national governments in influencing how nations see each other; nonetheless they maintain that: 'popular contacts now have a part to play in their own right, in that they may be utilized to reinforce such policies as European integration adopted at higher levels'. (1975, p. v.)

Interestingly, some public opinion studies have reported a distinctly more 'European' attitude amongst those who had travelled abroad in the last ten years.[12] Thus two questions were included in the questionnaire, to measure frequency of travel and duration of sojourn in other European countries. Notwithstanding the effects reported among the general public, it must be acknowledged that many, if not most, students (like those in the samples used) do now travel frequently (*cf.* Inglehart, 1971) and that, even if this has a positive effect, there may be too little variation in reported travel itself to yield significant correlations.[13]

3.7 Perceptions of economic policy and its outcomes

In contrast to the social-psychological variables introduced thus far, it may be that no such complex theorising is necessary to examine underlying attitudes to the European Community. Rather, the best predictors might be perceptions of economic policy and its outcomes. While the above measures of expectancy-value and utilitarian support, in particular, obviously address economic issues, it can be argued that they demand no knowledge of community achievements. An argument in favour of social-psychological measures is, indeed, that they do *not* require knowledge of sometimes complex economic policy. Nonetheless, to allow respondents to make more specific evaluations of the Community, and to see whether these judgements do affect overall attitudes, two sets of questions called for ratings of common policy (e.g. agriculture, transport) and some of its effects (e.g. increased agricultural productivity; harmonization of national transport costs within each of the member states).

3.8 Information and knowledge about the Community

The level of respondents' information and knowledge about the Community can be taken further by asking about newspaper readership, intention to take an interest in Community affairs in the future, and the perceived image of the Community in the mass media. More objectively, a knowledge test was constructed with items of varying difficulty. This last measure avoids the problems of response-biases sometimes encountered in opinion polls and attitude questionnaires, and allows for a test of the hypothesis that knowledge and attitude are (positively or negatively) correlated. It seems to the author that far too little attention has been paid to objective assessments of knowledge in studies of political attitudes, and that such information might provide a basis for future work on attitude change and public information campaigns.

Having now introduced the variables measured in the research, and given their theoretical rationale, we can turn to a description of the study in terms of the samples tested and the exact details of the questionnaire used.

3.9 Description of the study

3.9.1 Samples and respondents

Respondents were a total of 545 university students drawn from the four largest European Community countries: W. Germany (128); Italy (141); France (147); and the U.K. (129). At least two universities were used in W. Germany (Kiel, Tübingen), France (Paris VII, Tours) and the U.K. (Bristol, Kent, University College London), but only one in Italy (Bologna). The mean age of students was between 20 and 22 years of age, with the mean in Italy slightly lower and that in France slightly higher. There were rather more female than male students in the total sample, but with comparable ratios in each country. Students were drawn from faculties of social science, arts and natural science, but predominantly from the former.[14] Details of the samples are presented in Appendix A, Table A.1. Recruitment procedures were identical in the four countries and in line with standard social-psychological practice. Respondents were asked to participate, on a voluntary basis, in a questionnaire study of 'social attitudes' (no mention of the European Community was made in poster advertisements). No respondents refused to complete the questionnaire.[15]

Clearly these samples are *not* representative of the Community as a whole, nor of its citizens; nor are they intended to be. Studies with students (e.g. Inglehart, 1967, 1970a) and with subsets of member states (e.g. Deutsch *et al.*, 1957; Inglehart, 1970a,b; Merritt and Puchala, 1968) are widely found in the literature on social and political science. A focus on the four largest countries is most frequently found, partly because as Wildgen and Feld (1976) explain, 'it is simpler to compare four large countries than nine (now ten) countries of various sizes running from major powers to mini states'. (p. 82.)

Students could be characterised as an elite, because some will almost certainly have a direct or indirect effect on the operation of Community institutions or of Community policy, by virtue of positions in the national governments or the civil service. However, having examined and differed from the 'elitist' view of public opinion, the obtained samples are considered simply as educational elites, a status which has specific advantages for the research. In particular, the more specific, complex and extensive the set of questions a researcher seeks to pose, the higher the intellectual skills necessary to answer in a well-reasoned and consistent manner. Given the aim of developing and testing an explanatory model of European attitudes, preference was given to richness of information, rather than the representatives of the samples (see Himmelweit *et al.*, 1981).

Notwithstanding the above points, the use of university students (as in most social-psychological research) can be criticised on the grounds that students are not representative of the general population. Thus it may be argued that the attitudes reported and explored in this study are not typical of the population at large in the four countries. However, the purpose of the study is to go one step *beyond* what the normal survey studies on attitudes to Europe produce. We know about the distribution of these attitudes from the highly representative samples used in the *Euro-baromètre* research (see Chapter 2). What is needed now is to *explain* these attitudes. The best defence (as will be spelled out, below) for the analysis and interpretation of data based on students is that these results from students in the different countries are not different from those in the large and representative studies.

There remains, however, the problem that the kind of sampling one has used has reduced variables that could be important theoretically to the level of a constant. For example, the present samples, 'controlled' for social class and education, may rule out of consideration questions of politico-economic shaping of individual attitudes. Certainly, one should not expect correlations reported below to parallel exactly those in the general population. Kerlinger

(1984) has compared the attitude structure of elites and mass publics, and reports a clearer and more coherent factor structure in the former; however, he did still report a clearly interpretable factor structure in his mass sample. Kerlinger also emphasises that only a few questions can be asked in any one public opinion survey with a representative sample; this grossly restricts one's options for studying attitude *structure*.[16]

3.9.2 *The questionnaire*

Respondents were asked to complete an extensive questionnaire for a 'study on what ordinary citizens know, think and feel about the European Community or E.E.C., sometimes called the Common Market'. It was emphasised that opinions were of interest, and that respondents would remain anonymous.[17]

The questionnaire contained both 'open-end' and 'closed-end' questions, each of which have a number of advantages and disadvantages (see Oskamp, 1977). Open-end questions elicit the full range, depth and complexity of a respondent's view, a luxury almost never afforded in public opinion polls. Distortion caused by questionnaire wording is minimal, and a researcher can ascertain whether important viewpoints or topics have been overlooked. Disadvantages of such questions are the difficulty, unreliability and sheer time-demand of coding, especially where respondents use four different languages. In contrast, closed-end questions are easy to score and relatively objective, when used in the form of multi-point Likert-type scales; these questions measure the extent of a respondent's agreement (or disagreement) with each item, rather than simply obtaining a yes–no answer. However, careless wording may bias responses and the selection of items may restrict the views of respondents. Where both types of question are used, a 'funnel sequence' is recommended, whereby broad open-end questions precede more specific closed-end questions.[18]

Open-end questions
Three open-end questions, giving respondents about half a page to respond on each, tapped:

(A)   overall view of the Community, advantages and disadvantages, successes and failures;
(B)   basic principles and goals of the Community;
(C)   attitude to and information about one major common policy.

In questions (A) and (B) respondents were asked to try to give reasons for their answers.[19]

Closed-end questions

These questions were arranged in 11 sections (D–N in the questionnaire reproduced in Appendix B) so that questions on related issues were grouped together and summary scores calculated to increase reliability.[20] Thus the reported results focus on summary scores, rather than a very lengthy and less reliable analysis of over 100 individual judgements. To guard against response biases (e.g. social desirability; response extremity; acquiescence), positively and negatively worded items were interchanged where appropriate, and in equal numbers. It was not practical to produce several versions of the questionnaire with the sections ordered differently, thus the same carefully considered order of sections was always used. It should therefore be acknowledged that this elicitation procedure may itself produce certain patterns of response. For example, previously non-salient beliefs may become salient once elicited, or mere elicitation of certain ideas and issues may change a person's overall attitude. The order of questions was as follows:

(D)   *Expectancy-value analysis of attitudes.* Thirteen[21] items concerning political and economic goals of the Community (e.g. strengthening Europe's role in the world; establishing a custom's union) were first evaluated on 7-point scales (scoring: extremely good, $+3$; extremely bad, -3). Respondents then rated how probable they thought it was that the Community was bringing about each of the goals (scoring was manipulated as bipolar: probable, $+3$; improbable, -3; and unipolar: probable, 7; improbable, 1).

(E)   *Achievements of common policy.* Five areas of common policy (e.g. agriculture, transport) were rated for their success (scoring: extremely unsuccessful, 1; extremely successful, 7).

(F)   *Effects of common policy.* Ten specific economic effects (e.g. increased agricultural productivity; speaking with a single voice) were rated for the success with which they had been brought about (scoring: extremely unsuccessful, 1; extremely successful, 7).

(G)   *Utilitarian support.* Respondents rated their agreement with eight items concerning 'gains' (e.g. personal gain) and 'losses' (e.g. net budget contribution) associated with Community membership. Scoring (1–7 to 7–1) was reversed on four items to produce high scores for strong agreement with pro-E.E.C. statements.

(H)   *Affective support.* Respondents endorsed eight items relating to affective support for the Community (e.g. 'I feel a strong sense of solidarity'; 'I do not have confidence'). Scoring (1–7 to 7–1) was reversed on half the items to produce high scores for strong agreement with pro-E.E.C. statements.

(I)   *National stereotypes.* Respondents ascribed ten personality traits to any percentage (0%–100%) of people from their own and the three other countries. Given the length of the questionnaire, this section was limited to five positive and five negative traits which had been shown to be used in describing these four nationalities (see Buchanan and Cantril, 1953; Karlins *et al.*, 1969). Each of the traits was then evaluated (scoring: extremely good, $+3$; extremely bad, -3).

(J)   *National images.* Descriptions of one's own and three other countries were made in terms of ten (five positive, five negative) characteristics, using ratings from 0–9 to indicate the degree to which each country was believed to possess each characteristic.[22] Each of the characteristics was then evaluated (scoring: extremely good, $+3$; extremely bad, -3).

(K)   *Beliefs about international relations.* Helfant's (1967) 'Survey of opinions and beliefs about international relations' was adapted for each of the four countries to measure support for cooperative international relations. Responses were made on 7-, rather than 5-, point scales, to be comparable with other questionnaire items and to avoid confusing the respondents.[23] Scoring (1–7 to 7–1) was reversed on half the items so that high scores indicate a positive orientation towards cooperative international relations.

(L)   *Miscellaneous.* A number of items, the theoretical background to which has been discussed above, were grouped in this section for convenience.

Active interest. One item measured intention to take an active interest in Community affairs in the coming years (scoring: extremely likely, $+3$; extremely unlikely, -3).

Perceived inequity: Perceived beneficiaries from and contributors to the Community. Four items asked which member state benefits *most* and *least* from the Community; and which contributes *most* and *least* to the Community. Responses were classified nominally, by country given as response.

Liking. Expressed liking for own and three other nationalities was scored from 7 (very much) to 1 (not at all).

Verdicts on the Community. Two questions asked whether the Community had become too big to be effective; and whether the respondent's own country should vote to leave. Responses were yes/no.

Confidence in national government. Confidence in one's national government's handling of economic affairs was assessed on a 7-point scale for comparison with item 5 in Section H (scoring: extremely confident, 7; not at all confident, 1).

Mass media. Perceived description of the Community in the mass media was rated on a scale from extremely positively (7) to extremely negatively (1).

Attitude ambivalence. Respondents were asked to judge the Community, first, only on its positive qualities (ignoring its negative qualities); this 4-point scale was scored from 'no feelings in favour' (0) to 'strongly in favour' (+3). A second item asked the respondent to focus only on negative qualities (ignoring the Community's positive qualities); this 4-point scale was scored from 'strongly against' (−3) to 'no feelings against' (0).[24]

Overall attitude. The criterion variable for the whole study, overall attitude to the Community, was assessed on a 7-point scale from 'strongly against' (−3) to 'strongly in favour' (+3).

(M)   *Personal and demographic details.* Standard questions served to classify respondents by age, sex, country of birth, nationality, name of university, faculty, whether politics or economics had been studied and for how long,[25] and for which political party they would vote if a general election were held tomorrow.

Contact. Two items measured time spent (extremely long: 6; no time at all: 0) and frequency of travel (extremely frequently: 6; never: 0) in other European countries.

Newspapers. Respondents were asked to list the newspapers they read regularly.

(N)   *Knowledge test.* This final section made explicit the shift from assessment of (subjective) opinions to (objective) knowledge. Ten items ranging from quite simple to very difficult were scored 1 (correct) or 0 (incorrect).

3.9.3 Procedure
Pilot study
Pilot studies were run to pre-test the complete questionnaire. This led to small modifications and clarifications, and provided a check on comprehensibility, complexity and completion-time. It was also used to ensure a spread of difficulty in the knowledge test items.

The study
Data were collected simultaneously in all four countries in the last two weeks of November 1983. Respondents participated on a voluntary basis and completed the questionnaire (about one hour in length) under the supervision of assistants.

3.9.4 Caveats
This section has made clear the limitations of the study in terms of samples, respondents, questions asked and date of data-collection. It is usual in such

cross-national surveys to offer some caveat concerning the functional equivalence of items: does a given question, asked in translated form in each country, tap the same underlying issue or attitude? Alternatively, should one attempt to pose exactly the same questions in each country or, rather, simply ask relevant questions for each country? The answer is simple: at the outset it was not known *what* was relevant, that is what the study intended to uncover. It is also accepted that comparability is not necessarily consequent upon use of the same items, because there may be cross-national differences in interpretation. The author is, however, aware of the effects of wording in both cross-national psychological studies (see Manaster and Havighurst, 1972, pp. 19–21) and surveys of political attitudes (Greenstein, 1976). Ideally, the back-translation method should be used to overcome subtle problems of translation in cross-cultural research (see Brislin, 1980), although it was not feasible in this study. However, great efforts were made to control for such effects, and to ensure a reliable measurement instrument, by working together in each country with social psychologists and bilinguals. The author can therefore express confidence in the reliability and validity of the results.

3.10 Summary

There appear to be firm theoretical foundations for a social-psychological approach to the study of Community attitudes. However, the contribution of social psychology has so far been minimal, although as Wober (1981) has argued: 'Psychologists should see this context as an important one in which to make a contribution that can be both analytic, and empirical.' (p. 181.) Wober himself carried out a modest public opinion-type poll of 813 people in the U.K., using a 16-item attitude questionnaire.[26] Factor analysis yielded three factors (accounting for a total of 40% of the variance) which Wober named 'political', 'cultural' and 'economic'. These dimensions are, of course, constrained by the item input, but Wober does not claim to have uncovered *the* structure of Community attitudes. Rather, he has shown, simply but importantly, that 'attitude towards Europe' is not a homogeneous construct, but a multi-dimensional structure. Unfortunately, factor scores were not related to an overall measure of attitude and showed almost no relationship to voting turn-out in the European elections. This suggests that, notwithstanding the empirical support for a multivariate approach, social psychologists still have a long way to go before they can claim to have ascertained the 'inner structure' of attitudes towards Europe.

The present analysis (centred on the study of social representations; attitudes; stereotypes and images; perceived inequity; the effects of contact; perceptions of economic policy and its effects; and knowledge) should provide a more satisfactory picture of the 'inner structure' of Community attitudes and should eschew the critique that most research on international attitudes is unsophisticated and descriptive (Oskamp, 1977). Most important, this approach does justice to the complexity of European attitudes, or at least allows for them to be complex, and will focus on the interrelationships between various perceptions.

4 Social representations of the European Community: Content-analyses of open-ended responses

> For the most part, the business of the European Community tends to be largely economic and consequently rather obscure. Tariffs, taxes, agriculture, cartels are very complicated subjects and, despite their intrinsic significance, not entirely comprehensible to the politician or interesting to the man in the street.
>
> (L. N. Lindberg and S. A. Scheingold, 1970)

The first stage of the present study was a content-analysis of open-ended responses to three general questions at the beginning of the questionnaire. This chapter opens with a brief discussion of some of the principles and problems of content-analysis, and the results of one comparable study known to the author. The present findings are then examined and discussed.

4.1 Content-analysis

Content-analysis has been described as 'a research technique for the objective, systematic, and quantitative description of the manifest content of communication'. (Berelson, 1952, p. 18.) The major strength of the technique lies in its analysis of unstructured responses in terms of various specified categories. However, in their choice of response categories researchers must be careful not merely to find what they seek and, instead, to find the middle ground between very general, but banal, and very narrow, but idiosyncratic, categories. As Berelson noted, 'content-analysis stands and falls by its categories'. (*op. cit.* p. 147.)

At the outset some strengths and shortcomings of the approach can be illustrated with reference to the study by Bacot-Decriaud and Plantin (1982). These authors analysed a written questionnaire completed by 746 French civil servants (*cadres*), whom one would expect to be relatively well-informed.[1] 49% of these respondents replied to the question: 'On parle beaucoup d'intégration européenne, qu'est-ce, pour vous, l'intégration européenne?' Only 9% of responses were negative, and these fell into four main categories: 'loss of identity and national independence' (2%); 'denunciation of a Europe of profit and multi-nationals' (2%); the view that Europe could only be 'a source of grave problems' (2%), and the description of Europe as 'la grande illusion' (3%).[2] Writing about what the European Community meant for them, respondents cited 'a common economic policy' (12%); 'harmonisation of social policies' (7%); 'free circulation of goods and capital, and a coordinated commercial policy' (5%). Finally, for the present summary, (8%) of these respondents mentioned 'political cooperation' and 5% conceived of integration in terms of a 'bloc in opposition to other powers'.

From this presentation of selected results, it is obvious that Bacot-Decriaud and Plantin have followed the standard procedure of analysis in terms of exact frequency counts. This analysis is based on the number of respondents, rather than the frequency of every occurrence of a given response. The latter analysis is, in fact, sometimes taken as a valid indicator of such characteristics as focus of attention, intensity, and importance (Holsti, 1969), but it is a much more complicated procedure (as is analysis in terms of the order in which responses are given, or the intensity of expression). It should also be noted that Bacot-Decriaud and Plantin's respondents showed apparently very little agreement, or consensus. This may, in part, be due to the narrow width of categories used, an issue which Holsti identifies as the paradox of content-analysis: 'as categories and units of analysis become more complex, they are likely to become both more useful and less reliable'. (*op. cit.*, p. 660.) The researcher should certainly think hard about whether response categories containing two per cent of the responses are of interest, for theoretical or practical reasons, or whether responses should be collapsed into broader groupings. Given the findings of this previous study, it was decided to simplify the analysis and to try to build broader response categories which would allow for meaningful cross-national comparisons.

4.2 Procedure

Coding was a time-consuming affair, limited by financial, practical and temporal constraints, and complicated by the nature of four different linguistic samples. Originally a small subset of answers were analysed by one coder in Italy and the author, to explore possible categories and their defining attributes. A final set of categories was then agreed, with criteria for inclusion (see examples in Appendix C), after discussion with all four coders.

Each coder was given 50 (25 male, 25 female) randomly selected answer-sheets from one country. Each unique response was written on a different index card, and the respondent's identification was written in the top corner. In this way it was ensured that a respondent's answer was coded only once in the same category, even if a point was repeated. Cards for the five basic sections (see below) were kept separate and then organised in terms of the category list. It was simply not possible to compute reliability scores, given four different coders using four different languages, which was another reason for keeping categories broad and objective. In this way, categories were clearly defined and the task rendered more one of objective counting than subjective coding (see Budd, Thorp and Donohew, 1967). Finally, it was decided not to pursue an analysis in terms of the order of the ideas mentioned in an answer, because similar responses sometimes occurred for the three different questions. For example, one respondent might give as a disadvantage of the Community, high prices of agricultural produce. Another respondent might give the same reply but in answer to the question about common policy. Because agricultural policy was so dominant, this problem was easily solved. All responses to questions one and two which related to agriculture were coded as responses to question three. Thus the findings below are presented in five major sections, with a summary table for each:

> overall view of the Community;
> positive aspects of the Community ('advantages' and 'successes');
> negative aspects of the Community ('disadvantages' and 'failures');
> principles, goals and aims of the Community;
> view of agricultural policy.

4.3 Results

Although all identifiable categories are included in the tables below, the discussion will focus on responses given, first, by at least 10% of all respondents; and, second, by 10% of the respondents in any country. This is a somewhat arbitrary and conservative criterion, but one which maintains a focus on ideas or views about the Community which are not completely idiosyncratic. After much thought it was decided not to compute statistics to compare response frequencies in the four countries. The percentage of respondents who gave no answer was quite high, especially in Italy and France, thus making inferences about reliability dubious. Given this problem, we cannot state that the absence of a response in either of these countries means that the issue is unimportant; and where at least 10% of respondents in these countries have answered, it may be that the view in question is especially important only to this minority.

4.3.1 Overall view of the Community
Responses to the question: 'What do you think of the E.E.C.?' are given in Table 4.1. Unfortunately this general view was not always given, as some

Table 4.1. *Overall view of the European Community*

Category	W. Germany		Italy		France		U.K.		All	
	N	%	N	%	N	%	N	%	N	%
1.1 neutral/ambiguous	4	8	10	20	5	10	1	2	20	10
1.2 negative	8	16	3	6	6	12	8	16	25	12.5
1.3 positive	15	30	17	34	9	18	11	22	52	26
1.4 conditional positive	9	18	16	32	7	14	15	30	47	23.5
No answer	14	28	4	8	23	46	15	30	56	28
Total	50	100	50	100	50	100	50	100	200	100

Note:
N denotes total number of responses in a category.

respondents simply began listing positive and negative aspects of the Community. However, it was possible to build four broad categories.

The majority response in every country except the U.K. was positive, emphasising themes of unity and security:

> I think the EEC is a very good idea from a point of view of: 1/. World unity – the more countries find themselves in a 'club' the more they are likely to help each other and not fight with each other.
> 2/. Economical security – hopefully, countries in a good financial situation should help poorer countries. (F, 173)

as well as genuine enthusiasm:

> I am in favour of the Common Market, principally, I suppose for cultural and ideological reasons; it represents at least a partial approach to the ideal of mediaeval Christendom. It is incredible that nations which, only one generation ago, were engaged (and had been many times previously) in war should now be co-operating within a united political matrix, however loose. (M, 253)

On this measure the Italians are most positive, followed by the W. Germans, the British and the French, but the large number of respondents who did not answer prevents any confident prediction of overall attitudes in the structured questionnaire

While encouraging for the Community, the number of positive respondents should be seen alongside those in perhaps the most interesting category – 'conditional positive'. These respondents (nearly a quarter of the total sample) distinguished between theory and practice to pass a more qualified judgement on the Community. They supported the aims and principles of the Community, but were disappointed with the reality:

> I think the principle of the EEC is a good one, but one which has not always worked. (F, 179)

> I think the 'idea' of the EEC is very good... but in practice these ideas
> seem constrained by rigid bureaucracy and political in-fighting. (F, 185)

> In theory it's a good idea but in practice seems to degenerate into a series
> of nationalistic squabbles.[3] (M, 499)

In comparison with the first two categories, the number of explicitly negative
responses was very small, but might be higher in W. Germany and the U.K.,
than in France and Italy. The negative minority were, however, sometimes
highly critical:

> I believe that the EEC is an odious bureaucratic mess. I cannot see any
> advantages in the format at the present time... (it) is the oracle of
> nationalism.... (M, 168)

Finally, a small number of respondents – although large in Italy – were
neutral or ambivalent, seeing both positive and negative aspects of the
Community, but not wishing to commit themselves.

4.3.2 Positive aspects
Pooling the perceived 'advantages' and 'successes' of the Community, four
broad categories emerged (see Table 4.2). The most widely cited positive
aspect of the Community is 'European cooperation' (17% of all respondents),
although this is far more important in W. Germany than in the three other
countries. As can be seen from the other sub-parts of category 2.2., what
exactly economic policy is, is not very clear.

Other kinds of cooperation – cultural, technical and scientific – are also
given support, as is the widely enjoyed 'freedom of travel'. Perhaps all these
aspects help to build a sense of 'European unity and identity', mentioned
especially by the W. Germans and British. Although less important overall,
it should be noted that a high percentage of both W. Germans and British
positively evaluate 'helping other member states'.

Respondents are also aware of commercial policy and, interestingly, the
Italians and French mention the 'expansion of free exchanges', while the
W. Germans and British support the 'dismantling of quotas and tariffs'.
Finally, the role of the Community in international affairs is expressed in
two categories. Only the French do not mention 'European foreign policy',
and only the W. Germans do not mention the building of a 'block against
the superpowers'.

Overall, there is no great consensus on the positive aspects of the
Community, although a variety of instances are given. It is, at least,
encouraging to note that Community cooperation and international affairs
were mentioned, although these are still less frequently cited than are commercial and economic matters. This suggests that the European *Economic*
Community, although many respondents still use this term (or Common

Table 4.2. *Positive aspects of the European Community*

Category	Country of respondent									
	W. Germany		Italy		France		U.K.		All	
	N	%	N	%	N	%	N	%	N	%
2.1. Commercial policy										
2.1.1. expansion of free exchanges	—	—	10	20	8	16	2	4	20	10
2.1.2. dismantling quotas and tariffs for trade	11	22	3	6	2	4	12	24	28	14
2.1.3. unification and expansion of markets	2	4	3	6	2	4	3	6	10	5
2.1.4. harmonization of laws, norms	2	4	2	4	3	6	4	8	11	5.5
2.2 Economic policy										
2.2.1. economic cooperation	17	34	6	12	6	12	5	10	34	17
2.2.2. common monetary policy	4	8	—	—	2	4	—	—	6	3
2.2.3. production and supply of goods	—	—	2	4	—	—	2	4	4	2
2.3. Community cooperation										
2.3.1. cultural, technical and scientific cooperation	11	22	4	8	8	16	6	12	24	14.5
2.3.2. freedom of travel	9	18	1	2	4	8	7	14	21	10.5
2.3.3. European unity/identity	9	18	1	2	5	10	7	14	22	11
2.3.4. help other member states	10	20	3	6	1	2	4	8	18	9
2.3.5. build peace	1	2	1	2	—	—	3	6	5	2.5
2.4. International affairs										
2.4.1. European foreign policy	6	12	3	6	—	—	9	18	18	9
2.4.2. block against the 'superpowers'	—	—	5	10	5	10	4	8	14	7
No advantages	—	—	1	2	—	—	4	8	5	2.5
Unclassified	2	4	5	10	—	—	6	12	13	6.5
No answer	—	—	12	24	15	30	1	2	28	14

Notes:
N denotes total number of responses in a category.
Absence of responses is indicated by a dash.

Table 4.3. *Negative aspects of the European Community*

Category	Country of respondent									All	
	W. Germany		Italy		France		U.K.				
	N	%	N	%	N	%	N	%	N	%	
2.1. Commercial policy											
2.1.1. negative effect on prices	6	12	—	—	4	8	5	10	15	7.5	
2.1.2. import–export restrictions	5	10	3	6	2	4	3	6	13	6.5	
2.1.3. forced harmonisation	—	—	1	2	—	—	4	8	5	2.5	
2.2. Economic policy											
2.2.1. bureaucracy and centralisation	10	20	3	6	1	2	12	24	26	13	
2.2.2. imbalance between rich/ poor countries	5	10	8	16	3	6	6	12	22	11	
2.2.3. 'we' pay too much	4	8	—	—	—	—	8	16	28	14	
2.2.4. interference with 'natural' supply and demand	5	10	—	—	—	—	—	—	5	2.5	
2.2.5. expensive support of weak members	3	6	—	—	—	—	—	—	3	1.5	
2.2.6. anti-socialist policy	—	—	—	—	—	—	3	6	3	1.5	
2.3. Community cooperation											
2.3.1 too much nationalism/ protectionism	15	30	3	6	4	8	11	22	33	16.5	
2.3.2. competition between members	19	38	4	8	6	12	5	10	34	17	
2.3.3. goals not achieved	9	18	—	—	—	—	2	4	11	5.5	
2.3.4. failure of peace/nuclear threat	—	—	1	2	—	—	1	2	2	1	
2.3.5. still border/passport controls	2	4	—	—	—	—	2	4	4	2	
2.3.6. Franco–British conflict	—	—	—	—	4	8	3	6	7	3.5	
2.4. National Sovereignty											
2.4.1. Loss of national sovereignty identity and independence	8	16	3	6	6	12	9	18	26	13	
No disadvantages	—	—	—	—	—	—	—	—	—	—	
unclassified	4	8	4	8	1	2	6	12	15	7.5	
No answer	—	—	14	28	18	36	—	—	32	16	

Notes:
N denotes total number of responses in a category.
Absence of responses is denoted by a dash.

Market), is now viewed in the wider sense of a European Community with political, as well as economic, aims.

4.3.3 Negative aspects

Perceived 'disadvantages' and 'failures' of the Community can be classified in terms of similar categories to those used for positive aspects, although here 'Community cooperation', or the lack of it, dominates (see Table 4.3.). Around 17% of the total sample complain that there is too much 'nationalism and protectionism', and that 'competition', not cooperation, between member states prevails. For the French and the British, the highly publicised Anglo-French conflicts are mentioned specifically in several answers. The W. Germans are by far the most critical with respect to the lack of cooperation, followed by the British, then the French and the Italians. Although one expects the British to complain about 'loss of national sovereignty, identity and independence', this category was used in all countries, albeit especially by the French and W. Germans.

Criticism of, and disappointment with, economic policy was also evident, and centred on three main issues. Familiar complaints about 'bureaucracy and centralisation' were raised especially by the British and the W. Germans, while the 'imbalance between rich and poor countries' was criticised by over 10% in all countries except France. Primarily the British, but also the W. Germans, raised the complaint that '"we" pay too much' (into the Community) a point not raised at all in France or Italy. Although not mentioned in other countries, 10% of the W. German sample also criticised Community policy's interference with '"natural" supply and demand'. Commercial policy was least cited, yet over 10% in W. Germany and the U.K. complained about the 'negative effect on prices'. In addition, the W. Germans were especially critical of 'import–export restrictions', while a handful of die-hard Britons bemoaned the demise of imperial measures and such petty irritations as 'cream puffs that don't contain cream'.

Overall, respondents seem most dissatisfied with the lack of solidarity or cooperation between Community countries. They do criticise economic and commercial policy, but the strongest agreement among countries is revealed in judgements of the competitive, nationalist and protectionist attitudes of individual member states.

4.3.4 Principles, goals and aims

Respondents' knowledge of, or beliefs about, the reasons why the Community was established are presented in Table 4.4. Responses were classified in terms of four broad categories – general; trade and economic policy; political cooperation; and defence.

Some respondents gave very vague, and somewhat redundant, answers

Table 4.4. *Principles, goals and aims of European Community*

Category	W. Germany N	%	Italy N	%	France N	%	U.K. N	%	All N	%
					Country of respondent					
3.1. General										
3.1.1. benefit/protect interests of members	—	—	13	26	6	12	9	18	28	14
3.1.2. build an efficient Europe	16	32	1	2	1	2	5	10	23	11.5
3.2. Trade and economic policy										
3.2.1. promote trade	19	38	18	36	23	46	28	56	88	44
3.2.2. economic alliance	—	—	—	—	7	14	—	—	7	3.5
3.2.3. reduce inequalities between rich and poor member states	12	24	3	6	3	6	4	8	22	11
3.2.4. large markets, economies of scale	—	—	7	14	3	6	5	10	15	7.5
3.2.5. third trading block	6	12	—	—	2	4	6	12	14	7
3.2.6. stabilise prices and supply	11	22	—	—	3	6	4	8	18	9
3.2.7. exchange goods and persons	3	6	—	—	7	14	6	12	16	8
3.2.8. harmonisation, standardisation	4	8	—	—	3	6	6	12	13	6.5
3.3. Political cooperation										
3.3.1. cooperation/shared identity	12	24	25	50	15	30	19	36	71	35.5
3.3.2. greater world role for Europe	13	26	4	8	14	28	4	8	35	17.5
3.4. Defence										
3.4.1. peace and mutual defence	1	2	1	2	—	—	9	18	11	5.5
Unclassified	6	12	—	—	1	2	10	20	17	8.5
No answer	2	4	11	22	4	8	4	8	21	10.5

Notes:
N denotes total number of responses in a category.
Absence of responses is indicated by a dash.

(as shown in categories 3.1.1. and 3.1.2.); one would hardly form a Community which conflicted with its members' interests, or in order to build an inefficient Europe. The simple answer 'to promote trade' was given by the most respondents, but there was scant evidence of more specific ideas relating to trade and economic policy. Interestingly, different ideas attained prominence in different countries: for the W. Germans, reducing inequalities between rich and poor member states and stabilising prices and supply; for the Italians, large markets and economies of scale; for the French and British, exchange of goods and persons.

As noted above, non-economic and specifically political aspects of the Community also receive attention – the development of shared identity through cooperation, and a greater world (political) role for Europe. Only the British saw defence and mutual peace as an important aim of the Community.

Overall, few respondents mentioned the more specific ideas behind the Community. Very general ideas predominated and are found in nearly half the respondents, but more exact information is held only by a minority of respondents and its content varies across countries.

4.3.5 The Common Agricultural Policy
Categories of responses to the Common Agricultural Policy (C.A.P.) are shown in Table 4.5., the most striking feature of which is the extent to which one aspect of the policy predominates. More than one person in four, considering all respondents, and over 10% in all countries except Italy (where 40% did not answer) mentioned the problem of 'surpluses', 'excesses', 'stock-piles' or 'over-production'. Given the number of responses here, it was possible to classify further into those respondents who simply mentioned the problem, and those who used metaphorical language:

> The proliferation of gluts, mountains and lakes of agricultural produce, brought about by 'quota' buying tactics by the administration is a waste. (M, 160)

> I hear about butter mountains and wine lakes and have seen reports of tons of apples and tomatoes being wasted because if they were put into circulation, prices would fall and hence profits. (M, 166)

The importance of this language is discussed below.

Given the number of respondents in W. Germany and the U.K. who wrote about agricultural surpluses, further analyses were computed to relate these views to two closed-end ratings which formed part of the questionnaire: overall attitude to the Community, and rating of the success of the C.A.P. In both countries, respondents were split into three groups: those who wrote about 'surpluses'; those who used metaphorical language; and those who

Table 4.5. Common Agricultural Policy

Category	Country of respondent									
	W. Germany		Italy		France		U.K.		All	
	N	%	N	%	N	%	N	%	N	%
4.1. Surpluses problem										(27.5)
4.1.1.1. surpluses/excesses of food	9	18	2	4	5	10	10	20	26	13
4.1.1.2. surpluses described with metaphorical language (e.g. butter 'mountain', milk 'lake')	10	20	—	—	—	—	19	38	29	14.5
4.1.2. irresponsible policy for Third World	11	22	—	—	—	—	8	16	19	9.5
4.1.3. selling cheap butter to non-members	—	—	—	—	—	—	4	8	4	2
4.2. Subsidies/support buying/ guaranteed prices	17	34	8	16	8	16	12	24	45	22.5
4.3. Frictions between member states	—	—	7	14	11	22	10	20	28	14
4.4. Negative evaluation of C.A.P.	—	—	6	12	7	14	11	22	24	12
4.5. Expensive policy for 'us'	3	6	5	10	1	2	5	10	14	7
4.6. Small farmers suffer	2	4	—	—	—	—	7	14	9	4.5
4.7. Inefficient techniques favour small farmers	—	—	—	—	—	—	5	10	5	2.5
4.8. High consumer prices	—	—	—	—	1	2	3	6	4	2
4.9. C.A.P. favours agricultural countries	—	—	2	4	1	2	2	4	5	2.5
Unclassified	12	24	2	4	1	2	5	10	20	10
No answer	4	8	20	40	15	30	9	18	48	24

Notes:
N denotes total number of responses in a category.
Absence of responses is indicated by a dash.

did not mention the problem. Sample sizes for the three groups in W. Germany and the U.K. were 9, 10, 30; and 9, 19, 21, respectively. Although t-tests for all possible pairwise comparisons were computed, only two significant differences emerged. In W. Germany, overall attitudes of those who mentioned surpluses ($M = -0.78$) were negative, and significantly different from those who did not ($M = 0.67$), $t(37) = -2.33$, $p < 0.025$. In the U.K. those who used metaphorical language judged the C.A.P. to be less successful ($M = 2.21$) than did those who made no mention of the problem ($M = 3.29$), $t(38) = -2.33$, $p < 0.05$. Bearing in mind that one group in the U.K. ($N = 9$) and two groups in W. Germany ($N = 9$, $N = 10$) are very small, these analyses do reveal a limited, but consistent, effect. Although the language used may not be so important, there is a trend for those who are aware of the 'surpluses problem' to have more negative attitudes towards the Community, or its agricultural policy.

Related aspects of the over-production problem which were mentioned were the irresponsibility of this policy with a view to the Third World (noted by W. Germans and Britons), and a few Britons who criticised the selling-off of cheap butter to the U.S.S.R. Linked to surpluses, indeed identified by many as the cause, are the questions of subsidies, support buying and guaranteed prices. Several respondents specified a close relationship of cause and effect between policy and outcome.

> I feel it (the C.A.P.) is too expensive.... The system whereby a target price (where greatest deficiency occurs) is set, and then an intervention price which the EEC pay to farmers, means that the EEC commodity prices are much higher as a rule than world prices, thus 'butter mountains' are created. This is wastage which third World countries could use. (F, 186)

while others reacted more viscerally:

> Agricultural policy – unworkability of free import and export of dairy products, mountains, lakes and the disgustingly large subsidy given to French farmers. I don't think much of it – bring back New Zealand butter and Danish bacon. (F, 234)

This last response, by a Briton, shows criticism of the French, and frictions between member states were mentioned by many respondents in all countries except W. Germany.

Three other aspects of the perception of agricultural policy merit discussion. Quite a high proportion of respondents, except in W. Germany, simply gave a negative evaluation of the policy (e.g. 'a farce', 'a ridiculous situation', 'an unmitigated disaster') and in Italy and the U.K., in particular, the policy was seen as 'expensive for us'. Finally, categories 4.6. and 4.7. show, to some extent, how effectively the Community in general, and agricultural policy in particular, functions as a scapegoat for all countries and all causes.

It is blamed on the one hand for making 'small farmers suffer'; and on the other hand for 'inefficient techniques which favour small farmers'.

Overall, the view of this most important common policy – indeed the only one to be mentioned by more than a handful of respondents – is damning. Respondents obviously have heard, and assimilated, a great deal of negative information about the policy, often couched in terms of appealingly simple imagery. Some of the implications of this view are explored below.

4.4 Discussion

Although caution has been expressed with regard to the reliability of the above content-analyses, a number of interesting and important points emerge from the investigation of common-sense views about the European Community.

4.4.1 From specialised knowledge to social representations

It was noted earlier (Section 3.1.) that transformation is essential for the transmission of knowledge from specialists to citizens. One can, then, first compare the official aims of the Community with the social representations identified in the four countries.

Four immediate objectives of the Community, entrenched in the Treaty of Rome, were mentioned at the beginning of this work; the establishment of a customs union; the four great freedoms; common policies for agriculture and transport; and the creation of a European Social Fund. Considering first the results presented in Table 4.4. above, only 8% of all respondents included in their answer about the Community's principles and aims the (freedom of) exchange of goods and persons (category 3.10). Looking at respondents' other answers, 14% were aware of the customs union (dismantling of quotas and tariffs for trade; see Table 4.2., category 2.1.2.); and at least 30% mention some aspect of the Common Agricultural Policy (see Table 4.5.). Transport policy and the European Social Fund were not mentioned. However, the most widely shared ideas were the very general aims of promoting trade and cooperation towards a shared identity. These findings suggest that only a small minority of citizens have a clear picture of the Community. However, the proportion of respondents able to identify some Community principles compares favourably with the results of Bacot-Decriaud and Plantin's (1982) study, using different samples and questions, where few respondents spontaneously mentioned key aspects of economic or political policy. It was interesting to note the importance attached to political as well as economic matters in the present sample, suggesting that the Community is no longer seen as a purely economic creation.

Although the European Community may be an 'obscure object of desire', this does not inhibit respondents from positive and negative judgements on Community effects and outcomes. The main positive dimensions were 'economic cooperation' and 'European unity and identity', but both were cited by only about 10% of all respondents. Negative perceptions were predominantly in terms of dissatisfaction with the unilateral actions of independent-minded member states, the ghosts of nationalism and protectionism. This criticism was accompanied by complaints about bureaucracy and centralisation, negative effects on consumer prices, and one of the two negative dimensions obtained by Bacot-Decriaud and Plantin – loss of identity and national sovereignty. The other negative dimension from this previous study – regarding a Europe of profit and multi-nationals – was less important, but did appear in Table 4.3., category 2.2.6. The W. Germans and British were certainly the more critical, of those who answered the question. This effect was strongest on the question of payment to the Community, an issue – even a *cause célèbre* – raised by neither the French nor the Italians. This apparent perception of 'inequity' would lead us to predict less favourable attitudes towards the Community in W. Germany and the U.K., a point followed up in Chapter 5.

The core of the social representations, and here too especially for the W. Germans and British, is the C.A.P. Here respondents revealed the greatest amount of knowledge about the working of policy and its effects; they also had a clear, negative evaluation in W. Germany and the U.K. The striking use of metaphorical language can be seen as an example of what Moscovici and Hewstone (1983) called 'figuration' in social representations. This tendency to substitute metaphors and images for complex notions is worth considering in more detail.

4.4.2 Social representations and common-sense metaphors: the mental 'landscape' of the Community

We should not be surprised at the preponderance of metaphorical thinking in these responses. Lakoff and Johnson's (1980) fascinating book demonstrates convincingly just how prevalent such thinking is. They argue that:

> metaphor is pervasive in everday life, not just in language but in thought and action. Our ordinary conceptual system, in terms of which we both think and act, is fundamentally metaphorical in nature. (Lakoff and Johnson, 1980, p. 3)

Metaphor is so important because, as Moscovici says about social representations in general, the unfamiliar is rendered familiar:

> Because so many of the concepts that are important to us are either abstract or not clearly delineated in our experience... we need to get a

grasp on them by means of other concepts that we understand in clearer terms (spatial orientations, objects, etc.). (*op. cit.*, p. 115)

The use of metaphor means that one kind of experience, thing or object is understood in terms of another. Understanding the C.A.P. in terms of landscape imagery – mountains, lakes and so on – is thus an example of what Lakoff and Johnson call a *structural* metaphor (one concept is structured in terms of another). This kind of thinking becomes important when we realise that, by making us see an issue in certain terms, metaphors also obscure other aspects of the concept (particularly aspects which are inconsistent with the metaphor). Furthermore, these metaphors can even assume the power of defining what is real. To modify an argument from Lakoff and Johnson, suppose a newspaper announces that 'the C.A.P. is directly responsible for the butter mountain'. Is this claim true or false? Even to address oneself to the question requires accepting at least the central parts of, if not also the language of, the metaphor.

The metaphorical language used is not, of course, a primordial aspect of the collective unconscious of European citizens. A more reasonable hypothesis is that the imagery, in particular, and the focus on agriculture, in general, have come from the mass media.

4.4.3 The origin of social representations

Although it would be interesting to examine the role of the mass media in relation to Community attitudes, a content-analysis of the press alone would constitute a volume in itself.[4] Nonetheless, an informal analysis of the press undertaken by the author, since the inception of this project, suggests that two central aspects of the social representations recorded – bureaucracy and agriculture – are supported, if not suggested, by the national press.

Consider first bureaucracy, a term which, in its popular sense, represents all that is commonly deplored in the day-to-day experience of organisations (Coombes, 1970). According to Crozier (1964) the word: 'evokes the slowness, the ponderousness, the routine, the complication of procedures, and the maladapted responses of "bureaucratic" organisations to the needs which they should satisfy, and the frustrations which their members, clients or subjects consequently endure'. (p. 3.) Distanced from Brussels, and lost in the sea of legislation, for some people the Community connotes a pile of paperwork, in seven languages, attended to in the free time between rounds of diplomatic cocktail parties. Economies of scale are replaced by bureaucracies of scale, supported by newspaper images of the European Commission like the following:

> To be sure, the European Commission is a strange creature. It reminds one of a huge hamster cage where creatures of various size and

importance spin round in wheels which give enormous traction but no forward movement. (*The Observer*, 2 January, 1983)

Thus the bureaucratic image of the Community is entrenched.[5]

The centrality of the Common Agricultural Policy is predictable both from its premier position in the Community's finances, and from the consequent attention it receives in the media. Its evaluation seems to be consistently and markedly negative, and while it is not the place of this work to draw the line between economic truth and falsehood it is reasonable to suggest that respondents are influenced by massive media attention to the C.A.P. and Community budget contributions (the issue of 'we pay more'), often treated together as in the following British editorial:

> It is manifestly unjust that Britain, a relatively poor member in terms of income per head, should be expected to pay more than any other country save West Germany – and then see too much of the money used to subsidise farm products which we have to import at too high a price. (*The Observer*, 19 June, 1983)

or consisting of articles written in ways which reinforce or extend the metaphors:

> Early last Tuesday morning, a team of 10 agricultural ministers of the European Community scrambled up the last slope of Europe's brooding 900,000-tonne butter mountain and claimed this virgin peak in the name of economy and European solidarity.
> The climb has taken years and the relays of ministers attempting it had frequently lost their way. Less than an hour before the peak was conquered, the ministers, not obviously roped together, had been glimpsed, through a gap in the fog of words, wandering rather aimlessly about, apparently unaware of which way was up. When the triumph came therefore, it was as unexpected as it was glorious, and news of it quite stunned the team of foreign ministers on the adjacent British EEC budget molehill, who had been scrabbling around in the mist for hours. (*The Times*, 15 March, 1984)

Indeed, backed by media attention, 'the Community has increasingly become the stage on which national rivalries are fought out'. (Slater, 1983; p. 77.) Thus the repeated references to wine, lamb or cod 'wars', hijacked British lorry-drivers and so on. As one more responsible newspaper editorial commented:

> unless you pinch yourself hard, a couple of lorryloads of lamb carcases gone astray, mixed gently with a little musty tasting milk, becomes an epic in the glowing tradition of Agincourt, Crecy and Waterloo. (*The Guardian Weekly*, 22 January, 1984)

Several respondents explicitly mentioned the role of the media in disseminating the metaphors and images in terms of which they have come to view the Community:

> The common agricultural policy is most mentioned by the media. There is constant reference to wine lakes, butter mountains etc. and to unfair subsidies being paid to farmers in certain countries.... (F, 185)

> the policies of the EEC about which one hears the most are tragically only those which cause trouble and internal disagreement – i.e. the fisheries policy, and those regulations which lead to such anomalies as butter mountains. (M, 253)

Dalton and Duval's (1981) analysis of Community news from 1972–79 also reports that problems associated with the C.A.P. were ubiquitous. The policy's effects on British consumers and farmers were criticised and, according to these authors, constitute a 'major handicap for the Community's public image'. (p. 10.) Robinson (1981; cited in Wober, 1984) has also noted that news stories on Europe have tended to focus on conflicts about farm produce, subsidies and stockpiles. The media's promulgation of metaphorical images is an example of a tendency (noted by Lippmann, 1922) in modern communication systems to condense information into brief slogans. Lippmann viewed such slogans as a 'wall of stereotypes' between citizens and the issues to which they should respond,[6] and he wondered whether, and how, citizens could possibly make rational, democratic decisions given this diet of simplistic information. Against this critical viewpoint, it must also be noted that social representations, as here studied, may aid, rather than prevent, understanding. Arguably, without the aid of simplifying imagery few respondents would have come to understand the relationship between support buying, intervention prices and agricultural excesses. The impact of these simplifying images must also be kept in perspective. It is important to note that the last respondent quoted, even though he wrote about 'butter mountains', described the Community in glowing terms as the contemporary version of 'mediaeval Christendom' (see above). It is then not surprising that only a slight relationship was found between use of such metaphors and both overall attitude and rating of the C.A.P. (see discussion, below, of 'use' and 'mention' in social representations).

Notwithstanding the attention paid to the media here, they cannot shoulder all the blame for negative evaluations of the C.A.P. Common-sense views are also influenced by 'experts' (in this case, presumably, economists), politicians and 'opinion leaders' in general, many of whom are critical of what Holland (1980) calls the 'agricultural albatross'. Thus Swann (1981), in his treatment of '*The economics of the Common Market*', states boldly that the C.A.P. 'does not make sense economically'. (p. 169.) Similarly, Macfarlane (1981) describes the policy as one:

> which takes up three-quarters of the EEC Budget and involves paying
> subsidies to inefficient small farmers to pile up great agricultural surpluses
> nobody wants or can afford to buy. (Macfarlane, 1981, p. 150)

Even Edward Heath, the U.K.'s Charlemagne prize-winner and Euro-devotee,
has written that:

> The expenditure of 30 per cent of the budget to subsidize sales of surplus
> food on to the world market is crippling the Community's finances,
> contributing to an unprecedented dispute over agriculture with the United
> States, and damaging the production of food in developing countries.
> These and other anomalies of the C.A.P. can and must be reformed....
> (*The Times*, 5 January, 1983)

Thus it is easy to see why the British and the W. Germans (for whom
comparable quotations and sources could be given) view the C.A.P. as so
central, and so disastrous. The question remains – why is this not so, or less
so for the French and the Italians? Part of the answer may lie in the relative
gains made by both these countries from the Community's agricultural
policy; this might also result in less, and less intense, media coverage and
the absence of metaphorical language. Both explanations are plausible, and
not mutually exclusive, but the validity of the former lies in the domain of
the economist (see Chapter 7), and that of the latter in an extensive
content-analysis of the European press.[7]

4.4.4 *The importance of social representations*
Having devoted such time and attention to the analysis of what have been
called 'social representations', it is now incumbent upon the author to
explain why such common-sense beliefs are felt to be so important. To begin
with, consider Potter and Litton's (1985) distinction between 'use' and
'mention' of social representations. Do respondents only 'mention' agricultural surpluses (i.e. report that these receive media attention), or do they
'use' these ideas themselves? Moscovici (1976) emphasises the role of social
representations in facilitating, indeed permitting, communication and it may
be that individuals are 'forced' to use the metaphorical representation when
discussing Community matters with people whose only common-sense
representation is of this type. Even for those people who do not spontaneously
'mention' 'lakes' and 'mountains', the use of the metaphors in the media
may ensure that they play a role later. Active expression of complex ideas
and knowledge is generally much less common than 'passive' comprehension.
But as Sears (1969) points out, even respondents who cannot articulate their
ideas, for example those who did not answer at all or those who made no
mention of the problem, may possess mental structures which provide a
context for organising incoming information, seeking further information

and generating explanations. These mental structures are important, in short, because at a fundamental level they guide the way people think about the world. As Lakoff and Johnson argue:

> In all aspects of life, not just in politics or in love, we define our reality in terms of metaphors and then proceed to act on the basis of metaphors. We draw inferences, set goals, make commitments, and execute plans, all on the basis of how we in part structure our experience, consciously and unconsciously, by means of metaphor. (Lakoff and Johnson, 1980, p. 158)

This is the argument for studying social representations, including their metaphorical images, however difficult that may turn out to be (see Hewstone, 1985).

4.5 Conclusion

It may be argued that the relative lack of information apparent from the content-analyses fails to meet the necessary conditions for a subsequent study of social attitudes and their structure. This argument, however, ignores the phenomenon of 'opinion without information' (see Lane and Sears, 1964, chapter 6; Rogers, Stuhler and Koenig, 1967, p. 247) and the distinction between competence and performance. This phenomenon can be illustrated with one respondent's answer to the question about common policy:

> I have heard and read very little about any common policies of the E.E.C. The only thing that I vaguely recollect is something about France refusing to take British lamb, and yet Britain having still to succumb to pressures of the E.E.C. in taking French apples! Come to think of it, I now remember that I have heard many rumours (by English dairy-owners and workers) that if the E.E.C. chose to, they could force us (England) to take much 'long life milk' which is imported ever increasingly at the cost of door-to-door delivery of milk being lost in England – not to mention many milkmen's jobs! My attitude to this policy is that there is something wrong going on whenever, or whoever it is that makes the decisions and puts the proposals forward. [sic] (F, 184)

The response is quoted in full because it seems to show how the respondent is thinking. She admits, first, her lack of knowledge; then she recollects a vague rumour; she ends up expressing her attitude to the policy. If this kind of response is not idiosyncratic, and research suggests it is not, then the following analysis of attitudes needs no defence. As Almond and Verba wrote (describing their respondents in a study of political attitudes in the U.S., U.K., W. Germany and Mexico): 'the willingness to express opinions is widespread, affecting even the uniformed... even the cognitively incompetent feel free to express opinions' (1963, p. 98) and Lane and Sears (*op. cit.*) even speak of a 'drive toward opinionation'. (p. 66.)

The analysis thus far has focussed on *content*, revealing some of the richness, but also the poverty, of common-sense thinking about the Common Market. These data were, of course, collected simultaneously with those reported below, so that the content-analysis could not be used to suggest items for the questionnaire. However, with the single exception of bureaucracy, all the main issues arising here had been included in the questionnaire. While it is possible that an item on bureaucracy might have correlated highly with overall attitude, it should not be assumed. The weak relationship between citing the agricultural surpluses issue and later ratings was discussed above; bureaucracy was raised by far fewer respondents, a small minority, and is therefore unlikely to be a crucial factor excluded from the study.

Comparing the four samples, there is some evidence for more critical views of the Community in W. Germany and the U.K., but such conclusions cannot be stated reliably with so many French and Italian respondents giving no answer. Such firm statements and confident cross-national comparisons will, therefore, be reserved for the following analyses of closed-end questions and the *structure* of European attitudes.

5 The social psychology of the European Community: cross-national comparisons

'the success of the Community as a durable political entity could not be guaranteed if the arrangement was seen as benefiting some states or areas at the expense, or to the exclusion, of others. The latter point gathers added force when it is remembered that economic difficulties could be accentuated by political, linguistic, cultural and religious divisions.'

(D. Swann, 1981)

5.1 Introduction

The aim of this chapter is to present the results for all parts of the questionnaire separately, and to compare social perceptions and knowledge in the four countries. Intercorrelations between items and sections, especially the correlation of variables with overall attitude and the selection of a best subset of predictor variables, are dealt with primarily in Chapter 6.

These results are provided in the same order as that followed in Chapter 3, above, in which the present social-psychological approach was outlined. Responses are grouped according to social-psychological notions addressed by, and the theories underlying, the questions asked. Details of scoring were set out earlier (Chapter 3), but in each case summary scores are clearly explained and information is provided at the foot of tables to clarify the findings reported.

Providing the complete set of results from such a large number of statistical analyses in a readable form is a difficult, if not impossible, task. To make this somewhat easier, for reader and writer, a number of tables appear in the appendices, rather than the text. The pattern followed with all responses is the same: a one-way analysis of variance (ANOVA) was computed to compare scores across the four nations tested; only when a significant main effect was uncovered were *post hoc* (t) tests (two-tailed) computed for all pairwise comparisons between nations.

Of course, these tests were computed with knowledge of the basic assumptions to be satisfied for parametric statistical analyses: e.g. interval scaling; normal distribution; and homogeneity of variance.

As a number of attitude researchers have pointed out, a common limitation shared by all attitude methodologies is that the response scales used are ordinal rather than equal-interval (see Oskamp, 1977). Thus one cannot assert that the actual distance between two attitudinal values on a scale (e.g. $+3$ and $+2$) is equal to the distance between two other adjacent values (e.g. $+2$ and $+1$). The distances are numerically equal, but they may not be psychologically equal. Although it would be technically correct to use nonparametric, distribution-free statistics with such data (and *not* to add or multiply scores together, and compare mean scores), parametric analyses are, in practice, almost always used. The assumption of interval scaling could be checked using methods of psychophysical scaling (see Stevens, 1946, 1959), but this assumption is so widely accepted in psychological research that the present study undertook no such preliminary analyses (see Dawes, 1971). Furthermore, simulation studies attest to the robustness of analysis of variance techniques (Baker, Hardyck and Petrinovich, 1966). The latter assumptions – normal distribution of scores and homogeneity of variance – were first checked visually – by inspection of frequency distributions – and then later with Levene's test of unequal variances. To improve readability of the text, only the significance of the effect (and not the value of t and the degrees of freedom) is reported, given the cumbersome nature of six pairwise comparisons for each analysis.

Finally, for those readers for whom (like Disraeli) there are 'lies, damned lies and statistics' a conservative criterion of statistical significance has been adopted. Only effects significant at less than 0.01 are treated as substantial, and all *post hoc* tests included Bonferonni's correction factor (here a significance level of 0.01 implies that all comparisons together do not exceed this strict level). In certain cases significance levels of 0.05 are reported, where an effect is particularly interesting, but it is emphasised that these effects are less reliable.[1]

5.2 Results

5.2.1 Attitudinal measures
Overall attitude
As measured by a single item criterion, overall attitudes to the Community were positive in all four countries, and highest in France and Italy (where they were significantly different from attitudes in W. Germany and the U.K.; $F(3,532) = 15.58, p < 0.001$). Although the full range of responses, from -3 to $+3$, was used in each country, the variance in responses was greater in the latter two countries (see Table 5.1 and Fig. 5.1). Given that overall attitude is the criterion measure for the whole study, the score we are trying to predict, it will be interesting to note which other variables reveal the same

Table 5.1. *Overall attitude to the European Community*

	Country of respondent				
	W. Germany	Italy	France	U.K.	All
Mean score	0.59[a]	1.29[b]	1.34[b]	0.37[a]	0.92
Standard deviation	1.57	1.12	1.13	1.84	1.49
Sample size	128	136	143	129	536

Notes:
Means with different superscripts are significant at $p < 0.01$. Range of scores: -3 to $+3$.

pattern of more pro-Community ratings in France and Italy, than in W. Germany and the U.K.

Expectancy-value analysis of political and economic goals. Ratings of value and expectancy
The two separate parts of the model – evaluations of the goals and expectancies of their achievement – were analysed separately using ANOVA. Looking first at the *evaluations*, one solitary item (number 4, for the W. Germans) was (slightly) negatively evaluated, all others were positive (see Table 5.2). Across all four nations, two items were particularly positively evaluated – 'achieving lasting peace in Europe' and 'achieving greater mutual understanding between nations' – but on most items there were marked cross-national differences in ratings, yielding a significant main effect in the ANOVA, $F(3,529) = 14.92, p < 0.001$. The Italians were clearly the most positive in their evaluations of the Community's goals, significantly more so than the other three countries. Interestingly, the British were slightly more positive than the French and the W. Germans, and were clearly not against the ideas behind the Community.

A quite different picture emerged from the ratings of *expectancies*. In contrast with evaluations, many goals received negative ratings and the number of negative expectancies varied considerably across countries (W. Germany, 8; Italy, 4; France, 2; U.K., 10). Across all four countries there was recognition that 'the European Community is strengthening Europe's role in the world', but that it would improbably bring about a 'United States of Europe', 'dismantle quotas and all barriers to trade' or 'ensure that competition is not distorted within the EEC' (see Table 5.3). ANOVA on these ratings yielded a significant main effect, $F(3,533) = 17.86, p < 0.001$, and revealed where, or how, the British and the W. Germans differed from the French and the Italians. The former are pessimistic, or unconvinced, about the Community's achievement of these goals.

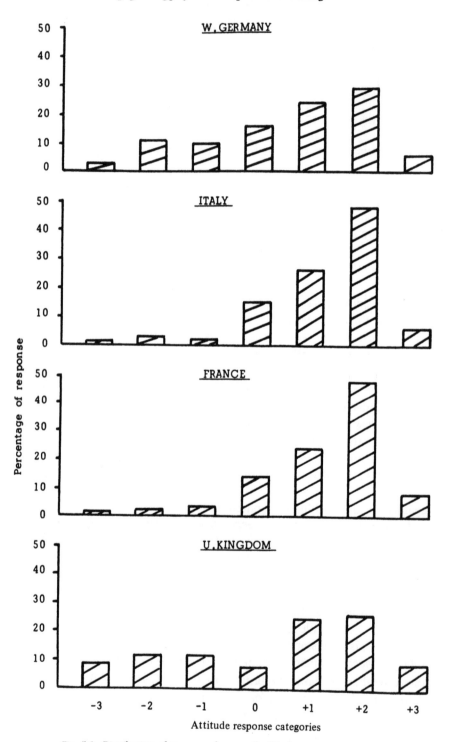

Fig. 5.1. Distribution of responses for overall attitude measure.

Table 5.2. *Mean evaluation of political and economic goals*

Item	Country of respondent				
	W. Germany	Italy	France	U.K.	All
1. United States of Europe	1.27	1.41	0.82	0.79	1.07
2. Europe's role in the world	0.98	2.81	2.01	1.44	1.68
3. Lasting peace	2.61	2.84	2.27	2.64	2.59
4. Economic expansion	−0.28	2.11	1.86	1.85	1.43
5. Mutual understanding	2.65	2.66	2.25	2.41	2.49
6. Third block	0.47	0.17	0.76	1.07	0.61
7. Customs union	1.68	2.02	1.24	1.54	1.61
8. Dismantling quotas	1.06	1.14	0.90	0.92	1.00
9. Common commercial policy	0.75	1.77	0.16	0.93	0.90
10. Free movement	1.84	1.66	1.40	1.52	1.60
11. Competition not distorted	1.50	2.01	1.68	1.48	1.67
12. Goods produced as suited	0.89	1.92	0.42	1.53	1.18
13. Large-scale market	0.34	1.31	1.13	0.49	0.84
Mean sum of evaluations	15.77[a]	22.93[b]	16.93[a]	18.55[a]	18.58
Sample size	127	137	141	128	533

Notes:
Range of scores: + 3 (extremely good); − 3 (extremely bad). Means which do not share a common superscript are significant at $p < 0.001$ except Italy–U.K. ($p < 0.01$).

Table 5.3. *Mean expectancy that the European Community is bringing about political and economic goals*

Item	Country of respondent				
	W. Germany	Italy	France	U.K.	All
1. United States of Europe	−1.31	0.29	−0.37	−0.92	−0.56
2. Europe's role in the world	0.78	0.70	1.35	0.35	0.81
3. Lasting peace	−0.68	0.06	0.48	−0.31	−0.09
4. Economic expansion	−0.45	−0.04	0.08	−0.57	−0.23
5. Mutual understanding	0.52	0.43	0.95	−0.42	0.39
6. Third block	−0.56	−0.36	0.31	−0.57	−0.28
7. Customs union	0.06	0.44	0.56	0.15	0.31
8. Dismantling quotas	−0.88	−0.26	−0.17	−0.49	−0.44
9. Common commercial policy	0.40	0.16	0.38	−0.02	0.23
10. Free movement	−0.10	0.54	0.37	0.13	0.25
11. Competition not distorted	−0.93	−0.20	0.15	−0.95	−0.45
12. Goods produced as suited	−0.36	0.43	0.37	−0.63	−0.02
13. Large-scale market	0.63	0.15	0.55	−0.15	0.30
Mean sum of probabilities	−2.88[a]	2.09[b]	5.01[b]	−4.40[a]	0.13
Sample size	128	136	144	129	537

Notes:
Range of scores: + 3 (probable); − 3 (improbable). Means which do not share a common superscript are significant at $p < 0.001$ except W. Germany–Italy ($p < 0.01$)

Comparison of different computational models of expectancy-value

To assess the expectancy-value model, correlations were computed between the independent and combined (both multiplied and added) components of the model and overall attitude. According to Fishbein and Ajzen (1975), who report studies to support their claim, attitudes can be estimated more accurately by considering both belief strength and evaluation of related attitudes (i.e. $\Sigma b_i e_i$) than by using only the sum of beliefs (Σb_i) or the sum of evaluations (Σe_i). Thus the best correlation should be achieved by summing the products of expectancies and values (these products are not obtained by multiplying average belief strength by average attribute evaluation, but by computing the products separately for each respondent). However, as discussed earlier (Chapter 3), there are alternatives to the multiplicative model and Fishbein and Ajzen discuss other combinatorial rules, such as the mean of the belief–evaluation products (i.e. $A_O = \Sigma b_i e_i / n$). They point out, though, that given the methodology of most studies, estimates of attitude obtained by these two methods would be perfectly correlated.[2] An alternative method is to eschew the multiplicative model in favour of a simple additive one (i.e. $\Sigma b_i + e_i$). The problem then becomes, how to compare these multiplicative and additive models? According to Schmidt (1973), such comparisons are empirically ambiguous, because the multiplicative model is itself problematic. Multiplication of scales, if it is to be logically meaningful, requires the existence of a true rational zero point on both measures entered into the product (i.e. the expectancy and value scales; see Lord and Novick, 1968, chapter 1). Schmidt questions whether the scales used in such research have a rational zero point, and suggests that the measures are at best interval scales. If this is so, then transformations of the form $X + b$ (where X is the scale score and b is some positive or negative constant) change the location of the arbitrary zero point (but do not affect the rank order and equal interval properties, and the standard deviation, of the scale). Schmidt demonstrates convincingly that such transformed measures of expectancy and value could influence the correlation between the product ($\Sigma e \times v$) and a third variable (e.g. overall attitude).

The impact of such transformations for the multiplicative model is seen in Table 5.4. Following Fishbein and Ajzen's method of bipolar scoring (-3 to $+3$) for both components, one obtains the correlations reported in the top line of the Table. These correlations are moderately high and are significant, with the exception of Italy. If one then rescores the expectancy component on a unipolar scale (1–7; consistent with the notion of subjective probability), this constitutes a transformation of the general form $X + b$ (where $b = 4$). Just as Schmidt demonstrated, this transformation has dramatic effects (except in the case of France); the correlation with overall attitude for all respondents together rises from $+0.30$ to 0.46 (a difference

Table 5.4 *Comparison of computational models based on expectancy-value: correlations with overall attitude*

Computational model	Country of respondent				
	W. Germany	Italy	France	U.K.	All
Multiplicative model ($\Sigma e \times v$)					
Bipolar scoring for both components	+0.31[b,c]	+0.13[b]	+0.27	+0.32[b,c]	+0.30[c]
Unipolar scoring for expectancy	+0.49[a]	+0.30[a,c]	+0.32	+0.59[a]	+0.46[a]
Unipolar scoring for expectancy (standard scores)	+0.49[a]	+0.31[a,c]	+0.33	+0.59[a]	+0.47[a]
Additive model ($\Sigma e + v$)					
Bipolar scoring for both components	+0.49[a]	+0.37[a]	+0.30	+0.54[a]	+0.46[a]
Unipolar scoring for expectancy	+0.49[a]	+0.37[a]	+0.30	+0.54[a]	+0.46[a]
Unipolar scoring for expectancy (standard scores)	+0.52[a]	+0.37[a]	+0.29	+0.55[a]	+0.48[a]
Independent components					
Sum of values (Σv)	+0.43[a,c]	+0.30[a,c]	+0.28	+0.48[a,c]	+0.39[a,b,c]
Sum of expectancies (Σe)	+0.38[b,c]	+0.25[b,c]	+0.23	+0.35[b,c]	+0.35[b]
Sample size	127	129	135	128	519

Notes:
Comparisons within columns take account of correlated samples (product–moment correlations transformed to Z-scores), correlations with a different superscript are significantly different ($p < 0.01$).
All correlations significant $p < 0.001$, except 0.25 and 0.23 (both < 0.01) and 0.13 (n.s.).

in explained variance of about 12%). It is important to emphasise here that the best set of correlations is *not* obtained with the method of scoring preferred by Fishbein and Ajzen (1981). They want scores at the two extremes (a negative value × a negative expectancy; or a positive value × a positive expectancy) to have the *same* force $(-3 \times -3 = +9;$ $+3 \times +3 = +9)$. However, as Mitchell (1974) notes, scoring the expectancy component as a probability (1–7) alters this model completely; negative values $(-3) \times$ negative expectancies (1) now result in a contribution of -3 to overall attitude; positive values $(+3) \times$ positive expectancies (7) result in a contribution of $+21$ to overall attitude.

In contrast to the striking effect on the multiplicative model, Schmidt also showed that such $X+b$ transformations leave the correlation between $(\Sigma e + v)$ and the third variable unchanged. He concludes that the nature of the measurement scales used in studies of the expectancy-value model appears to be interval at best. The correlations for the additive model, reported in Table 5.4, are again consistent with Schmidt's findings. Whether the expectancy component is scored on a bipolar or unipolar scale makes *no difference* to the correlations with overall attitude (which are quite high).

A third computational comparison (and one not considered by Schmidt) involves the use of standard scores. Given the greater variability of scores when using a multiplicative model, increased variance could have adversely affected the obtained correlations. However, as shown in Table 5.4, use of standard scores yielded no significant improvement on the multiplicative or additive models.

A final computational possibility is that the independent contributions of the two components, value and expectancy, are examined, and then compared with the other models. As shown in Table 5.4, the correlations between both individual components and overall attitude are significant, although considerably higher in the case of 'sum of values' (Σv). In fact, Fishbein and Ajzen (1975, p. 227) give one exception to the rule that the sum of products is the best estimate of attitude; when the evaluations are all positive, or all negative, they report that the sum of expectancies will tend to be highly correlated with the attitude score. Although, as noted above, almost all items were positively evaluated (and expected to be so, given that they were chosen from the Community's stated goals), it was the sum of evaluations which actually tended to yield the higher correlations. It is interesting to note that *in no case* was the correlation yielded by the best computational model significantly higher than that yielded by the sum of evaluations.

Given the set of correlations reported in Table 5.4, how should one choose the best expectancy-value model for use in further analyses? Comparisons between the correlations in the columns of the Table were computed (using

Olkin's 1967, test; see Bortz, 1979), although these tests are conservative, due to the correlated samples. Such tests, however, did not decide in favour of the predictive validity of either a multiplicative or an additive model, both appeared valid under specific circumstances. This issue is, therefore, considered further in the discussion, below.

A final set of correlations was computed between the components of the expectancy-value model. Components of the model were generally highly intercorrelated, but this was not always so. Although Fishbein and Ajzen's approach does not assume that evaluations and beliefs are positively correlated, this was found to be the case for both the W. Germans and the French, but not the Italians and the British. Correlations between sum of evaluations and sum of expectancies (beliefs) were as follows: W. Germany ($N = 127, r = +0.37, p < 0.001$); Italy ($N = 133, r = +0.14$, n.s.); France ($N = 139, r = +0.45, p < 0.001$); U.K. ($N = 128, r = +0.17$, n.s.)[3].

International relations
Total scores derived from Helfant's (1967) 'Survey of opinions and beliefs about international relations' also distinguished between the four nations, $F(3,532) = 31.73, p < 0.001$. Follow-up tests showed that the W. Germans were most inclined towards cooperative international relations, although all scores were high (see Table 5.5).

Attitude ambivalence
Attitude ambivalence was measured as the discrepancy between the two ratings focussed on only positive and only negative aspects of the Community. Attitudes were more ambivalent in W. Germany and the U.K. than in Italy and France, $F(3,507) = 23.54, p < 0.001$.

This score can be understood by looking at the two individual ratings from which it is calculated (see Table 5.6). It is interesting to note that respondents from all four countries can be positive *and* negative about the Community, given an appropriate focus of attention. However, the difference between the countries lies in the propensity to be negative, which is stronger for the W. Germans and the British, $F(3,507) = 26.70, p < 0.001$; there is no difference in positive ratings, $F(3,507) = 1.14$, n.s.

These judgements apparently cause respondents some difficulty, as seen by the drop in sample size. For this reason the variable was excluded from further analyses (in Chapter 6); simple correlations with overall attitude were not, in any case, significant (W. Germany, $N = 125, r = +0.15$; Italy, $N = 132, r = -0.02$; France, $N = 127, r = +0.11$; U.K., $N = 123$, $r = +0.17$).

Table 5.5 *Mean scores on Helfant's 'Survey of Opinions and Beliefs about International Relations'*

Item		Country			
	W. Germany	Italy	France	U.K.	All
1.* The U.K. should give up trying to be on friendly terms with other countries	6.92	6.55	6.48	6.36	6.58
2. If the U.K. is friendly towards other countries they are not as likely to be aggressive towards us	5.57	4.96	5.41	5.19	5.28
3.* Only foolish dreamers believe that international friendliness can accomplish anything in the modern world	5.95	4.94	5.04	5.54	5.36
4. In international relations it is just plain common sense to 'love thy neighbour as thyself'	5.09	3.59	4.40	4.78	4.44
5. The U.K. should send food and materials to any country that needs them	5.52	4.82	5.12	4.93	5.09
6.* We shouldn't risk our happiness and well-being by getting involved with other countries	5.27	5.07	4.88	5.40	5.14
7.* Helping foreign countries is a waste of money	6.56	5.68	5.95	6.03	6.04
8.* International good will is essential to the welfare of the United Kingdom	5.63	5.61	5.16	5.67	5.51
9.* We should get even with any country that tries to take advantage of the U.K.	4.94	2.76	4.42	5.12	4.28
10.* We can't have 'peace on earth, good will to men', because other nations are not of good will	5.02	4.06	3.99	4.61	4.40
11. Being friendly with other countries will do more good than harm	6.16	5.84	5.68	5.10	5.70
12. We should try to help all nations, whether we get anything special out of it or not	5.66	4.89	4.78	5.20	5.11
13.* Other countries are always getting us into wars	5.81	4.39	3.74	5.36	4.77
14. Being friendly with other nations is a real help in solving international problems	6.39	5.83	4.57	5.69	5.59
15.* Other nations are often plotting against us	5.93	4.87	4.65	5.25	5.15
16. All sensible people believe in trying to be friendly with other countries	5.38	5.68	5.21	5.45	5.43
Mean total	91.80[a]	79.69[b]	79.63[b]	85.65[c]	84.00

Notes:
Range of scores: 1 (strongly agree), 7 (strongly disagree) for items marked with asterisk. Reversed scoring for other items.
Means with different superscripts are significant at $p < 0.001$.
Items shown are from the British version of the questionnaire.

Table 5.6. *Mean attitude ambivalence*

	Country of respondent				
	W. Germany	Italy	France	U.K.	All
View of the European Community:					
1. Considering only its positive qualities	2.01[a]	1.86[a]	1.90[a]	1.98[a]	1.94
2. Considering only its negative qualities	−1.90[a]	−1.19[b]	−1.44[b]	−1.94[a]	−1.61
Ambivalence score (1–2)	3.91[a]	3.04[b]	3.34[b]	3.93[a]	3.54
Sample size	125	132	131	123	511

Notes:
Range of scores for item 1: 0 to +3; item 2: −3 to 0. Means with different superscripts are significant ($p < 0.001$).

Summary

Considered together, the various measures bearing on attitudinal judgements provide a rather consistent picture. On three measures (overall attitude; sum of expectancies; and attitude ambivalence) the French and the Italians were distinctly more pro-European than the W. Germans and the British. The Italians gave most positive evaluations of the Community's goals; and the W. Germans were most inclined towards cooperative international relations; but the dichotomy of Latin sisters vs Anglo-Saxons and Teutons predominates. As we shall see, this pattern reappears on several other variables and appears to be one of the major cross-national effects.

5.2.2 Stereotypes, liking and national images
Stereotypes
Mean attribution of ten traits to each of the four nationalities is presented in Appendix D, Table D.1; this Table shows a reluctance of respondents to ascribe traits in this way to high percentages of the respective populations. However, the emergence of traditional stereotypes – the 'industrious' W. Germans, the 'passionate' French and Italians, the 'reserved' British – suggests that respondents can and do stereotype to some extent. There is at least a *pattern* to the responses. Evaluations of the traits are shown in Appendix D, Table D.2.

Percentage ratings were multiplied by evaluations and summed over the ten traits to calculate each respondent's stereotype of his/her own and the other three nationalities. For example, if the trait 'intelligent' were ascribed to 60% of the British and evaluated +2, a score of +120 would be one of ten such scores making up the British stereotype.[4] Mean summary scores for auto- and hetero-stereotypes are shown in Table 5.7. These scores are

Table 5.7. *Mean stereotyping scores*

Nationality judged	Country of respondent			
	W. Germany	Italy	France	U.K.
The W. Germans	*−55.08*	67.82	132.33	19.97
The Italians	−40.43	*181.35*	−25.35	−87.27
The French	−24.47	103.94	*5.72*	−60.22
The British	−63.24	63.71	−25.84	*−17.77*
Mean stereotyping score	−10.03[a]	108.10[b]	−23.84[a]	21.38[a]
Sample size	127	133	139	127

Notes:
Stereotyping scores are calculated by multiplying the percentage of the nationality judged to hold the trait by the evaluation of the trait. Range of scores: −300 to +300.
Means with different superscripts are significant at $p < 0.001$.
Values given in italic denote judgement of one's own group

relative, so that scores for one's own group must be interpreted in the light of scores for other groups. The Italians are clearly the most ethnocentric, or positively inclined towards their own people, while all three other nationalities view at least one other group as more positive or less negative than the ingroup.

A 'stereotyping' or 'ethnocentrism' score was calculated using the following formula:

$$\text{ingroup score} - \text{mean outgroup score}$$

or

$$\text{mean } IG - (\text{mean } OG_1 + \text{mean } OG_2 + \text{mean } OG_3)\,/3$$

This formula is based on the assumption that someone who views the ingroup more positively (or less negatively) than outgroups *in general*, is more ethnocentric than someone who perceives no such difference.

ANOVA computed on these scores yielded a significant main effect, $F(3,522) = 14.30, p < 0.001$, with the Italians clearly different from all three other countries. The W. Germans and the French actually have negative scores; for the W. Germans this is due to less negative perception of the Italians and the French, while the French are extraordinarily positive about the W. Germans.

Liking
A related, and perhaps less contentious, way of measuring ethnocentrism is to ask people how much they like their own and other nationalities. Preference for own people was calculated as the difference between liking for one's own national group and other national groups in general.

Table 5.8. *Mean liking for own and other nationalities*

Nationality judged	Country of respondent				
	W. Germany	Italy	France	U.K.	All
The W. Germans	*4.28*	3.69	4.95	4.64	4.39
The Italians	5.14	*5.98*	4.56	4.34	5.01
The French	5.54	4.28	*4.71*	4.31	4.70
The British	4.87	3.77	4.22	*5.06*	4.45
Mean preference for own people	-0.90^a	2.07^b	0.14^c	0.63^c	—
Sample size	128	141	147	128	544

Notes:
Range of scores 1–7. Preference for own people is the difference between rating for own nationality minus the mean of the three outgroup scores.
Mean preference scores with different superscripts are significant at $p < 0.001$.
Values given in italic denote judgement of one's own group.

Table 5.9. *Mean national images*

Country judged	Country of respondent			
	W. Germany	Italy	France	U.K.
W. Germany	*9.94*	39.99	30.64	34.44
Italy	-5.44	*13.79*	-6.19	1.97
France	5.76	32.89	*17.91*	21.89
U.K.	1.17	35.17	11.62	*24.22*
Mean preference for own land	9.44^a	-22.23^b	5.87^a	4.79^a
Sample size	126	132	138	122

Notes:
Overall scores are calculated by multiplying ratings (0–9) by evaluations. Range of scores: -27 to $+27$.
Means with different superscripts are significant at $p < 0.001$.
Values given in italic denote judgement of one's own group.

These scores followed a similar pattern to those for stereotyping (see Table 5.9). ANOVA revealed a main effect across countries, $F(3,540) = 91.46, p < 0.001$, with the Italians once again most, and the W. Germans least, inclined towards their own people.

Images
National images of the four countries are shown in Appendix D, Table D.3, and evaluations of the ten characteristics used to describe countries are reported in Appendix D, Table D.4. As with the stereotypes, some expected dimensions characterised each country – W. Germany was seen as 'pros-

perous', Italy as *not* 'politically stable' (whereas the U.K. is), and France as 'politically independent'.

These ratings were multiplied by evaluations of the characteristics, as for the stereotypes, to calculate a score for each country. Mean preference for own country was calculated as the difference between 'own land' score and mean 'other land' score (see Table 5.9). ANOVA computed on these scores revealed a significant main effect, $F(3,514) = 70.57, p < 0.001$. As before, Italy was significantly different from the other three countries, but this time because the national image, in complete contrast to the national stereotype, was (relatively) negative.

Summary
Data on stereotyping and liking revealed the same picture of the Italians' strong preference for their own people; none of the other three countries could be characterised so simply in this manner, although the W. Germans appeared least ethnocentric on both scores. The data for national images were quite different, supporting the idea that stereotypes and images measure different perceptions. The Italians viewed all three other countries more positively than they did Italy; the W. Germans had a very positive view of their land; but the British and French rated W. Germany higher than their homelands.

5.2.3 Perceived inequity
Perceptions of inequity were analysed, first, in terms of which member states were believed to benefit most and least from, and contribute most and least to, the Community.

Benefits most
Very few respondents thought that their own country benefited most from the Community (see Table 5.10). However, responses were not random and there was considerable agreement within each country. According to the W. Germans and the French, it is the British who benefit most; according to the Italians, it is the W. Germans; and according to the British, it is the French.

Benefits least
A large majority of the W. Germans, Italians and British all gave their own country as a response to this question, thus satisfying one of the preconditions for the perception of inequity (see Table 5.11). The French split their replies fairly evenly between their own country, Italy and W. Germany.

Table 5.10. *Which Member State benefits most from the Community?*

Response		W. Germany	Italy	France	U.K.	Row total
				Country of respondent		
0. (Non-EEC)	N	8	1	4	20	33
	%	6.9	1.1	3.0	15.5	7.1
1. U.K.	N	37	12	62	0	111
	%	31.9	13.8	46.6	0	23.9
2. France	N	17	21	5	59	102
	%	14.7	24.1	3.8	45.7	21.9
3. Greece	N	11	2	7	10	30
	%	9.5	2.3	5.3	7.8	6.4
4. Italy	N	25	4	16	14	59
	%	21.6	4.6	12.0	10.9	12.7
5. Belgium	N	0	1	0	5	6
	%	0	1.1	0	3.9	1.3
6. Holland	N	1	3	2	1	7
	%	0.9	3.4	1.5	0.8	1.5
7. Denmark	N	1	0	2	6	9
	%	0.9	0	1.5	4.7	1.9
8. Ireland	N	2	0	0	4	6
	%	1.7	0	0	3.1	1.3
9. Luxembourg	N	0	0	1	1	2
	%	0	0	0.8	0.8	0.4
10. W. Germany	N	14	43	34	9	100
	%	12.1	49.4	25.6	7.0	21.5
Sample size		116	87	133	129	465

Notes:
Percentages given as a proportion of those who answered the question.
N denotes total number of responses of a given type.
Values given in italic denote judgement of one's own group.

Table 5.11. *Which Member State benefits least from the Community?*

Response	N/%	Country of respondent				Row total
		W. Germany	Italy	France	U.K.	
0. (Non-EEC)	N	9	0	5	26	40
	%	7.6	0	3.9	20.3	8.8
1. U.K.	N	14	0	14	64	92
	%	3.0	0	10.9	50.0	20.2
2. France	N	9	1	21	3	34
	%	7.6	1.2	16.4	2.3	7.5
3. Greece	N	9	12	15	7	43
	%	7.6	14.8	11.7	5.5	9.5
4. Italy	N	15	58	31	9	113
	%	12.7	71.6	24.2	7.0	24.8
5. Belgium	N	2	0	4	1	7
	%	1.7	0	3.1	0.8	1.5
6. Holland	N	1	1	1	1	4
	%	0.8	1.2	0.1	0.8	0.9
7. Denmark	N	5	0	2	0	7
	%	4.2	0	1.6	0	1.5
8. Ireland	N	2	2	5	2	11
	%	1.7	2.5	3.9	1.6	2.4
9. Luxembourg	N	2	2	1	1	6
	%	1.7	2.5	0.1	0.8	1.3
10. W. Germany	N	50	5	29	14	98
	%	42.4	6.2	22.7	10.9	21.5
Sample size		118	81	128	128	455

Notes:
Percentages given as a proportion of those who answered the question.
N denotes total number of responses of a given type.
Values given in italic denote judgement of one's own group.

Table 5.12. *Which Member State contributes most to the Community?*

Response		Country of respondent				Row total
		W. Germany	Italy	France	U.K.	
0. (Non-EEC)	N	1	0	0	24	25
	%	0.8	0	0	18.8	5.6
1. U.K.	N	6	8	15	*50*	79
	%	5.0	11.6	11.6	*39.1*	17.7
2. France	N	0	4	*36*	2	42
	%	0	5.8	*27.9*	1.6	9.4
3. Greece	N	0	0	1	0	1
	%	0	0	0.8	0	0.2
4. Italy	N	0	*13*	4	0	17
	%	0	*18.8*	3.1	0	3.8
5. Holland	N	0	4	2	0	6
	%	0	5.8	1.6	0	1.3
6. Denmark	N	0	0	1	1	2
	%	0	0	0.8	0.8	0.4
7. W. Germany	N	*114*	40	70	51	275
	%	*94.2*	58.0	54.3	39.8	61.5
Sample size	N	121	69	129	128	447

Notes:
Percentages given as a proportion of those who answered the question.
N denotes total number of responses of a given type.
Values given in italic denote judgement of one's own group.

Contributes most

The second part of the equity 'equation' is the perception that one contributes more than one gains. A massive majority of the W. Germans felt that their country contributed most, while a large number of Italians, French and British agreed with them (see Table 5.12). The British were, however, split equally into two groups, with a large number also asserting that the U.K. contributed most.

Contributes least

While very few respondents thought that their own country contributed least, the pattern of responses was not so clear on this item (see Table 5.13). The W. Germans cited Italy and the Italians pointed to the U.K.; the French were undecided between Italy and the U.K.; while the British named France, followed by Italy and Greece.

Perceived inequity for one's own country

Given the large number of respondents (especially in W. Germany and the U.K.) who gave their own country as the minor beneficiary and the major contributor, it was decided to classify respondents according to a 2×2 table of perceived inequity.

For example, those who perceived their own country to contribute most *and* benefit least were considered to perceive high inequity; those who perceived only one of these conditions were considered intermediate; and those who perceived neither were classified as 'no perceived inequity' (see Table 5.14(a)). Many Italians did not answer these questions and thus the Italian data are not discussed here.[5] In all other countries missing data were not a problem. Of those who answered all four questions, the percentages perceiving high inequity were as follows: W. Germany, 40.7%; France, 7.7% U.K.: 27%. This again shows greater satisfaction with the Community in France, than in W. Germany or the U.K.

Two-tailed *t*-tests were computed to compare the overall attitudes of those respondents who perceived different levels of (or no) inequity. In W. Germany only a weak test is possible, because so few respondents perceived no inequity (itself an interesting finding), and no significant differences in attitude were found. In France too, no effects were insignificant, but there was a trend for those few who perceived high inequity ($M = 0.67$) to have less positive attitudes than those who perceived intermediate or no inequity ($Ms = 1.52, 1.42, 1.25$). Only in the U.K. was there a clear, strong effect in support of equity theory. The attitudes of those who perceived high inequity were negative ($M = -0.46$) and significantly different from those who perceived no inequity ($M = 0.96$), $t(82) = 3.62, p < 0.001$.

Table 5.13. *Which Member State contributes least to the Community?*

Response		W. Germany	Italy	France	U.K.	Row total
				Country of respondent		
0. (Non-EEC)	N	11	4	7	33	55
	%	9.2	6.3	5.4	25.8	12.5
1. U.K.	N	15	27	39	2	83
	%	12.6	42.9	30.2	1.6	18.9
2. France	N	3	7	2	30	42
	%	2.5	11.1	1.6	23.4	9.6
3. Greece	N	32	8	22	21	83
	%	26.9	12.7	17.1	16.4	18.9
4. Italy	N	41	7	31	21	100
	%	34.5	11.1	24.0	16.4	22.8
5. Belgium	N	0	1	2	3	6
	%	0	1.6	1.6	2.3	1.4
6. Holland	N	0	1	2	2	5
	%	0	1.6	1.6	1.6	1.1
7. Denmark	N	1	2	2	2	7
	%	0.8	3.2	1.6	1.6	1.1
8. Ireland	N	7	3	5	6	21
	%	5.9	4.8	3.9	4.7	4.8
9. Luxembourg	N	9	0	7	7	23
	%	7.6	0	5.4	5.5	5.2
10. W. Germany	N	0	3	10	1	14
	%	0	4.8	7.8	0.8	3.2
Sample size		119	63	129	128	439

Notes:
Percentages given as a proportion of those who answered the question.
N denotes total number of responses of a given type.
Values given in italic denote judgement of one's own group.

Table 5.14. *Perceived inequity*

(A) Perception that one's own country benefits least/contributes most

Own country benefits least		Own country contributes most			
		No		Yes	
		N	%	N	%
(a) W. Germany (N = 118)	No	5	4.2	63	53.4
	Yes	2	1.7	48	40.7
(b) Italy (N = 61)	No	18	29.5	1	1.6
	Yes	30	49.2	12	19.7
(c) France (N = 117)	No	71	60.7	25	21.4
	Yes	12	10.3	9	7.7
(d) U.K. (N = 128)	No	49	38.3	15	11.7
	Yes	29	22.7	35	27.3

Notes:
N denotes total number of responses in each cell of the 2 × 2 table.
Values given in italic denote perception of high inequity.

(B) Perceived ratio of outcomes: inputs for own and 'average other' country

Perceived ratio of outcomes: inputs	Country of respondent			
	W. Germany	Italy	France	U.K.
For own country	0.17	0.61	0.20	0.13
For average 'other country'	7.00	1.06	1.21	1.44
Perceived inequity	0.02	0.57	0.17	0.09

Note:
For sample sizes see Tables 5.10–5.13.

Overall, then, there was only limited support for this first analysis of perceived inequity, tests being hindered by unequal cell sizes. While quite high numbers of respondents in W. Germany and the U.K. did perceive high inequity, it was only in the latter country (where large numbers of respondents could also be classified as perceiving no inequity) that a clear relationship between perceived inequity and overall attitude could be shown.

The perceived ratio of outcomes: intputs
The equity theory analysis thus far has looked only at the perceived contributions and benefits for each of the four member states examined. However, it is essential for the application of equity theory to *compare* the states with each other: 'How does my state's ratio of contributions: benefits compare with the same ratio for other states?' One way to measure this more social and comparative kind of perceived inequity would be to calculate the ratio of benefits and contributions for one's own country, and to compare this with the average ratio of other countries, as perceived by nationals of

the same country. This calculation is consistent with equity theory's computational formula (see Chapter 3) whereby the ratio of outcomes: inputs is compared for two parties, i.e.:

$$\frac{O_A}{I_A} = \frac{O_B}{I_B}$$

This formula confirms the perception of inequity if the resultant score is less than unity. As an example, consider the calculation using data from the W. German respondents: Tables 5.10 and 5.11 report relative frequencies for how many respondents perceive each country to benefit from ('outcomes') and contribute to ('inputs') the Community. One can take the frequency of *most* and *least* mentioned as an index, by giving *most* a value of 10 and *least* a value of 1. Thus for W. Germany, in Table 5.10, 12.1% of the W. Germans said that W. Germany was the country that benefited *most* from the Community; in Table 5.11, 42.4% of the W. Germans said that W. Germany benefited *least* from the Community. Thus the value for outcomes would be: $(12.1 \times 10) + (42.4 \times 1) = 162$. One can do the same calculation for inputs. For W. Germany, in Table 5.12, 94.2% of the W. Germans said that Germany contributes *most* to the Community; and in Table 5.13, 0% said that W. Germany contributes *least*. Thus the value for inputs would be: $(94.2 \times 10) + (0 \times 1) = 940$. Thus for W. Germans judging W. Germany, the ratio of perceived outcomes to inputs = 162/940.

One must now consider how the W. German respondents perceived the other three countries. In the case of Italy, Table 5.10 shows that 21.6% of the W. Germans perceived Italy to benefit *most*; while Table 5.11 shows that 12.7% perceived Italy to benefit least. Thus the value for outcomes would be: $(21.6 \times 10) + (12.7 \times 1) = 233$. The same calculation for inputs reveals that 0% of the W. Germans think that Italy contributes *most*, while 34.5% think Italy contributes *least*. Thus the value for inputs $= (0 \times 10) + (34.5 \times 1) = 35$. The ratio of perceived outcomes to inputs for Italy is thus 233/35. Similar calculations for the W. Germans' perceptions of France and the U.K. yield ratios of 158/3 and 323/63, respectively. Thus the average ratio of outcomes: inputs for other countries is 238/34. Overall perceived inequity for the W. German 'scrutineers' can then be calculated as: $162/940 \times 34/238 = 0.02$.

Using the same procedures, perceived inequity for respondents of the other three countries is – Italy, *0.57*; France, *0.17*; U.K. *0.09*. Thus respondents in each country feel a certain degree of inequity (scores are less than unity), but the inhabitants of some countries perceive more inequity than do the inhabitants of others. The Italians are least dissatisfied, followed by the French; once again, the W. Germans and the British are most dissatisfied. The true extent to which respondents considered that their own country was

Table 5.15. *Has the Community become too big to be effective?*

Response		Country of respondent				Row total
		W. Germany	Italy	France	U.K.	
No	N	102	110	62	102	376
	%	81.0	82.7	43.7	79.7	71.1
Yes	N	24	23	80	26	153
	%	19.0	17.3	56.3	20.3	28.9
Sample size		126	133	142	128	529

Notes:
Percentages given as a proportion of those who answered the question.
N denotes total number of responses of a given type.

a net contributor, compared with other countries, is evident from Table 5.14(b). Note, particularly, that the perceived ratio of outcomes: inputs is, in every case, lower for one's *own* country, a phenomenon discussed at more length, below.

Has the Community become too big to be effective?
Although we have seen that some respondents perceive inequity in varying degrees, very few appear to relate this to the size of the Community (see Table 5.15). Only in France, perhaps with an eye on the accession of Spain and Portugal, did a majority agree with this item. Two-dimensional chi-square analyses yielded a significant difference between countries for both 'no' ($\chi^2(3) = 20.6, p < 0.001$) and 'yes' ($\chi^2(3) = 50.6 p < 0.001$) responses, with the effect due primarily to the numbers of French who answered affirmatively.

Should your country leave the Community?
Again, notwithstanding complaints and disaffection, few respondents would leave the Community, if given the opportunity (see Table 5.16). As so often before, there is support for this 'exit' option among the British, but the vast majority of all respondents do not seriously entertain the possibility. Two-dimensional chi-square analyses revealed that the difference between countries was limited to 'yes' responses ($\chi^2(3) = 35.5, p < 0.001$) and clearly due to the high frequency of British responses in this category.

Summary
Testing predictions from equity theory was hampered by missing data and a skewed pattern of responses. Using an individual index, support for the theory was only clear where it was possible to provide a fair test although

Table 5.16. *Should your country leave the Community as soon as possible?*

Response		W. Germany	Italy	France	U.K.	Row total
				Country of respondent		
No	N	115	121	140	92	468
	%	91.3	92.4	95.9	73.0	88.5
Yes	N	11	10	6	34	61
	%	8.7	7.6	4.1	27.0	11.5
Sample size		126	131	146	126	529

Notes:
Percentages given as a proportion of those who answered the question.
N denotes total number of responses of a given type.

a group index provided a clear demonstration of the value of equity theory
for such an analysis. In view of the pattern of data, no further cross-
tabulations were computed for questions relating to the effectiveness of the
Community and desire to leave. These latter questions revealed considerable
support for the Community, with the exception of respondents from two
countries (France and the U.K.).

5.2.4 Support for the European Community
Utilitarian support
Mean ratings of utilitarian support – gains and losses associated with
Community membership – are shown in Table 5.17. While scores in each
country were well below the maximum, there was evidence of broad
utilitarian support. Highest ratings were obtained on items 6 and 8:
respondents did *not* feel forced to give too much money to poorer groups
in developing countries, and they did *not* think that their own country had
become less competitive economically. ANOVA revealed a significant main
effect, $F(3,535) = 10.91, p < 0.001$, and *post hoc* tests showed that utilitarian
support was significantly lower in the U.K. than in the other three countries.
Considering the content of individual items, British dissatisfaction centred
on the contentious issues of net budget contribution and the Common
Agricultural Policy.

Affective support
Interestingly, levels of affective support were almost exactly the same as
those for utilitarian support (see Table 5.18). In all countries ratings
were highest on the same item: respondents strongly *dis*agreed with the
statement that their country should not help out another member state
in economic difficulties. ANOVA yielded the same main effect,

Table 5.17. *Mean ratings for utilitarian support*

Item	W. Germany	Italy	Country France	U.K.	All
1.* I personally, have gained from the EEC	4.23	3.54	4.08	3.65	3.88
2. The U.K.'s net contribution to the EEC budget is excessive	3.84	4.21	3.67	2.64	3.60
3.* The U.K. has benefited from the EEC	4.70	4.15	5.05	3.72	4.42
4. Through the U.K.'s membership of the EEC you are subsidising poorer groups in other EEC countries	2.81	4.12	2.88	3.21	3.26
5.* The U.K. has gained from the Common Agricultural Policy	4.02	3.59	3.93	2.76	3.58
6. Through the U.K.'s membership of the EEC you are forced to give too much money to poorer groups in developing countries	5.75	4.21	4.81	5.16	4.96
7.* The U.K. has gained from the Community Regional Fund	3.49	4.14	4.17	4.13	3.99
8. The U.K. has become less competitive economically as a result of the EEC	4.74	4.09	4.65	4.35	4.46
Mean total	33.58[a]	32.07[a]	33.19[a]	29.61[b]	32.14
Sample size	128	137	145	129	539

Notes:
Range of scores: 1 (strongly disagree), 7 (strongly agree) for items marked with asterisk. Reversed scoring for other items.
Higher scores indicate more pro-EEC ratings.
Range of total scores: 8–56.
Mean totals with different superscripts are significant at $p < 0.001$ except Italy–U.K. ($p < 0.01$).
Items shown are from the British version of the questionnaire.

Table 5.18. *Mean ratings for affective support*

Item	W. Germany	Country Italy	France	U.K.	All
1. The EEC has increased national rivalries in Europe	4.84	4.34	4.19	3.90	4.31
2.* I feel a strong sense of solidarity with developments in the EEC	2.97	4.55	4.56	2.97	3.80
3. The EEC interferes with the national government of the U.K.	4.87	4.01	3.65	3.81	4.07
4.* The EEC can be trusted to look after the interests of the U.K.	3.71	3.90	3.61	2.47	3.44
5. I do not have confidence in the EEC's handling of economic affairs	3.61	3.81	4.76	3.26	3.89
6.* I am more loyal to the interests of the EEC than to the interests of the U.K.	4.00	2.84	3.55	2.50	3.23
7. The U.K. should not help out another member state in economic difficulties	5.98	5.61	5.47	5.65	5.67
8.* The people of the U.K. should be willing to make personal sacrifices to help out another member state in difficulties	5.07	4.77	3.93	4.41	4.53
Mean total	35.05[a]	33.73[a]	33.77[a]	28.97[b]	32.92
Sample size	128	139	145	127	541

Notes:
Range of scores: 1 (strongly disagree), 7 (strongly agree) for items marked with asterisk. Reversed scoring for other items.
Higher scores indicate more pro-EEC ratings.
Range of total scores: 8–56.
Mean totals with different superscripts are significant at $p < 0.001$.
Items shown are from the British version of the questionnaire.

Table 5.19 *Mean confidence in the Community's and national government's handling of economic affairs*

	Country of respondent				
	W. Germany	Italy	France	U.K.	All
1. The Community	3.61[b]	3.79[b]	4.76[a]	3.26[b]	3.88
2. The national government	3.11[b]	3.06[b]	4.26[a]	3.01[b]	3.88
Difference (1−2)	0.50	0.73	0.50	0.25	0.50
Correlation of difference with overall attitude	−0.23*	−0.05	−0.08	−0.17	—
Sample size	128	139	147	129	543

Notes:
* $p < 0.01$.
Range of scores: 1 (not at all confident); 7 (extremely confident).
Means with different superscripts are significant at $p < 0.01$.

$F(3,537) = 20.60, p < 0.001$, due to lower support in the U.K. British respondents' ratings were especially low on items 2, 4 and 6 and they clearly differed from the other respondents in disagreeing that the Community could be trusted to look after their national interests.

Shift of loyalties
Item 5 for affective support, which measured confidence in the Community's handling of economic affairs, was compared with a similarly worded item (see L.9 in questionnaire: Appendix B) assessing confidence in the national government's economic skills. It is clear from Table 5.19 that the French expressed most confidence in the Community, $F(3,546) = 21.37, p < 0.001$; however, they were also more confident about their national government, $F(3,539) = 18.60, p < 0.001$. A difference score takes account of this response tendency and shows that, while respondents in all four countries tended slightly towards higher ratings of the Community, they did not differ significantly in this respect, $F(3,539) = 1.06, n.s.$

In each country *more* confidence was expressed in the Community than in the national government, and this difference was significant ($p < 0.01$) in all countries except the U.K.[6] This variable was not included in later multiple regressions (see Chapter 6), because it is based on one item already used in the measure of affective support. Therefore simple correlations with overall attitude were computed for respondents in each country separately. This correlation was significant only for the W. Germans (see Table 5.19), which would appear to rule it out as a key predictor of Community attitudes.

Table 5.20. *Mean 'contact' ratings*

Item	Country of respondent				
	W. Germany	Italy	France	U.K.	All
1. Time spent in other European countries	2.58[a]	1.19[b]	1.89[c]	2.65[a]	2.06
Sample size	127	138	145	129	539
2. Frequency of travel abroad in Europe	3.57[a]	1.23[b]	2.20[c]	2.89[d]	2.44
Sample size	127	139	144	129	539

Notes:
Range of scores: 0 (no time, never) to 6 (extremely long/frequently).
Means which do not share a common superscript are significant at $p < 0.001$.

Summary

The picture presented by all three measures was entirely consistent. While levels of utilitarian and affective support were quite high, and there was some evidence of a shift of political loyalties towards the Community, the British were always significantly different from, and less pro-European than, respondents in the other three countries.

5.2.5 Contact

Two items assessed self-reported contact opportunities with members of other European countries (see Table 5.20). First, the W. Germans and the British reported significantly more time spent in other European countries than did the Italians and the French, $F(3,535) = 31.78, p < 0.001$. The Italian ratings were lowest of all. Second, the same pattern of results appeared for the item measuring frequency of travel in Europe, $F(3,535) = 56.89, p < 0.001$. All contrasts were significant, with the W. Germans reporting most, and the Italians least, travel.

5.2.6 Economic perceptions
Common policy

Five policy areas in which Community countries work together were assessed for their achievements. Judgements of policy success were not enthusiastic, although there were significant differences between all four countries, $F(3,538) = 41.88, p < 0.001$ (see Table 5.21). The French perceived most policy successes, followed by the Italians, the British and the W. Germans. Some key to the surprisingly negative view in W. Germany is the high proportion of environmentalists (those who vote for the '*Grünen*') in the sample, and the growing nation-wide support for the party. Policies

Table 5.21. *Mean ratings of common policy*

Item	Country of respondent				
	W. Germany	Italy	France	U.K.	All
1. Agricultural	2.86	3.62	4.57	2.95	3.54
2. Transport	4.20	4.25	3.38	3.92	3.93
3. Energy	3.05	3.78	4.01	3.70	3.65
4. Environmental protection	1.99	3.69	4.32	3.51	3.42
5. Defence	2.72	3.60	4.52	3.17	3.54
Mean total	14.87[a]	18.96[b]	20.80[c]	17.25[d]	18.09
Sample size	127	139	147	129	542

Notes:
Range of scores: 1 (extremely unsuccessful); 7 (extremely successful).
Range of total scores: 7–35.
Mean totals with different superscripts are significant at $p < 0.001$, except Italy–France $(p < 0.01)$ and Italy–U.K. $(p < 0.01)$.

of environmental protection and defence were very negatively rated in W. Germany.

Effects of Community policy
Ratings of the Community's success in bringing about 10 more specific political and economic effects are shown in Table 5.22. Although total scores were much less than the maximum, specific positive effects were perceived – for example, freedom of movement for Community citizens and increased trade between member states. However, there was considerable variation between the four countries and ANOVA yielded a significant main effect, $F(3,534) = 5.84, p < 0.001$. *Post hoc* tests revealed that the British, in a now familiar pattern, gave lower ratings than did the respondents in the other three countries.

Summary
It is interesting to see what different pictures are provided by the two sets of economic perceptions. While the Germans are most critical of common policy, they show a tendency to be most laudatory about specific effects achieved by the Community. It is also worth emphasising the differentiation of responses to the individual items in Tables 5.21 and 5.22. Respondents would appear to have definite views about the nature and effects of common policy, rather than simply global evaluations of 'the Community'.

Table 5.22. *Mean ratings of the effects of Community policy*

Item	Country of respondent				
	W. Germany	Italy	France	U.K.	All
1. Increased agricultural productivity	5.16	4.28	3.31	4.37	4.25
2. Reasonably priced agricultural produce for the consumer	3.44	3.36	4.25	2.93	3.52
3. Harmonisation of national transport costs within each of the member states	3.77	3.82	3.91	3.21	3.69
4. Increased efficiency of industries	4.59	3.95	3.67	3.23	3.86
5. Freedom of movement for EEC citizens to work elsewhere in the EEC	3.98	4.29	4.91	4.51	4.44
6. Speaking with a single voice when the EEC acts on the world stage	2.91	3.35	4.32	2.50	3.31
7. Reducing travel restrictions in the EEC	5.02	4.19	3.58	4.86	4.38
8. Increasing trade between member states	5.21	5.05	3.10	4.87	4.52
9. Reducing inequalities between regions of the community	3.69	3.37	4.31	3.14	3.65
10. Providing social security benefits for EEC citizens who work in other member states	3.96	3.71	3.67	3.83	3.79
Mean total	41.75[a]	39.34[a]	39.06[a]	37.46[b]	39.38
Sample size	126	138	145	129	538

Notes:
Range of scores: 1 (extremely unsuccessful); 7 (extremely successful).
Range of total scores: 7–70.
Mean totals with different superscripts are significant at $p < 0.001$.

Table 5.23. *Mean intended active interest in Community affairs in coming years*

	W. Germany	Italy	France	U.K.	All
			Country of respondent		
Active interest	-0.22^a	$0.45^{b,c}$	0.83^c	$-0.05^{a,b}$	0.28
Sample size	125	140	147	129	541

Notes:
Range of scores: -3 to $+3$. Means which do not share a common superscript are significant at $p < 0.001$ except W. Germany/Italy ($p < 0.01$).

Table 5.24. *Mean perception of the Community in the mass media*

	W. Germany	Italy	France	U.K.	All
			Country of respondent		
Perceived media view of the Community	3.80^b	4.42^c	$4.09^{b,c}$	3.09^a	3.87
Sample size	128	139	147	128	542

Notes:
Range of scores: 1 (extremely negatively), 7 (extremely positively). Means which do not share a common superscript are significant at $p < 0.01$.

5.2.7 Interest and knowledge
Although almost all respondents reported regularly reading a newspaper, thus preventing any analysis in terms of this measure, differences did arise from ratings of intended active interest, mass media image of the Community, and a knowledge test.

Active interest
ANOVA on this measure of behavioural intention yielded a main effect, $F(3,537) = 10.88, p < 0.001$, but with no clear pattern of differences between the nations (see Table 5.23). There was only a tendency for the French to be most, and the W. Germans least, interested. It should, however, be noted that, consistent with above findings, the Italians and the French were on the positive side of the mid-point, while the British and the W. Germans were on the negative side.

Perceived media image
The image of the Community perceived in the mass media was quite different for respondents of the four countries, as revealed by a significant ANOVA

main effect, $F(3,538) = 28.70, p < 0.001$ (see Table 5.24). The only clear effect to emerge was the especially negative view in the U.K.[7]

Knowledge

Mean scores for the ten-item knowledge test revealed a remarkable *lack* of knowledge in all countries (see Table 5.25). ANOVA yielded a significant main effect. $F(3,540) = 16.57, p < 0.001$, due to the especially low level of knowledge in Italy.[8] One can, however, hardly talk about knowledge being 'better' in the other three countries – where only about two out of 10 questions were answered correctly.

Further analyses of these scores were computed using Guttman's (1944, 1950) scalogram technique, which enables the construction of a uni-dimensional and cumulative scale in which the items can be monotonically arranged in terms of their difficulty. The idea is that the ten knowledge test items can be ordered so that respondents who correctly answer an item in, say, position four on the scale, also correctly answer all items that are lower in order (i.e. items 1, 2 and 3). Strict criteria determine whether the scale can be considered unidimensional and cumulative: a 'coefficient of reproducibility' of at least 0.90, and a 'coefficient of scalability' of at least 0.60. The percentages of correct answers in Table 5.25 reveal that items covered a range of difficulty, and that they can to some extent be ordered in terms of increasing difficulty (although the order varies between countries). However, the Guttman statistics do not allow strong inferences about unidimensionality. Coefficients of reproducibility attain the criterion in each country (indicating less than 10% inconsistent responses), but coefficients of scalability do not reach an acceptable level.[9]

Although the scale cannot unequivocally be described as uni-dimensional and cumulative, the ordering of responses in terms of difficulty does highlight both areas and lacunae of knowledge, as well as cross-national differences. For example, very few respondents knew who Mr Piet Dankert was (he *was* President of the European Parliament); while most respondents (but not those in Italy) were aware of the prime position of agriculture in the Community's finances.

Summary

These analyses of information and knowledge reveal a mixed pattern of results. The Italians and French show slightly more interest in Community affairs; the British view of the Community in the mass media is most negative; and the Italians are least knowledgeable. Overall, however, the picture is one of low interest and low knowledge, indicating the Community's lack of saliency in the minds of its citizens.

Table 5.25. *Mean scores on knowledge test*

Item	Country of respondent				
	W. Germany	Italy	France	U.K.	All
1. Which common policy accounts for the largest percentage of the EEC budget?	62	11	51	69	48.3
2. How many member states are there in the EEC?	30	31	50	32	36.8
3. How many countries were there in the original 'Common Market'?	30	21	48	34	33.3
4. Which treaties form the basis of the EEC?	15	6	29	32	20.5
5. Name the member states of the EEC	11	10	16	12	12.3
6. Name three of the major decision-making institutions of the EEC	18	3	5	11	9.3
7. What is the position held by M. Gaston Thorn?	13	3	3	16	8.8
8. What is the name of the convention which covers the EEC's economic relationship with African, Caribbean and Pacific states?	6	0	6	4	4
9. When were the EEC treaties ratified?	2	1	10	2	3.8
10. What office is held by Mr Piet Dankert?	5	2	2	3	3
Mean number of correct answers	1.91[a]	0.88[b]	2.20[a]	2.13[b]	1.78
Range of scores	0–10	0–7	0–8	0–9	
Guttman statistics					
coefficient of reproducibility	0.90	0.95	0.89	0.88	0.90
coefficient of scalability	0.40	0.47	0.50	0.30	0.44
Sample size	127	141	147	129	544

Notes:
Data presented are the percentages of correct answers.
Answers scored 1, correct, 0, incorrect (max: 10).
Means with different superscripts are significant at $p < 0.001$.
Items are ordered in terms of increasing difficulty for the sample as a whole.

5.2.8 Effects of respondents' sex and political affiliation
Thus far the analysis has centred exclusively on cross-national differences at the expense of other demographic variables. Two such variables which were analysed, but have been relegated to the background, are respondents' sex and political affiliation.

Sex

The overall sample consisted of 256 males and 288 females, which totals were used, ignoring national differences, to test for sex effects on all the major scores considered thus far. Only two, related, measures yielded significant effects for sex. Males ($M = 0.59$) intended more than females ($M = 0.43$) to take an active interest in Community affairs, $F(1,532) = 14.05, p < 0.001$. Males ($M = 2.30$) also attained higher scores on the knowledge test than did females ($M = 1.30$), $F(1,542) = 45.34, p < 0.001$. These effects were considered further by means of 4(countries) × 2(sex) ANOVAs. For both interest ($F(532) = 3.44, p < 0.025$) and knowledge ($F(3,535) = 2.35, p < 0.08$) there was a slight, but not substantive, interaction, although in the case of knowledge the sex difference occurred only in Italy.

These effects of sex are consistent with other literature on political attitudes, which reveals greater interest in political affairs among males than females (see Etzioni, 1969; Sears, 1969; but *cf.* Himmelweit *et al.*, 1981; Inglehart, 1970b), and with the findings of the *Euro-baromètre* series. However, given the limited nature of sex differences here and the equivalent male/female ratio in each country, these results will not be considered further in the present work.

Political affiliation

The first problem encountered in classifying respondents by their chosen political party in a 'general election tomorrow' was the number who gave no answer (due to indignation, indecision, suspicion or apathy). The second problem was the variety of political affiliations given (especially in Italy). Despite these problems, comparisons between the major groupings in each country (in terms of relative frequency of the response, not electoral standing) were made for the criterion measure of overall attitude. Results were as follows:

W. Germany. ANOVA yielded no main effect, $F(1,100) = 2.81$, n.s., between those who voted SPD ($N = 40$) vs *Grünen* ($N = 62$), both expressing positive attitudes ($Ms = +0.93$ and $+0.40$, respectively).

Italy. Approximately equal numbers of Christian Democrats ($N = 21$) and Communists ($N = 26$) were compared using ANOVA, yielding a significant main effect, $F(1,45) = 10.61, p < 0.01$. Both groups held positive attitudes, but the Christian Democrats ($M = 1.86$) were more pro-Community than the Communists ($M = 0.96$).

France. Respondents were collapsed into political 'Left' (P.S. and P.C.; $N = 62$; $M = +1.53$) and 'Right' (R.P.R. and U.D.F.; $N = 16$; $M = +1.63$), with, unfortunately, very unequal numbers. ANOVA yielded no significant main effect, $F(1,76) = < 1$,n.s.

U.K. Conservative ($N = 24$), Labour ($N = 41$) and Liberal/SDP Alliance ($N = 42$) voters were compared using ANOVA, $F(2,104) = 8.34$,$p < .001$. *Post hoc* tests revealed only a significant difference between the most positive Liberal/SDP voters ($M = +1.14$) and the negative Labour voters ($M = -0.42$),$t(104) = -4.07$,$p < 0.001$. Conservative voters were intermediate, but positively inclined ($M = +0.25$).

These results clearly do indicate effects for political affiliation in Italy and the U.K.[10] However, it is only in the latter country, and then only for Labour Party voters, that political affiliation corresponds with a difference between positive and negative attitudes. Considering the four countries together, political affiliation is obviously not a major factor in predicting Community attitudes (a point supported by *Euro-baromètre* polls)[11], nor one that could be adequately treated in the present work.

5.2.9 *A methodological note on cross-national differences*
Before discussing the data on cross-national differences, it is necessary to address one key methodological issue: are observed differences between the four nations factual or artefactual? One possibility is that the Italians and French are more positive about the Community because they are always positive (or use response scales in this way).[12] In other words, cross-national differences could be due to a 'positivity' bias (see Zajonc and Burnstein, 1965) on the part of the Latin sisters. This claim can be convincingly scotched by three lines of empirical evidence:

(1) Considering only the data for overall attitude (i.e. Table 5.1 above), the reported differences could arise because everyone is positive about the Community, but the French and Italians are more so. Dichotomising the responses, from a 7-point scale to 'positive' vs 'negative', and excluding those respondents with a score of 0, this claim is obviously not upheld (see Appendix D, Table D.5). While less than 10% of respondents in Italy and France are negative, approximately 30% in both other countries are negative. A two-dimensional chi-square analysis revealed that the major effect is for differences in the relative frequency of negative attitudes ($\chi^2(3) = 40.5$,$p < 0.001$,two-tailed), such responses being much more frequent among the W. Germans and British, than the French and Italians.

(2) If the French and Italians are always more positive, then this difference should also emerge when good and bad concepts are rated by the

four nationalities. Such data are provided by evaluations of the dimensions along which stereotypes and images were rated (see Appendix D, Tables D.2 and D.4). Multivariate analyses of variance on both sets of ratings revealed a significant main effect; for stereotypes, Multivariate $F(3,539 = 6.11, p < 0.01$; for national images, Multivariate $F(3,535) = 32.46, p < 0.001$. However, follow-up ANOVAs on each dimension separately revealed no clear pattern. It is certainly *not* the case that the French and Italians are generally more positive, or less negative, nor that their responses form one 'pair' and those of the W. Germans and British another, quite distinct, unit.

(3) The preceding point is reinforced by the complete set of results discussed in this chapter. The Italians and French were *not* more positive on all ratings, and response patterns varied from one section of the questionnaire to the next.

In sum, the empirical evidence quashes any claim that the cross-national differences reported are artefactual. Rather, the extent to which two nations, the Italians and French, appear more pro-European is interpreted as a true reflection of attitudes: genuine enthusiasm for the Community, on the one hand; disillusionment and dissatisfaction, on the other. That the four countries may differ in terms of the complexity and structure of their views is another, empirical, question which is considered in detail in Chapter 6. Viewing the world, or Europe, differently is not, however, a methodological artefact.

5.3 Discussion

The differentiated pattern of responses reported above – both in terms of differences between countries and between responses to the various questions asked – supports the claim of a more sophisticated analysis of attitudes towards the European Community. These findings are now discussed and their implications elaborated, following the same outline in which results were presented above. Finally, the results are related back to the *Eurobaromètre* findings and the institutional support accorded to the Community in each of the four countries studied (see Chapter one).

5.3.1 Attitudes: the Community's 'credibility gap'

Overall attitude to the Community is one of the core variables in the study and is the criterion variable we are trying to predict. On this measure the French and Italians were shown to be more positive towards the Community than were the W. Germans and the British. As we have seen, this dichotomy between pairs of nations was quite fundamental and consistent in the pattern of results as a whole.

Attitudes were also considered in terms of value and expectancy components, orientation to international relations, and attitude ambivalence; these results are now discussed.

Expectancy-value analysis of attitudes
Separate analyses of evaluations and expectancies provided quite different pictures of the four nations examined. The goals of the Community were positively evaluated in all countries, but the real difference between countries appeared in the ratings of expectancy. The Italians and French were optimistic, or satisfied, the W. Germans and the British were pessimistic, or disillusioned. These two sets of ratings would appear to measure that gulf between rhetoric and reality which has already appeared in open-end responses (see Chapter 4) classified as 'conditional positive' (e.g. 'the EEC is a good thing in principle, but...'). This chasm is sometimes referred to in politics as the 'credibility gap', a term now used to assess political promises or undertakings of any kind.[13] The public are apparently now getting used to the great claims, followed by long periods of inactivity. The phenomenon is illustrated by the following extract: 'The European parliament voted by a two-thirds majority for a motion calling for a new EEC treaty committing member states to a major advance towards federation. The chances of such a treaty being adopted in the foreseeable future are nil.; (*The Economist*, 8 October, 1983.)

Both evaluations and expectancies are important, as shown by correlations between these ratings, individually and in various combinations, with overall attitude. It is, however, difficult to specify the *best* combinatorial expectancy-value model.

As Mitchell (1974) and others have pointed out, certain assumptions are being made about the mathematical attributes of the variables when aggregated scores are generated. Namely, when the sums or products of values and expectancies are summed, additive and multiplicative assumptions are made. The main issue for the multiplicative model is that scales used do not meet the criteria for ratio scales. Schmidt (1973) reviewed several studies indicating mixed results for the multiplicative vs additive model. His own transformational analyses indicated that correlations based on the additive model are more stable. The problem for the multiplicative model is the absence of a 'true rational zero point' on both the measures entered into the product (i.e. the Σe_s and Σv_s) and hence the dubious assumption of ratio scale measurement. Schmidt therefore suggests that it is easy, but pointless, to 'prove' the superiority of the multiplicative model, by moving the arbitrary zero point. The transformation applied to the present data (simply adding 4 to the bipolar expectancy rating, thereby forming a unipolar scale) supported Schmidt's point, that perfectly legitimate transformations (of the form $X + b$) of interval measures of expectancy and value can considerably alter conclusions drawn about the apparent performance of multiplicative and additive models. Such transformations had no effect on the performance of the additive model, but did affect the correlations produced by the multiplicative model. Schmidt concludes that 'a meaningful test of the multiplicative expectancy-valence models is not possible using the measures and operations employed by researchers in this area to date'. (1973, p. 249.) Thus the present analyses could be used to support a multiplicative *or* additive model (in the case of unipolar scoring of expectancy); or only an additive model (in the case of bipolar scoring of expectancy).

Notwithstanding his critique, Schmidt (1973) acknowledges that the use of multiplicative scores may be justified in terms of 'practical validity criteria', i.e. where the purpose of the study is purely practical prediction and not to demonstrate the theoretical meaningfulness of the multiplicative model. But such scores should not be used as validational evidence for the underlying multiplicative relationship: i.e. the procedures do not follow 'fundamental measurement criteria'. (see Hackman and Porter, 1968; Mitchell, 1974.)

Given these viewpoints, and the rating scales used in the present study, we are in no position to provide a 'test' of the multiplicative model. Furthermore, for practical reasons, items were based on the Treaty of Rome and were, as expected, almost without exception positively evaluated. Interest was centred on whether respondents even valued the original aims of the Community, and thought that they were being achieved. This use of only positive items may limit the efficacy of the multiplicative model because multiplication must be given a chance to make a difference (Insko *et al.*, 1970). For example, using the multiplicative model and bipolar scoring the Community would be viewed positively if it were seen as improbably achieving negative goals ($-3 \times -3 = +9$); using the additive model the same ratings would result in a negative view ($-3 + -3 = -6$). However, the aim of the study was to identify the combinatorial rule which provided the best estimate of overall attitude. The empirical evidence clearly supports both multiplicative and additive models, and yet one model must be chosen for subsequent analyses. The additive model has been chosen for various reasons.[14] First, it does not make the assumption of ratio-scaling and correlations yielded by this model are clearly more stable. This additive model does, however, share with the multiplicative model the assumption that all scores (sums or products) are equally weighted and, according to Mitchell, this assumption has not been tested. However, while Wyer (1970) has suggested weighting items, Fishbein and Ajzen (1975) report that the inclusion of perceived importance ratings tends to attenuate the prediction of attitudes. 'Weighting' is, at least psychologically, already implied by ratings of evaluation and expectancy, and is therefore redundant. Second, the use of an additive model avoids the erroneous conclusion that the Fishbein–Ajzen model has received support. Notwithstanding the importance of the Fishbein-Ajzen approach, it must be noted that their bipolar scoring multiplicative model fared particularly badly in three out of four countries. This raises considerable doubts about the scoring of expectancies on a bipolar scale.[15]

Having adopted an additive (i.e. two-component) model, it should be noted that the correlations yielded by sum of values alone were quite high and never significantly lower than those yielded by the best computational models. The additive model has been used, because the percentage of variance explained is slightly higher, but the relatively small differences might suggest that the time-consuming task of completing two sets of ratings is unnecessary. As Insko *et al.* (1970) point out, using both sets of ratings may correlate more highly with attitude simply because the increased number of items improves reliability. Future research – using positive and negative items – will have to decide whether the two-component model is justified, or whether as Insko *et al.* suggest, respondents may adjust their beliefs and their evaluations so as to conform to the multiplicative (or additive) rule (note, however, that while Σv and Σe were significantly correlated for the Germans and French, this was not so for the Italians and British).

To summarise, the expectancy-value approach (leaving aside combinatorial issues) does appear useful in focussing attention on what respondents value and what they expect. It is then, perhaps, the contrasting picture of the four countries in these respects (see Tables 5.2 and 5.3) that argues for the use of this approach in political behaviour in general (see Fishbein and Coombs, 1974) and in studies of European Community attitudes in particular. Fishbein and Azjen (1975) argue that the elicitation of each respondent's salient beliefs increases the magnitude of correlations (see Fishbein, 1963; Jaccard and Davidson, 1972) with total evaluation levelling off after 5–9 beliefs. Nonetheless the invariant set of 13 items used in the present study allows for cross-national comparisons and obviously does relate to the criterion variable of interest. For each of four independent samples, the adopted additive model has obvious practical validity – accounting for between 9 and 29% of the variance in attitudes. However, it must be emphasised that the obtained results say nothing about the process of attitude formation. Computational models have been identified which can predict overall attitude quite well, but this is not the same as saying that any model was *used* by a single individual (van der Pligt and

Eiser, 1983). The impact of this criticism is most evident in the scoring transformations which can be used to provide support for either a multiplicative *or* an additive model.

International relations and attitude ambivalence
While the above analyses showed the Italians to be most positive in evaluating the Community's goals, and the Italians and French to score higher on the sum of expectancies a different picture emerged from the scale measuring attitudes towards international relations. Here all nations scored highly, but the Germans had the highest scores. The pairs of countries divided again on attitude ambivalence, where an interesting effect was shown. When asked to focus explicitly and exclusively on negative aspects of the Community, the Germans and British revealed a greater propensity to think negatively about the Community. However, no relationship was found between attitude ambivalence scores and overall attitude.

Summarising the picture from all three attitudinal measures, the Italians and French appeared most positively inclined towards the Community, followed by the Germans, and then the British.

5.3.2 Ethnocentrism
The data concerning these three variables – stereotypes, liking and images – provided contrasting pictures which help to map out the way people view nations and nationalities in Europe. In the case of stereotypes and images, it must be emphasised that only ten out of the universe of attributes were used. However, in the case of stereotypes these were based on previous research and for both sets of judgements equal numbers of positive and negative characteristics were used.

Although respondents did not show any strong tendency to stereotype, the individual stereotyping measure computed did reveal cross-national differences, with the Italians most positively inclined towards their own people. Exactly the same effect was found for judgements of liking. This result is interesting in view of the Italians' pro-European view noted on almost all measures. Apparently, being pro-European does not rule out national chauvinism. This recalls Mathew's (1980) proposal that the Community may be rated positively if judged to be good for one's own nation (see Chapter 2, above). The limited tendency to stereotype others and to prefer one's own nationality could be attributed to the Community's existence, or to the liberal background of the student respondents. The results certainly provide very little support for Sumner's (1906) idea of a universal tendency ('ethnocentrism') to see one's own group positively, and a 'view of things in which one's own group is the center of everything, and all countries are scaled or rated with reference to it'. (p. 13.)

If the Italians are chauvinistic, the Germans show the opposite tendency.

While they share with the French and the British a tendency to stereotype some other groups more positively than their own group (nationality), on the liking measure they have a clear negative score for their own group which sets them apart from the other three countries. Other studies have also reported evidence that W. German school and university students may not have a very positive view of the German nationality. In the study by Schönbach, Gollwitzer, Stiepel and Wagner (1981), school pupils preferred the Italians to the W. Germans; students tested by Dannenberg and Winter (1975) rated the W. Germans more negatively than both the Americans and the Russians; and Jonas and Hewstone (in press) reported more positive stereotypes of, and liking for, both the Italians and the French, than the W. Germans, by W. German university students. These results are consistent with those from *Euro-baromètre*, revealing low levels of national pride among the W. Germans, and could be seen as the social psychological residue of the post-war generations of W. Germans who have been nurtured on a diet of historical shame and the dangers of nationalism.

Quite a different picture emerged from the analysis of national images, supporting the separate assessment of views about nation and nationality. On this measure the Italians showed the lowest, and the W. Germans slightly the highest, preference for own country. While the Italians could see their people positively, they characterised their country as neither 'economically and industrially developed', nor 'politically stable'. On these dimensions, and others, the W. Germans viewed the 'fatherland' very positively.

Taking these three measures together, one cannot say that nationalism, ethnocentrism or patriotism is dead, or even dying. However, preference for one's own land or people is quite limited and, given the pattern of Italian responses throughout the questionnaire, may not even interfere with support for a supra-national entity.

5.3.3 Perceived inequity

As noted above, it was not possible to provide an optimal test of intra-individual hypotheses from equity theory, in view of the pattern of responses. However, in the one country where responses allowed for such tests (U.K.), the prediction from the theory was strongly upheld. Thus perceptions of costs and benefits, or gains and losses, do bear some relationship to Community attitudes. This one finding alone, important because of the vexed British relationship with the Community, is relevant for the reasons outlined by an economist in the quotation at the head of this chapter. It was also found that, consistent with other findings, large numbers of respondents in W. Germany and the U.K. were classified as perceiving high inequity. Obviously, the question of net contributions to the Community budget will have to be settled sooner, rather than later.

The findings of a second equity theory analysis proved much more successful, both in terms of understanding the social psychology of the Community, and in demonstrating that equity theory can be applied to wider social issues. Responses concerning which country benefited most and least from, and contributed most and least to, the Community were used to compare the ratio of perceived outcomes: inputs for each country. Interestingly, these ratios were always less than unity when one's *own* country was judged. Furthermore, when this ratio for own country was compared with the ratio for other countries in general (the average for the other three countries), the ratio was again always less than unity. Thus all four sets of respondents did perceive inequity in their dealings with the Community, especially the W. Germans and the British.

The finding that respondents from all four member states think that their country is worse off than the average other state may come as no surprise to political commentators. It is, however, the opposite of Codol's (1975) P.I.P. (*primus inter pares*) effect. Whereas Codol reported, in a number of studies, that people tend to think that they are better than the average other, here every member state seems to think that it is *worse off* than the average other member. It is a particularly crass example of self-interest and one that might have been expected from politicians, but not students. Jaspars (pers. comm.) has christened this effect, appropriately, the *pauper inter pares* effect.[16]

While it was decided not to consider the relationship between perceived inequity and the two questions asking for a 'verdict' on the Community, the latter questions are interesting in their own right. Only in France did a substantial number, indeed a majority, of respondents agree that the Community had become too big to be effective. It is interesting to note that in several *Euro-baromètre* polls (e.g. nos. 8, 10 and 13) the French have consistently withheld support for membership of the Community by Greece, Portugal and Spain (now all members). It appears from the present data that the French are still worried about the influx of cheap southern mediterranean agricultural produce and, despite their unquestioning support for the Community, are not above protecting their own national interests.[17]

As Rutherford (1981) has argued, 'in (continental) Europe the Common Market is popular and taken for granted. In the U.K. it seems to be neither of these'. (p. 1.) He goes on to point out that in other countries almost no one would think of conducting an opinion poll about leaving the Community. In the U.K. this happens all the time. The results for this item bear out his view – only among the British do a sizeable minority (27%) choose this option. This should still be a worrying figure for the Community and it obviously remains a task to convince such citizens that membership is worthwhile.

5.3.4 Utilitarian and affective support

Items measuring utilitarian support also bear on notions of gain–loss and almost all respondents answered these closed-end questions, where many had declined to identify particular countries as beneficiaries and contributors. Someone once wrote that the benefits of belonging to the European Community were like flying saucers: a lot of people talked about them, precious few could claim to have actually seen them, and those who did were generally disbelieved. However, our respondents clearly did see benefits of Community membership and, in particular, agreed that their own country had become more competitive economically as a result of Community membership. Interestingly, although Mathew's (1980) measures of support were criticised above (Chapter 2), the results here parallel those he calculated from *Euro-baromètre* polls. While he found a difference between 'new' and 'old' member states for both kinds of support, the present analyses yielded significant differences between the U.K. and the other three countries. Wildgen and Feld (1976) also reported that, while 'affective-institutional' support in France and the U.K. was slightly lower than in Italy and W. Germany, 'utilitarian-performance' support was much lower in the U.K. than in all three other countries. In line with the results reported so far (in both this section and Chapter 4), the British were most dissatisfied with their budget contribution and with the Common Agricultural Policy. Although these data cannot be used to consider the temporal relationship between utilitarian and affective support, it was noted that both levels of support were almost exactly the same. The Community now has substantial utilitarian and affective support in W. Germany, Italy and France, as measured by these items and with respect to these citizens.[18] The relationship between these two types of support is considered below (in Chapter 6).

One item from the section on affective support measured confidence in the Community's handling of economic affairs; this was compared with a similar item tapping confidence in the national government. Analyses revealed that in all countries except the U.K., respondents actually expressed *more* confidence in the Community. This might be taken as some indication of a shift in political (but, note, not necessarily emotional) loyalties, of the type discussed by neo-functionalists see Haas, 1968). Taken together with the support findings, this must be considered good news for the Community, even if the relationship between 'loyalty' and Community attitudes was only significant in W. Germany.

5.3.5 Contact

Having seen that Community views are generally more positive in Italy and France, it is interesting and somewhat surprising to report that on both contact measures (time spent and frequency of travel) it was the W. Germans and British who were more cosmopolitan. This suggests a minor influence, if any, of contact on Community attitudes, although intrasubject correlations (computed in Chapter 6) can best address this issue. Following writers like Kelman (1965c) and Inglehart (1971), it is probably more realistic to consider that international travel plays a general, eye-opening role and influences attitudes only indirectly, as we shall see below.

5.3.6 Common policy and its effects
Respondents' judgements of common policy achievements were not particularly enthusiastic. Following the pattern of open-ended results, the W. Germans and British were clearly dissatisfied with the Community's main common policy – agriculture. Only the French judged the policy successful and, again, they and the Italians were more pro-Community on this measure.

It was noted earlier, that Piet Dankert accounted for the negative public image of the Community in terms of citizens' lack of knowledge about the effects of Community policies. Despite this view, responses to the items on political and economic effects were differentiated and evidenced some knowledge. For example, on average all respondents judged the Community successful in giving citizens 'freedom of movement to work elsewhere in the Community' and in 'reducing travel restrictions in the Community'[19] although the British were again least impressed. On the other hand, Dankert may have been correct in his assertion that, 'opinions about the EEC are all too often shaped by persons who combine impatience with a short memory'. (Dankert, 1983, p. 3.) Consider the low ratings given by the British, who enjoyed Community support during the Falklands crisis, for the item 'speaking with a single voice when the EEC acts on the world stage'. Perhaps, if respondents and citizens in general are so fickle or forgetful, ratings of these specific effects will have very little influence on Community attitudes.

5.3.7 Dark areas of ignorance
Although the effect was not significant, the respondents from Italy and France again differed from those in W. Germany and the U.K. when asked about interest in the Community. While the former did intend to take an interest in Community affairs in coming years, the latter made no such pretences or promises. If this response seems now predictable for the British, they also reported an especially negative view of the Community in the mass media. It is, of course, not possible to state the direction of this relationship. Negative press reports could generate negative attitudes; but those with negative attitudes could also seek out (with little difficulty) negative news stories about the Community. It would certainly be interesting, although the

author knows of no relevant research, to investigate whether, and how, the media image of the Community actually differs in various countries.

As noted earlier, general knowledge of politics and current affairs is low; clearly the European Community is no exception. Results of the 'knowledge test' provided striking evidence of a lack of knowledge, which certainly justifies borrowing the term 'dark area of ignorance' (Kriesberg, 1949) to describe the average respondent's cognitive map of the Community. If students are so poorly informed, one wonders where the 'attentive public' (Almond, 1960) of Europe is to be found. That respondents in Italy were significantly less knowledgeable is almost an epiphenomenon; we are talking here about a difference between 'chronic know-nothings' (Sears, 1969) and the plain ignorant.[20] That only 12.3% of all respondents could name exactly all ten member states is staggering and, for the Community, disappointing. Even the British, for whom Community matters were made salient via the referendum and fairly continuous political debate, appear to have enjoyed no spin off in terms of increased knowledge. Given the preponderance of metaphorical language (and, perhaps, thought; see Lakoff and Johnson, 1980) among British respondents (see Chapter 4), one might wonder whether the acquisition of knowledge is impeded by a 'wall of stereotypes' as Lippmann (1922) believed.

The ten knowledge items were chosen to provide a gradient of difficulty and to relate to issues which respondents were expected to know about (rather than, for example, questions about the underlying theory of customs unions and economies of scale). Particularly suprising, given the tendency towards 'personification' in social representations and the media's inclination to personalise politics (see Lane, 1959; Lazarsfeld *et al.*, 1948), is that knowledge of personalities was so low. Sears (1969) even suggests that 'persons' represent very simple stimuli, easily cognised and retained, unlike most political stimuli which are abstract and complex. Yet, in the sample as a whole only 8.8% of respondents knew who Gastorn Thorn was; and only 3% knew what office was held by Piet Dankert. It may be that other personalities – Prime Ministers, Presidents, Chancellors and Foreign Ministers – dominate the minds of the electorate, but this lack of knowledge about major figures in the Community bureaucracy is nonetheless surprising.

One can only speculate as to why knowledge is so low. It may simply be that Community matters are too complex to be of interest to most people. Thus Noelle-Neumann argues that such data reveal, 'how grossly boring the European machinery – that intricate system of cross-national linkages and institutions – must be' (1980, p. 58) for its citizens. Alternatively, starved of direct participation in Community decision-making, except via the innocuous parliamentary assembly, citizens may simply feel that the whole business is too remote, and beyond their ken or control. Whether this lack of knowledge relates to Community attitudes is considered below; but it merits attention in any case by a Community which wants an 'attentive public' as a resource for further steps towards European integration.

5.3.8 National profiles

Having reported cross-national differences, it is now incumbent upon us to provide some explanation for the observed pattern of responses. This is achieved, first, by summarising the findings into a 'profile' for each of the four countries. This highlights the judgements in terms of which each country was set apart from the others. The profile of each country is then related back to the results of public opinion surveys, and to the levels of institutional support for the Community in each of the four member states.

The W. Germans are significantly the most positive in their orientation towards cooperative international relations, and they even show negative ethnocentrism (preference for others and not their own people) on measures of stereotyping and liking (although not for national images). However, they are most negative in their evaluation of common policy (probably due to the influence of the environmentalist, *Grünen*, party on ratings of defence and environmental protection).

The Italians are the most enthusiastic in evaluating the goals of the Community, but unlike the W. Germans they have not eschewed preference for their own countryfolk. They are the most ethnocentric in terms of stereotypes and liking, although they view the country of Italy critically. Perhaps it is because they see their own country, as opposed to people, so negatively that they embrace the Community so warmly. This may be Barzini's (1983) image of a people fed up with *Il Malgoverno*, investing their hope in the European Community version of *Il Buongoverno*. The Italians are, however, the least knowledgeable (a finding which parallels their frequent failure to respond to the open-ended questions in Chapter 4).

The French are significantly different from the other three countries on only two measures. They judge common policies to be most successful, but are also the only nation of which a majority believe that the Community has become too big to be effective.

While these countries of continental Europe were distinct and independent on only a handful of responses, it was the British who were unmistakably 'out of step', 'behind' or 'different' on seven measures. Just as British politicians over the years have held back in their support for the Community, so did the British respondents in this study. The list of responses on which they are distinct reads like the six deadly (non-European) sins: only they have a large minority who believe that the country should leave the Community; they have lower levels of utilitarian and affective support; they show no shift of political loyalty towards the Community; they judge the effects of Community policy to be least successful; and, whether cause or consequence, they judge the mass media view of the Community to be especially negative. Evidently, the British are still very much the villains of the piece (and perhaps also the 'peace').

Alongside the clear effect for the British, the major cross-national effect observed was that between France and Italy vs W. Germany and the U.K. On five measures the French and Italians are significantly more pro-European in outlook: more positive overall attitude; higher expectancies that the Community is bringing about valued political and economic goals; less attitudinal ambivalence about the Community (due to their reluctance or inability to focus on negative aspects); and higher ratings of intention to take an active interest in the Community. In addition there is a lesser tendency to view the Community as inequitable. Finally, the French and Italians reported less international travel and contact.

From this social-psychological analysis of Community knowledge and attitudes, the four nations fall into three groups. France and Italy lead the European movement, followed with some misgivings by the W. Germans; the British, consistently critical on several dimensions, are apparently still not convinced that membership of the Community is a natural part of their political life. Rather than seek to explain these differences in terms of 'national character' (see Duijker and Frijda, 1960; Inkeles and Levinson, 1969), the present approach prefers to attribute them to differences in institutional support.

Consider, first, the findings of public opinion surveys; it is clear that the results from student samples are broadly comparable to those from the general public. This confirmation of earlier findings, based on a more exact questionnaire, is itself an important result which justifies the more wide-ranging discussion which follows (see Chapter 7). The finding of Italian enthusiasm is consistent, although among students nothing separates the Italians from the French in this respect. The W. Germans, while not negative, reveal that 'noncommital benevolence' referred to by Noelle-Neumann (1980, p. 99) and would appear to be principled, not passionate, Europeans. Overall, the British are, just, positive, and this fact must be emphasised; but, just as in the *Euro-baromètre* polls, it would seem premature to count on their unqualified support. This pattern of responses across countries appears to match the picture of institutional support sketched earlier (see Chapter 1). Perhaps French support has been given a fillip by President Mitterand's efforts, while Chancellor Kohl's paymaster-role has made the topic of budget contributions and Community 'pay-outs' a more frequent aspect in his speeches and the public's mind. It is, however, only in the U.K. where a national head of government has fought head-on with the Community for 'my money back' (see also Chapter 7). Surely this has helped to ensure that public acceptance of and support for the Community in the U.K. has never been allowed to crystallise. The pot is continually stirred and the British public will presumably withhold support until or unless the issue of net budget contributions is settled and the national government regards the European Commission, not to mention other member states, as friend, not foe.

5.3.9 Conclusion

In conclusion, the interesting and differentiated pattern of results justifies the novel and more detailed analysis of 'common sense and the Common market'. Views about the Community have been shown to be item-specific, and not global, a finding which suggests that further analysis in terms of underlying structure would be worthwhile. It is to this issue, analysed with multivariate rather than univariate statistical techniques, that we now turn.

6   Predicting attitudes towards the European Community: towards a model of underlying structure

> Although no theory can be verified, since there will always be alternative theories that imply the same predictions, one can at least proceed by eliminating or modifying the inadequate ones. In constructing such theories, the scientist is always confronted with the dilemma of how much to oversimplify reality. On the one hand, simple theories are easier to construct and evaluate. On the other hand, more complex ones may stand a better chance of conforming to reality.
>
> (H. M. Blalock, 1971)

6.1 Introduction

Thus far the statistical treatment of questionnaire items has been limited to analysis of individual variables. While these analyses constitute an important and useful stage of understanding the data, in particular the issue of cross-national differences, the analysis can still be criticised on the same grounds as were some public opinion surveys – namely, that the *interrelations* between variables are ignored. It is this next step, to look at the structure of views about Europe, that is the focus of this chapter. To that end a series of multivariate analyses are used – factor analysis, multiple regression, path analysis and discriminant analysis – to treat a large number of the questionnaire variables together, in the same analysis (see Andrews, Klem, Davidson, O'Malley and Rodgers, 1974). The present approach, using a variety of multivariate analyses, can be seen as analogous to Campbell and Fiske's (1959) notion of 'convergent validation' and Garner, Hake and Eriksen's (1956) concept of 'converging operations'. If this battery of statistical procedures converges on the same underlying attitudinal structure, then this agreement constitutes a confirmation of the proposed model of Community attitudes.

Each of the multivariate techniques has been selected for a specific reason, because different techniques highlight different aspects of the data – for example, the simplicity–complexity of views about the Community; the best combination of variables which can be used to predict overall attitudes; the pattern of effects, direct and indirect, that underlies the relationship between predictor variables and overall attitude; and the accuracy with which respondents can be classified as holding positive or negative attitudes. A brief explanation accompanies the use of each technique, to help justify and illustrate why each analysis was undertaken and what it reveals. For these analyses the two basic assumptions are, for significance testing, a multivariate normal distribution; and for regression models, a linear relationship between the variables examined. While no direct tests of these assumptions were made, checks of the uni- and bi-variate distributions revealed no curvilinear trends.

6.2 The factorial structure of questionnaire responses
6.2.1 Factor analysis
In concluding, above, that cross-national differences were genuine and not artefactual, it was acknowledged that the four nations might differ in terms of the underlying structure of their views about the Community. To consider further the possibility that views in the four countries vary in terms of simplicity–complexity, factor analyses were computed. Factor analysis (see Kim and Mueller, 1978a,b) was used here to reduce a mass of data, with the aim of perceiving some underlying pattern of relationships, or some structure. This technique has been described by Himmelweit *et al.* as one that: 'involves looking at the matrix of intercorrelations among all items under consideration in the attempt to extract factors which more or less represent "families" (a family is a set of items which are relatively highly correlated with each other and relatively poorly correlated with items outside the family'. (1981, p. 138.)

Principal components factor analysis was computed, with varimax rotation, for each national sample separately, on the 31 items in the following four sections: common policy; effects of policy; utilitarian support; and affective support. The analysis was restricted to these 31 items, with sample sizes of approximately 130, to ensure a satisfactory ratio of dependent variables to respondents (see Gorsuch, 1980). To simplify the solution, analyses were limited to five factors with eigenvalues greater than one.

6.2.2 Results of factor analysis
Results of the four factor analyses are presented in Table 6.1. Of course, having chosen items grouped in four sections of the questionnaire, it is true that input to factor analysis was already structured. However, it is immediately clear from Table 6.1., and for present purposes more interesting, that respondents in the four countries saw the Community quite differently. For the W. Germans and the British, 'support' was the major factor to emerge, with both utilitarian and affective items loading above 0.50. For the Italians, the first factor was comprised of 'common policy and its effects'. Perhaps most interesting, the first factor for French respondents contained all four, and no other, items that dealt with 'agriculture'.

Table 6.1. *Loadings on first factor of principal components factor analysis*

	Country of respondent			
	W. Germany	Italy	France	U.K.
Common Policy				
1. Agriculture			0.80	
2. Transport		0.65		
3. Energy		0.67		
4. Environmental protection				
5. Defence		0.60		
Effects of Common Policy				
1. Agricultural productivity		0.68	0.52	
2. Agricultural produce		0.72	0.55	
3. Transport costs		0.63		
4. Efficiency of industries				
5. Freedom of movement		0.61		
6. Speaking with a single voice		0.54		
7. Reducing travel restrictions				
8. Increasing trade				
9. Reducing inequalities		0.57		
10. Social security benefits		0.66		
Utilitarian support				
1. Personal gain				0.54
2. Budget contribution				0.59
3. Country benefits	0.60			
4. Subsidise poor groups in other EEC countries			−0.76	0.56
5. Gain from C.A.P.				
6. Money to poorer groups in developing countries				
7. Gain from C.R.F.				
8. Less competitive	0.71			0.65
Affective support				
1. Increased national rivalries	0.53			0.62
2. Solidarity				0.62
3. Community interferes	0.63			0.53
4. Trust				0.63
5. Not confident				0.70
6. More loyal to Community				0.56
7. Should not help others	0.53			
8. Personal sacrifices				
Number of items with loadings greater than 0.50	5	10	4	10
Factor name	'support'	'Community policy and effects'	'agriculture'	'support'
Percentage variance accounted for	10.84%	17.54%	9.47%	13.74%
Sample size	126	135	142	129

Notes:
Items are presented in full in Appendix B.
Only factor loadings greater than 0.50 are shown.

If the content of these first factors does reveal cross-national differences, the complexity of views across countries is quite comparable. Although the Italians, especially, and British to some extent appear to have a rather less differentiated view (in terms of the percentage of variance accounted for by the first factor), it cannot be claimed that the nations differ substantially in the complexity of their views about the Community. Further evidence for this statement was provided by the very similar percentages of variance accounted for by all five factors in each country (W. Germany, 48%; Italy, 49%; France, 42%; U.K., 46%).

6.2.3 Discussion

This initial analysis corroborates Wober's (1980) conclusion that views about the European Community are multi-, rather than uni-, dimensional. In each of the four countries the first rotated factor accounted for between nine and 18% of the variance, which argues against any global tendency for respondents to see the Community in simple 'good–bad' terms (see also Feld and Wildgen, 1976). What is interesting is that the factorial structure uncovered, while similar in W. Germany and the U.K., was quite different for the Italians and French. This finding provides further support for the pattern of cross-national differences that emerged in Chapter 5. The relatively differentiated structure that emerged also suggests that respondents did complete the questionnaire in a thoughtful fashion, thus justifying the time spent here in trying to provide a clearer picture of their views about the Community.

6.3 Prediction of overall attitudes I: selection of variables
6.3.1 Multiple regression
Multiple regression is a general statistical technique that analyses the relationship between a dependent or criterion variable (in this case overall attitude to the Community) and a set of predictor variables (see Achen, 1982; Kerlinger, 1973). For present purposes multiple regression has two main uses:

(1)   As a simplifying tool, to give a summary of the overall contribution of the predictor variables to variation in the dependent variable (i.e. the relationship between the variables measured in the questionnaire and overall attitude). This involves finding the best linear prediction equation, and then evaluating its predictive accuracy.

(2)   As a tool for examining the structure of the complex interrelations of a set of variables.

   The first, descriptive, use is dealt with in this section; the second, model-building, approach ('path analysis') is covered in Section 6.4.

6.3.2 Initial regression analyses: selecting predictor variables

A first run of multiple regression analyses included all possible predictors. Many of these, such as sex and political affiliation (as dummy variables), did not improve prediction and were therefore dropped in subsequent analyses. The first all-inclusive analyses also resulted in large drops in the size of samples, due to missing data.[1] Further runs of the analysis excluded those variables which markedly reduced sample size in any country. In this way the study maintained a theoretically interesting set of predictor variables, and sample sizes of at least 100 respondents in each country. This set of predictors consisted of 13 variables: active interest; knowledge; time spent in other European countries; sum of expectancies plus values; common policy; utilitarian support; affective support; stereotyping score; preference for own country (national image); international relations; liking; effects of community policy; and travel in Europe.

Basic input to multiple regression analysis is the matrix of correlations between these 13 variables (see Appendix E, Tables E.1–E.4); most important here are the correlations between individual predictors and overall attitude (see the bottom line of the correlation matrices). It is clear that several variables correlated significantly with overall attitude and that one variable yielded the highest positive correlation in each country – affective support. Thus there is one basic commonality between nations. The other variables which correlated highly with the criterion in all countries were: sum of expectancies plus values; common policy; and utilitarian support.[2]

Several variables also had consistently low correlations with overall attitude – for example, knowledge;[3] the contact variables ('time' and 'travel'); stereotyping; liking and preference for own country[4] – and would not appear to be central to public information and election campaigns. However, these variables may still play a role in a general model of Community attitudes, as is seen below. These simple correlations do not identify the independent effects of the predictor variables, some of which are highly intercorrelated. Thus further analyses must be undertaken to provide a more succinct model of attitudes towards the Community. To this end, multiple regression was used to compute a single measure of the relationship between the overall attitude and all the predictor variables taken together (Andrews *et al.*, 1974).

6.3.3 Results of multiple regression analyses in four independent samples

Using multiple regression might be termed an attempt to worship the twin gods of explanation and prediction. The adjusted R^2 statistic (adjusted for the number of independent variables in the equation and the number of cases) is used here as a conservative measure of explanation, indicating the proportion of variance explained.[5] Prediction accuracy 'in absolute units' (Kim and Kohout, 1975) is reflected by the standard error of estimate for the regression equation, which has the same unit of measurement as the dependent variable. Both statistics are reported below.

Multiple regression with all possible subsets (see Frane, 1981) was computed to identify the 'best' subset of the 13 predictor variables, using the maximisation of R^2 as a criterion.[6] Table 6.2 shows that the best subset in each of the four countries, except France, explained a large percentage of the variance (see adjusted R^2). Absolute prediction was, however, somewhat more accurate in Italy, where overall attitudes predicted from the eight-variable best subset would only differ from actual scores by, on average, 0.85 units on the (7-point) attitude scale. In all countries a good degree of predictive accuracy was indicated by the value of the standard error. It should also be noted that (because not all predictor variables included in the equation are significant) the best subset procedure is an over-inclusive approach. This is to be expected, because the 'maximising R^2' criterion includes all variables which contribute minimally to R^2 (i.e. which have an F-to-enter above 1). Closer analysis of the smaller subsets of best predictors revealed that in every country two- or three-variable equations were almost as good as those provided by the 'best' subset. In other words, relative gain with increasing number of independent variables is small. Kerlinger acknowledges this point in writing that, 'because many variables of behavioral research are correlated, additional variables may prove redundant with the first 3–4 of the equation'. (1973, p. 625.)

Although Table 6.2 shows clear differences between the four countries with respect to the variables included in the best subset, the measures of affective and utilitarian support, and expectancy-value yielded the highest standardised regression coefficients (beta weights). The inclusion and weight of variables in the equation is dependent on their correlation with other variables. Thus in the U.K., for example, affective support alone yielded a value of $R^2 = 0.37$; however, it correlated highly with other variables (e.g. sum of expectancy-value; utilitarian support) and is not significant in the best subset (this important issue of the interrelations between predictor variables is treated in the following section). Generally, it is interesting to note that measures of utilitarian and affective support were highly correlated in every country (W. Germany, $+0.52$; Italy, $+0.50$; France, $+0.33$; U.K., $+0.77$), although they both entered the best subset, except in W. Germany. The fact that the two variables, at least as measured here, were so highly intercorrelated is considered in more detail, below.

Table 6.2. Multiple regression with 'best' possible subset of predictor variables for overall attitude

Predictor variables	Country of respondent				All
	W. Germany	Italy	France	U.K.	
Active interest	0.15*	0.12	0.14	0.17*	0.17**
Knowledge	0.10	-0.17*	-0.10	-0.12	-0.08*
Time spent in other European countries		0.10			0.04
Sum of expectancies plus values	0.21*	0.15	-0.18*	0.24**	0.20**
Common policy	0.19*		0.15	0.15*	0.06
Utilitarian support	0.46**	0.12	0.15	0.26**	0.12**
Affective support	0.09	0.38**		0.18	0.33**
Preference for own country		0.18*	0.10		0.07
International relations		0.13	-0.20	0.13	0.09*
Liking	-0.11			0.21**	0.09*
Effects of community policy			0.21		
Stereotyping score			-0.12	0.10	
Travel					-0.10*
Dummy 1 (U.K./rest)					-0.10*
Dummy 2 (W. Germany/rest)					-0.19**
Multiple R	0.69	0.63	0.50	0.76	0.66
Adjusted R^2	0.45	0.35	0.18	0.55	0.42
Standard error of estimate	1.15	0.85	1.04	1.44	1.27
Number of variables in equation	7	8	9	9	10(+2)
Sample size	117	107	115	118	457

Notes:
**$p < 0.01$.
*$p < 0.05$.
Scores are standardised regression coefficients (beta weights).

6.3.4 The 'best' subset of predictor variables for all respondents

To select variables for use in the path analysis reported below, the same multiple regression was computed for all respondents together, with three dummy variables to measure the influence of nationality. This analysis provided a ten-variable best subset (excluding two dummy variables, for W. Germany and the U.K.). It should be noted that this subset is still over-inclusive (three variables are not significant) and the BMDP program (see Frane, 1981) advises that all variables selected for the final equation should have significant *t*-statistics for their standardised regression coefficients. However, all variables were retained, with appropriate caution, for path analyses which are both comprehensive and comparable across samples (in terms of number of predictors and sample size).[7] The inclusion of all ten variables can also be defended on theoretical grounds, following Achen's (1982) advice that, 'any choice among competing regressions is to some extent arbitrary. No choice makes sense outside a theoretical context in which a variety of competing explanations have been tried'. (p. 67.) Thus variables were chosen in such a way that the statistical tool remained the slave and not the master.

The two significant dummy variables which appear in the best subset (see Table 6.2.) were significant and have been used to justify separate path analyses, albeit with exactly the same predictor variables, for each country. This has advantages in terms of comprehensibility – the effects of dummy variables are difficult to 'see' – and also provides four independent 'tests' in the attempt to build a model of Community attitudes.

6.3.5 Discussion

Multiple regression analyses revealed considerable overlap between the set of predictor variables as intuition, theory and previous statistical work (Kerlinger, 1973) would lead one to believe. From the set of 13 variables it was possible to identify a relatively small subset which could successfully be used to account for the variation in, and to predict the absolute value of, overall attitudes.

The accuracy of explanation and prediction was not equivalent across national samples, which may perhaps be due to such factors as differential variation in the predictor and/or criterion variables, or the omission of particular variables which predict attitudes in a given country. Notwithstanding this cross-national variation, it was still possible to explain between 18% and 55% of the variation in attitudes towards the Community, or 42% for the sample as a whole. These are highly satisfactory results in terms of specifying the structure of Community attitudes, and indicating which predictors are most important. However, multiple regression is still limited insofar as it:

> assigns to each independent variable some of the explainable variance in
> the dependent variable which that independent variable shares with other
> independent variables. (Andrews *et al.*, 1974, p. 18)

Thus we may know *which* variables predict attitudes, but not *how*, in terms
of direct or indirect effects. We now want a statistic (e.g. path coefficient):

> which measures the additional proportion of the total variance in the
> dependent variable explainable by each independent variable, over and
> above what the other independent variables can explain. (*ibid.*)

In other words, we want to know whether, for example, utilitarian and
affective support can really be treated as independent influences on overall
attitude, and whether they have a direct or indirect effect. To answer these
questions, path analysis was used.

6.4 Prediction of overall attitudes II: path-analytic models
6.4.1 *Path analysis*

Multiple regression analyses are still limited to the estimation of direct effects
of a set of independent or predictor variables on the dependent variable. Use
of multiple regression techniques in conjunction with a causal theory, path
analysis (see Blalock, 1964; Kerlinger and Pedhazur, 1973), shifts the
emphasis to a description of the entire structure of linkages between
predictor variables and dependent variables. The general aim of path analysis is the specification of a causal model, based on information about relationships of correlation between the variables (Brandstädter and Bernitzke,
1976). Both direct and indirect effects of one variable on another are
measured, and the relative importance of alternative paths of influence can
be estimated. Thus path analysis has important advantages for model-testing,
and the very act of constructing a path diagram and thinking about the
direction of effects may be of heuristic value in itself (Asher, 1983; Duncan,
1966). It is, however, up to the researcher to propose a model. This involves
specifying the relationships between the predictor variables and the ultimate
dependent variable of interest, and between the prior variables themselves.

    Causation cannot, of course, be demonstrated directly, but the variables
can be arranged in a plausible order. This 'weak order assumption' is the
basic prerequisite for path analysis. To have confidence in a model it must
be possible to order the variables in a temporal sequence and this is not
always easy, or even possible, to do, especially when, as in the present study,
the data are drawn from a cross-sectional survey. For the present data, for
example, does active interest precede knowledge, or *vice versa?* In fact, with
the subset of ten variables derived from multiple regression, almost all that
one can say with some degree of confidence is that people learn stereotypes
at a very young age (see Lambert and Klineberg, 1967), and thus that liking

and images can probably be considered causally prior to the other variables. Caution is also in order, because this study was openly exploratory – its aim being to generate and test various models. It was thus not possible to follow exactly Asher's (1983) advice on the use of causal modelling: 'begin with a model in which one has substantial confidence'. (p. 10.) However, the variables were generated on the basis of previous theoretical work, and considerable thought was given to the ordering of variables in the first path models constructed. Having then tested various models on one sample, it was possible to test the chosen model on the other samples with reasonable, if not substantial, confidence (this is essentially analogous to a 'split-sample' strategy for testing hypotheses which were generated using one sample on a further sample; see Macdonald, 1977).

The application of path analysis can be considered in four steps (see Brandstädter and Bernitzke, 1976), each of which is considered in the following pages:

(1)   proposal of a hypothetical causal model;
(2)   path-diagrammatic representation of the causal model;
(3)   estimation of path coefficients on the basis of empirical correlations between the model's variables;
(4)   reproduction of the correlations obtained in the path-analytic solution.

6.4.2 Path-analysis methodology.[8]

Selection of independent variables

A first set of path analyses was computed using the ten predictor variables which appeared in the best subset of multiple regression using all respondents. However, these analyses contained path coefficients greater than unity, probably indicating the problem of multi-collinearity (Asher, 1983). Essentially this means that correlations between the 'independent' variables were too high (the variables were not independent of each other). In these analyses the problem was primarily due to the overlap between four variables: utilitarian support; affective support; judgements of common policy; and international relations.

Asher (*op. cit.*, p. 52) suggests three practical solutions to this problem:

(1)   Eliminate one or more of the highly correlated independent variables from the regression equation.
(2)   Combine the collinear variables into an index or scale.
(3)   Use factor analysis to identify a smaller number of less correlated indicators.

Given the theoretical interest in keeping utilitarian and affective support separate, option (3) was attempted first. Factor analysis with varimax rotation was computed on the 16 support items, and limited to five factors. Although a number of items loaded satisfactorily on their intended factor, the pattern varied from country to country and this argues against using the factor structure for all respondents together (see Appendix E, Table E.5). The exclusion of items without clear loadings on only one factor is also unattractive, because some of the best predictor items are then lost. It should, furthermore, be noted that the factors which emerged were rather mixed. For example, looking at the factor structure for all respondents together, the quintessential affective support item ('sense of solidarity') in fact loaded highly on a factor with gain (personal, national, from the Common Agricultural Policy, and from the Community Regional Fund), which is explicitly utilitarian. It would therefore appear that the utilitarian-affective distinction, while theoretically appealing, has no empirical basis on the strength of these items and the present samples. Thus Asher's second suggestion was taken up, and the two separate bases of support were collapsed into an index of 'support'.

Path analyses were computed again, but still there were path coefficients above unity. It was therefore necessary to follow option (1) as well and exclude two collinear variables – common policy and international relations – which were not major predictors of attitude, as shown by a modest reduction of the value of R^2 in the new analysis.[9]

Ordering the variables
Variables were ordered in three blocks, beginning with the 'basic' social-psychological variables, assumed to be developmentally and causally prior to the others: liking; national image; and time spent in other European countries ('contact'). The second block of variables consisted of the three core summary scores from the questionnaire: support; sum of expectancies plus values; and knowledge. Finally, placed immediately prior to the dependent variable, overall attitude, was active interest. This analysis allows only for links in one direction, *from* the basic social-psychological variables, the summary scores and active interest *to* overall attitude, and not *vice versa*; in addition, the basic social-psychological variables can influence the summary scores, and the latter can in turn influence active interest. It may be objected that the unidirectional causality of this recursive model is artificial; however, this simplification of reality is orthodox. As a number of methodologists point out, the recursive model is a fairly standard approach and is considerably less problematic than non-recursive path analysis which retains the notion of reciprocal causation (see Blalock, 1971; Macdonald, 1977).

Within blocks, variables were ordered on theoretical grounds, again allowing for influence in a specified direction. 'Liking' was entered first, given the developmental primacy of national prejudices and preferences, followed by 'national image'. 'Contact' was chosen as the third variable in the first group, because it was assumed that many respondents travelled before they developed ideas about the Community. In the second group of variables, 'support' was chosen first, given its general nature and its centrality in the political science literature. The more specific 'expectancy-value' measure was entered second, followed by knowledge. 'Active interest' was entered alone in the third group, because according to Fishbein and Ajzen (1975), this behavioural intention can be predicted from the expectancy-value measure.

Interpreting the path-analytic models

The path-analytic model used consisted of a series of multiple regressions in which first overall attitude, and then each of the remaining variables, served as criterion variable. The number of predictor variables was successively reduced to the number of predictors considered to be causally prior. Path diagrams are presented separately for each of the four countries, in view of the significant effects of (W. German and British) dummy variables in the earlier multiple regression.

The strength of paths in each figure is indicated by the size of standardised path coefficients, based on simultaneous regression to all preceding variables. This path coefficient represents the direct effect of the predictor variable on the dependent variable (i.e. with the effects of all other variables partialled out). A path coefficient approaching the value of unity denotes a strong direct effect. The variance explained by the direct effect is the fraction of the variance that would be found if all other causal variables were held constant (Land, 1969). In the figures, one-way arrows lead *from* each determining variable *to* each variable dependent on it. To facilitate interpretation of the figures, path coefficients which are not significant ($p > 0.05$) have been omitted, except for marginally significant paths to overall attitude.[10] Where a predictor variable has an indirect effect, on overall attitude for example, this may be evident from the fact that the simple correlation between the two measures is substantially higher than the path coefficient (for a direct effect this is not so). An indirect effect is the amount of covariation due to variation that the designated variable shares with other correlates of the criterion variable. The indirect effect can be computed as the difference between the correlation and the path coefficient for the direct effect. Thus where a correlation is relatively high and a path coefficient relatively low, the indirect effect tends to be strong.

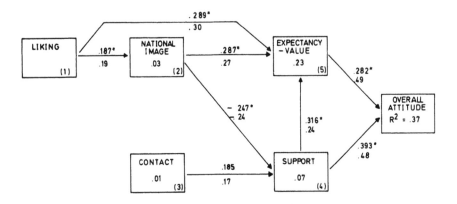

Note. Path coefficients given to three significant figures (* = p < .01); correlations given to two significant figures. Adjusted R^2 for successive variables is reported inside the boxes. Numbers in parentheses denote order of variables in the analysis (variables not shown: knowledge, 6, and active interest, 7). Standard error of estimate for overall attitude = 1.22.

Fig. 6.1. Path analysis with overall attitude as dependent variable (W. German sample, N = 120).

6.4.3 Results of path analyses in four independent samples

The results of path analyses computed for each country separately are shown in Figures 6.1–6.4.

Federal Republic of Germany (adjusted $R^2 = 0.37$, standard error of estimate = 1.22)

Only two variables, expectancy-value and support, had a significant direct effect on overall attitude. The path coefficient for support is the highest of all, and this variable also exerted an indirect influence on attitudes via the expectancy-value measure. Having identified two main predictors, it is also clear from Figure 6.1 that both expectancy-value and support were, in turn, influenced by prior variables. National image had a direct effect on both predictors, although the signs of the correlations are different. A positive image of one's own country was positively related to expectancy-value score, but negatively related to support. The latter relationship is the more intuitively correct, because one would not expect support for the European Community to be associated with an ethnocentric view of one's own country. Contact also had a direct effect on support, indicating that the more travelled respondents expressed more support for the Community. Finally, national image was related to liking, as one would expect: people who like their own nationality more, tend to have a positive image of their own country. Liking also had a direct effect on expectancy-value, which parallels the effect of national image.

This path diagram thus shows how well overall attitudes can be accounted

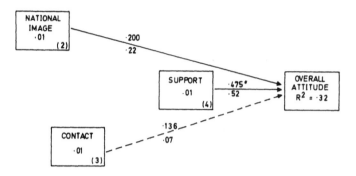

Note. Path coefficients given to three significant figures (* = $p < .01$); correlations given to two significant figures. Adjusted R^2 for successive variables is reported inside the boxes. Numbers in parentheses denote order of variables in the analysis (variables not shown: liking, 1, expectancy-value, 5, knowledge, 6, and active interest, 7). Standard error of estimate for overall attitude = 0.86. Broken line indicates non-significant direct path ($p < .10$, $> .05$) to overall attitude.

Fig. 6.2. Path analysis with overall attitude as dependent variable (Italian sample, $M = 117$).

for by these seven variables (two of which are not shown), and identifies support as the major predictor. It is, however, interesting that the basic social-psychological variables – liking, national image and contact – although having no direct impact on attitudes, did relate to the best predictors.

Italy (adjusted $R^2 = 0.32$, standard error of estimate = 0.86)
The path diagram for Italian respondents, see Figure 6.2, is very simple and yet also accounts for a large percentage of variance in the criterion variable, and predicts to a fine degree. Support, as for the W. Germans, was the major predictor, with a very large and highly significant path coefficient for its direct effect on attitude. There were no indirect effects, although national image also had a direct effect on attitude. Interestingly, the sign of the correlation for this effect is positive, while for the W. Germans it was negative. This is consistent with the view stated earlier, that for Italians the Community may be viewed positively because it is good for their own country. Finally, contact had a marginally significant direct effect on attitude, indicating again some effect of European travel on pro-European views.

France ($R^2 = 0.12$, standard error of estimate = 1.09)
As in W. Germany and Italy, the strongest direct effect on overall attitude came from support (see Figure 6.3). Also following the model for W. Germany, support had an indirect effect, although only marginally significant, via expectancy-value. This latter variable, and active interest, also exerted

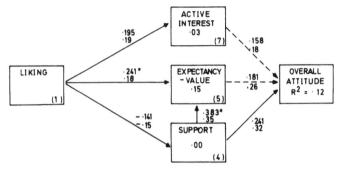

Note. Path coefficients given to three significant figures (* = p < .01); correlations given to two significant figures. Adjusted R^2 for successive variables is reported inside the boxes. Numbers in parentheses denote order of variables in the analysis (variables not shown: national image, 2, contact, 3, and knowledge, 6). Standard error of estimate for overall attitude = 1.09. Broken line indicates non-significant direct paths (p < .10, > .05) to overall attitude.

Fig. 6.3. Path analysis with overall attitude as dependent variable (French sample, M = 120).

non-signficant direct effects on overall attitude. All three variables having some impact on attitudes could be traced back to liking. Preference for one's own people was positively associated with active interest and, as in W. Germany, the expectancy-value score; the relationship between liking and support, however, was negative. Increased liking for one's own nationality was associated with decreased support for the Community.

This model is quite simple but, unlike that for Italy, is disappointing in terms of accounting for variance in the dependent variable. This may be partly due to the weaker effect of support in the French sample and, as was seen in the earlier factor analysis, the first factor for French respondents was comprised of items concerning agriculture, not support. However, ratings of the success of, or gains from, this policy were not particularly highly correlated with overall attitude (-0.20 and $+0.16$, respectively). Alternatively, this low value of R^2 may indicate that some central aspect of French views about the Community has been omitted in the present study.

U.K. ($R^2 = 0.55$, standard error of estimate = 1.22)
The most successful model, in terms of variance accounted for, was also the most complex, as shown in Figure 6.4. Five predictors had significant direct effects on overall attitude, three of them highly significant. Consistent with the picture gleaned from the three other countries, support was again the major predictor, acting directly on attitude and indirectly via both expectancy-value and active interest. The next most important predictors were expectancy-value, which acted directly and also indirectly, and the behavioural intention measure of intended active interest. The effect of

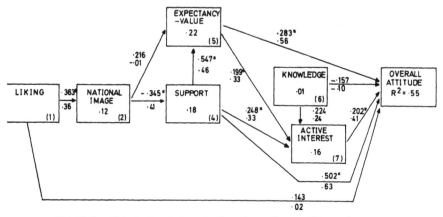

Note. Path coefficients given to three significant figures (* = p < .01); correlations given to two significant figures. Adjusted R² for successive variables is reported inside the boxes. Numbers in parentheses denote order of variables in the analysis (variable not shown: contact, 3). Standard error of estimate for overall attitude = 1.22.

Fig. 6.4. Path analysis with overall attitude as dependent variable (U.K. sample, N = 120).

expectancy-value on active interest is thus consistent with Fishbein and Ajzen's (1975) model, whereby the estimate of attitude also predicts behavioural intention.

In addition, liking had a direct positive effect on attitudes, which parallels the direct effect of national image for the Italians. For the British, liking for one's own people does not stand in the way of pro-Community attitudes. The final direct effect, for knowledge, was negative. Increased knowledge appears weakly associated with more negative attitudes, although knowledge also acted indirectly via active interest, which was positively related to attitudes. This effect of knowledge should, however, be interpreted with caution, and may be an artefact. Due to the distribution of knowledge scores, we do not really know how highly knowledgeable respondents view the Community.

Thus support, especially, and expectancy-value dominate this model in terms of both direct and indirect effects. They were both, in turn, influenced by the basic social-psychological variables – national image and liking. Preference for one's own country was positively associated with support for the Community (in contrast to the finding in W. Germany), but negatively associated with expectancy-value; liking for one's own people was positively associated with preference for one's own country.

Reproduction of the obtained correlations
As noted above, while path analysis will not prove causality when using correlational data, it allows one to test whether the data are consistent with

a specified causal model (or models). However, a procedure is needed to evaluate the adequacy of the model(s) specified. This procedure asks the question, to what extent can the model reproduce the actual correlation between variables? Discrepancies between the reproduced and original correlational matrices indicate that the theoretical causal structure is *not* compatible with the obtained correlational data. In practice the criterion used for determining whether deviations between original and reproduced correlations are 'significant' is whether the correlations differ by more than 0.05 or 0.10 (see Asher, 1983; Brandstädter and Bernitzke, 1976).

For the present study chi-square analyses were used to compare the original and reproduced correlation matrices (see separate appendix F, Tables F.1–F.4, for details) and thus provide a measure of 'goodness of fit'. In no sample was there evidence for a difference between original and reproduced correlation matrices (W. Germans, $\chi^2(14) = 0.92$; Italians, $\chi^2(12) = 0.39$; French, $\chi^2(11) = 0.89$; British, $\chi^2(17) = 0.73$).[11] It should, however, be emphasised that this support for the model only confirms its plausibility; it does not establish its empirical validity. There will normally be several models that yield identical predictions, and although a model with more causal arrows will better reproduce the original correlation matrix, it will not necessarily have higher empirical validity.

6.4.4 Discussion

The results of the four path analyses are impressive in terms of both predictive accuracy and explained variance, accounting for between 30% and 55% of the variance in attitudes, except in France. The results are also parsimonious, in providing such statistics on the basis of only seven independent variables. Of course, all but two of these variables are composite measures, but the analyses have nonetheless successfully separated the wheat from the chaff, in terms of predictors.

The exact nature of the path-analytic model varies across the four countries, but commonalities are apparent. There are three key variables on which to focus our attention – support; expectancy-value; and active interest. Support has the strongest direct path to attitudes in every country, and is especially influential in W. Germany, Italy and the U.K. It is also a key mediating variable, having an indirect effect via one or two other variables in both W. Germany and the U.K.

The expectancy-value total score is also highly significant in W. Germany and the U.K., marginally so in France, but not at all in Italy. Active interest is only significantly related to attitudes in the U.K. (although marginally so in France), where it relates to both knowledge and expectancy-value. The results across countries are also consistent in pointing to the influence of the basic social-psychological variables. Only in Italy and the U.K. did national image and liking, respectively, have direct effects on attitude, but in all countries except Italy there were significant direct paths from one or more of these variables to the more central measures of support and expectancy-value. Thus the marriage of general social-psychological views about peoples and countries to more specific judgements about the Community is successful.

Notwithstanding the generality (cross-national validity) of a model centred on support and expectancy-value, differences between countries were also evident. Moreover, the four nations could be subdivided in the same way as for the univariate analyses. In Italy and France, the model of attitudes was limited to three or four predictor variables, with an emphasis on support. In W. Germany and the U.K., however, five and six predictors, respectively, constituted the model and indirect effects were much more in evidence. It is particularly interesting to note the importance of the expectancy-value measure, in addition to support. This finding suggests a more critical and differentiated view on the part of W. German and British respondents, who judge the Community as a function of its stated goals and the extent to which they are being achieved.

To return to the poor performance of the model in the case of the French sample, it is of course to be expected that not all variation can be explained. Following Blalock (1971), there are at least three possible reasons for the obtained results: (1) the 'wrong' set of predictors has been used, where the 'right' set would increase the percentage of variance explained; (2) there may be a very large number of relevant predictors and many more of these need to be considered simultaneously to improve explanation; and (3) the 'right' set of predictors may have been used, but error may have arisen due to inadequate measurement.[12] Given the performance of the model using the other sets of data, the third possibility seems unlikely, thus leaving the broad option of including more predictors. Further analyses on the French sample (including those variables highlighted by factor analysis) still failed to achieve a substantial improvement in prediction; this suggests that new variables might be included in a further study. It is interesting to note that other authors have also found differences between French and other national samples, in terms of political attitudes. Converse and Dupeux (1962) reported that voter loyalty is lower in France than in the U.S. and they suggested that subtle ideological differences might blur the partisanship of the electorate. Greenstein and Tarrow (1969) have also reported on the distinctiveness of political socialisation in France. It may, then, be that future work should look in more detail at French political beliefs and understanding in general.

In sum, path analyses deliver a clear, concise message about the underlying structure of Community attitudes. The model is not exactly the same for the four independent samples, but the basic similarities attest to its generality. This increases confidence in the importance of key variables, support and expectancy-value, on which attention is centred throughout this volume.

6.5 Classification of respondents with positive and negative attitudes
6.5.1 Discriminant analysis
To complete the multivariate analyses, step-wise discriminant analyses (Jennrich and Sampson, 1981; Klecka, 1980) were computed. The aim of discriminant analysis is to weight and linearly combine the discriminating variables, in this case the same ten independent variables derived from regression, so as to help distinguish between 'groups' of interest, in this case those respondents with positive and negative overall attitudes to the Community.[13] The full set of independent variables was retained, because the step-wise procedure begins by selecting one most discriminating variable and does not encounter the problem of multi-collinearity. This analysis does then give a useful indication of what the single, major classificatory variable is.

Discriminant analyses were computed for the German and British samples, because only these countries contained a substantial number of respondents with negative attitudes (see Appendix D, Table D.5). A positive–negative, rather than median-split, criterion was used, because the practical issue is not so much whether someone is more or less positive or negative about the Community, but whether he or she is 'for' or 'against' (respondents with scores of 0 were excluded from this analysis). Discriminant analysis provides two very useful pieces of information (see Himmelweit *et al.*, 1981) which will help any reader to understand which variables are central, and how successful they are in classifying respondents:

(1)   a measure of the *overall accuracy* of the classification, in terms of the percentage of respondents correctly classified by the analysis, broken down by the two 'groups' of interest;[14]

(2)   a measure of *which independent variable* (that selected first) contributes most to the classification.

6.5.2 Results and discussion
Very high percentage accuracy of classification, for both national samples, was achieved (see Table 6.3). The accuracy is almost equally high for respondents with positive and negative attitudes. As expected, following multiple regression and path analyses, support – and specifically 'affective' support – emerged as the most powerful classificatory variable (always having the largest F-to-enter). In fact, using only the summary score of eight items originally intended to measure affective support, the percentage

Table 6.3 *Accuracy of classification of W. German and British respondents with positive and negative attitudes, using discriminant analysis*

(A) W. Germany

Actual attitude	% correct	No. of cases classified into each group	
		Negative attitude	Positive attitude
Negative	75.9	22	7
Positive	78.6	15	55
Total	77.8	37	62

Note:
Independent variables used in best classification (in order of F – to remove): affective support; common policy.

(B) U.K.

Actual attitude	% correct	No. of cases classified into each group	
		Negative attitude	Positive attitude
Negative	82.1	32	7
Positive	81.9	13	59
Total	82.0	45	66

Note:
Independent variables used in best classification function (in order of F – to remove): affective support, active interest; common policy; liking.

accuracy in W. Germany and the U.K. was almost as high as that achieved for the optimal discriminant function (75.8% and 78.4%; *cf.*, Table 6.3). Interestingly, in W. Germany affective support alone did not predict those with positive attitudes (72.9%) as well as those with negative attitudes (82.8%), while the reverse was true in the U.K. (81.9% and 71.8%). It is in accounting for both types of respondent that the optimal solutions are superior.

Thus discriminant analyses provide a further measure of the importance of support in classifying respondents with positive and negative attitudes. As noted earlier, this measure of 'affective' support is not pure, in the sense of distinct from utilitarian support. However, the results of these analyses underline that, in the two countries where negative attitudes were widely found, the items selected as measures of affective support (and of which the content is intuitively 'affective', e.g. 'solidarity', 'trust' and 'confidence') are most powerful in classifying respondents according to the valence of their overall attitudes towards the Community.

6.6 Conclusions

Using a series of multivariate techniques, it has been possible to build a general model of attitudes towards the European Community. This understanding of Community attitudes has implications for further studies on attitude development and change, and suggests a number of variables that should be included in future studies of public opinion about Europe.

Considering first the findings of factor analysis and multiple regression, it was shown that respondents in the four countries do not differ in the relative complexity of their views, but that they do perceive matters somewhat differently. Using the predictor variables identified by multiple regression, path analysis clarified matters further. It showed, first, that the distinction between utilitarian and affective support, while conceptually appealing and useful, was not empirically tenable. This finding corroborates the conception of Wildgen and Feld, that: 'The two sources of support are not necessarily orthogonal or uncorrelated. Indeed, the two in actual day-to-day politics are often hard to distinguish.' (1976, p. 78.) It may still be quite possible to generate items which are distinct measures of utilitarian and affective support, but this was not demonstrated in the present study (as shown by a factor analysis on the 16 support items). Rather than forcing the issue, it was decided to collapse the items into a 'support index' and this did prove a powerful, indeed by far the most powerful, predictor of Community attitudes.

The role of support was clear in each of the four path analyses. The correlations between overall attitude and the individual items of the support index indicate further which issues form the basis of Community attitudes (see Appendix E, Table E.6). For the section originally titled affective support, correlations were highest in general for the three items measuring 'solidarity', 'trust' and 'confidence'. For the section originally conceived as an index of utilitarian support, correlations were highest in general for the two items measuring 'personal gain' and 'own country has benefited'. These latter correlations, which are especially high for the British sample, reinforce the view that, 'favourable economic payoffs are conducive to – and perhaps even essential to – the processes of national and supranational integration'. (Inglehart and Rabier, 1978, p.69.)

The path analyses also partly upheld the attitudinal approach of Fishbein and Ajzen (1975), albeit using an additive (rather than multiplicative) combination of expectancies and values. The expectancy-value measure yielded strong direct paths to overall attitude for both W. Germans and Britons, and was marginally significant in France. Only in the U.K. did this measure also have a direct effect on active interest, which in turn had a direct effect on attitude. The influence of active interest, although limited to the

British, is consistent with Handley's (1981) finding that when saliency of European affairs is increased (e.g. in election campaigns), attitudinal support for Europe tends also to increase. Feld and Wildgen (1976) also reported that of three measures of cognitive mobilisation – knowledge, interest and media exposure – interest accounted for the most variation in support for European unification. Correlations between overall attitude and individual expectancy-value ratings were also computed (see Appendix E, Table E.7) and revealed high correlations for several items. The most important goals were 'bringing about a United States of Europe', 'strengthening Europe's role in the world' and 'achieving greater mutual understanding between European nations'.[15]

To some extent, the study can claim success in simply identifying these linkages between support, expectancy-value, active interest and overall attitude. It was therefore an added bonus to find that the causal model could be traced back further. The basic social-psychological variables of liking, national image and contact (time spent in other European countries) tended to relate to the main variables.

That contact had a direct effect on overall attitude or support (in Italy and W. Germany respectively) is particularly interesting. Of course, it could be argued that attitudes or support would lead people to undertake foreign travel, but it seems reasonable to assume that many people travel in Europe *before* their ideas about the Community develop. Thus, following Inglehart (1971), at least part of this linkage would appear due to an influence from travel to attitudes (hence the ordering of variables in path analysis). As noted earlier, travel has also been accorded an important role in international relations by other scholars (see Deutsch's pluralist approach, and his, 1961, notion of 'social mobilization'; and Kelman's, 1965a, functionalist approach with its emphasis on social interaction). The present findings accord contact a more modest, but more specific, role. They would seem to support further research like that of Farquarson and Holt (1975), dealing with the building of 'Europe from below' by means of twin towns, sporting and educational exchanges and so on.

Liking for own and other nationalities (which was related to stereotypes; see correlation matrices in Appendix E, Tables E.1–E.4) might be considered a measure of what Lindberg and Scheingold (1970) call 'identitive support' – a link with other peoples of the Community, not just political institutions. Apparently such support, like contact and national images, plays only a limited role in influencing overall attitudes, but did nonetheless appear in the path diagrams.

The other variable included in path analyses – knowledge – had negligible impact on attitudes, except in the U.K. In this country knowledge had a direct, but negative, effect, indicating that the more knowledgeable were less positively inclined towards the Community.[16] Although this result may be unreliable, it may occur because issues arising from Community membership became so highly politicised in the U.K. that opponents of membership have become better informed. This variable may then have worked in the same way as cognitive mobilisation, as discussed by Inglehart (1970b). Cognitive mobilisation only increases awareness of the content of, for example, the mass media. If the message is then negative, the more highly cognitively mobilised (or knowledgeable) may be less 'European'.

The final discriminant analyses in W. Germany and the U.K. provided further evidence for the importance of support. In both countries the items originally chosen to measure affective support proved the most accurate in classifying respondents according to positive or negative attitudes. This finding suggests that, to (re)capture the hearts and minds of its opponents, the Community will have to work to improve levels of solidarity, trust and confidence. This general idea of solidarity, central to the work of Inglehart (e.g. Inglehart, 1970b; Inglehart and Rabier, 1978), is considered in more detail below.

In conclusion, the multivariate approach, treating large numbers of variables simultaneously in one analysis, has delivered its payload. Some predictors of Community attitudes have been identified, and a general model developed which can be applied to each of these four member states. In considering the model, one should ask what kind of theory is necessary or useful in this area (see Blalock, 1971). The model advanced follows Blalock's guide in its focus on a small number of variables that are directly linked to the dependent variable of interest, or that are indirectly linked to overall attitude by only one or two steps in a causal sequence. It is argued that such a model goes beyond common sense, but can also lead to specific hypotheses which could be tested in future research. As Blalock writes: 'Don't be afraid to oversimplify reality. It will then always be possible to introduce complexities a few at a time.' (1971, p. 196.) Thus the major aim of the present work has been realised. The implications of these findings for future research, public information campaigns and the Community's well-being are now considered in the final chapter.

7 Conclusion: findings and implications

> If Europe sometimes seems like a dream come untrue, it is because the
> dream is open to so many interpretations.
>
> *(The Times,* 9 March, 1985)

As was emphasised in the opening chapter, Europe is 'a historical concept,
emerging from the crucible of the past 15 centuries'. (Battaglia, 1957, p.
2.) Thus Spinelli (1966) refers to the idea of unifying Europe as a spectre
in search of incarnation. The European Community or Common Market is
the contemporary version of this spectre and since its founding it has been
one of the centrepieces of political and economic debate. Its value is still
fiercely contested by supporters and detractors within the member states (see
Kaiser, Merlini, Montbrial, Wellenstein and Wallace, 1983), while there is
no shortage of countries seeking to become members themselves.

The verdict on the Community, even by its supporters, is sometimes harsh.
Thus Piet Dankert (1983) has argued that: 'The European Community is
in a bad way. Mobility and dynamism have given way to stagnation and
passivity.' (p. 8.) Inevitably, such views have filtered down to (if not bubbled
up from) the citizens of the Community themselves. How do they view the
Community? Inglehart (1984), reviewing public opinion from 1970–84 in
a report for the Commission of the European Communities, paints a
depressing picture: 'What is perceived, is a process of endless bureaucratic
infighting; the European spirit seems to have died sometime during the
1960s. The European movement no longer captures the imagination of the
most educated and politically involved stratum to the extent that it once did.'
(p.17.) Thus the level of *attitudinal* integration would appear to be low. The
present work has used a social-psychological approach to investigate this
phenomenon in greater depth and to attempt to provide a model of the
structure underlying Community attitudes. Such a model, if successful,
should be of use in understanding how and why Community attitudes
develop, and in implementing changes to improve the attitudinal basis of
support for the Community.

Although there has clearly been no paucity of economic or political
comment on the European Community, there had been almost no input of

a social-psychological nature prior to the present work. This is the vacuum that this study has attempted to fill. It is in some sense ironic that social psychologists have contributed so little to the debate. In his pioneering exposition of the value of social psychology for the study of international relations, Kelman suggested that one of: 'the problems to which social-psychological research will increasingly address itself... (are) the ideological underpinnings for such supranational agencies as the European Economic Community'. (Kelman, 1965*a*, p. 12.) The present study has been concerned with that broad area outlined by Kelman which involves the study of social attitudes, opinions, images, beliefs and values (rather than, for example, cross-national contacts between individuals from the different Community countries). These attitudes are certainly individually held, but as Kelman emphasised they are socially determined (see also Eiser, 1982). Thus the foregoing chapters have paid considerable attention to the larger societal context within which attitudes develop. Maintaining this broad approach, this final chapter highlights the key findings of the research and spells out some central implications for research and practice.

7.1 Findings
7.1.1 Social representations and social attitudes
The first stage of the empirical research uncovered some of the common-sense ideas about the Community which were spontaneously generated in response to open-ended questions. Most respondents were able to list both positive and negative aspects of the Community, while a small number of them were wildly enthusiastic or vehemently negative. Knowledge of the principles and goals of the Community was however limited, although views about one common policy – agriculture – were richer and, notably, more negative in content. This finding is consistent with Slater's (1983) analysis of 'popular indifference' to the Community: 'There is little public understanding of or interest in the Community. Clearly, the work of the Community is not something that has captured the imagination or interest of the public. A difficult problem for the Community is that where it has attracted public attention, the publicity is all too often negative.' (p. 77.) More than one person in four (taking all respondents together) mentioned the issue of agricultural surpluses and it must be seen as a problem for the Community that where knowledge was found – the terminology of food 'surpluses', 'support buying' and 'intervention prices' – it formed part of predominantly negative evaluations. This knowledge about the Common Agricultural Policy (C.A.P.) was often couched in simple, and simplistic, metaphorical language – the imagery of butter 'mountains' and wine 'lakes' – appearing to corroborate Lakoff and Johnson's view that: 'Metaphor is one of our most

important tools for trying to comprehend partially what cannot be comprehended totally.' (1980, p. 193.) This dominance of agricultural policy in common-sense views is partly predictable from the central role of agriculture in the Community's finances, and from the consequent attention paid to this issue by the press, politicians and other opinion leaders. If the Community is to improve its public image (see below), then it would do well to improve its agricultural policy first.

Chapters 5 and 6 dealt with responses to closed-end questions about the Community, including its peoples, policies and effects. Using questions on a whole range of issues, it was possible to explore the relationships between different sets of judgements, and to assess the impact on overall attitudes of both general views of nations and nationalities and specific reactions to particular political and economic issues (see Kelman, 1965a). It was thus possible to examine the underlying structure of Community attitudes (see also Inglehart, 1970a).

Responses to several items intended to measure 'utilitarian' and 'affective' support indicated quite high levels of support for the Community, which might constitute what Easton referred to as a: ' "reservoir" of support upon which a system may draw credit in times when things are going badly'. (1965a, p. 249.) The distinction between the two types of support was not, however, borne out empirically. It would seem premature, although not necessarily impossible, to insist on this dichotomy as long as responses to both types of support are so highly interrelated, as shown by both simple correlational and factor analytic techniques. The latter analyses were particularly impressive in revealing how items which should intuitively load on different factors – e.g. 'solidarity' and 'personal gain' – did, in fact, sometimes load on the same factor. A priority for future research, given the conceptual appeal of this distinction, must be the construction of independent and orthogonal scales to measure utilitarian and affective support. In the absence of such an instrument, it is more accurate to speak generally of 'support'.

While some of the support items, especially those intended to measure affective support, tap what Handley (1981) called 'diffuse affective orientations' (pp. 348–9), judgements of common policy and its effects were more specific and led to highly differentiated responses. This replicates Lipsey's (1979) finding, that different issues of Community membership elicit different (including positive and negative) views from respondents. Perhaps the most striking finding to all except the most cynical 'anti-Marketeers', was the very low level of knowledge. Taken together with the large number of respondents who failed to provide open-ended answers, and those whose responses were glibly superficial, this result provides further evidence of the Community's lack of salience for even its most educated citizens.

Using multiple regression techniques to select, and exclude, predictor variables, the major predictors of overall attitude were examined by means of path analysis. This latter analysis was used to determine whether those variables conceived to be 'causally prior' act directly or indirectly on the criterion variable (see Kerlinger and Pedhazur, 1973).[1] Of course, many other variables could also have been assessed, but the present demands on respondents were already high. In fact, a subset of predictor variables provided a highly satisfactory prediction and explanation of overall attitudes. The path-analytic models varied somewhat across national samples, but were consistent in pointing to the impact of three variables: active interest, sum of expectancies plus values and, especially, support. Significantly, there was also a role for basic social-psychological variables – contact, liking and national image – as predictors of the key variables, support and expectancy-value. These analyses are parsimonious and were indeed computed to reduce the data. However, the exclusion of certain variables does not necessarily mean that they were not correlated with overall attitudes (see the correlation matrices in Appendix E, Tables E.1–E.4). Multiple regression selects variables which make an independent contribution to the prediction equation, and path analyses separate direct and indirect effects. The simple correlations between, for example, international relations, common policy ratings or policy effects and overall attitude were often significant; but these variables also correlated highly with other variables, which themselves were better predictors of overall attitude.[2] One purpose of the present study, and one for which some credit can be claimed, was to sift these predictor variables and identify those on which attention should be focussed; this focus should not, however, be taken to imply the irrelevance of other variables.

Overall, these results offer some encouragement to the Community, especially the fact that mean attitudes in each country were positive (the modal response for all respondents being $+2$; see Figure 5.1). However, respondents were hardly passionate in their support for the Community (especially in W. Germany and the U.K.), although enthusiasm might have been expected on two counts. First, a very high proportion of university students would be classified as 'opinion leaders', and these politically more active citizens have in the past shown especially high levels of support for a united Europe, favourability to Community membership, willingness to make personal sacrifices, and interest in Community affairs (see *Eurobaromètres*, nos. 10 and 16; and Slater, 1983). Second, these students are 'young', and the optimism of youth is proverbial. At least since Aristotle it has been recognised that youth:

> have exalted notions because they have not yet been humbled by life or learned its necessary limitations; moreover their hopeful disposition makes them think themselves equal to great things – and that means

> having exalted notions. They would always rather do noble deeds than
> useful ones; their lives are regulated more by moral feeling than by
> reasoning. (cited by Inglehart, 1977, p. 66)

Consistent with Aristotle's argument, Inglehart (1967, 1970*b*) has reported
that the young are more enthusiastic about, and have a more stable
commitment to, European integration. This European outlook, Inglehart
argues, is not simply superficial, but reflects a fundamental change in values
and attitudes, and the emergence of a European supranational identity
(Inglehart, 1977). Discordant with the view of both Aristotle and Inglehart,
Noelle-Neumann (1980) reported no more support for Europe among the
young than the older generation, and Handley (1981) even found that the
young were *less* pro-European. Using the most recent data, Inglehart (1984)
found that the young tend still to be relatively more pro-European, but that
this effect had weakened over the years and did not hold for all member
states. Integrating these findings, it is hard to say whether today's students
represent the vanguard or the rearguard of the European movement. Either
way, these are the coming generations and Noelle-Neumann (*op. cit.*) is
surely correct to argue that a lack of support among youth would not augur
well for the future of the European Community. This support has, however,
been identified in the present samples, which suggests that there is no
immediate crisis (insofar as the present samples are broadly representative
of students throughout the Community); although the support findings did
vary cross-nationally and must be considered alongside those for overall
attitude, which revealed quite high numbers of respondents in W. Germany
(29%) and the U.K. (36%) who expressed negative views. This issue of
cross-national differences is now considered in more detail, focussing
primarily on the lower levels of support in the U.K.

At this point it is as well to make explicit, once again, that the data
reported in the present study clearly parallel the findings from the much
larger, representative and longer-term surveys of *Euro-baromètre* (reviewed
in Chapter 2). It is this fact, notwithstanding the specific nature of the
student sampled investigated, that is used to justify the more discursive
stance taken in this final chapter. Thus a more wide ranging analysis of
cross-national differences in attitudinal support, the Community's impact on
its citizens, and the implications of the present research is now attempted.

7.1.2 Cross-national differences: the 'British problem'
Considering the complete set of questionnaire data, the European Community
evidently appeals to the Italians, the French and the W. Germans; this is
especially clear for the important measures of support, on which these three
countries have significantly higher levels than do the British. Some of the
reasons for this support have already been discussed, and part of the

historical explanation given. These findings are largely consistent with those of the *Euro-baromètre* series (see Chapter 2), although public opinion has not always followed this pattern. As Inglehart (1967) notes, the W. Germans used to be most favourable (they now lag behind the French and Italians) and once upon a time the British were more favourable than the French towards European unification (see Merritt and Puchala, 1968). Why do the British of today appear to hold the Churchillian view of relations with continental Europe, that 'we are with them, but not of them'?

Having restricted respondents to those with homogeneous educational backgrounds, it is not surprising that cross-national differences were predominant. Furthermore, the finding that the British were different on several measures might appear to support Inglehart's claim that: 'The most important line of cleavage for or against European integration, then, is based on nationality: today as was true a decade ago, the publics of the six original member nations are markedly more pro-European than the publics of the four newer member nations.' (1984, p. 13.) However, this view that national differences are more important predictors of European attitudes than, for example, are political affiliations, social class, age, occupation and religion (see Deutsch, 1967; Mathew, 1980) can, and has been, improved upon. Long-term membership of the Community may be more important than short-term economic fluctuations (see Inglehart and Rabier, 1978), but it is not the ultimate variable. Consider the impact of the dummy variables for nationality in the multiple regression based on all respondents (see Table 6.2). First, the dummy variable for W. Germany was more significant than that for the U.K.; second, both variables had less impact than the set of eight items intended to measure affective support. Rabier (in press) also found that the 'length of membership' variable was relatively unimportant in accounting for voting turn-out in the second direct elections to the European Parliament. He proposed that this measure of integration into the Community is no longer a key variable. It would appear to be more specific and, for practical purposes, more significant, to report that the British are distinguished by lower levels of support and that, as we have seen, support is the main predictor of attitudes. The British and the W. Germans were also less positive in their ratings of value-expectancy, due to their pessimism about the achievement of Community goals. Both these questionnaire variables would appear to have more practical utility than does the nationality variable.

Thus national differences are not denied, indeed they permeate this research. Rather, they are broken down into more specific components. Put differently, the focus now becomes, not 'why are the British different?', but 'why do the British lack support for the Community?' This discussion centres on the British, rather than the W. Germans, although a large minority of both samples had negative overall attitudes. There are three reasons for this choice. First, the British were set apart from all three other countries on several measures, while the W. Germans were not. Second, while a large portion of the W. Germans had negative attitudes, the mean levels of support (for both measures separately, see Tables 5.17 and 5.18) in W. Germany were quite high and, in fact, slightly higher than in both Italy and France. Thus there is no immediacy to the W. German 'problem' if, indeed, it exists. Third, the Community has been troubled by, and attentive to, the problem of negative public opinion in the U.K. for years. It *is* a problem for Community solidarity.

The dimensions of the problem are various and complex, and could surely be the topic for a different book. The discussion here is restricted to brief illustration of six factors which appear to be possible, and interactive rather than mutually exclusive, bases for the low levels of British support for the Community: history; financial problems of the budget and agriculture; politicians past and present; relations with France and the French; the role of the press; and the Community as scapegoat.

History

History is not, as Coleridge suggested, 'a lantern in the stern which shines only on the waves behind us'. History also influences the way people think and act many years later. Some background has already been given in the introductory chapter. Here it may be reiterated that the various countries of Europe had different reasons for joining the Community, or not. Among these were the repercussions of World War II, as Robertson (1959) explains: 'The disillusionment of defeat... bred the need for a new faith and the European idea struck a responsive chord in many quarters. It was precisely where old loyalties remained strong – in Britain – that the appeal for a United Europe evoked least response.' (p. 5.) It is because the U.K. joined the Community late that 'length of membership' has always been a convenient and obvious variable with which to explain the independence of British public opinion. However, length of time is a very vague concept until and unless researchers being to identify *what* has happened in that time to drive a wedge between the opinions of the 'new' and 'old' members. In any case, 'sheer passage of time' (Inglehart and Rabier, 1978, p. 78) would not seem to be the key variable, because the favourability of attitudes does *not* increase monotonically as a function of time (see Figures 2.1 and 2.2).

It is more useful to look at what happened at different periods of time, whereupon it becomes obvious that the period in which the British have been affiliated to the Community has paralleled the decline of 'Great' Britain. These 11 lean years have been difficult in terms of economic adjustment. It is hardly surprising that, given appropriate support from politicians and the press, the Community has been blamed for, and leaving the Community is seen as the cure for, all economic ills from inflation to unemployment. As Inglehart has written:

> The man in the street would not, of course, make an expert analysis of the effects of the EEC (indeed, the experts have difficulty doing so). But, in a general sense, as he finds his own standard of living rising while his country is a member, he might well attribute some part of this rise to the effects of the Common Market and, consequently, become more pro-European. We might regard this as a process analogous to 'spillover'. Conversely, then, deteriorating economic conditions should tend to produce a gradual decline in Europeanism.[3] (1970*b*, p. 67.)

This observation brings us to the second factor which has arguably had an adverse effect on British support – economic aspects of the Community which are seen as unfair by Britons.

Financial problems of the budget and agriculture
The possibilities for negative 'spillover', as conceived by Inglehart, are writ large for the British on two fronts – the Community budget and the Common Agricultural Policy. Interestingly, both of these topics received attention in open-ended responses (see Chapter 4). The budget issue appeared in the catch-phrase 'we pay too much', while agricultural policy was criticised as over-productive, wasteful and 'expensive for us' by some British respondents. The British (along with the W. Germans) also rated the C.A.P. negatively when asked to judge the achievements of common policy (see Table 5.21), and were adamant that their net contribution to the E.E.C. budget was excessive (see Table 5.17). The two issues are obviously interrelated, because more than 70% of the Community budget is spent on agriculture (Harrod, 1983), and for British respondents both ratings were significantly correlated with overall attitude (see Appendix E, Table E.6 and this chapter, note 2).

The U.K. and its national representatives may have irritated, and alienated, other member states in the long-running budget argument. However, there seems to be a powerful consensus that the U.K. and W. Germany are the big losers from the Community (both contributing more to the Community's finances than they receive).[4] Inglehart (1984) argues that this fact 'almost certainly contributes to the widespread British perception that their membership in the Community is disadvantageous and *inequitable*'. (p. 11, emphasis added.) The analyses computed to test predictions from equity theory certainly bore out Inglehart's view (see Table 5.14). Those Britons who perceived their country to be both the major contributor to *and* the minor beneficiary from the Community held significantly different attitudes from those who perceived no inequity. Furthermore, the attitudes of the former were negative, while those of the latter were positive. The message of this analysis, which due to sample reduction could not be used in the multivariate analyses, is that economic perceptions do have an impact on Community attitudes in the U.K.

Politicians past and present

Economic and other decisions are, of course, taken by national politicians. These representatives therefore have the capacity to be opinion makers *par excellence*. The British have certainly been influenced over the years by such leaders as Churchill, Bevin, Attlee, Macmillan, Heath and Wilson. The war of words continues and some Labour politicians argue forcefully against the Community. Thus ex-minister Peter Shore has maintained that changes due to the European Community: 'involved the transfer from a democratic and sovereign U.K. Parliament of law-making, tax-gathering and treaty-making powers to non-elected institutions in Europe, no longer accountable to the people of this land. The damage to the democracy, to the prosperity and the self-confidence of the British people has been, and will continue to be, immense.' (*The Times*, 4 January, 1983.) It would surely be hard to find any deputy in Italy, France or W. Germany expressing such strong anti-Community views.

The role of Britain's current leader, Margaret Thatcher, is less direct, but no less histrionic. Mrs Thatcher has arguably done today, for British public opinion about Europe, what Charles de Gaulle did in France in the 1960s. She has rent the Community and carried public opinion with her. From the present analyses (including those limited analyses for political affiliation), the Prime Minister cannot be accused of turning these respondents, especially those who vote Conservative, against the Community. She has been more subtle than that. She has made pro-Europeans in a land of patriots feel less than patriotic, and she has certainly done nothing to encourage a sense of European solidarity, as a political leader in her position could have done (see Inglehart and Rabier, 1978). Spurred on by headlines such as 'Euro leaders gang up on Maggie',[5] she appears to have sought, and found, in the Community a basis for awakening that little-England streak in public opinion:

> The Prime Minister had never been closely identified with the European cause.... She was pro-European when she could relate it to defence, with which the Community has little if anything to do, but that was about all. She had fought publicly for an even better budget solution than the government finally accepted... she must have been aware that popular feeling about the Community accorded with her own personal instinct. She did not appear to be someone who would lightly abandon this link with popular sentiment for the sake of closer ties with Europe....
> (Rutherford, 1981, pp. 19–20)

With such leaders in power, British public opinion should never be considered a mystery. Rather, in the light of the present government and some sections of the opposition, evidence of any support must be an unexpected bonus for the Community.

Relations with France and the French

Over the years, helped on by the de Gaulle vetoes, British Community relations with France have been tumultuous.[6] This constitutes a problem for the Community to the extent that such conflictual relations act as a barrier to the development of identitive support. According to Handley, the notion of identitive support (see Lindberg and Scheingold, 1970) conveys the idea that 'a feeling of solidarity among the *peoples* of a set of countries is a necessary condition in the creation of a political community'. (Handley, 1981, p. 338; emphasis added.) Following Handley's use of the degree of mutual trust as a measure of this kind of support, the results of the *Euro-baromètre* series draw attention to an interesting phenomenon. Over the four years, 1976–80, there has been a significant decrease in mutual trust between the British and French (a finding which is the starting point for the analysis by Cohen-Solal and Bachmann, 1983). By the same logic that credits the Community with the increased mutual trust between France and W. Germany (see Inglehart and Rabier, 1982), the Community should also be held responsible for the negative trend in Franco-British relations.

There are various ways to analyse this phenomenon, but it is surely exacerbated by press coverage of such events as the lamb 'war' (see below).[7] In the present study, Franco-British antagonisms had no apparent effect on the three measures which might be related to identitive support. There was no evidence of mutual negative stereotypes, low ratings of liking, or negative images of each other's country. However, the Franco-British conflict did appear when respondents were asked to say which member state benefits most from and contributes least to the Community. For the former question, both groups cited each other; for the latter question, responses were shared between countries, but again both mentioned each other. Overall these results may be encouraging for the Community, to the extent that continued conflicts have not yet galvanised that chauvinistic streak in public opinion by generating negative outgroup stereotypes. These British respondents would not obey Admiral Lord Nelson's order, to 'hate a Frenchman as you hate the devil'. However, the responses to questions about contributors and beneficiaries do reveal the old antagonism, and here it might be appropriate for the Community to instruct its citizens about which countries really are the winners and losers (see below).[8]

Data recently analysed by Hewstone and Young (1985) provide some support for the importance attached to Anglo-French relations. Asked if they thought there had been an improvement (7) or worsening (1) in relations between the U.K. and each of the three largest member states, respondents significantly perceived an improvement in relations with both W. Germany

(5.16) and Italy (4.22), but a worsening (2.31) in the case of France. Furthermore, the latter item alone correlated $+0.39$ ($p < 0.01$) with overall attitude to the Community. A further series of questions asked how important (1–7) various factors were in explaining the U.K.'s relationship with the Community. Two items relating to Anglo-French relations were perceived as among the most important: 'The U.K.'s original attempts to join the Community were vetoed by the French' (5.22) and: 'Membership of the Community has increased rivalry between the French and the British' (5.33).

The role of the press

The impact and content of the press have already been referred to at several stages of this work. The justification for an analysis of the press, and especially of the British press, is given by Inglehart (1970b): 'The British are *least* European, despite the fact that they show the highest rates of media exposure and are the most likely to have opinions of any of the nationality groups. Presumably the *content* of communications relevant to Europe has been less favourable here than in other countries.' (p. 53.) The press, like politicians, are 'opinion makers' (Rosenau, 1961), and if we want to understand why public opinion about the Community takes the form it does, then we must turn to a content-analysis of the national press.

   Surprisingly, the scope of available research is very limited, although what work has been done is informative. For example, Cohen-Solal and Bachmann (1983) compared French and British coverage of two major, but very different, events: The France–England rugby match of 1981, and the 19th European Council meeting at Maastricht, in March of the same year. Their analysis reports that whereas French newspaper articles were oriented towards Europe as a whole, the British papers were much more national-oriented. A corpus of openly aggressive expressions comprised the British coverage, and this was about the summit, not the rugby! Cohen-Solal and Bachmann even identified a 'lexicon of war' – reporting in terms of combat ('attack'; 'break'), treason ('cheat'; 'betrayed') and threat ('accuse'; 'warn') – with expressions which were absent from French coverage. Interestingly, in view of Mrs Thatcher's provocative role, this content-analysis also reported a chauvinistic view in many of the headlines: 'Quand ils parlent de l'Europe, les Britanniques perdent leur flegme. "Seule contre tous" proclame leur presse, qui célèbre la vaillante petite Maggie, luttant toute la nuit contre le loup européen.' (Cohen-Solal and Bachmann, 1983, p. 82.) These authors, far from succumbing to chauvinism themselves, are also highly critical of the French press. Why, they ask, do the most lucid and acerbic political commentators in France become suddenly credulous on the topic of England or Mme Thatcher? There is no attempt to understand or explain the British point of view. Instead, the orchestrated attack by the press on Mrs Thatcher is described as 'ce concert Thatcherophobe' (p. 97) and the authors refer to, 'une anglophobie naive et calme qui s'insinue dans les colonnes de chaque quotidien'. (p. 123.)

Thus the British and French press appear to fuel the fires of protectionism and nationalism. These extracts also emphasise the interplay between the various factors considered in this section – history, politics, economics and the press – all of which mould public opinion in general and negative British views in particular. Evidently, more extensive content-analyses of the press throughout the Community would be a very useful complement to further studies of public opinion.

The Community as scapegoat

Writing in 1981, Himmelweit *et al.* concluded that 'in the next election' leaving the European Community would be an issue of concern to parties and candidates in the U.K., but would not be a vote-catcher, 'unless of course the recession can be convincingly attributed to the U.K.'s membership – not an easy task!'. (p. 201.) In spite of this view, we have seen that politicians, newspapers and the public in the U.K. have displayed a marked propensity to ascribe, if not recession *per se*, all manner of economic ills to membership of the Community. As Rutherford (1981) wrote: 'The Common Market was probably as useful a scapegoat as any for prevailing discontents.' (p. 12.) This function fulfilled by the Community, and the Commission more specifically in this instance, has been described by Shank in the following passage:

> The Commission provides a very convenient alibi for national politicians when unpleasant decisions have to be taken. When there is money to be distributed or favourable decisions to be announced, on the other hand, national politicians like to take the credit. By and large, the mass media in all the member states of the EEC remain highly nationalistic, so journalists listen to their own country's ministers rather than to Commission officials when preparing their stories. Inevitably, therefore, the Commission tends to get bad press... national governments find the Commission a convenient whipping boy when things are going badly, and have no wish to see it as a possible rival in public esteem in their home countries. (*The Times*, 7 July, 1978, cited by Mathew, 1980, p. 164)

This role played by the Community brings together the various dimensions considered in this attempt to explain negative public opinion in the U.K. All these influences help to ensure that, for Britons, the Community is not yet accepted as a permanent aspect of the political scenery. According to Donovan (1973), the real dispute between the U.K. and the Community goes beyond economics: 'The economics are too contradictory and each citizen can find an expert to back his prejudice. The real dispute goes deeper, it touches our separateness, our sovereignty, our suspicion of foreigners and the fact that one day we may have to defer to them.' (p. 43.) However, this argument with heavy overtones of 'national character' does not accord with the facts of this study. The economic argument is simpler, more straightforward and has a firmer factual basis. Far from being condemned, as President Mitterand put it, 'by history and geography', to tread their solitary path, the British are not so mystical. The British respondents in this study did value the basic political and economic goals of the Community (see Table 5.2), and if any nation appears firmly opposed to the Community it is Denmark, not the U.K.[9] What irks the British is their financial relationship with the Community – viz. the budget and C.A.P. – which is perceived as inequitable. The budget issue is the 'British problem' that must be solved; whereupon the problem of British public opinion might no longer exist.

The British problem, however defined, must be solved, because it is destroying the Community. Thus one British journalist has argued that the continentals now hold a view of the 'mean-minded and intolerably insular British who are preventing the Community from living happily ever after'. (*The Times*, 30 March, 1984). Judging from public opinion studies, he would appear to be correct. In a French poll for the magazine *Le Nouvel Observateur*, the British came out badly and Mrs Thatcher was detested. In the most recent *Euro-baromètre* poll (no. 21, 1984), several countries voiced anti-British sentiment (see Inglehart, 1984). In answer to the following question: 'Are there any countries, including your own, which you would prefer not to be in the Community?', only one country, the U.K., received a large number of negative votes. Among respondents from each of the three other countries of interest here, there was a large increase since 1976, when the question was last asked (W. Germany, 19–33%; Italy, 7–18%; France, 15–41%; U.K., 9–12%). In the present study there was no evidence of negative feelings towards the U.K. or the British on stereotypes, liking or national images; but at a national level the country's relationship to the Community is perceived negatively. The W. Germans and French gave the U.K. as the country which 'benefits most', while the Italians and many French gave the U.K. as the country which 'contributes least'. These views are worrying at a time when public opinion might be a critical resource for further steps towards European integration. This is not to say, however, that the Community has failed to win the support of the present respondents, at least to some extent. The following section evaluates the Community's success in this respect, and argues for a less ambitious criterion of public support than some integrationists have used.

7.1.3 The Community's impact on its citizens: the death of nationalism, the birth of new loyalties, or a growing sense of solidarity ?

According to several writers, one of the Community's original aims was to eradicate pernicious nationalism. Thus Lindberg and Scheingold (1970) talk of a bold attempt 'to lower the barriers of nationalism' (p. 1), while Benoit (1961) argues that the idea of the European Community, 'implied such a sharp break with the pervasive assumptions of traditional nationalism that until the last moment, and beyond it, few persons could believe it would happen'. (pp. 57–68.)

In order to assess the decline of nationalism, some clarification of the term is required and two aspects may be distinguished: '(1) The feeling of belonging to a group united by common racial, linguistic, and historical ties, and usually identified with a particular territory. (2) A corresponding ideology which exalts the nation state as the ideal form of political organization with an overriding claim on the loyalty of its citizens.'[10] On the face of it, nothing seems inherently undesirable about the first type of nationalism (with the proviso that the word 'ethnic' replace the inaccurate word 'racial'), although some politicians and writers might view both types as barriers to the development of a completely integrated federal Europe. Certainly, restricting nationalism to the former type, rather than eradicating it completely, would seem a more realistic aim. The question then becomes, as posed by Kohn (1957): 'Will it be possible to de-emphasize nationalism, to disintensify its emotional appeal, and to reduce it to proportions compatible with a supranational order... will it be possible to bring nationalism in the West back to those attitudes which characterised it at the time of its rise in the eighteenth century?' (p. 32.)

Euro-baromètre evidence for national pride was reviewed earlier and high percentages of respondents were classified as 'very' or 'fairly' proud (especially the British). From the present study, it was noted that about 17% of all respondents complained of 'nationalism and protectionism' in their open-ended answers (see Table 4.3). However, on measures of stereotyping, liking and national images, evidence of nationalism was limited. The Italians did show national pride in their judgements of stereotypes and liking, but their national image was less positive than were their views of the other countries: respondents in the other three countries showed very little evidence of this form of nationalism or ethnocentrism. Moreover, while the Italians were proud in this sense, they were consistent supporters of the Community, a finding which questions the necessity or value of dispelling benign nationalism.

It would appear, then, that nationalism is still present, but not prevalent. Kurt Tucholsky, the W. German satirist, viewed European pride in terms of both belonging to one group, and *not* belonging to others:

'Worauf man in Europa stolz ist
Dieser Erdteil ist stolz auf sich,
und er kann auch stolz auf sich sein.
Man ist stolz in Europa:
*
Deutscher zu sein
*
Franzose zu sein
*
Engländer zu sein
*
Kein Deutscher zu sein
*
Kein Franzose zu sein
*
Kein Engländer zu sein[11]

The present responses were not so stark, but nor was nationalism dead.

The issue of national pride is obviously closely connected with that of the development of new loyalties. The question of interest here was posed by Deutsch *et al.* (1967): 'Are nation-states and national policies in Western Europe being superseded by supra-national loyalties, interests and institutions?' (p. vii.) This is a particularly important issue for the functionalist and neo-functionalist schools of integration, which contend that community loyalties will slowly replace national loyalties (e.g. Haas, 1968; Robertson, 1959). From *Euro-baromètre* polls, there was little evidence that Community citizens (especially the British) had come to think of themselves as 'citizens of Europe'. The present study bears out this view, using different measures. Item six in the section on affective support asked respondents to indicate their degree of agreement with the statement: 'I am more loyal to the interests of the EEC than to interests of (respondent's own country).' Results were disappointing for anyone awaiting the emergence of supra-national loyalty. From the mean scores (see Table 5.18), the W. Germans showed agreement, but in all other countries this view was not endorsed. As noted earlier, a measure of loyalty shift was also calculated by assessing confidence in the economic skills of both the national government and the Community (see Table 5.19). Here, somewhat surprisingly, responses were more positive towards the Community. In all countries except the U.K., respondents expressed more confidence in the Community.

Overall, these responses reveal no strong tendency to eschew national pride or shift from national to supra-national loyalties. They tend to support Aron's view that the 'old' nation-states will not be, or have not yet been, replaced by the 'new' Europe:

'Will the old nations, with their centuries-old concern for national sovereignty, survive? Is the passion with which the public supports national athletic teams a symbol of a nationalism which raises still another insurmountable obstacle to block federation? Yes and no. I believe that consicousness of the nation remains infinitely stronger than a sense of Europe. I do not perceive any European nationalism beyond an aspiration to a degree of autonomy in relation to the U.S. and, especially, to the rejection of the bloody quarrels of the past.... The old nations still live in the hearts of men, and love of the European nation is not yet born – assuming that it ever will be'. (Aron, 1964, pp. 60–1)

This same view has been expressed by Deutsch (1967), that Europe remains a Europe of nation states (but see Inglehart, 1967). Surely this will be so, as long as the European Community falls short of complete integration and unification. Indeed, this nationalism is part of social life, embedded in phrases such as: 'La France sera toujours La France'; 'There will always be an England'; and 'Deutschland über alles'.[12] The best one might hope for, then, is the development of 'multiple loyalties' (Guetzkow, 1955). After all, Haas (1968) emphasised that shifts towards supra-national loyalty need not be accompanied by the sloughing off of old national loyalties. As Guetzkow explains, the two identities will complement, not contradict, each other, provided they 'are furnishing compatible solutions to different needs'. (*op cit.*, p. 39.)

Given the foregoing, a less ambitious and idealistic goal for the Community would be to engender positive attitudes and earn the support of its citizens. On these criteria, the Community has much better grounds for claiming success. Building a sense of solidarity has long been seen as one of the Community's goals, as Robert Schuman acknowledged: 'Europe will not be made all at once, or according to a single general plan. It will be built through concrete achievements which first create a *de facto* solidarity....' (Declaration, 9 May, 1950, cited in Harrison, 1974.) By solidarity we mean here that 'sense of community' envisaged by several writers (e.g. Deutsch *et al.* 1957; Easton, 1965*a*; Harrison, 1974; Taylor, 1972) and described by Easton as, 'a we-feeling among a group of people – they are a political entity that works together and will likely share a common political fate and destiny'. (*op. cit.*, p. 332.)

From the *Euro-baromètre* series, there are two measures which relate closely to this conception of solidarity. First, the willingness to make some personal sacrifice to help out another member state in economic difficulties. As noted in Chapter 2, while many citizens are willing to make this gesture (in the abstract at least), the numbers have fallen in recent years. Second, there is the sense of mutual trust between nationalities which, with the exception of Franco-British relations, has risen steeply from 1970 to 1980 (see Inglehart and Rabier, 1982). From the present study, levels of 'support' (affective and utilitarian, in terms of intuitive content) were reasonably high in all countries, but lower in the U.K. Looking at specific items of an affective nature (see Table 5.18), respondents in all countries disagreed with an item suggesting that they 'should *not* help out another member state in economic difficulties' (means were over 5.0 in each country). As in the *Euro-baromètre* polls, respondents voiced somewhat less agreement with an item asking whether the people of their country 'should be willing to make personal sacrifices to help out another member state in difficulties'. Three other items were also chosen to exemplify the idea of solidarity and revealed rather low ratings of 'solidarity', 'trust' and 'confidence' in the European Community.

Summarising these results on solidarity, the Community can claim modest commitment from its citizens and the emergence of a supra-national identity (noted by Inglehart, 1977) may be mooted. Notwithstanding this 'European feeling (Hewstone, 1984), it is surely too early to see this 'sense of solidarity' as a firm basis of diffuse support on which the Community can rely. It is certainly a long way from Winston Churchill's poetic vision of a Europe: 'where men and women of every country will think as much of being European as of belonging to their native land and wherever they go in this wide domain will truly feel "here I am at home!"'

How important is it for the Community to engender, or nurture, this sense of solidarity? According to many theorists (e.g. Deutsch), this feeling is a necessary, but not sufficient, component in the building of a political community. One should also note Katona's (1975) work on 'psychological economics', showing that measures of trust and confidence in the government had as important an influence on economic behaviour as did fiscal measures themselves. Evidently, this support must be strengthened if the Community is to rely upon it, and one must emphasise again that levels of support are limited, considering the superior level of education of these respondents. The Community must, then, act now to build on existing foundations, and it is to this topic of education and change that we now turn, to consider some major implications of the present study.

7.2 Implications

It is hoped that the present work has implications for the European Community and its empirical study. This section concentrates on four broad areas which appear particularly important – education and public information; citizen participation; future polls of public opinion; and finally, the relevance of social psychology for the study of European integration.

7.2.1 *Awakening the European public: education, public information and attitude change*

Having noted several negative trends in public opinion (for example, in willingness to help others by means of a personal sacrifice; and in the perceived development of understanding between member states), it is obvious that the Community must act to halt the tide. What is to be done, and how?

One possibility is radical political change. According to Inglehart (1984):

> Probably, only a bold new departure can recapture the imagination and support of the most dynamic segments of the European public. If it is pursued vigorously, the proposed European Union might rekindle a European spirit, and provide a sense of purpose that is palpably lacking. Bringing about a European Union would not be easy; it will unquestionably give rise to opposition and could even split the Community, in a worst-case scenario. But the gamble is worth taking: if the Community allows itself to stagnate further, as it has during the past decade, it seems likely to become a moribund and largely meaningless institution. (Inglehart, 1984, p.20)

This is certainly a bold proposal and one justified by the view that public opinion about foreign affairs usually follows, rather than leads, the official policy (Etzioni, 1969; Rosenberg, 1967). It is, however, very ambitious and at a time when support for the Community has been sapped. A less radical, more pragmatic, proposal would be to win back the public via education and public information. This follows Handley's (1981) view that the Community has not cared for its public image, and must make an active effort to stimulate interest in Community affairs. As Oskamp (1977) notes, there is no clear agreement concerning the processes of attitude formation and the key factors in attitude development. However, one can usefully consider strategies for 'awakening' the European publics under the headings of 'education', 'public information campaigns' and 'attitude change'.

Education

Considering first education, one may note Madariaga's (1960) view, that: 'il y a deux moyens de faire des Européens: par l'éducation des nouveaux et par la rééducation des anciens.' (cited in Rabier, 1966, p. 24.) This emphasis on education has also been apparent in the work of Inglehart (e.g. 1970*b*) showing that education is a more powerful predictor of pro-European attitudes than is occupation or social class. Yet, as already stated, although respondents in the present study were university students, predominantly middle class and highly educated, they were not euphoric about the Community. More must be done to build support for the Community, than simply educating its citizens.

One obvious possibility is to begin education about the Community (even if only in general terms) at a very young age. Bissery (1972) asked 11- and 12-year olds to draw a map of Europe from memory. She reported striking departures from 'geographical reality', the absence of a global image of Europe and, usually, a national or regional 'socio-centrism'. Bissery suggested that the possibility of forming a geographical representation of Europe might be a pre-condition for forming a European 'consciousness', and that the failure to draw 'Europe' was a sign of non-recognition of Europe. It might, then, be possible to begin building a European consciousness with such young children.

Other researchers, as noted earlier, have found that many children as young as 6 or 7 years old have developed strong emotional and cognitive associations about their nation, its leaders, and national symbols (e.g. Easton and Dennis, 1969; Lambert and Klineberg, 1967). Interestingly, young children seem predisposed (cross-nationally) to view politicians positively as 'benevolent leaders' (see Greenstein, 1965, 1975; Hess and Torney, 1967), and the Community could attempt to announce its existence to children at this propitious moment. Research on children's political ideas has also examined the development of support (Easton and Dennis, 1969) and the dawn of a 'sense of community' (Adelson and O'Neil, 1966). Such measures could be used in a Community-wide study of the input and impact of teaching in this domain, to compare and contrast what, and how, children in the different member states learn about 'Europe'.

Future educational programmes aimed at enhancing the image of the Community should also build on some basic principles of social cognition – such as 'generalisation of affect' and the 'organisation and polarisation of news'. (See Katona, 1975.) Thus the Community should seek to ensure that positive aspects of the Community are learned first, with the hope that this positive affect will generalise to other domains in which the Community is judged. This proposal is consistent with research on the development of international attitudes, which suggests that children may establish an evaluative preference prior to possessing any information about other countries (e.g. Johnson, Middleton and Tajfel, 1970). Such positive aspects of the Community could also serve as reference points around which news is organised, so that incoming information would be assimilated to positive, not negative, knowledge structures. In this general vein, the Community would do well to ensure that it becomes known as the 'European Community' and not the 'Common Market'. As Swann (1981) argues, the Community is more than a common market, because it calls for common policies and harmonisation of economic and political policy; psychologically more important, the restricted term Common Market has been shown to be held by those with less support for the Community (see *Euro-baromètre*, no. 21).

Thus the Community could begin a more active educational campaign in schools and among its younger citizens.

Public information campaigns
An alternative, or complement, to the education of the young is the re-education of the old. This strategy has some justification in findings which have related children's prejudices (e.g. Epstein and Kormorita, 1966) and political views (e.g. Hyman, 1959; but see Connell, 1972; Jennings and Niemi, 1968) to those of their parents. In other words, change the views of the children by changing their parents' attitudes. Whatever the strength of this parent–child relationship, public information campaigns are important in their own right as attempts to change the views of the adult population, although somewhat surprisingly this topic is one for which the Community has shown little appetite. As Handley (1981) concluded: 'It is somewhat surprising to note that the Community undertakes very little widespread interest-stimulating activity, or at least in a more efficacious manner.' (p. 361.) Notwithstanding this view, the Community has shown some activity in this respect. It does provide information, or feedback, in response to the findings of *Euro-baromètre* polls,[13] and it is has formed committees to attend to the problem. Thus the Irish Prime Minister, Dr Garrett FitzGerald (speaking in the European Parliament at Strasbourg in July, 1984), promised that under Irish presidency of the Community he would follow up the idea of a committee to strengthen the identity of the Community. This committee would be directed towards: 'making the Community a reality in the eyes of its citizens, for many of whom it remains today a somewhat remote concept'. (Reported in *The Guardian*, 26 July, 1984). How effective this committee will be, remains to be seen. The same broad aims of making the Community more visible to the public, and highlighting the more tangible benefits of membership, were also stated in the Tindemans Report of 1974 (see Slater, 1983).

Committees and public information campaigns must, of course, have a reasoned and empirically founded basis. In this respect, public opinion polls may guide campaigns and the findings of the present, more specific, study should also prove useful. At the outset of this research it seemed likely that factors such as knowledge of the Community and assessment of its effects would influence Community attitudes. Following the model of attitudes developed in Chapter 6, three rather different variables suggested themselves as candidates for the major roles in any public information campaign: support; values and expectancies associated with Community goals (dealt with below); and active interest.

Much has already been said about support, and there is no need or wish to be prolix. However, the two items measuring intuitively 'utilitarian' support (personal gain; own country's benefit) and the three items from the section on 'affective' support (solidarity; trust; confidence) should be central to any new campaign aimed at winning over the public. In terms of gains and benefits, the Community must put its fiscal house in order and then ensure that the public is made aware of this achievement. The need for such action is nowhere more urgent than in the U.K. Only for the British sample were correlations between overall attitude and utilitarian support items highly significant (personal gain $r = +0.61$; country has benefitted, $r = +0.59$; see Table E.6).[14] In all other countries these predictors were considerably less powerful than three measures of affective support – solidarity, trust and confidence. In terms of solidarity, trust and confidence, the Community should emphasise these values in communications to its citizens, and avoid a myopic focus on the economic benefits of membership.

The third variable which emerged from the model of Community attitudes, albeit tentatively, was active interest. This variable only had a significant impact in the United Kingdom (and a marginal effect in France) but Handley (1981) has shown that when interest in Community affairs is increased (as in an election campaign), the general public tends to increase its support for European unity. An augmentation of citizens' interest, like knowledge, is in any case a desirable goal for a Community which wants or needs an 'attentive public'.[15] At present, the Community's public – even the educational elites studies here – appears opinionated, not informed. According to Lane and Sears (1964) this is a general phenomenon, and should not be attributed to an especially apathetic electorate in Europe. Lane and Sears argue that: 'modern society has divorced the pressure to have an opinion from the pressure to be informed; it has kept the one and eroded the other'. (p. 63.) This can be seen in the present study. Of 545 respondents, nine (1.65%) gave no overall attitude; yet 129 (23.7%) had a knowledge score of nought out of 10, and a staggering 518 (95.2%) had a score of five or less. If there is a psychologically realised Europe, it appears to be of the heart (solidarity) and not the head (knowledge). The Community should therefore act to educate its citizens and increase the salience of the Community – via advertising campaigns, competitions or otherwise. It may be that knowledge must reach a certain level before its impact is felt, or that the present study used an inappropriate dependent variable.[16] Future research must reconsider this question. Whatever the outcome, an informed or attentive public should be a goal for the Community, and could be a resource: 'Because what people think (about economic policy) influences their response to government actions, every effort should be made to induce them to reflect upon the problem, to understand the government's proposed solution as being in their best interest, and so to provide willing cooperation.' (Katona, 1975, p. 348.)

Staying with the theme of knowledge, a central aspect of this social-psychological approach has been the distinction between objective and subjective knowledge (as encapsulated in the notion of 'social representation', see Chapters 3 and 4). It is not always possible to identify objective knowledge – for example, does the Community 'increase national rivalries' or 'interfere with national government'? – but even where facts are available, the public may be ignorant, or wilfully negligent, of them. Here again the Community should give feedback, as can be illustrated with two issues.

First, consider the Community Regional Fund, intended as a counterweight to the budget contribution made by each member state (Swann, 1981). Given the ill will generated by the issue of budget contributions (as seen in the analyses based on equity theory), it is in the interests of the Community to ensure that citizens are also aware of what their country gains here. According to Swann (*op. cit.*), the fund (set up from January 1st, 1975) was to divide available money, for the countries of interest here, as follows: W. Germany, 6.4%; Italy, 40%; France, 15%; U.K., 28% (the remainder being shared by the, then, five other member states). Item 7 of the section on utilitarian support asked respondents if their country had gained from this fund; mean responses were as follows: W. Germany, 3.49; Italy, 4.14; France, 4.17; U.K., 4.13 (the responses of the W. Germans being significantly lower than those of respondents in the three other countries).[17] This shows that the W. German respondents, at least, were accurate in a relative sense. Yet the responses of Italians and Britons showed no recognition of their substantial gains from the Community, in comparison with France. In short, cross-national differences in ratings of relative gain are not in proportion to actual gains.

Item 2 in the same section of the questionnaire asked respondents if they felt that their country's net contribution to the Community budget was 'excessive'. This is, of course, a subjective term – in excess of what? According to equity theory, it might be in excess of gains from the Community, or a ratio of payments to gains which was in excess of that for other countries. Considering a variety of sources, the actual rank order of the present four countries, in terms of gross or net budget contributions, is clear: W. Germany; U.K.; France; Italy.[18] Respondents' agreement (1) or disagreement (7) with this item was as follows: W. Germany, 3.84; Italy, 4.21; France 3.67; U.K., 2.64 (the British showing significantly less disagreement than respondents in the other three countries).[19] These responses provide further evidence of the saliency of the budget issue in the U.K., because although the W. Germans apparently pay more, they appear less concerned than the British (however, the subsequent analysis of perceived inequity revealed that the W. German respondents were just as aware as the British; see Table 5.14(b)). The Italians, who pay considerably less than the other three countries, show only slightly more disagreement than the others. Again, common-sense perceptions are not in proportion to the 'economic reality' and feedback should aim to rectify this misperception.

These findings on perceived inequity should be worrying for the Community. As Homans (1976, p. 232) points out, if all parties are to accept a distribution of outcomes as fair, they must agree on three different points: (1) that outcomes ought to be proportional to inputs; (2) on what kinds of outcomes and inputs are to be legitimately taken into account in applying the rule; and (3) in their assessment of the amounts of these inputs made by, and the outcomes received by, each party. Homans notes also that agreement on point (1) is more likely than on points (2) or (3). The contribution of equity theory to the present analysis is that it has drawn attention to a kind of running sore in citizens' perceptions of the Community that will have to be treated. Either the Community explains why it sees the present system as fair, or it revises the system. It would in either case do well to address its citizens on this issue, following Adams and Freedman's (1976) view, that 'it is not foolishly optimistic to believe that a public understanding of inequity would make a difference in ameliorating conflicted relationships'. (p. 55.)

In this section some limited suggestions have been made for bolstering support, clarifying the goals of the Community and their achievement, stimulating interest, and increasing knowledge about the Community. More could be said about how, exactly, this information could be provided by the Community (e.g. in a form consistent with the common-sense views of citizens, rather than in dull, abstract statistics), but this is premature until the Community decides to pursue this course. For until now it has declined to discuss 'net' budget contributions and shown little inclination to educate its citizens towards, for example, paying a little more in order to help poorer countries (e.g. Italy and Ireland), rather than thinking only in terms of the economic gains to be derived from a larger market. Some specific proposals have been made, with a view towards a more honest and informative relationship between the Community and its citizens. It is not, however, assumed that the envisaged public information campaign would have immediate, or dramatic, effects. As Slater has argued: 'National governments have themselves found it increasingly difficult to satisfy a fickle public. In a general desire for decentralized democracy, there is no good reason why the Community should expect to find it any easier.' (1983, p. 87.)

In addition to Slater's pessimistic view, it must be stated that many scholars have misgivings about the impact of public information campaigns. The problem with such information (or propaganda) as identified by Stephan and Stephan (1984) is that those people who do not wish to be influenced by it, will avoid it (Cooper and Jahoda, 1947) and, if they are exposed to such information, will distort it (Berelson and Steiner, 1964). Thus public information campaigns often fail (Hyman and Sheatsley, 1947), or succeed only in 'preaching to the converted' (Titchenor, Donohue and Olien, 1970). This is not the place to plan such a campaign for the Community, but if and when it is initiated, it should of course be based on careful consideration of the advantages and disadvantages of various media, in relation to such criteria as attention, comprehension, yielding, retention and action (see Klapper, 1960, 1963). Klapper's studies on the effects of mass communication are, however, optimistic in one sense. He reported that attitude change produced is more commonly a small change in the extremity or intensity of the attitude, than a 'conversion' from 'for' to 'against' (or *vice versa*). As noted in the present study, and the review of *Euro-baromètre* findings, the public is generally positively inclined towards the community already, and it ought to be possible for a carefully conceived campaign to exploit this predisposition.

Attitude change
While the preceding section dealt with information campaigns in general, one can also make a number of more specific statements about changing attitudes. Although attitude change has been well researched in social psychology, the vast literature offers no easy recipes for applied research; as Eagly and Himmelfarb concluded their review, 'there are few simple and direct empirical generalisations that can be made concerning how to change attitudes'. (1974, p. 594.) Nonetheless, one should share the view recently expounded by Eagly and Chaiken (1984), that theories of persuasion should possess obvious applied value for the design of information campaigns. How, then, could one attempt to change attitudes to the European Community?

Having opted for an expectancy – value analysis of attitudes (and despite the critical issues raised) it is consistent to explore the implications of such an approach as a theory of attitude change. Once again, we can consider first Fishbein and Ajzen's claims (Ajzen and Fishbein, 1980; Fishbein and Ajzen, 1975, 1981). According to their expectancy-value model attitude (A) is viewed as determined by the sum of a person's salient beliefs about an object's attributes (b), multiplied by his or her evaluations (e) of these attributes (i.e. $A = \Sigma b_i e_i$). It follows that attitudes will only be changed in a more positive direction when the persuasion attempt results in summed expectancy-value products that are more positive than the summed products prior to the influence attempt. Thus attitude change requires a change in the information base underlying attitudes. Attitudes could be changed by altering one or more of the existing salient beliefs; by introducing new salient beliefs; or by changing an individual's evaluations of the attitude object's attributes (Fishbein and Ajzen, 1975). There are thus two possible foci of influence attempts: beliefs about the attitude object (e.g. persuade citizens to view the Community's creation of a 'United States of Europe' as 'very likely') and/or attribute evaluations (e.g. persuade citizens to evaluate the idea of a 'United States of Europe' as 'very good'). According to Fishbein and Ajzen, the most commonly used strategy is to direct the influence attempt to target beliefs which are assumed to be primary determinants of attitude. However, the impact of this influence attempt will depend on evaluations of the attribute linked to the belief. Thus change of a belief linking the attitude object to a neutral evaluation would leave $\Sigma b_i e_i$ unaltered and no change in attitude would result. Alternatively, an influence attempt could fail by changing two beliefs that were linked to differently valenced attributes (increasing positive *and* negative effects would cancel each other out). Attempted change of attribute evaluations requires equal care. Fishbein and Ajzen propose change of evaluations associated with a salient belief about the attitude object, but once again there is the danger that changes may cancel each other out because overall attitude change depends on the impact of persuasion on the total information base underlying attitude (1975, p. 339).

Depending on the attitude domain in question, the evaluative or cognitive components of attitude may be crucial in predicting someone's overall attitude (see Smith and Clark, 1973). Eagly and Chaiken (1984) report that less research has addressed the problem of changing attitudes by changing attribute evaluations (as opposed to beliefs), and such attempts have met with little success in changing either evaluations or overall attitudes. This may be, as Eagly and Chaiken point out, because evaluations of attributes are often well-grounded in extensive prior learning. However, Rosenberg (1960) used hypnotic suggestion to change the affective component (feelings towards) of issues such as U.S. foreign economic aid. He then found resulting parallel changes in the cognitive components of value importance and perceived instrumentality (i.e. cognitive reorganisation followed induced affective change). These changes were also shown to remain stable for a full week, until the hypnotic suggestion was removed, at which time they rapidly reverted, although they did not return immediately to their original level. The general absence of research on changing evaluations may be convenient for the present task because, as reported in Chapter 5, evaluations of the Community were generally positive, and it was beliefs – especially for the British – that were pessimistic. These results suggest that beliefs might be the best focus for any programme of attitude change.

Beliefs, of course, are central to Fishbein and Ajzen's conceptual framework. They argue that overall attitude is determined by a person's salient beliefs about the attitude object, and that the formation of one belief may lead to the development of other inferential beliefs. If beliefs are taken as paramount, the first major problem is to identify the *primary beliefs* for a given attitude, based on the salient beliefs associating the attitude object with a set of attributes. The beliefs which one is trying to change are termed *target beliefs* (these should be, or be related to, primary beliefs) and research has shown that change in a target belief can produce change in a logically related belief (see Dillehay, Insko and Smith, 1966; Holt, 1970; Holt and Watts, 1969; McGuire, 1960). Studies have also shown that attitude change is related to change in beliefs. Carlson (1956), in a study of attitudes towards the abolition of housing segregation, found that attitude change was positively related to change in the subjective probability (belief) that desegregation would lead to certain goals. Research on advertising is also relevant, having shown that exposure to advertisements can bring about changes in beliefs about products and product use, and corresponding changes in attitudes towards the use or purchase of products (Lutz, 1975, 1977; Mitchell and Olson, 1981; Pomazol, 1983; see Eagly and Chaiken, 1984).[20]

Returning specifically to the present study of attitudes, which beliefs need to be changed in order to influence overall attitude to the Community? Fishbein and Ajzen propose that a change in an individual's attitude could be engendered by changing the beliefs that were already salient prior to the individual receiving any message, or by making salient certain beliefs that were not previously salient. Fishbein and Ajzen's recommendations for careful pre-testing of salient beliefs should help to ensure that communications do not include arguments that merely reiterate respondents' pre-existing beliefs. There is, however, still the question of whether to try to change already salient beliefs or to introduce new beliefs in the hope that these will become salient (Eagly and Chaiken, 1984). In fact, because the method of eliciting salient beliefs was not used in this study, all one can do is use the beliefs actually investigated.[21] Arguably, the present set of beliefs will still be of some use, following Fishbein and Ajzen's suggestion that, 'when the dependent variable is the attitude toward an institution, for example, beliefs about that institutions's attributes or characteristics are some of the primary beliefs at which the influence attempt can be directed'. (1975, p. 389.) The obtained measures of belief broadly fit this description and could thus serve as the basis for an attitude change programme.

A table of the expectancy-value products would reveal which items contribute most to the overall attitude score. However, given the competing claims of additive vs multiplicative models, let us focus on the data for evaluations and expectancies which are entered into the model (see Chapter 5, Tables 5.2 and 5.3). The present study chose a set of goals based on the Treaty of Rome, and reported a fairly strong consensus that these goals were positively valued. However, respondents often did not *expect* them to be achieved by the Community. Here is an obvious place where clear and honest feedback should be given to citizens on what has so far been achieved. Moreover, the Community should avoid making great claims about its goals, when these have little realistic chance of being reached. Sophisticated citizens are evidently not impressed by mere rhetoric.

For the British respondents, whose attitudes were least positive, we have noted already how many of the beliefs are negative (given bipolar scoring of beliefs; see Table 5.3). Obviously, one aim of an attitude change programme based on expectancy-value conceptions could be to change the negative beliefs associated with the most positively evaluated items. For example, target beliefs might include changing British respondents' perceptions in the direction of greater likelihood that the Community was bringing about 'lasting peace', 'mutual understanding' and a European market where 'competition is not distorted'. The correlations between individual expectancy-value items (for the additive model) are shown in Appendix E (Table E.7). These correlations could also guide choice of target beliefs.

In opposition to pessimistic views of voters as ill-informed, unthinking and unaffected by political campaigns, the Fishbein–Ajzen approach is more optimistic. They argue (Fishbein and Ajzen, 1981), that when attention is paid to the beliefs and attribute evaluations that underlie, for example, attitudes towards candidates, then campaigns can and do have impact on the voter. Their analysis of American political elections demonstrates that even in the last months of a presidential campaign, one can identify changes in voters' evaluations of issues and their beliefs about candidates. Perhaps most important, changes in beliefs were not random, but were in most cases in the direction of more accurate perceptions of what candidates stood for.

Despite the present suggestions for attitude change programmes based on an expectancy-value model, Eagly and Chaiken's (1984) recent review of cognitive theories of persuasion finds some fault with this approach. They argue that expectancy-value models have no explicit way to predict the effects of a number of variables in persuasion (e.g. source, recipient and contextual variables) and cite evidence that the effects of messages on attitudes are not always mediated by changes in beliefs, as defined by expectancy-value products (e.g. Mitchell and Olson, 1981). Notwithstanding these shortcomings, an expectancy-value approach to attitude change could, at least, lead to an active, constructive attempt to bring European citizens up to date with the Community's achievements and could help to direct communications more effectively towards those underlying beliefs most needing change. Thus an expectancy-value approach has important implications for the choice of arguments to include in any messages that the Community sends to its citizens.[22]

Notwithstanding the difficulties involved in attempting to inform the European public, and make attitudes more positive, the Community should now take a more active stance (nurturing, rather than just measuring, attitudes), if it is to be assured of future attitudinal support. According to Lang and Lang (1959), the mass media help to define what is 'real' by *selecting, emphasising* and *interpreting* particular events; these processes then direct the public to form attitudes on these issues. It is now up to the Community to take cognisance of this fact and to try to capture the minds of its citizens. One concrete benefit of a successful attempt at this goal is that the Community's electorate might shake off its apathy and participate more fully in elections; it is to this issue that we now turn.

7.2.2 Awakening the European electorate: apathy and voting turn-out
Elections to the European Parliament
As John le Carré once wrote: 'The opposite of love is not hate. But apathy.' Few people hate the European Community, but many cannot be bothered to exercise their right to vote in direct elections to the European Parliament. Why?

Voting for European politicians (actually national politicians who sit in the European Parliament), like knowing about or being interested in European politics, must be considered against the background of what is known about political behaviour at a national level. Voting turn-out in national elections, except where voting is compulsory, is always short of 100%. As Himmelweit *et al.* explain: 'the majority of the electorate are little involved. They believe that their individual decision, being one of millions, makes little difference to the outcome, and the public as a collection of individuals does not see itself as having much influence on political events or even on the conduct of the party of their choice.' (1981, p. 2.)

Despite this knowledge of general political apathy, the problem in Europe is amplified. Turn-out for European elections is considerably lower than for national elections, as reported by Rabier (in press).[23] Part of the reason, as Rabier contends, is that people see the European election as less important than national elections; and Piet Dankert, as outgoing President of the Parliament, acknowledged that the disappointing turn-out in 1984 indicated that the Parliament had not established itself as a credible force in the eyes of the voters (see Rabier, *op. cit.*). Rabier also reported a significant influence on turn-out of factors such as cognitive mobilisation and attitude to European integration, variables which have also been found to influence Community attitudes. This suggests that variables identified in the present study may be relevant to voting turn-out as well.[24]

For example, the expectancy-value analysis of goals maps on to what some political scientists have said about the Community. Hrbek and Wessels (1984) propose that the criteria used to evaluate the European Parliament (EP) should include the 'hopes and expectations' (p. 27) generated before the elections, and the stated 'goals for policies' (*ibid.*). These authors also point to:

> the danger for the EP of not being taken seriously when most of these activities lead to nothing and have no visible outcome. Again we are confronted with the possibility of some long-term effect which, as it is uncertain, will not generate immediate support for the EP. *Frustrated expectations* about the effects of the EP-activities might grow to the extent that the EP becomes less interesting, less worthy for investing time and attention... An outburst of these activities with no direct results might result in a loss of reputation and legitimacy. (Hrbek and Wessels, *op. cit.*, p. 33, emphases added)

Other variables identified as predictors of Community attitudes – support, active interest and knowledge – may also help to explain why turn-out is so low, especially in the U.K. (see Rabier, 1985). In short, a more sophisticated analysis of attitudes to the European *Parliament* (a more specific focus than attitudes to the Community) should be undertaken before the next elections in 1989. We should not expect any simple overlap between the two attitudes, however, because of the Parliament's limited role. As Kohler (1984) has contended. 'It can be assumed that at least those who are aware of the European *Parliament*'s marginal role in the decision-making process of the Community may in spite of their overall positive outlook on the EC pay little attention to European parliamentary affairs.' (p. 442.) While agreeing with Kohler, that Community attitudes are not equivalent to attitudes to the Parliament, the approach and methodology of the present study could easily be adapted for a study of voting behaviour, following Himmelweit *et al.* (1981). Their research in Britain showed quite convincingly that different groups of voters were accurately defined by different attitudes, and that attitudinal measures were good predictors of future vote. There are, then, firm grounds for believing that a social-psychological approach could be used to provide a more detailed analysis and explanation of the disappointing and worrying low turn-out in European elections. However, any serious attempt to predict voting turn-out would first have to consider the relationship between attitudes and behaviour more closely.

Attitudes and behaviour

Early research on attitudes took as a working hypothesis or an implicit assumption that the relationship between attitudes and behaviour was isomorphic and positive (Perry *et al.*, 1976); by understanding a person's attitude one could predict his or her behaviour. Later and contemporary research overcame this period of optimism, or innocence, to ask the question: To what extent, if at all, are people's attitudes predictive of their behaviour? (Fazio and Zanna, 1981). In the course of the debate, views have been polarised. Reactions from some quarters were iconoclastic: Wicker (1971) considered aloud whether, 'it may be desirable to abandon the attitude concept' (p. 29) and Abelson (1972) entitled an article: 'Are attitudes necessary?' Other scholars challenged this scepticism and argued that moderately strong correlations between attitudes and behaviour could be observed when attitudes of some social importance and consequence were investigated in non-laboratory settings (see Fazio and Zanna, 1981; Jaspars, 1978; Kelman, 1974; Schuman and Johnson, 1976).

One of the reasons for employing an expectancy-value approach in the present work was that the Fishbein and Ajzen theory has had a major impact in the attitude–behaviour literature (see Ajzen and Fishbein, 1977). Although their approach and suggested resolution to the problem is not the only one, they have developed a theory which appears to have considerable relevance for the present topic.[25] This theory is grounded in a careful analysis of the attitude–behaviour relationship.

Fishbein and Ajzen (1975) proposed that predictability of a behaviour is increased by working with attitudes and behaviour defined at an equivalent level of specificity (what Bagozzi, 1981, calls the 'parallelism' between attitude and behaviour). Three kinds of behavioural criteria are outlined: specific behaviours performed at a single point in time are labelled *single-act criteria* (e.g. voting in June, 1984); an index based on single behaviours assessed at a number of points in time fulfills *repeated-observation criteria* (e.g. voting in European elections in both 1979 and 1984); an index based on different behaviours combined on a single or multiple observation basis fulfills *multiple-act critiera* (e.g. voting in the 1984 European election *and* attending a meeting organised by your local Member of the European Parliament). Fishbein and Ajzen argue that attitudes towards specific behaviours (e.g.: 'What is your attitude towards voting in tomorrow's referendum?') provide the best attitudinal predictors of single-act criteria; and attitudes towards general tendencies to engage in a specific behaviour (e.g.: 'What is your attitude towards voting in European elections?') provide the best predictors of repeated-observation critiera. Thus the degree of aggregation of the behavioural criterion is a key factor (Fishbein and Ajzen, 1974; Weigel and Newman, 1976): *general* attitudinal measures (such as those examined in the present study) should predict only *broad behavioural patterns*, but not specific behavioural acts.

Fishbein and Ajzen's (1975) re-analysis of research on attitudes and behaviour showed that previous studies had frequently used inappropriate 'attitudinal' predictors (i.e. the measures were not of attitude, or were of incorrect specificity) and had differed widely in terms of the behavioural criteria used. The thrust of their analysis is, then, that many of the studies purporting to be relevant to this issue were, in fact, of little relevance. Most studies which did at least obtain some measure of attitude and behavioural criterion attempted, with little success, to predict a single-act criterion or repeated-observation criterion from a traditional measure of attitude towards an object. In contrast, when attitude towards a behaviour, rather than an object, was used to predict single-act or repeated-observation criteria, significant findings were generally obtained. Consistent with their argument, Fishbein and Ajzen found that the magnitude of the attitude–behaviour relationship varied with the degree of correspondence between levels of attitudinal and behavioural specificity. Finally, and also consistently, significant relations were found between attitudes towards an object and multiple-act critiera. The upshot of this critical re-analysis of the literature was the development by Fishbein and Ajzen of a 'theory of reasoned action' which can now be considered in relation to voting behaviour.

The stated aim of the theory of reasoned action (see Fishbein, 1980; Ajzen and Fishbein, 1980) is to account for behaviour of various kinds by referring to a relatively small number of concepts contained within a single theoretical framework. The theory is based on the assumption that most individuals use available information in a systematic and rational way. The immediate determinant of an action is viewed quite simply as a person's *intention* to perform (or not perform) a behaviour. Fishbein and Ajzen identify two basic determinants of a person's intention, one personal in nature and the other more social. The personal factor is the individual's positive or negative evaluation of performing the behaviour, or his/her *attitude towards the behaviour* (i.e. the person judges performing the behaviour on a good–bad scale). The more social determinant of intention is the person's perception of the social pressures compelling performance of the behaviour. This factor is termed the *subjective norm* (i.e. the person's judgement of the likelihood – on a 7-point scale – that others (e.g. friends) would expect her to vote). In turn, the theory attempts to explain why people hold certain attitudes towards the behaviour and why they perceive certain subjective norms. Attitudes towards the behaviour, like attitudes towards an object (see Chapter 3), are seen as a function of beliefs and evaluations: the person's so-called *behavioural beliefs* about the consequences of performing a particular behaviour; and his or her *evaluation* of these consequences. Thus a person's attitude toward voting in the European election would be a function of his/her beliefs about the consequences of this behaviour (e.g.: 'Voting will very probably imply acceptance of the European Parliament as a legitimate political authority') and his/her evaluations of these consequences (e.g.: 'Acceptance of the European Parliament as a legitimate political authority is a good thing').

Subjective norms are conceived as determined by so-called *normative beliefs* regarding the expectations of relevant others, and the person's

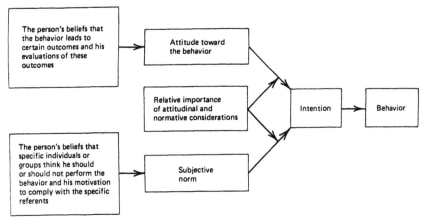

Note: Arrows indicate the direction of influence.

Fig. 7.1. Factors determining a person's behaviour. (From I. Ajzen and M. Fishbein, *Understanding Attitudes and Predicting Social Behaviour*. Englewood Cliffs, N.J.: Prentice-Hall, 1980.)

motivation to comply with these expectations. These central concepts have been organized into an explanatory model by Ajzen and Fishbein (1980), as shown in Figure 7.1. In a recent publication Fishbein and Ajzen (1981) describe each step in the model as representing a different level of explanation for a person's behaviour:

> At the most global level, behaviour is assumed to be determined by intention. At the next level, these intentions are themselves explained in terms of attitudes toward the behaviour and subjective norms. The third level explains these attitudes and subjective norms in terms of beliefs about the consequences of performing the behaviour and about the normative expectations of relevant referents. In the final analysis, then, a person's behaviour is explained by reference to his or her beliefs. Since people's beliefs represent the information (be it correct or incorrect) they have about their worlds, it follows that their behaviour is ultimately determined by this formation. (Fishbein and Ajzen, 1981, p. 281)

As in their model of attitudes, Ajzen and Fishbein suggest that these components are combined mathematically, multiplying each pair together, weighting them appropriately and then adding the two products. The determinants of behaviour can be represented symbolically in the following equation:

$$B \cong BI = (\sum_{j=1}^{n} b_i e_i) \, w_1 + (\sum_{j=1}^{m} nb_j mc_j) \, w_2 \qquad (4)[26]$$

where: B is overt behaviour; BI is intention to perform the behaviour; b_i

is the belief (perceived probability) that performing the behaviour will lead to consequence i; e_i is the evaluation of consequence i; nb_j is the perceived expectation of referent group j; mc_j is the motivation to comply with referent group j; n is the number of salient consequences; m is the number of salient normative beliefs; and w_1 and w_2 are empirically determined regression weights.

There is considerable empirical support for the theory of reasoned action (see Ajzen and Fishbein, 1980). Although some research (Bentler and Speckart, 1979) has reported a direct effect of attitudes on behaviour, Bagozzi (1981) found the classic sequence proposed by Fishbein and Ajzen, whereby attitude influences behaviour only through its impact on intentions. The ultimate effect of attitude on behaviour was, however, relatively small. There has also been some debate about whether the normative and personal influences on behavioural intentions have been satisfactorily separated (see Miniard and Cohen, 1981) and whether an additional component, 'personal normative beliefs', adds significantly to the model's predictive ability (see Pagel and Davidson, 1984). Most recently, Pagel and Davidson's comparison of three expectancy-value models of behaviour concluded that the Fishbein–Ajzen model did better than (vs Rosenberg, 1956) or at least as well as (vs Beach *et al.*, 1979) its competitors (when beliefs were scored on a unipolar scale). Thus the Fishbein–Ajzen approach to behaviour appears valid.

The theory has now been applied to voting behaviour in a number of different studies; these show that a person's intention to vote for any given candidate in an election (and actual voting for that candidate) is a function of the person's attitude towards and subjective norms with respect to voting for the candidate (Ajzen and Fishbein, 1980, chapter 14; Fishbein and Ajzen, 1981; Fishbein and Coombs, 1974).[27] Fishbein and Ajzen's view of the voter from this perspective is a rather respectful one, which argues that: 'voters are aware of both the advantages and disadvantages of voting for a given candidate and that their voting decisions take these considerations into account. This is an eminently rational strategy for making a choice vote. It is neither frivolous nor arbitrary to attempt to maximize the likelihood of achieving valued outcomes.' (1981, p. 290.) Flattering though this view is, we should recall van der Pligt and Eiser's (1983) point, that the expectancy-value model appears unlikely to be *descriptive* of how voters actually decide. However, the model has impressive predictive validity and interestingly voting behaviour is an area where almost perfect attitude–behaviour relations have been demonstrated (see Jaccard, 1981; Kelley and Mirer, 1974), and where the theory of reasoned action contributes an interesting approach. Although it has already been applied to elections in a number of countries, it has not been considered in relation to European elections (which are different in a number of respects). Given the insights contributed already by their expectancy-value analysis applied to European attitudes, use of the Fishbein–Ajzen approach to predicting voting behaviour seems a logical next step for research. It may, in fact, be that the kind of general attitudes measured in this study would correlate quite well with multiple-act criteria; but if we really want to apply social psychology to the prediction of voting next time around in the European elections, then the kind of analysis suggested by the theory of reasoned action would appear most appropriate.

7.2.3 Future polls of European public opinion

As long as the European Commission continues to sponsor the *Euro-baromètre* series, social scientists will be well provided with a mass of evidence on attitudinal aspects of European integration. It is hoped, however, that the present work will have some impact on the questions asked during the second decade of the series. Some key predictors of Community attitudes have been identified, albeit with samples of students. The ideal next step would be to ascertain whether variables such as support and the expectancy-value analysis of goals have the same impact in samples drawn from the general public. At the very least, key predictors and an overall measure of attitude should be included in forthcoming *Euro-baromètre* polls and, if successful, used in a time-series. Future work should also attempt to select items which unambiguously measure utilitarian *or* affective support, if this distinction is not to be discarded.

Although a number of important measures can be suggested, they cannot all be included in the *Euro-baromètre* series for reasons of time, space and economy. Accurate probability samples used in public opinion polling, especially when ten nations are involved, are difficult, time-consuming and expensive. A further recommendation, therefore, is that the Community invest more time and money in in-depth studies, like the present one (see also Bissery, 1972; Gallup International, 1964; Riffault and Tchernia, 1983). This is not an elitist argument against *public* opinion, but rather a plea for further detailed studies of European attitudes. Following Himmelweit *et al.*, it may be argued that: 'politicians and the media would gain more useful information if they were to commission rather fewer superficial polls and instead devoted resources to the building up of small panels, whose attitudes and beliefs could be sampled more searchingly.' (1981, pp, 215–16.) Ideally, these panels would be made up not only of students (as here), but of relevant interest groups, including, for example, farmers, businesspeople, consumers and so on.

All kinds of surveys have their strengths and weaknesses, the present study included. It is now important for different kinds of research to be considered complementary. Thus studies like this one may suggest variables of interest, and exclude others which appear to play only a limited, or negligible, role. Predictor variables identified can then be investigated in the mass public, to see whether they have general validity. Longitudinal work, testing the same sample or 'panel' of respondents over a number of months or years should also be on the agenda. Such work is laborious and demands great care and patience, but as Himmelweit *et al.* (*op. cit.*) have shown, it makes a unique contribution to our understanding of political behaviour. If one of the contributions of polls is to educate, then surely better polls will result in better education. The level of political discourse will be lifted above that of newspaper headlines, and we will begin to understand why people think and act in political life as they do.

Another exciting prospect for future research is a merging of the study of 'opinion makers' (e.g. Inglehart, Rabier, Gordon and Sørensen, 1980) with the study of opinion polls. As Dalton and Duval (1981) contend, the mass media act as an interface between foreign affairs and the mass public; the media generate, reinforce and change opinions. Starting from the observation that trends in public opinion are as volatile as changes in political events (see Deutsch and Merritt, 1965; Shepherd, 1975), Dalton and Duval set out to model the relationship between political events and foreign policy opinions, using time-series analysis. Having first analysed reporting about the European Community and demonstrated that for most months the balance of public events was negative, these authors then tested three models using, on the one hand, a time-series for 'events' and, on the other hand, a time-series for 'opinions'. Results favoured an 'opinion-decay' model. In this model events have an immediate effect on opinions, but opinions return to an equilibrium point only gradually, over several months. Taking nothing away from this sophisticated analysis, its overlap with the present research is obvious. As content-analytic measures of 'events' become more precise, so too must measures of 'opinion'. To give an example from the present study, detailed reporting an agricultural policy may have an effect on judgements of that policy, but not on overall attitudes towards the Community (because the link between assessment of the C.A.P. and overall attitude, as identified here, was slight). Thus conclusions about the effects of mass media may well be erroneous as long as researchers continue to use global and unspecific measures of how respondents view the Community. It seems to the present author that such a marriage of precise coding and attitudinal measures with a powerful statistical modelling technique would be a highly original contribution to the literature. It would certainly advance research much further than the very general statements about the press to which this volume too has been limited.

In sum, the present study has focussed on the nature and structure of attitudes rather than their processes of formation and change. Future work could address the latter issue with a richer array of measures, and could also proceed to a more challenging longitudinal study of how events influence views about the Community on a variety of specific dimensions.

7.2.4 *The relevance of social psychology for the study of European integration*

The final issue to be considered in this work concerns the relevance of social psychology. While other writers have enquired about the relevance of social psychology for an analysis of international relations (Etzioni, 1969; Kelman, 1965c), political behaviour (Sears, 1969) or voting (Himmelweit *et al.*, 1981), the present concern is more specific. Does social psychology have a contribution to make to attitudinal studies of European integration?

The benefits and limitations of a social-psychological approach have been eloquently stated by Himmelweit *et al.*:

> Social psychology, through its methodologies and theories, has a substantial contribution to make to the explanation of social phenomena, provided that researchers develop a sensitivity for the problems they investigate at the societal as well as the psychological level.... This involves more use of the insights of the other social sciences and of historical and comparative data than is currently the practice.... If social psychology is to make the contribution to the understanding of society and social change of which it is capable, then social psychologists must focus more on the study of social phenomena than they do at present, and must develop appropriate conceptual frameworks and methodologies for such studies. (Himmelweit *et al.*, 1981, pp. 187–8)

Methodologically, the major strengths of this work are the following: use of open-ended and closed-ended questions; a large set of multi-point rating scales with balanced wording; and the application of a set of multivariate statistical procedures.

Considering first the use of open and closed questions, various parallels between the two sets of data have been noted in the text (e.g. the British respondents' concern with perceived inequity; and the poor knowledge of the Italian respondents). Following Campbell and Fiske (1959), it should be noted that particular measurement approaches contain 'biases' and that the most efficient research strategy is to exploit, rather than seek to eliminate, these biases by means of multiple methods. Some of the advantages and disadvantages of the two methods have been dealt with already (Chapter 3); here it is simply argued that the adopted methodology has provided an interesting, innovative and consistent picture of respondents' attitudes to and knowledge about the Community.

The use of a large set of response scales allowed for detailed analysis of the structure of European attitudes. It is, unfortunately, in the nature of attitude and opinion research, that there is almost inevitably a trade-off between the adequacy of sampling and the sophistication of structural analysis. The present work, cognisant of the mass of data already yielded by opinion surveys, explicitly developed an extensive questionnaire to investigate attitudinal structure, and sought out respondents suited to the task. Because students are not representative of the general population, one should not expect the attitudinal structure of the two groups to be isomorphic (although they need not be dissimilar). However, the basic similarity in content between the attitudes studied here and those reported in the *Euro-baromètre* series suggests that the understanding of attitudes achieved by the present analysis has considerable relevance for our understanding of attitudes in mass publics. The exact nature of such an extrapolation remains, of course, a topic for further research.

The final aspect of methodology which should be highlighted, multivariate statistics, is closely linked to the quest for attitudinal structure. Although social psychology cannot claim to have invented multivariate statistical techniques, techniques such as factor analysis, multiple regression, path analysis and discriminant analysis are to be found increasingly in social-psychological research. As shown by the present study's use of multiple regression and path analysis, such techniques help to produce a mass of data to a manageable size, and draw attention, for example, to the small number of predictor variables which have a direct effect on attitudes. It may be safely predicted that, as the most modern multivariate methods for theory-testing (e.g. the 'analysis of covariance structures'; see Jöreskog and Sörbom, 1981) are increasingly applied to attitudinal research, so will the contribution of social psychology assume greater importance in the attempt to explain political and other attitudes (see Bagozzi and Burnkrant, 1979; Bentler and Speckart, 1979).

As outlined in Chapter 3, the content of the present questionnaire was based on existing theory in social psychology (and political science). Emphasis is placed here on just two contributions from social psychology, namely attitude theory and equity theory. The analysis of attitudes, based on Fishbein and Ajzen's (1975) expectancy-value approach, provided a good estimate of overall attitude and made clear how different the attitudes of people in the various member states are. This analysis has gone beyond the mere observation that the British like the Community less than does anybody else, and has shown that they arrive at this attitude on quite different grounds than do other respondents. Specifically, the British did not differ in terms of their evaluations of various economic and political goals (see Table 5.2), but they did clearly perceive the achivement of these goals as less likely (see Table 5.3). Thus although the present data led to a critical discussion of the Fishbein–Ajzen approach in computational terms, the distinction between values and expectancies was shown to be fundamental for an understanding of attitudes. The fact that expectancies proved the differentiating factor is consistent with Fishbein and Ajzen's (1981) application of their approach to the area of political attitudes and voting behaviour. As they acknowledged: 'A well-informed electorate should be able to agree on a candidate's expressed position with respect to a given policy, but voters may well disagree about the likelihood that he will be able to implement it.' (p. 288.) Further advantages accruing from the expectancy-value theoretical analysis of attitudes may be found in the implications for attitude change and attitude–behaviour relations, discussed above.

The different attitudinal basis of the British respondents was also evident from the finding that their level of utilitarian support was lower than that of the other three samples, and that the correlation between such items and overall attitude was highly significant only for the British. This result was consistent with the glaring perception of inequity by British and W. German respondents, both of which groups held less positive attitudes. By looking at the perceived ratio of contributions and benefits for each of the four member states, and comparing these with each other, it was possible to determine perceived inequity. To some extent this analysis put the complaints of the British in a somewhat different perspective, because the W. Germans too were very dissatisfied. However, the finding that every member state thinks it is worse off than the average other member (the *pauper inter pares* effect) contributes perhaps the most striking insight into the way people perceive their country's relationship with the Community. The equity theory analyses thus made clear that the whole issue of inputs to and outcomes from the Community has an important psychological dimension.

The application of social-psychological theory has therefore brought to bear upon a practical social issue a general social-psychological perspective, contributing some novel insights to this area. Theoretically, it is also very important to have material of this kind since it provides us with external validity for both attitude and equity theories. Notwithstanding these theories, it might be claimed that the theoretical framework or 'meta-theory' guiding this research was rather narrowly conceived. In discussing the functions of attitudes (Chapter 3), it was stated that the utilitarian function of attitudes (developing favourable attitudes towards objects that are rewarding, and unfavourable attitudes towards objects that are unrewarding) seemed most relevant. This same notion of utilitarianism, or a cost–benefit analysis, can be seen to underlie the expectancy-value analysis, equity theory and the notion of utilitarian support. However, it must be remembered that other less rational, theoretical perspectives were also represented in the questionnaire. Some, such as affective support, proved very influential; others, such as stereotypes about national groups and the images of different countries appeared less central, but not irrelevant. Obviously, there are many other questions that could be raised in future research – the relationship between national and European identification; the relationship between political–economic variables, on the one hand, and social-psychological variables, on the other hand; the role of socializing agents (family, peers, the mass media) in shaping the development of Community attitudes; and patterns of consumer behaviour in a European market. All these topics seem worthy of future attention, but they could not have been considered in one study.

In the above quotation, Himmelweit *et al.* (1981) also argue that social psychologists should make more use of the insights of other disciplines. In this respect the present volume's bibliography speaks for itself. Many of the references are from the literature of political science, not social psychology, and these have played a fundamental role in the conception, execution and reporting of this research. Specifically, much has been gained from the literature, both empirical and theoretical, on opinion polls, and from political science writings on utilitarian – and affective – support.

The role of social psychology that emerges is both modest and essential, as Kelman (1965c) argued. Social psychology complements, but does not, cannot and should not replace other social science disciplines in the study of European integration. This can be seen in the marriage of political science notions (utilitarian and affective support) with social-psychological concepts (expectancy-value; equity) to provide a clear explanation of overall attitudes. The implication is that social psychology can and should form part of the study of attitudinal integration in Europe, but it will be for further research to chart fully these contributions. If and when that happens, the present work will have made its contribution.

Appendix A
Characteristics of national samples

Table A.1. *Characteristics of national samples I: age, sex, faculty*

		Country of respondent			
		W. Germany	Italy	France	U.K.
(A)	Age (years) mean:	23.9	19.8	23.0	22.2
(B)	Sex				
	Male:	58	73	70	55
	Female:	69	68	77	74
	No answer:	1			
(C)	Faculty				
	Social sciences:	110	72	109	103
	Arts:	6	5	17	13
	Natural science:	12	64	21	13
	Sample size	128	141	147	129

Table A.2 *Characteristics of national samples II: political affiliation*

(A) W. Germany

Political party	N	%
1. Social Democrat (SPD)	40	31.3
2. Christian Democrat (CDU)	6	4.7
3. 'Green' (Grüne)	62	48.4
4. Free Democrat (FDP)	3	2.3
Not given	17	13.3
Total	128	100

(B) Italy

Political party	N	%
1. Christian Democrat (DC)	21	15.6
2. Communist Party (PCI)	26	18.4
3. Socialist Party (PSI)	4	2.8
4. Social Democrat (PSDI)	4	2.8
5. Republican Party (PRI)	8	5.7
6. Social Movement (MSI)	6	4.3
7. Liberal Party (PLI)	1	0.7
8. Party of Proletarian Unity (PLUP) Proletarian Democracy (DP)	10	7.1
9. Radical Party (PR)	2	1.4
Not given	59	41.1
Total	141	100

(C) France

Political party	N	%
Union for French Democracy (UDF)	8	5.4
Ecology Party	8	5.4
Assembly for the Republic (RPR)	8	5.4
Socialist Party (PS)	54	36.7
Communist Party (PCF)	8	5.4
Not given	61	41.5
Total	147	100

(D) U.K.

Political party	N	%
Conservative	24	18.6
Labour	41	31.8
Liberal/SDP Alliance	42	32.6
Communist	5	3.9
Not given	17	13.1
Total	129	100

Note:
N denotes the total number of responses of a given type.

Appendix B
English-language version of the questionnaire

Questionnaire on your views about the European Economic Community

The questions in this booklet form part of a study on what ordinary citizens know, think and feel about the European Economic Community or EEC, sometimes called the Common Market.

If this questionnaire is to serve its intended purpose, it is important that every question be answered. Please attempt to work through all the questions in their given order – please do not look ahead to see what questions come next. It is also important that you *write clearly*, otherwise we may not later be able to read exactly what you have written. Please give full answers to all the questions, these will help us very much in our enquiry. There are no right or wrong answers. We are only interested in your personal opinion. Also, the results will be treated as confidential and you can remain anonymous. There is no need to write your name on the questionnaire. Thank you, in advance, for your help.

There are quite a few questions to answer, so do not spend too much time puzzling over an answer. Remember, we are interested in your *opinions*. Each new section of the questionnaire begins with a few lines to explain more clearly the specific task. If you read this advice carefully, you should find the task easy and, we hope, interesting.

A. What do you think of the EEC? What are its advantages and disadvantages, successes and failures? Please try to give reasons for your answers.

    – Please write clearly –

B. What are the basic principles and goals of the EEC? Why was the Community founded?

    – Please write clearly –

C. About which common policy of the EEC have you heard or read the most? What have you heard and read, and what is your attitude to that policy? Please try to give reasons for your answers.

    – Please write clearly –

227

D. This section of the questionnaire is made up of two different parts, each requiring you to make ratings.

In making your ratings, please remember the following points:

(1)   Place your marks in the middle of the scale-points. *Not* on the boundaries:

extremely :____: ____: :_X_: :____: :____:X :____: :____: extremely
   good   this   *not* this   bad

(2)   Be sure to answer *all* items.
(3)   Never put more than *one* check mark on a single scale.
(4)   If you change your answer, correct it *clearly* by crossing out the old answer.

Part 1

Please *evaluate* 14 political and economic goals, i.e. say how good or bad *you* think they are. Your view will be indicated by where you place a X on the scale. If you think a goal is *good*, then you place a X near to this word. If you think a goal is *bad*, then you place a X near to this word. The distance between the X and each word conveys your evaluation. Place a X in the centre if you are undecided. For example, if you thought a goal was *extremely* bad, you would place your X like this:

extremely :____: :____: :____: :____: :____: :____: :_X_: extremely
   good   bad

    If you thought a goal was *quite good*, you would place your X like this:
extremely :____: :_X_: :____: :____: :____: :____: :____: extremely
   good   bad

Now please *evaluate* each of the following 14 goals.

1.   Bringing about a 'United States of Europe'
    extremely :____: :____: :____: ____: :____: :____: :____: extremely
       good   bad

2.   Building a defence against communism
    extremely :____: :____: :____: ____: :____: :____: :____: extremely
       good   bad

3.   Strengthening Europe's role in the world
    extremely :____: :____: :____: ____: :____: :____: :____: extremely
       good   bad

4.   Achieving lasting peace in Europe
    extremely :____: :____: :____: ____: :____: :____: :____: extremely
       good   bad

5.   Bringing about economic expansion and steadily increasing the standard of living of people throughout the EEC
    extremely :____: :____: :____: ____: :____: :____: :____: extremely
       good   bad

6.   Achieving greater mutual understanding between European nations
     extremely :___: :___: :___: ___: :___: :___: :___: extremely
     good   bad

7.   Providing a third block, between the two 'superpowers'
     extremely :___: :___: :___: ___: :___: :___: :___: extremely
     good   bad

8.   Establishing a customs union with free movement of goods between member
     states
     extremely :___: :___: :___: ___: :___: :___: :___: extremely
     good   bad

9.   Dismantling quotas and all barriers to trade
     extremely :___: :___: :___: ___: :___: :___: :___: extremely
     good   bad

10. Establishing a common customs tariff and a common commercial policy
     towards third countries
     extremely :___: :___: :___: ___: :___: :___: :___: extremely
     good   bad

11. Free movement of persons, goods, services and capital between EEC states
     extremely :___: :___: :___: ___: :___: :___: :___: extremely
     good   bad

12. Ensuring that competition is not distorted within the EEC
     extremely :___: :___: :___: ___: :___: :___: :___: extremely
     good   bad

13. Countries producing goods for which they are most suited
     extremely :___: :___: :___: ___: :___: :___: :___: extremely
     good   bad

14. Creating a market of large-scale production and consumption (like American
     and Soviet markets)
     extremely :___: :___: :___: ___: :___: :___: :___: extremely
     good   bad

     – Please make sure that you have answered all the questions –

Part 2

Now please rate how *probable* you think it is that the EEC is *bringing about* each of
the goals. As before, your view will be indicated by where you place a X on the scale.
If you think it is *probable* that the EEC is bringing about a goal, then you place a
X near to this word. If you think it is *improbable* that the EEC is bringing about a
goal, then you place a X near to this word. Place a X in the centre if you are
undecided. For example, if you thought it only *slightly probable* that the EEC was
bringing about a goal, you would place your mark like this:

               probable :___: :___: : X : ___: :___: :___: :___: improbable

If you thought it *extremely improbable* that the EEC was bringing about a goal, you would place your X like this:

probable :___: :___: :___: ___: :___: :___: :_X_: improbable

Now please rate how *probable* it is that the EEC is bringing about each of the following 14 goals.

1.   The EEC is bringing about a 'United States of Europe'
      probable :___: :___: :___: ___: :___: :___: :___: improbable

2.   The EEC is building a defence against communism
      probable :___: :___: :___: ___: :___: :___: :___: improbable

3.   The EEC is strengthening Europe's role in the world
      probable :___: :___: :___: ___: :___: :___: :___: improbable

4.   The EEC is helping to achieve lasting peace in Europe
      probable :___: :___: :___: ___: :___: :___: :___: improbable

5.   The EEC is bringing about economic expansion and steadily increasing the standard of living of people throughout the EEC
      probable :___: :___: :___: ___: :___: :___: :___: improbable

6.   The EEC is helping to achieve greater mutual understanding between European nations
      probable :___: :___: :___: ___: :___: :___: :___: improbable

7.   The EEC is providing a third block, between the two 'superpowers'
      probable :___: :___: :___: ___: :___: :___: :___: improbable

8.   The EEC is establishing a customs union with free movement of goods between member states
      probable :___: :___: :___: ___: :___: :___: :___: improbable

9.   The EEC is dismantling quotas and all barriers to trade
      probable :___: :___: :___: ___: :___: :___: :___: improbable

10.   The EEC is establishing a customs tariff and a common commercial policy towards third countries
      probable :___: :___: :___: ___: .:___: :___: :___: improbable

11.   The EEC is bringing about free movement of persons, goods, services and capital between EEC states
      probable :___: :___: :___: ___: :___: :___: :___: improbable

12.   The EEC is ensuring that competition is not distorted within the EEC
      probable :___: :___: :___: ___: :___: :___: :___: improbable

13.   The EEC is encouraging countries to produce goods for which they are most suited
      probable :___: :___: :___: ___: :___: :___: :___: improbable

14.   The EEC is creating a market of large-scale production and consumption (like American and Soviet markets)

probable :____: :____: :____: ____: :____: :____: :____: improbable

– Please check that you have left no gaps –

E. Please rate how you see the achievement of EEC common policy in the following areas. Indicate your view by placing a X on the scale for each of the following 5 items. Place a X in the centre if you are undecided.

1.   In my opinion the *agricultural* policy of the EEC has been:

extremely :____: :____: :____: ____: :____: :____: :____: extremely
unsuccessful   successful

2.   In my opinion the *transport* policy of the EEC has been:

extremely :____: :____: :____: ____: :____: :____: :____: extremely
unsuccessful   successful

3.   In my opinion the *energy* policy of the EEC has been:

extremely :____: :____: :____: ____: :____: :____: :____: extremely
unsuccessful   successful

4.   In my opinion the *environment protection* policy of the EEC has been:

extremely :____: :____: :____: ____: :____: :____: :____: extremely
unsuccessful   successful

5.   In my opinion the *defence* policy of the EEC has been:

extremely :____: :____: :____: ____: :____: :____: :____: extremely
unsuccessful   successful

F. How successful or unsuccessful do you think the EEC has been in bringing about the following effects? Please indicate your view by placing a mark on the scale for each of the 10 following items. Place a X in the centre if you are undecided.

1.   Increased agricultural productivity

extremely :____: :____: :____: ____: :____: :____: :____: extremely
unsuccessful   successful

2.   Reasonably priced agricultural produce for the consumer

extremely :____: :____: :____: ____: :____: :____: :____: extremely
unsuccessful   successful

3.   Harmonization of national transport costs within each of the member states

extremely :____: :____: :____: ____: :____: :____: :____: extremely
unsuccessful   successful

4.   Increased efficiency of industries

extremely :____: :____: :____: ____: :____: :____: :____: extremely
unsuccessful   successful

5.   Freedom of movement for EEC citizens to work elsewhere in the EEC

extremely :____: :____: :____: ____: :____: :____: :____: extremely
unsuccessful   successful

6.   Speaking with a single voice when the EEC acts on the world stage
      extremely :____: :____: :____: ____: :____: :____: :____: extremely
      unsuccessful   successful

7.   Reducing travel restrictions in the EEC
      extremely :____: :____: :____: ____: :____: :____: :____: extremely
      unsuccessful   successful

8.   Increasing trade between member states
      extremely :____: :____: :____: ____: :____: :____: :____: extremely
      unsuccessful   successful

9.   Reducing inequalities between regions of the community
      extremely :____: :____: :____: ____: :____: :____: :____: extremely
      unsuccessful   successful

10.   Providing social security benefits for EEC citizens who work in other member
      states
      extremely :____: :____: :____: ____: :____: :____: :____: extremely
      unsuccessful   successful

      – Please make sure that you leave no gaps –

G. In this section we are interested in what you see as the gains and losses associated
with EEC membership. Please indicate your agreement or disagreement with each
of the statements by placing a X on each of the scales, at the point corresponding
to your attitude. Place a X in the centre if you are undecided.

1.   I, personally, have gained from the EEC
      strongly :____: :____: :____: ____: :____: :____: :____: strongly
      agree   disagree

2.   The United Kingdom's net contribution to the EEC budget is excessive
      strongly :____: :____: :____: ____: :____: :____: :____: strongly
      agree   disagree

3.   The United Kingdom has benefitted from the EEC
      strongly :____: :____: :____: ____: :____: :____: :____: strongly
      agree   disagree

4.   Through the United Kingdom's membership of the EEC you are subsidising
      poorer groups in other EEC countries
      strongly :____: :____: :____: ____: :____: :____: :____: strongly
      agree   disagree

5.   The United Kingdom has gained from the Common Agricultural Policy
      strongly :____: :____: :____: ____: :____: :____: :____: strongly
      agree   disagree

6.   Through the United Kingdom's membership of the EEC you are forced to give
      too much money to poorer groups in developing countries
      strongly :____: :____: :____: ____: :____: :____: :____: strongly
      agree   disagree

7. The United Kingdom has gained from the Community Regional Fund
strongly :___: :___: :___: ___: :___: :___: :___: strongly
agree   disagree

8. The United Kingdom has become less competitive economically as a result of the EEC
strongly :___: :___: :___: ___: :___: :___: :___: strongly
agree   disagree

– Please ensure that you have omitted no questions –

H. The questions in this section deal with the relations between independent countries and the EEC. Please indicate how much you agree or disagree with each statement. Place a X at one of the 7 points on each scale to indicate your view. Place a X in the centre if you are undecided.

1. The EEC has increased national rivalries in Europe
strongly :___: :___: :___: ___: :___: :___: :___: strongly
agree   disagree

2. I feel a strong sense of solidarity with developments in the EEC
strongly :___: :___: :___: ___: :___: :___: :___: strongly
agree   disagree

3. The EEC interferes with the national government of the United Kingdom
strongly :___: :___: :___: ___: :___: :___: :___: strongly
agree   disagree

4. The EEC can be trusted to look after the interests of the United Kingdom
strongly :___: :___: :___: ___: :___: :___: :___: strongly
agree   disagree

5. I do not have confidence in the EEC's handling of economic affairs
strongly :___: :___: :___: ___: :___: :___: :___: strongly
agree   disagree

6. I am more loyal to the interests of the EEC than to the interests of the United Kingdom
strongly :___: :___: :___: ___: :___: :___: :___: strongly
agree   disagree

7. The United Kingdom should not help out another member state in economic difficulties
strongly :___: :___: :___: ___: :___: :___: :___: strongly
agree   disagree

8. The people of the United Kingdom should be willing to make personal sacrifices to help out another member state in difficulties
strongly :___: :___: :___: ___: :___: :___: :___: strongly
agree   disagree

– Please check that you have left no spaces –

I. In this section we are interested in how you describe people from your own and from certain other European countries.

Before ascribing some characteristics to various nationalities, please note the following example. To the left you will see the name of a characteristic, for example *friendly*. At the top are the nationalities.

Please enter in the proper space the percentage of the population of each country that *you believe* to possess the stated characteristic. Note the example:

	Inhabitants of Country A	Inhabitants of Country B	Inhabitants of Country C	Inhabitants of Country ...
friendly	70	40	...	...
...	...	...	...	...

Thus you would have indicated a belief that 70% of the people of country A and 40% of the people of country B could accurately be characterized as being friendly by placing the numbers '70' and '40' in the appropriate spaces. Please attempt to fill in a number for each nationality before going on to the next line and the next attribute.

In the questionnaire you are welcome to use all possible percentages, from 0 to 100. It is of course clear that it may sometimes be difficult to arrive at a precise number. In cases of doubt please enter your best guess; statistical accuracy is not expected. Do, please, write the numbers clearly. When you are filling out this particular questionnaire you do not have to place the % sign after the number you have selected. Please check that you have filled in a number from 0 to 100 in each of the boxes.

	The British	The French	The Germans	The Italians
intelligent				
progressive				
conceited				
reserved				
domineering				
industrious				
aggressive				
passionate				
quick-tempered				
extremely nationalistic				

Now, please *evaluate* each of the 10 characteristics, indicating how good or bad you think it is to possess each characteristic. Place a X in the centre if you are undecided.

1. intelligent
    extremely :___: :___: :___: ___: :___: :___: :___: extremely
    good   bad

2. progressive
    extremely :___: :___: :___: ___: :___: :___: :___: extremely
    good   bad

3. conceited
    extremely :___: :___: :___: ___: :___: :___: :___: extremely
    good   bad

4. reserved
    extremely :___: :___: :___: ___: :___: :___: :___: extremely
    good   bad

5. domineering
    extremely :___: :___: :___: ___: :___: :___: :___: extremely
    good   bad

6. industrious
    extremely :___: :___: :___: ___: :___: :___: :___: extremely
    good   bad

7. aggressive
    extremely :___: :___: :___: ___: :___: :___: :___: extremely
    good   bad

8. passionate
    extremely :___: :___: :___: ___: :___: :___: :___: extremely
    good   bad

9. quick-tempered
    extremely :___: :___: :___: ___: :___: :___: :___: extremely
    good   bad

10. extremely nationalistic
    extremely :___: :___: :___: ___: :___: :___: :___: extremely
    good   bad

    – Please leave no gaps –

J. This section is concerned with the characteristics of various countries. In a column on the left side of the page are listed various characteristics, along the top of the page are the names of 4 European countries.

Working across one line at a time, please fill in the degree to which you believe that each country possesses each characteristic in the appropriate space. In doing this please select from the numbers 0 1 2 3 4 5 6 7 8 9. If you believe the country to be *totally without* a characteristic you should answer with the number 0. The more you believe a country to possess a particular attribute, the higher should be the number that you enter. If you believe a country to be *very strongly characterized* by the attribute in question, please enter the number 9. The example shows how the numbers are to be entered; for instance, it has been indicated that country A is extremely prosperous.

	Country A	Country B	Country C	Country ...
prosperous	9	3	6	...
...				...

Please enter a number for each country before going on to the next line and the next characteristic. Please fill in the questionnaire *completely*, as this is important for the proper analysis of the results. Please write the numbers very clearly and check carefully that you have placed a number from 0 to 9 in each of the boxes.

	United Kingdom	France	Germany	Italy
prosperous				
has a great deal of communist influence				
aggressively militaristic				
politically stable				
has few economic problems				
undemocratic				
politically independent				
powerless				
economically and industrially developed				
infertile country				

Now please *evaluate* each of the 10 characteristics of countries, indicating how good or bad each characteristic is. Place a X in the centre if you are undecided.

1.   prosperous
        extremely :___: :___: :___: ___: :___: :___: :___: extremely
            good   bad

2.   has a great deal of communist influence
     extremely :___: :___: :___: ___: :___: :___: :___: extremely
       good   bad

3.   aggressively militaristic
     extremely :___: :___: :___: ___: :___: :___: :___: extremely
       good   bad

4.   politically stable
     extremely :___: :___: :___: ___: :___: :___: :___: extremely
       good   bad

5.   has few economic problems
     extremely :___: :___: :___: ___: :___: :___: :___: extremely
       good   bad

6.   undemocratic
     extremely :___: :___: :___: ___: :___: :___: :___: extremely
       good   bad

7.   politically independent
     extremely :___: :___: :___: ___: :___: :___: :___: extremely
       good   bad

8.   powerless
     extremely :___: :___: :___: ___: :___: :___: :___: extremely
       good   bad

9.   economically and industrially developed
     extremely :___: :___: :___: ___: :___: :___: :___: extremely
       good   bad

10. infertile country
     extremely :___: :___: :___: ___: :___: :___: :___: extremely
       good   bad

– Please make sure that you have evaluated each characteristic –

K. This section deals with beliefs about international relations. Please put a X on each of the scales below, to show how much you agree or disagree with each statement. Put a X in the middle if you are undecided.

1.   In my opinion the United Kingdom should give up trying to be on friendly terms with other countries.
     strongly :___: :___: :___: ___: :___: :___: :___: strongly
       agree   disagree

2.   I think that if the United Kingdom is friendly towards other countries they are not as likely to be aggressive towards us.
     strongly :___: :___: :___: ___: :___: :___: :___: strongly
       agree   disagree

3.   In my opinion, only foolish dreamers believe that international friendliness can accomplish anything in the modern world.
      strongly :____: :____: :____: ____: :____: :____: :____: strongly
      agree   disagree

4.   I feel that in international relations it is just plain common sense to 'love thy neighbour as thyself'.
      strongly :____: :____: :____: ____: :____: :____: :____: strongly
      agree   disagree

5.   I believe that the U.K. should send food and materials to any country that needs them.
      strongly :____: :____: :____: ____: :____: :____: :____: strongly
      agree   disagree

6.   In my opinion, we shouldn't risk our happiness and well-being by getting involved with other countries.
      strongly :____: :____: :____: ____: :____: :____: :____: strongly
      agree   disagree

7.   I think that helping foreign countries is a waste of money.
      strongly :____: :____: :____: ____: :____: :____: :____: strongly
      agree   disagree

8.   In my opinion, international good will is essential to the welfare of the United Kingdom.
      strongly :____: :____: :____: ____: :____: :____: :____: strongly
      agree   disagree

9.   It is my belief that we should get even with any country that tries to take advantage of the United Kingdom.
      strongly :____: :____: :____: ____: :____: :____: :____: strongly
      agree   disagree

10.   I feel that we can't have 'peace on earth, good will to men', because other nations are not of good will.
      strongly :____: :____: :____: ____: :____: :____: :____: strongly
      agree   disagree

11.   I think that being friendly with other countries will do more good than harm.
      strongly :____: :____: :____: ____: :____: :____: :____: strongly
      agree   disagree

12.   It is my feeling that we should try to help all nations, whether we get anything special out of it or not.
      strongly :____: :____: :____: ____: :____: :____: :____: strongly
      agree   disagree

13.   I think that other countries are always getting us into wars.
      strongly :____: :____: :____: ____: :____: :____: :____: strongly
      agree   disagree

14. I think that being friendly with other nations is a real help in solving international problems.
strongly :____: :____: :____: ____: :____: :____: :____: strongly
   agree   disagree

15. It is my belief that other nations are often plotting against us.
strongly :____: :____: :____: ____: :____: :____: :____: strongly
   agree   disagree

16. In my opinion, all sensible people believe in trying to be friendly with other countries.
strongly :____: :____: :____: ____: :____: :____: :____: strongly
   agree   disagree

   – *Please answer all questions* –

L. This section contains a few other questions on European attitudes and views relating to the EEC. The questions vary in format, so please work carefully through them in the order in which they are presented.

1. Do you intend to take an active interest in EEC affairs in the coming years?
extremely :____: :____: :____: ____: :____: :____: :____: extremely
   likely   unlikely

2. In your opinion, which member state benefits *most* from the EEC?
   _____

3. In your opinion, which member state benefits *least* from the EEC?
   _____

4. In your opinion, which member state contributes *most* to the EEC?
   _____

5. In your opinion, which member state contributes *least* to the EEC?
   _____

6. How much do you like each of the following nationalities?
   (a) The British
   not at all :____: :____: :____: ____: :____: :____: :____: very much
   (b) The French
   not at all :____: :____: :____: ____: :____: :____: :____: very much
   (c) The Germans
   not at all :____: :____: :____: ____: :____: :____: :____: very much
   (d) The Italians
   not at all :____: :____: :____: ____: :____: :____: :____: very much

7. Do you think the EEC has become too big to be effective?
   YES/NO

8. Do you think the United Kingdom should vote to leave the EEC as soon as possible?
   YES/NO

9.   How confident are you in the United Kingdom government's handling of economic affairs?

extremely :___: :___: :___: ___: :___: :___: :___: not at all
   confident   confident

10.   How do you feel the EEC is described in the mass media?

extremely :___: :___: :___: ___: :___: :___: :___: extremely
   positively   negatively

11.   Considering only the positive qualities of the EEC and ignoring its negative qualities, how much in favour of the EEC do the positive qualities make you feel? For example, think about your attitude towards ice cream. Although you may be against eating ice cream, when you think of its positive qualities – ignoring its negative qualities – you realize that ice cream tastes good, especially on a hot day. Thus, even though you are against eating ice cream, there may be qualities of ice cream which are positive. If you cannot think of any positive qualities of the EEC, then you should indicate that you have 'no feelings in favour'. Otherwise, mark the scale at a place which represents the degree to which these qualities make you feel in favour of the EEC.

:____: :____: :____: :____:
no feelings   slightly   moderately   strongly
in favour   in favour   in favour   in favour

12.   Considering only the negative qualities of the EEC and ignoring its positive qualities, how much against the EEC do the negative qualities make you feel? For example, think about your attitude towards ice cream. Although you may have a favourable attitude towards ice cream, when you think of its negative qualities – ignoring its positive qualities – you realize that ice cream has unwanted calories and contains a lot of sugar. Thus, even though you are favourable, there may be qualities of ice cream which are negative. If you cannot think of any negative qualities of the EEC, then you should indicate that you have 'no feelings against'. Otherwise, mark the scale at a place which represents the degree to which these qualities make you feel against the EEC.

:____: :____: :____: :____:
strongly   moderately   slightly   no feelings
against   against   against   against

13.   Overall, what is your attitude towards the EEC?

:____: :____: :____: :____: :____: :____: :____:
strongly   moderately slightly   neutral or slightly   moderately strongly
against   against   against   undecided   in favour   in favour   in favour

M. This section concerns some more personal details about yourself to provide us with a clearer picture of your background. The questions are not all of the same type, so please work carefully through them in the order presented.

1.   How old are you? _____ years

2.   What sex are you? _____ male   (place a X beside one)
                       _____ female

3.   In which country were you born? _____

4.   What nationality are you? _____

5.   At which university are you studying _____

6.   What subject are you studying _____

7.   Have you ever studied politics or economics?   YES/NO
     If YES, for how long?   _____years

8.   For which political party would you vote if there were a general election
     tomorrow? _____

9.   How much time have you spent in other European countries?
     an extremely 6   5   4   3   2   1   0   no time
       long time   at all

10. How frequently do you travel abroad in Europe?
     extremely 6   5   4   3   2   1   0   never
       frequently   at all

11. What newspaper(s) do you read regularly?

N. In this final part of the questionnaire we are no longer interested in your opinions,
but your knowledge about the EEC. Please try to answer the following questions
about the EEC. If you don't know an answer, just write 'don't know'.

1.   How many member states are there in the EEC? _____

2.   Name as many as you can:

3.   Name 3 of the major decision-making institutions of the EEC. Try to get their
     names exactly right.
     a._____
     b._____
     c._____

4.   What is the position held by Mr Gaston Thorn? _____

5.   Which common policy accounts for the largest percentage of the EEC budget?
     _____

6.   What office is held by Mr Piet Dankert? _____

7.   What is the name of the convention which covers the EEC's economic
     relationship with African, Caribbean and Pacific states? _____

8.   How many countries were there in the original 'Common Market'? ___

9.   Which treaties form the basis of the EEC? _____

10. When were they ratified? _____

Appendix C
Content-analysis coding scheme
(supplement to Chapter 4)

Appendix C: Examples of responses categorised according to content-analysis scheme.

1. Overall view

1.1.   neutral
a)   'my view is ambiguous'
b)   'has certain advantages and disadvantages'

1.2.   negative
a)   'I object to its ridiculous nature'
b)   'an odious mess'

1.3.   positive
a)   'a good idea'
b)   'I like it'

1.4.   conditional positive
a)   'a good idea, but in practise...'
b)   'in principle good, but...'
c)   'in theory good, but ineffectual'
d)   'it would be good, if...'

2A. Positive aspects of the European Community

2.1.   commercial policy
2.1.1. expansion of free exchanges
a)   'free exchanges are encouraged'
b)   'free trade between member States'

2.1.2. dismantling quotas and tariffs for trade
a)   'trade barriers lowered'
b)   'absence of trading restrictions'

2.1.3. unification and expansion of markets
a)   'larger market for goods'
b)   'guaranteed market for producers'

2.1.4. harmonisation of laws, norms
a)   'consistency in laws'
b)   'common laws'

2.2.   economic policy
2.2.1. economic cooperation
a)   'financial support for each other'
b)   'good economic relations'

2.2.2. common monetary policy
a)   'common monetary policy'
b)   'unification of currency'

2.2.3. production and supply of goods
a)   'greater availability of goods'
b)   'certainty of supply'

2.3.   Community cooperation
2.3.1. cultural, technical and scientific cooperation
a)   'increased communication and cooperation'
b)   'provides a forum for discussion at the European level'

2.3.2. freedom of travel
a)   'do away with bureaucracy in travel'
b)   'freedom of movement for individuals at frontiers'

2.3.3. European unity/identity
a)   'sense of European unity'
b)   'breakdown of national stereotypes'

2.3.4. help other member states
a)   'help poorer members'
b)   'central fund for the financing of poorer EEC countries'

2.3.5. build peace
a)   'peace in Europe'
b)   'peace'

2.4.   international affairs
2.4.1. European foreign policy
a)   'acting with one voice on the world stage'
b)   'promotes a united European front'

2.4.2. block against the 'superpowers'
a)   'a bloc between the superpowers'
b)   'bastion against Russia'

2B. Negative aspects of the European Community

2.1.   commercial policy
2.1.1. negative effect on prices
a)   'ordinary people pay more'
b)   'this country now more expensive to live in'

2.1.2. import-export restrictions
a)   'disrupts a country's economy by cheap imports'
b)   'impinge on a particular country's own idea for exporting and importing goods'

2.1.3.   forced harmonisation
a)   'forced to change from imperial to metric measures'
b)   'petty laws lead to unrest'

2.2.   economic policy
2.2.1.   bureaucracy and centralisation
a)   'petty bureaucratic interference'
b)   'rigid and inefficient bureaucracy'

2.2.2.   imbalance between rich/poor countries
a)   'some countries have to bear a greater burden of contributions'
b)   'countries do not put in and get out equal shares'

2.2.3.   'we' pay too much
a)   'we put more in that we get out'
b)   'our proportion of the Community budget is too large'

2.2.4.   interference with 'natural' supply and demand
a)   'natural competition of free economy is distorted'
b)   'balance between supply and demand is altered'

2.2.5.   expensive support of weak members
a)   'support of the weak by the strong weakens the economy'
b)   'the poor don't bother about their deficits, because these are paid by the rich'

2.2.6.   anti-socialist policy
a)   'it bolsters the power of international capital'
b)   'it is a bosses club, which protects only the interests of powerful capitalists'

2.3.   community cooperation
2.3.1.   too much nationalism/protectionism
a)   'nationalistic squabbles'/'oracle of nationalism'
b)   'each nation is still out to get the best for itself'

2.3.2.   competition between members
a)   'EEC has failed to unite Europe'
b)   'quarrels about contributions'

2.3.3.   goals not achieved
a)   'failure to achieve stated goals'
b)   'goals of political unity not achieved'

2.3.4.   failure of peace/nuclear threat
a)   'Europe has become a battlefield for nuclear war'

2.3.5.   still border/passport controls
a)   'we still need passports'
b)   'the law governing passage across borders is not being implemented

2.3.6.   Franco-British conflict
a)   'conflicts between Britain and France'
b)   'heightened tension (Britain-France)'

2.4.   national sovereignty
2.4.1 loss of national sovereignty, identity, independence
a)   'loss of sovereignty'
b)   'EEC directives can be enforced against the wishes of U.K.'s democratically elected government'

3. *Principles, goals and aims of the European Community*

3.1.   general
3.1.1. benefit and protect the interests of members
a)   'to protect the interests of member states'
b)   'members should benefit'

3.1.2. build an efficient Europe
a)   'a more efficient united Europe'
b)   'to make Europe a less fragmented and more successful economic area'

3.2.   trade and economic policy
3.2.1. promote trade
a)   'to promote trade between members states'
b)   'to strengthen the world impact of member countries on trade'

3.2.2. economic alliance
a)   'to form an economic bloc'
b)   'to align the countries economically'

3.2.3. reduce inequalities between rich and poor member states
a)   'richer countries should help poorer'
b)   'distribution of resources among member countries'

3.2.4. large markets, economies of scale
a)   'to make Europe into one large market'
b)   'to increase economies of scale in industry'

3.2.5. third trading block
a)   'to create a third trade block'
b)   'to oppose U.S.S.R. and U.S.A.'

3.2.6. stabilise prices and supply
a)   'to stabilise prices and supply'
b)   'make prices stable'

3.2.7. exchange of goods and persons
a)   'exchange of goods, ideas, technology'
b)   'free movement of capital, goods and persons'

3.2.8. harmonisation, standardisation
a)   'standardisation of regulations'
b)   'standardisation of procedures in Europe'

3.3.   political cooperation
3.3.1. cooperation/shared identity
a)   'to give Europe a common identity'
b)   'to bring European countries closer together'

3.3.2. greater world role for Europe
a)   'to enable Europe to play a greater world role'
b)   'more political power for Europe'

3.4.   defence
3.4.1. peace and mutual defence
a)   'promote peace'
b)   'provide mutual defence'

4. *Common Agricultural Policy*

4.1.   surpluses problem
4.1.1.1. surpluses/excesses of food
a)   'huge agricultural surpluses'
b)   'over-production'

4.1.1.2. surpluses described with metaphorical language
a)   'wine lakes'
b)   'butter mountains'
c)   'butter, apple and milk mountains' (sic)
d)   'butter, meat and wine mountains' (sic)

4.1.2. irresponsible policy for Third World
a)   'excesses should be shared with, or given to, the Third world'
b)   'immoral when there is hunger in the Third world'

4.1.3. selling cheap excess to non-members
a)   'cheap butter sold to Russians'
b)   'excess sold off cheaply to non-EEC countries'

4.2.   subsidies/support buying/guaranteed prices
a)   'guaranteed prices to farmers'
b)   'subsidies to inefficient farmers'

4.3.   frictions between members states
a)   'French and British complain about each other'
b)   'policy leads to ill-will between nations'

4.4.   negative evaluation of C.A.P.
a)   'a farce'
b)   'an unmitigated disaster'

4.5.   expensive policy for 'us'
a)   'a raw deal for Britain'
b)   'isn't much good for G.B.'

4.6.   small farmers suffer
a)   'provides no help for small farmers'
b)   'small farmers suffer'

4.7.   inefficient techniques favour small farmers
a)   'promotes backward techniques'
b)   'does not encourage efficiency in farmers'

4.8. high consumer prices
a) 'keeps food prices up'
b) 'consumers pay too much'

4.9. C.A.P. favours agricultural countries
a) 'favours agricultural countries like France'
b) 'favours France'

Appendix D
Supplementary tables to Chapter 5

Table D.1. *Mean stereotypes of four nationalities*

	Country of respondent																
	W. Germany (N = 127)				Italy (N = 133)				France (N = 139)				U.K. (N = 127)			
					Nationality rated											
Traits	W. Germans	Italians	French	British	G	I	F	B	G	I	F	B	G	I	F	B
1. intelligent	56	53	55	55	60	63	58	56	59	47	53	51	55	44	49	50
2. progressive	40	41	44	33	57	53	55	40	59	43	49	40	55	36	43	42
3. conceited	54	41	45	50	65	51	63	65	45	54	51	54	56	51	59	52
4. reserved	47	27	37	57	59	31	48	74	49	30	40	54	49	25	36	65
5. domineering	52	41	46	46	74	38	47	59	58	42	51	53	58	41	50	47
6. industrious	66	48	52	56	78	54	58	63	68	36	45	55	69	41	47	49
7. aggressive	45	43	39	37	64	42	50	47	46	53	53	44	53	51	50	45
8. passionate	33	63	56	28	29	75	62	28	53	63	53	46	37	66	59	36
9. quick-tempered	41	59	49	27	59	55	53	43	43	52	50	46	44	66	54	37
10. extremely nationalistic	51	59	66	68	77	54	71	77	58	57	60	70	64	62	67	63

Note: All figures are percentages.

Table D.2. *Mean evaluation of stereotype traits*

Traits	Country of respondent				F	d.f.
	W. Germany	Italy	France	U.K.		
1. intelligent	2.38[a]	2.77[b]	2.45[a]	2.29[a]	9.85*	3,540
2. progressive	1.70[a]	2.24[b]	1.99[a,b]	2.00[a,b]	5.70*	3,540
3. conceited	−2.13[a]	−1.97[a]	−1.18[b]	−2.04[a]	16.51*	3,541
4. reserved	0.31	0.34	0.22	−0.14	3.14	3,541
5. domineering	−0.63	−1.04	−1.01	−1.06	2.23	3,541
6. industrious	0.99[a]	2.50[b]	1.96[c]	1.93[c]	51.73*	3,541
7. aggressive	−1.86[a]	−1.48[a,b]	−1.05[b]	−1.27[a,b]	6.21*	3,541
8. passionate	1.48[a]	0.78[b]	1.17[a,b]	1.03[a,b]	5.46+	3,541
9. quick tempered	−1.43[a]	−1.99[b]	−1.64[a,b]	−1.71[a,b]	4.13+	3,540
10. extremely nationalistic	−2.19[a]	−0.69[b]	−2.46[a]	−1.27[a]	36.25*	3,541
	127	133	139	127		

Notes:
Range of scores: + 3 (extremely good), − 3 (extremely bad).
Means without a common superscript are significant at $p < 0.01$.
Fs are significant at $p < 0.001$ (*) or $p < 0.01$ (+).

Table D.3. *Mean 'national images' of four countries*

	Country of respondent							
	W. Germany (N = 126)				Italy (N = 132)			
Characteristics	W. Germany	Italy	France	U.K.	W. Germany	Italy	France	U.K.
1. prosperous	7.59	4.03	5.52	5.27	7.33	5.32	6.34	6.21
2. communist influence	1.61	4.81	4.31	1.38	2.94	5.50	4.50	1.88
3. aggressively militaristic	4.48	3.42	4.78	5.53	5.66	2.96	4.90	5.57
4. politically stable	6.67	2.98	5.61	6.16	6.83	2.97	5.68	7.29
5. few economic problems	4.91	2.59	3.87	2.91	6.04	3.40	4.76	4.79
6. undemocratic	3.18	3.19	3.09	3.08	4.09	2.99	3.29	3.77
7. politically independent	3.08	3.90	4.66	4.32	5.57	3.90	5.61	6.04
8. powerless	3.97	4.28	3.45	3.48	3.96	4.74	3.90	3.76
9. economically and industrially developed	7.93	5.10	6.45	6.50	7.79	5.43	6.50	6.87
10. infertile country	2.50	3.14	2.27	3.17	4.67	4.53	4.27	4.92

	Country of respondent							
	France (N = 138)				U.K. (N = 122)			
Characteristics	W. Germany	Italy	France	U.K.	W. Germany	Italy	France	U.K.
1. prosperous	7.29	3.59	5.62	4.99	7.21	3.87	5.45	5.22
2. communist influence	2.27	4.55	3.52	1.32	2.43	5.02	4.19	1.69
3. aggressively militaristic	3.32	3.02	3.66	4.18	3.89	3.28	3.87	4.67
4. politically stable	5.99	2.67	4.85	6.10	6.38	2.96	5.09	6.78
5. few economic problems	5.03	2.22	3.03	2.79	4.78	2.53	3.52	3.13
6. undemocratic	2.80	2.88	2.46	2.76	3.63	4.10	3.78	3.95
7. politically independent	4.38	4.20	5.12	4.69	5.49	4.82	5.74	5.47
8. powerless	3.08	5.10	3.73	3.94	3.74	4.08	3.83	3.64
9. economically and industrially developed	7.59	4.10	6.25	5.36	7.74	4.92	6.29	6.75
10. infertile country	3.18	4.10	2.44	3.66	2.51	3.72	2.43	2.13

Note:
Range of scores: 0–9.

Table D.4. *Mean evaluation of national image characteristics*

Characteristics	Country of respondent				F	d.f.
	W. Germany	Italy	France	U.K.		
1. prosperous	0.98[b]	2.66[c]	1.95[a]	2.16[a]	65.40*	3,538
2. communist influence	-0.46	-0.57	-1.03	-0.57	3.00	3,541
3. aggressively militaristic	-2.52	-2.26	-2.45	-2.21	1.99	3,541
4. politically stable	1.51[a]	2.29[b]	1.44[a]	1.94[a,b]	13.01*	3,541
5. few economic problems	1.84[a]	2.48[b]	2.30[b]	2.42[b]	10.87*	3,541
6. undemocratic	-2.57	-2.55	-2.40	-2.40	1.11	3,541
7. politically independent	1.73[a,b]	2.26[a]	1.81[a,b]	1.28[b]	11.31*	3,540
8. powerless	-1.26[a]	-1.89[b]	-2.21[b]	-1.74[a,b]	11.33*	3,540
9. economically and industrially developed	1.09[a]	2.53[b]	2.10[c]	1.88[c]	44.10*	3,540
10. infertile country	-2.15	-2.39	-2.21	-2.23	1.00	3,539
Sample size	126	132	138	122		

Notes:
Range of scores: + 3 (extremely good), - 3 (extremely bad).
*F*s are significant at 0.001 (*)
Means without a common superscript are significant at 0.01.

Table D.5. *Relative frequency of negative and positive overall attitudes*

Response		W. Germany	Italy	France	U.K.	Row total	Chi square
					Country of respondent		
Negative	N	31	8	9	43	91	40.5**
	%	29.0	6.9	7.3	36.1	19.6	
Positive	N	76	108	114	76	374	9.8
	%	71.0	93.1	92.7	63.9	80.4	
Column total		107	116	123	119	465	50.3**
Percentage total		100	100	100	100	100	

Notes:
Percentages based on respondents whose attitudes were positive or negative.
** $p < 0.001$.

Appendix E
Supplementary tables to Chapter 6

Table E.1. Correlation matrix for multiple regression

Country: W. Germany
Sample size: 117
Critical values of Pearson product moment: (0.001): 0.30   (0.01): 0.24

	Active interest	Knowledge	Time spent in other European countries	Sum of expectancy + value	Common policy	Utilitarian support	Affective support	Stereotyping	Preference for own country	International relations	Liking	Common Policy effects	Travel
Knowledge	0.23												
Time	0.22	−0.03											
Sum e + v	0.31	0.21	0.14										
Common policy	0.07	−0.10	0.07	0.36									
Utilitarian support	0.15	0.23	0.12	0.08	0.10								
Affective support	0.20	0.14	0.17	0.32	0.21	0.52							
Stereotyping	0.08	−0.09	−0.05	0.16	0.09	−0.12	−0.08						
Preference own country	0.07	−0.18	0.08	0.27	0.17	−0.27	−0.15	0.29					
International relations	0.17	0.10	0.16	0.09	0.09	0.49	0.57	−0.19	−0.18				
Liking	0.04	0.05	−0.14	0.30	0.20	−0.13	−0.03	0.51	0.19	−0.19			
Common Policy effects	0.17	0.17	−0.11	0.33	0.41	0.40	0.23	0.01	0.06	0.14	0.06		
Travel	0.23	0.02	0.58	0.10	0.04	−0.02	0.16	−0.14	0.01	0.14	−0.07	−0.02	
Overall attitude	0.33	0.19	0.22	0.48	0.33	0.25	0.57	0.06	0.09	0.33	0.15	0.19	0.16

Table E.2. Correlation matrix for multiple regression

Country: Italy
Sample size: 107
Critical values of Pearson product moment: (0.001): 0.31   (0.01): 0.25

	Active Interest	Knowledge	Time spent in other European countries	Sum of expectancy + value	Common policy	Utilitarian support	Affective support	Stereo-typing	Preference for own country	Inter-national relations	Liking	Common Policy effects	Travel
Knowledge	0.13												
Time	-0.04	0.07											
Sum e + v	0.11	0.01	0.01										
Common Policy	0.12	-0.08	-0.20	0.52									
Utilitarian support	-0.01	0.10	-0.04	0.28	0.32								
Affective support	0.06	0.05	-0.03	0.32	0.25	0.50							
Stereotyping	-0.12	0.01	-0.03	-0.11	-0.15	-0.20	-0.13						
Preference own country	0.10	0.15	-0.12	-0.02	0.05	0.16	0.09	0.13					
International relations	-0.06	0.18	-0.01	0.01	-0.08	0.27	0.37	0.22	0.10				
Liking	-0.06	0.05	-0.03	-0.05	0.14	-0.06	-0.10	0.43	0.02	0.10			
Common Policy effects	0.09	0.01	-0.08	0.49	0.67	0.48	0.40	-0.13	0.13	0.03	0.16		
Travel	-0.10	0.11	0.71	-0.14	-0.30	-0.11	0.02	0.06	-0.12	0.20	0.08	-0.21	
Overall attitude	0.14	-0.07	0.05	0.31	0.23	0.39	0.54	0.01	0.22	0.28	-0.04	0.30	0.00

Table E.3. *Correlation matrix for multiple regression*

Country: France
Sample size: 115
Critical values of Pearson product moment: (0.001): 0.30   (0.01): 0.24

	Active interest	Knowledge	Time spent in other European countries	Sum of expectancy + value	Common policy	Utilitarian support	Affective support	Stereotyping	Preference for own country	International relations	Liking	Common Policy effects	Travel
Knowledge	0.11												
Time	−0.01	−0.11											
Sum e + v	0.18	0.16	−0.01										
Common Policy	−0.13	−0.01	0.10	−0.43									
Utilitarian support	0.03	0.05	0.04	0.14	−0.18								
Affective support	0.16	0.15	0.01	0.37	−0.35	0.33							
Stereotyping	0.30	0.10	−0.18	0.24	−0.17	−0.23	0.11						
Preference own country	0.10	0.05	0.09	0.08	0.07	−0.08	−0.04	0.22					
International relations	0.02	0.01	0.04	0.17	−0.06	0.33	0.33	−0.20	0.03				
Liking	0.22	0.07	−0.17	0.20	−0.12	−0.18	−0.08	0.57	0.16	−0.18			
Common Policy effects	−0.15	−0.14	0.10	−0.42	0.70	−0.28	−0.32	−0.25	−0.08	−0.05	−0.25		
Travel	0.02	−0.18	0.66	−0.05	0.05	0.03	0.01	−0.17	0.07	0.06	−0.14	0.07	
Overall attitude	0.20	−0.02	−0.08	0.26	−0.30	0.25	0.33	0.14	0.01	0.19	−0.07	−0.22	−0.10

Table E.4. Correlation matrix for multiple regression

Country: U.K.
Sample size: 118
Critical values of Pearson product moment: (0.001): 0.30   (0.01): 0.24

	Active interest	Knowledge	Time spent in other European countries	Sum of expectancy + value	Common policy	Utilitarian support	Affective support	Stereotyping	Preference for own country	International relations	Liking	Common Policy effects	Travel
Knowledge	0.26												
Time	0.14	0.07											
Sum e + v	0.32	0.14	0.11										
Common Policy	0.11	−0.10	0.00	0.33									
Utilitarian support	0.32	−0.01	0.21	0.36	0.16								
Affective support	0.29	−0.01	0.16	0.49	0.12	0.77							
Stereotyping	0.02	0.06	−0.19	−0.14	−0.10	−0.36	−0.43						
Preference own country	−0.11	−0.04	−0.15	−0.03	0.16	−0.39	−0.40	0.52					
International relations	0.17	0.04	0.05	0.26	−0.13	0.46	0.58	−0.25	−0.30				
Liking	−0.03	−0.09	−0.14	−0.06	−0.04	−0.27	−0.23	0.53	0.36	−0.24			
Common Policy effects	0.22	0.06	0.12	0.52	0.37	0.40	0.34	−0.16	−0.08	0.14	−0.03		
Travel	0.13	0.06	0.81	0.10	−0.09	0.11	0.10	−0.17	−0.10	0.03	−0.12	0.03	
Overall attitude	0.40	−0.07	0.15	0.54	0.29	0.58	0.61	−0.17	−0.09	0.38	0.04	0.44	0.15

Table E.5. *Principal components factor analysis of 'utilitarian' and 'affective' support: loadings on first two factors*

Support/items	W. Germany		Italy		France		U.K.		All	
	Factor 1	2	1	2	1	2	1	2	1	2
(a) *'Utilitarian' support*										
1. Personal gain	0.71		0.68				0.70		0.59	
2. Net budget contribution	0.53		0.70		0.62		0.56	0.68	0.62	
3. Country has benefited										
4. Subsidise other countries			0.79		−0.71				0.60	
5. Gain from C.A.P.					0.53					
6. Forced to give to developing countries	0.78									
7. Gain from Regional Fund	0.61		0.72		0.57				0.70	
8. Country less competitive				0.61				0.53		0.55
(b) *'Affective' support*										
1. EEC increased national rivalries		0.67								0.67
2. Sense of solidarity		0.70					0.79		0.52	
3. EEC interferes with national government				0.66	−0.52			0.83		0.67
4. EEC can be trusted				0.69			0.67			0.53
5. Do not have confidence						0.83	0.75			
6. More loyal to the EEC						0.54				
7. Should not help out others	0.57									
8. Willing to make personal sacrifices						0.61				
Percentage variance accounted for	17.8	12.0	17.0	13.9	13.0	10.8	18.9	14.2	13.6	12.1
Sample size	128		137		143		129		537	

Note:
Only factor loadings greater than 0.50 are shown.

Table E.6. *Correlations between individual support items and overall attitude*

Item	Country of respondent					
	W. Germany	Italy	France	U.K.	All
(a) 'Utilitarian' support					
1. Personal gain	0.25*	0.28*	0.22	0.61**	0.32
2. Budget contribution	0.15	0.29*	0.05	0.31**	0.25
3. Country has benefited	0.27*	0.27*	0.26*	0.59**	0.35
4. Subsidise poorer groups	−0.33**	0.09	−0.28*	0.16	−0.02
5. Gain from C.A.P.	0.19	0.27*	0.16	0.24*	0.22
6. Forced to give money	0.14	0.02	0.10	0.08	0.00
7. Gain from Regional Fund	0.09	0.25*	0.12	0.18	0.17
8. Less competitive economically	0.26*	0.22	0.16	0.39**	0.22
(b) 'Affective' support					
1. Increased national rivalries	0.25*	0.12	0.14	0.42**	0.22
2. Solidarity with EEC	0.52**	0.47**	0.12	0.53**	0.49
3. EEC interferes	0.32**	0.17	−0.08	0.25*	0.13
4. EEC can be trusted	0.28*	0.33**	0.06	0.44**	0.31
5. Do not have confidence	0.37**	0.38**	0.37**	0.50**	0.42
6. More loyal to the EEC	0.19	0.28*	0.08	0.23	0.17
7. Help out Member State	0.25*	0.11	0.24*	0.33**	0.20
8. Personal sacrifices	0.20	0.36**	0.25*	0.22	0.20
Sample size	117	107	115	118	457

Notes:
Pearson product moment correlations.
* $p < 0.01$.
** $p < 0.001$.

Table E.7. *Correlations between individual expectancy + value items and overall attitude*

Item		W. Germany	Italy	Country of respondent France	U.K.	All
1.	United States of Europe	0.37**	0.20	0.20	0.49**	0.36
2.	Europe's role in the world	0.47**	0.30*	0.03	0.29*	0.34
3.	Lasting peace	0.34**	0.19	0.22	0.36**	0.31
4.	Economic expansion	0.32**	0.09	0.22	0.37**	0.31
5.	Mutual understanding	0.40**	0.08	0.34**	0.42**	0.34
6.	Third block	0.27*	0.26*	0.07	0.19	0.19
7.	Customs union	0.29*	0.17	0.19	0.26*	0.23
8.	Dismantling quotas	0.15	0.17	0.15	0.24*	0.18
9.	Common commercial policy	0.23	-0.02	0.10	0.13	0.12
10.	Free movement	0.13	0.11	0.13	0.24*	0.15
11.	Competition not distorted	0.26*	0.23	0.11	0.34**	0.29
12.	Goods produced as suited	0.20	0.22	0.01	0.30**	0.21
13.	Large scale market	0.27*	0.12	-0.02	0.14	0.18
	Sum of expectancy + value	0.48**	0.31**	0.25*	0.54**	0.45
	Sample size	117	107	115	118	457

Notes:
Pearson product moment correlations.
* $p < 0.01$.
** $p < 0.001$.

Appendix F
Reproduction of the correlation matrix using estimates of path coefficients

As an illustration, consider a simple path model involving four variables (see Figure F. 1).

Theoretically, the correlation between variables X_1 and X_3 can be predicted from the sum of direct and indirect effects, in this case: direct effect is path coefficient a_{31} and indirect effect is denoted by the product of two path coefficients $(a_{21} \times a_{32})$. Following conventions for path analysis, the effect of variable X_1 on variable X_3 is given by the path coefficient a_{31} (see Duncan, 1966). The residuals associated with each variable are indicated by E and the appropriate subscript; and variables X_1 to X_4 are observed measures on a given scale (e.g., knowledge about the Community, support for the Community, etc.).

The model can be expressed in the following system of equations:

$$X_3 = a_{32}X_2 + a_{31}X_1 + E_3 \tag{1}$$

$$X_2 = a_{24}X_4 + a_{21}X_1 + E_2 \tag{2}$$

Substituting X_2 in equation (1) by equation (2) yields equation (3):

$$X_3 = a_{32}(a_{24}X_4 + a_{21}X_1 + E_2) + A_{31}X_1 + E_3 \tag{3}$$

The last structural equation can be used to derive, for example, the correlation between X_1 and X_3:

$$\text{correlation}(X_1,X_3) = \frac{\text{Covariance }(X_1,X_3)}{\text{standard deviation }(X_1)\text{ standard deviation }(X_3)}$$

Because the variables are standardized (with a standard deviation of 1) we need only deal with the covariance (X_1,X_3) in order to complete the correlation. Using equation (3) we have:

$$\text{Covariance }(X_1,X_3) = \text{Cov}[X_1, a_{32}(a_{24}X_4 + a_{21}X_1 + E_2) + a_{31}X_1 + E_3]$$
$$= \text{Cov}[X_1, a_{32}a_{24}X_4 + a_{32}a_{21}X_1 + a_{32}E_2 + a_{31}X_1 + E_3]$$

Using the distribution of covariances, yields:

$$= a_{32}a_{24}\text{ Cov }(X_1,X_4) + a_{32}a_{21}\text{ Cov }(X_1,X_1) + a_{32}\text{ Cov }(X_1,E_2) + a_{31}\text{ Cov }(X_1,X_1)$$

$$= \text{Cov }(X_1,E_3)$$

Since it is assumed that X_1 and X_4, X_1 and E_2, X_1 and E_1, respectively, are uncorrelated, it follows that Cov $(X_1,X_4) = 0$, Cov $(X_1,E_2) = 0$; and Cov $(X_1,E_1) = 0$; and since Cov $(X_1,X_1) = \text{Var } X_1 = 1$, then we can simplify:

$$= a_{32}a_{21} + a_{31}$$

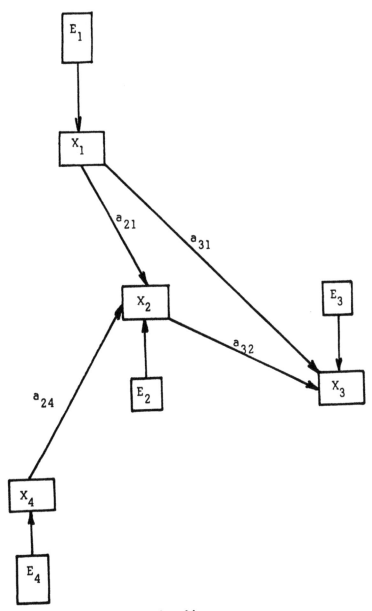

Fig. F.1. Simple four-variable path model.

i.e. the correlation between variables X_1 and X_3 can be predicted by multiplying together the indirect paths along the way (a_{32}, a_{21}; see Figure F.1 and e.g. Macdonald, 1977) and summing the result with the direct path (a_{31}).

This calculation can be illustrated for one simple case from the present German data. According to Figure 6.1 (see Chapter 6), the correlation between support and overall attitude consists of the following effects:

direct effect (0.393) + indirect effect $(0.316 \times 0.282) = 0.48$ (see the reproduced correlation between overall attitude and support in Table F.1).

The complete matrix of observed and reproduced correlations for each country, in turn, is shown in Tables F.1–F.4.

Table F.1. Matrix of 'observed' and 'reproduced' correlations from path analysis (W. German sample, N = 120)

	National image	Contact	Support	Expectancy value	Knowledge	Active interest	Overall attitude
Liking	0.19 (0.19)	-0.13 (0.00)	-0.09 (-0.07)	-0.30 (0.31)	0.08 (0.04)	0.04 (0.06)	0.15 (0.06)
National image		0.07 (0.00)	-0.24 (-0.23)	0.27 (0.21)	-0.16 (-0.15)	0.07 (0.04)	0.10 (-0.01)
Contact			0.17 (0.19)	0.14 (0.05)	-0.01 (0.04)	0.22 (0.20)	0.21 (0.13)
Support				0.24 (0.32)	0.20 (0.06)	0.20 (0.09)	0.48 (0.48)
Expectancy value					0.24 (0.27)	0.32 (0.27)	0.49 (0.32)
Knowledge						0.25 (0.19)	0.20 (0.03)
Active interest							0.33 (0.12)

Note: 'Reproduced' correlations are shown in parentheses.

Table F.2. *Matrix of 'observed' and 'reproduced' correlations from path analysis (Italian sample, N = 117)*

	National image	Contact	Support	Expectancy value	Knowledge	Active interest	Overall attitude
Liking	0.02 (0.00)	-0.06 (0.00)	-0.06 (0.00)	-0.04 (-0.02)	0.03 (0.00)	-0.07 (0.00)	-0.05 (-0.05)
National image		-0.06 (0.00)	0.10 (0.10)	-0.02 (0.04)	0.16 (0.16)	0.07 (0.02)	0.22 (0.22)
Contact			-0.07 (0.00)	-0.01 (-0.02)	0.09 (0.11)	-0.07 (0.01)	0.07 (0.08)
Support				0.33 (0.34)	0.04 (0.00)	0.03 (0.06)	0.52 (0.51)
Expectancy value					0.06 (0.00)	0.13 (0.13)	0.29 (0.14)
Knowledge						0.12 (0.13)	-0.06 (-0.13)
Active interest							0.14 (0.12)

Note: 'Reproduced' correlations are shown in parentheses.

Table F.3. *Matrix of 'observed' and 'reproduced' correlations from path analysis (French sample, N = 123)*

	National image	Contact	Support	Expectancy value	Knowledge	Active interest	Overall attitude
Liking	0.18 (0.19)	-0.17 (-0.17)	-0.15 (-0.14)	0.18 (0.19)	0.05 (0.03)	0.19 (0.20)	-0.05 (0.03)
National image		0.08 (0.12)	0.07 (0.00)	0.06 (-0.03)	0.00 (0.01)	0.06 (0.00)	-0.01 (0.00)
Contact			0.01 (0.00)	0.01 (0.00)	-0.07 (0.00)	0.03 (0.00)	-0.08 (0.01)
Support				0.35 (0.38)	0.12 (0.06)	0.10 (0.00)	0.32 (0.32)
Expectancy value					0.19 (0.16)	0.16 (0.00)	0.26 (0.21)
Knowledge						0.12 (0.00)	0.00 (0.02)
Active interest							0.18 (0.16)

Note: 'Reproduced' correlations are shown in parentheses.

Table F.4. *Matrix of 'observed' and 'reproduced' correlations from path analysis (U.K. sample, N = 120)*

	National image	Contact	Support	Expectancy value	Knowledge	Active interest	Overall attitude
Liking	0.36 (0.36)	−0.13 (−0.05)	−0.27 (−0.27)	−0.07 (−0.07)	−0.09 (0.03)	−0.05 (−0.10)	0.02 (−0.01)
National image		−0.16 (−0.13)	−0.41 (−0.36)	−0.01 (−0.01)	−0.07 (0.06)	−0.11 (−0.12)	−0.08 (−0.22)
Contact			0.19 (0.11)	0.08 (0.10)	0.09 (−0.02)	0.12 (0.08)	0.12 (0.12)
Support				0.46 (0.55)	−0.02 (0.09)	0.33 (0.34)	0.63 (0.70)
Expectancy value					0.09 (0.15)	0.33 (0.22)	0.56 (0.34)
Knowledge						0.24 (0.22)	−0.10 (−0.11)
Active interest							0.41 (0.20)

Note: 'Reproduced' correlations are shown in parentheses.

Notes

Chapter 1. The idea of Europe: dream and reality

1 Saint-Simon, with Augustin Thierry, even demanded the formation of an Anglo-French parliament, composed of two-thirds English and one-third French deputies, justifying this by the French need for guidance by the more experienced Englishmen (see Kohn, 1957).
2 In fact, the first use of the phrase 'United States of Europe' cannot be definitely attributed. It appears to have emerged around 1848, possibly in the speech of Cattaneo, Cobden, Mazzini or Hugo (see de Rougement, 1961; Renouvin, 1949).
3 Peter Shore, *The Times*, 4 January 1983.
4 E.E.C. Commission, Press Release, 22 May, 1961.
5 The Schuman Plan leading to the E.C.S.C. had as an ultimate objective to foster peace by making future war between France and W. Germany impossible (Coombes, 1970).
6 Barzini (1983) refers to these four nationalities as 'the imperturbable British', 'the mutable Germans', 'the quarrelsome French' and 'the flexible Italians'. Such characterisations should, however, succeed, not precede, empirical analysis.
7 I nonetheless apologise to my friends in 'the other six' for appearing to ignore their views.
8 See *The Sunday Times*, 18 March, 1984 and *The Observer*, 25 March, 1984. This question of gains-losses is dealt with in more detail below.

Chapter 2. Public opinion and European integration: a review and critique

1 See Liska (1964).
2 See Benoit (1961), Holland (1980) and Barzini (1983).
3 See Florinsky (1955), Lindberg and Scheingold (1970) and Graubard (1964).
4 See Rutherford (1981).
5 Quoted by Sampson (1961).
6 Quoted by Sampson (*op. cit.*).
7 Quoted by Holt (1972).
8 Quoted by Barzini (1983, p. 158).
9 Actual turn-out in the four countries was as follows: W. Germany, 56.8%; Italy (where voting is perceived as compulsory) 83.4%; France, 56.7%; U.K., 32.6%. This apparent lack of interest in the U.K. was accompanied by, if not due to, the less active role played by political parties and information agencies, compared with other Community countries (Lodge and Herman, 1980).

10 Rutherford (1981) argues that it is actually Denmark which is the 'deviant' country, its citizens' support for faster unification having barely reached double figures since its accession.

11 Although Mathew (1980) uses the term 'determinants', this is, strictly speaking, inaccurate; the relationships identified are correlational, and allow no inferences regarding causation.

12 Handley (1981) used six measures from *Euro-baromètre*: 'affective sentiment' for the idea of European unification; 'intensity' of attachment to the idea of uniting Europe; 'support for membership' of the European Community: 'saliency' of (interest in) the Community; 'degree of mutual trust' among Community countries; and 'identification' with a supra-national European unity.

13 Northern Ireland was not included in this 1973 sample, hence the term 'Great Britain is actually appropriate.

Chapter 3. Towards a social psychological analysis of 'Europeanism'

1 Farr (1984) suggests that Durkheim was himself influenced by Wundt, and that the latter's Völkerpsychologie (1917–26) is a collective psychology which also took cultural products as its object of study.

2 It is interesting to note that Durkheim advocated a branch of sociology concerned with such collective representations, and which he called 'social psychology' (Lukes, 1975, p. 8).

3 Perhaps one reason why definition has posed such a problem lies in the added difficulty of translating from French to English. As Lukes (1975) notes, the French word *représentation* does not translate literally as the English word representation; it maps out a different conceptual structure and means something to French people in a sense that is not true for its English counterpart and English people.

4 These responses were reported in 'Les nouvelles de Splash'. *Journal du Collège Anne Frank*, Miribel, France.

5 It may, however, be noted that Fishbein and Ajzen (1975) consider opinions as cognitive, and thus equivalent to beliefs, in contrast with attitudes which are evaluative.

6 There is, however, some confusion in Fishbein and Ajzen's (1981) chapter about how subjective probabilities are to be scored; on p. 291 one scale is scored 1–7, and two other scales are scored −3 to +3.

7 Not only do Fishbein and Ajzen (1975, p. 81) re-interpret competing theoretical approaches – e.g. learning theories, balance theory and theories of attribution – but they even argue that in all four standard attitude-scaling procedures (Guttman, Thurstone, Likert and the semantic differential) attitude scores are always obtained in accordance with an expectancy-value formulation.

8 I am grateful to Professor C. Insko for drawing my attention to this work.

9 The author has previously referred to the impact of such findings for apparently overly complex cognitive models in another area of social psychology – attribution theory (see Hewstone, 1983).

10 Interestingly, Palmerino et al. 1983) compare a number of major attitude theories and classify expectancy-value theories as 'primarily mindful' (p. 189).

11 The interested reader will find discussion of national and international images in all seven chapters of Part One (Kelman, 1965*b*).

12 See *Journal of Common Market Studies* (1963) and Inglehart (1970*b*).

13 Following the work of Bergius, Werbik, Winter and Schubring (1970), there may be a difference between contacts made with foreigners *within* one's own country, or when visiting abroad. This distinction was not followed up in the present study.

14 In Italy sample sizes for different faculties were large enough to test for statistical differences on all major questionnaire variables. None was found and thus the variable of faculty is hereafter ignored.

15 There still remains the possibility that 'university students' themselves are not comparable in the four countries. However, statistics on participation in higher education in different EEC countries do not suggest large differences in selection.

16 Interestingly, Kerlinger (1984) actually states that random samples of a whole country are not desirable samples for, for example, factor analytic purposes (citing Thurstone, 1947, p. xii).

17 While the European Community may seem an uncontentious topic, on visiting the universities in France the author was surprised to hear the suspicions of students and their reasons for declining to give political affiliation.

18 A disadvantage of this method, although the author finds it the only practicable solution, is that some respondents (especially in France and Italy) reported unease on being confronted immediately with their inability to write anything on the topic. To such respondents a 7-point scale is a refuge and a relief.

19 The exact wording of all questions is shown in the full questionnaire reported in Appendix B.

20 Following Scott (1968), multi-item assessment has advantages over single-item assessment. In particular, single items are subject to too much random response error and a composite score constructed from multiple items yields a better estimate of the intended attitude. Scott points out that adding the item scores together – a fairly standard procedure – implies that each item is a linear (or at least monotonic) function of the same attribute. This assumption can be checked by correlational analyses, correlating each item with the total scale score.

21 If 13 seems an unusual number, it is. Fourteen items were presented, but wording of an item on 'building a defence against Communism' had to be changed in the Communist town of Bologna. This item has therefore been deleted.

22 These characteristics had been used with success in a study of American students' perceptions of European nations and nationalities (Stapf, Stroebe and Jonas, 1984).

23 This change of response scale also avoids method-variance artifacts, so that the response scales for all variables entered into later multivariate correlational analyses (see Chapter 6) are identical.

24 This assessment of attitude ambivalence is exactly the same as that used by Kaplan (1972).

25 Respondents were excluded if they replied affirmatively to this item.

26 Several other responses were apparently assessed, but these are not reported in Wober's (1981) article.

Chapter 4. Social representations of the European Community: content-analysis of open-ended responses

1 In passing it may be noted that the response rate in this study (27%) raises serious doubts about the self-selection of those individuals who did reply.
2 All percentages reported are rounded up.
3 This idea of theory vs. practice is considered further, in Chapter 5, in relation to the expectancy-value analysis of Community attitudes.
4 Nonetheless, content-analysis of the press is an important part of studying common sense about the Common Market, what Cohen-Solal and Bachmann (1983) call the 'Europe of everyday life' – e.g. sporting contests, touristic voyages and international conferences. Their content-analysis of the British and French press for two major events – the France vs England rugby match in 1981 and the European Council at Maastricht in the same year – is fascinating. The role of the press is also dealt with in Dalton and Duval (1981) and Seymour-Ure (1976).
5 In fact, the Community has argued that it employs far fewer people per 100 000 Community citizens (seven 'Eurocrats') than do national governments (4200 civil servants; see 'The European Community: some questions and answers'. *European File*, nos. 5–6, 1984. Brussels: Commission of the European Communities). This comparison may, however, appear spurious since the powers and functions of the Community and national governments are not strictly comparable.
6 In this sense Lippmann's analysis of 'stereotypes' is far closer to Moscovici's (1961) notion of social representations than it is to the lists of group traits which have come to be called stereotypes.
7 However, French and Italian colleagues inform me that the landscape metaphors are less frequent in their national media. An alternative explanation lies in the relative knowledge of respondents in the four countries (see Chapter 5). This analysis of knowledge revealed a surprising ignorance in Italy about the premier position of agriculture in the Community's finances. Only 11% of the Italians knew that the C.A.P. accounts for the largest percentage of the Community budget, compared with a mean average of 61% in the three other countries.

Chapter 5. The social psychology of the European Community: cross-national comparisons

1 Notwithstanding the convention of accepting the 5% level as the 'maximal acceptable probability for determining statistical significance' (Cowles and Davis, 1982, p. 553), samples as large as those in the present study may result in the reporting of differences which are 'significant' but not 'substantive'. With odds of one in a hundred that a reported deviation is, in fact, due to chance, confidence in the reliability of the findings is increased.
2 Fishbein and Ajzen (1975) point out that dividing a variable by a constant (i.e. number of beliefs) produces a new variable that is perfectly correlated with the original variable. Furthermore, such a linear transformation has no effect on correlation coefficients.

3 The size of these correlations may be seen as support for Wahba and House's (1974) argument, that most psychological theories of expectancy suggest that the parameters of expectancy and value are not independent.

4 This multiplicative method is obviously open to the same criticisms as Schmidt (1973) has applied to the expectancy-value model. However, the percentage scale is a clearly unipolar measure of probability and this method of assessing stereotypes has considerable predictive validity. Jonas and Hewstone (in press) reported high correlations between this measure of stereotyping and criterion scores of both liking and intended contact.

5 In Italy only 61 respondents answered all four questions. However, results were in line with equity theory: overall attitude of those who perceived high inequity was less positive ($M = +0.33$) than of those who perceived no inequity ($M = +1.17$), $t(38) = -3.24, p < 0.01$.

6 Favourable ratings for the Community can hardly be explained in terms of political partisanship because, see Appendix A, comparable numbers of respondents in all countries except W. Germany indicated their affiliation with the government and opposition parties.

7 It is not possible to say whether this perception is a reflection or determinant of attitudes. However, following the earlier discussion of the press in relation to social representations of the Community, it is both interesting and consistent that the British perceived the Community image in the media to be so negative.

8 Given the relatively young mean age of the Italian sample, a median-split t-test was computed within this sample to compare the knowledge of 'young' and 'old'. The result was not significant, $t(139) = -1.23$, although the elder respondents were slightly more knowledgeable ($M = 1.03$ vs $M = 0.74$). This trend held for the full sample, using a similar analysis. $t(541) = 4.35, p < 0.01$. The 'young' overall, were slightly less knowledgeable than the 'old' ($M = 1.47$ vs 2.16).

9 'Minimum marginal reproducibility' is too high, probably reflecting the inherent cumulative interrelation of the variables used.

10 Attitudinal differences as a function of political affiliation, albeit slight, are treated in more detail in *Euro-baromètre*, no. 16, Inglehart (1984) and Inglehart and Rabier (1978).

11 Looking ahead to Chapter 6, this decision was supported by an initial run of mutliple regression analyses showing non-significant effects due to this factor, and a sharp drop in sample size.

12 I am grateful to Jos Jaspars for suggesting this possibility, and the appropriate analysis, to me.

13 See the entry for 'credibility' in *The Fontana Dictionary of Modern Thought*, London: Fontana Collins, 1977.

14 There is, however, one problem with the logic of the additive model – when an expectancy is zero. According to this model a value of $+3$, for example, added to an expectancy of 0 still contributes towards an overall positive attitude, whereas intuitively such a belief should form a neutral component of attitudes.

15 These doubts about the Fishbein–Ajzen model were confirmed in a more recent study (Hewstone and Young, in prep.) where attitudes based on modal salient beliefs (including equal numbers of positive and negative items) were compared in multiplicative and additive models, using bipolar and unipolar scoring of

expectancy. Once again (using a sample of 45 British students), the correlation based on the Fishbein–Ajzen model was very low (+0.08); although when expectancy was scored on a unipolar scale the correlation (+0.45) was not significantly different from that yielded by an additive model (+0.40).

16 It should be noted, however, that this effect is not limited to student respondents. Hewstone and Wober (1985), using a representative sample of 427 London adults, calculated a perceived inequity score of 0.06. Further evidence for the reliability of these scores comes from a recent study by Hewstone and Young (in prep.). Using a sample of 45 British students, they calculated a score of 0.12. Both values are obviously very close to the reported score of 0.09 for the British sample in the present study.

17 *Euro-baromètre* no. 10 also mentions that in the first European parliamentry election attention was drawn to future Spanish membership of the Community by both 'left' (P.C.) and 'right' (RPR) political parties. The issue has been more political and is more salient. *Euro-baromètre* no. 13 showed that even in 1980 more French respondents named Spain as a country seeking to join the Community, than named Greece (which joined in 1981).

18 The reader may note the apparent inconsistency between the W. German respondents' high perceived inequity and their relatively high level of utilitarian support. Unfortunately, it is not possible to say which measure is more valid, and they would appear to tap different beliefs and social knowledge. It may be that the two types of response exist in isolated 'opinion molecules' (Abelson, 1968), which only confront, and in this case contradict, each other in the course of such an enquiry.

19 Notwithstanding the Community's real achievements in this area, Barzini (1983) reports that on the eve of Sarajevo (1914) no passport was needed to go from one European nation to another.

20 Nonetheless, the fact that Italian respondents were less knowledgeable does replicate the finding reported by Mathew (1980). Using a different measure, he calculated that the following percentages of each country's general public possessed 'high' knowledge (W. Germany, 62%; France, 36%; Italy, 28%; U.K., 34%).

Chapter 6. Predicting attitudes towards the European Community: towards a model of underlying structure

1 Missing data for any one of the predictors result in the exclusion of that respondent from the analysis.

2 In France there is a negative correlation between judgements of common policy and overall attitude, a finding for which no ready explanation is available.

3 Even when a best-subset multiple regression analysis was computed using the ten knowledge items alone, it was not possible to explain more than approximately 5% of the variance in overall attitudes in any country.

4 It is possible that ethnocentrism – as measured by stereotypes, liking and images – would be greatly altered by adding ratings for the six other Community member states. However, as Inglehart and Rabier (1982) reported, images of small countries – especially Belgium, Holland and Luxembourg – are often very

vague; most respondents in the present study did at least have a clear picture of the nations and nationalities they were asked to judge.

5 Statements about how much variance is explained by given measures must, of course, be qualified by some statement concerning scaling of the variables (see Sechrest and Yeaton, 1982; Strack and Rehm, 1984). For example, the 'support' measure used in later analyses was based on 16 items, the expectancy-value measure on 26 (13 × 2), while contact was based on only one item. In addition, items used in parts of the questionnaire other than that for expectancy-value might have appeared more influential if they had also been rated in terms of both evaluation *and* expectancy. Statements about the percentage of variance explained therefore pertain to the *present* set of variables, scaled in *this* way.

6 Standard multiple regression, without the best subset procedure, was also computed and revealed almost exactly the same picture. Both the best multiplicative and additive measures of expectancy-value were also included in separate analyses, but the former was not a better predictor.

7 This best subset of ten variables excludes three variables – effects of community policy, stereotyping score and travel – which were included in the best subsets of individual countries. However, none of these variables was significant and, given the over-inclusiveness of the best subset approach, they were not considered in the path analyses.

8 I am grateful to an anonymous reviewer for the Alexander von Humboldt-Stiftung for suggesting this approach.

9 The fact that 'international relations' was dropped from the analysis, because less powerful than other variables, should not obscure the fact that broader internationalism tended to correlate with 'Europeanness'. This same finding was reported by Inglehart (1970a).

10 Note that the value of R^2 reported is based on *all* the predictor variables, and not only those with significant effects.

11 The degrees of freedom for these chi-square analyses vary as a function of the number of path coefficients in the model which are set to zero.

12 This last possibility may be linked with the fact that different correlations obtained in different populations may be due to differences in variation. However, as noted earlier, the French sample was very similar to the Italian sample in this respect (e.g. the restricted variation in overall attitude noted in both samples; see Figure 3.1), and the model performed well using the latter data.

13 Both forward and backward selection of variables by the step-wise procedure were used: at each step the variable that adds the most to the separation of the groups is entered into (or the variable that adds the least is removed from) the discriminant function. In fact, both methods always provided the same best set of classifying variables.

14 Himmelweit *et al.* (1981) also acknowledge some of the disadvantages of discriminant analysis. For example, it focuses on those variables that differentiate *across the board* between the different groups, and not those variables which might matter to particular individuals.

15 It should be emphasised that these correlations may be viewed as objective measures of importance, but that they provide no evidence as to causality; it is therefore inappropriate to assume that a high correlation (between any ques-

tionnaire item and overall attitude) indicates an important determinant of attitude.

16 In contrast, Mathew (1980) reported a relatively high positive correlation between Community support and knowledge in all member states. However, his measure of knowledge required respondents, the general public, only to name the member states of the Community.

Chapter 7. Conclusion: findings and implications

1 The single-item criterion for overall attitude can be criticised as possibly less reliable than a measurement based on, for example, four evaluative semantic differential scales (see Ajzen and Fishbein, 1980). However, analyses using both types of criterion (by Hewstone and Young, 1985) identified exactly the same set of predictors, and found that the two measures correlated $+0.79$.

2 Given the attention paid to the Common Agricultural Policy in respondents' open-ended answers, it is consistent that of correlations between judgements of the five common policies and overall attitude, those yielded by agriculture were the highest: W. Germany $(N = 117)$, $r = 0.25$, $p < 0.01$; Italy $(N = 107)$, $r = 0.25$, $p < 0.01$; France $(N = 115)$, $r = -0.20$, $p < 0.05$; U.K. $(N = 118)$, $r = 0.21$, $p < 0.05$.

3 See Haas (1985) for a discussion of 'spillover'.

4 Unfortunately, the figures cited by journalists and economists vary quite widely. For example, one newspaper article (without explaining its calculations) gives the U.K. and W. Germany as the major 'losers' out of the EEC, followed by France. These three members states gain £1.2 million, £1.2 million and £11 million respectively, from, but all put more money into, the Community (*The Observer*, 25 March, 1984). Another set of figures states that W. Germany (-40) is the largest loser, followed by the U.K. (-16) and France (-7); of the four countries studied here, only Italy is given as a winner $(+24)$. Amounts are given in European Currency Units and represent a nation's gain or loss from the Community budget per head of the nation's population in 1982 (*The Sunday Times*, 18 April, 1984).

5 Headline in the *Sun* 'newspaper', reported by Cohen-Solal and Bachmann (1983).

6 Inglehart (1970b) even suggests that the British response to the vetoes may represent an ironic self-fulfilling prophecy. Rejected on the grounds that they were not sufficiently 'European', the British may now be flaunting this trait.

7 The 'lamb war' refers to France's defiance of the Court of Justice ruling, that she should allow U.K. sheep meat into the French market.

8 According the *The Sunday Times* (18 April, 1984), neither France (-7) nor the U.K. (-16) make anything like the gains out of the Community of Ireland $(+203)$, Greece $(+69)$, Denmark $(+51)$, Belgium/Luxembourg $(+44)$, Italy $(+24)$ or the Netherlands $(+17)$. And yet, those British respondents who identified France as the major beneficiary were doing no more than giving the same answer as the sample of Labour Party Members of Parliament investigated by Featherstone (1981). 76% of these politicians identified France as the member state benefitting most from the Community, 60% gave W. Germany and yet only

25% named Ireland. According to Rutherford (1981), Conservative M.P.s are no better, being 'not averse to beating the anti-European drum, especially when it concerned the French'. (p. 19.)

9 Denmark is the only one of the ten member states which does not have a majority in favour of efforts to unify Europe (Inglehart, 1984); and whose percentage support for faster unification has barely reached double figures (Rutherford, 1981). However, the Danish are more positive about Community membership than are the British.

10 'Nationalisn', in the *Fontana Dictionary of Modern Thought* (London: Fontana/Collins, 1977).

11 Kurt Tucholsky *'Zwischen Gestern und Morgen'* (Hamburg: Rowohlt, 1952).

12 The author is aware of no comparable phrase in Italian and is assured by Italian colleagues that no such phrase exists!

13 See, for example. *'True or false? Questions about the European Community'* (nos. 13–14, 1980) and *'The European Community: Some questions and answers'* (nos. 5–6, 1984), both published in the *European File* series by the Commission of the European Communities, Directorate-General for Information, Brussels.

14 Further evidence concerning the importance of utilitarian support for British respondents was provided by Hewstone and Wober (1985); see also Wober, 1984). Using a representative sample of London's adults a multiple regression analysis was computed to predict overall attitudes to the Community; predictors included four-item summary scores based on utilitarian support, affective support and the effects of Community policy (taken from the present questionnaire). The regression analysis yielded an adjusted R^2 of 0.44, with the measure of utilitarian support the best predictor (< 0.001).

15 There is, perhaps, one potential disadvantage in increasing interest in Community affairs, given that a circular relationship exists between knowledge, interest and attention to the media (Atkin, Galloway and Nayman, 1973). Attention to the media leads to increased knowledge and interest in the topic; and high levels of knowledge and interest stimulate further attention to the (sometimes very negative) media.

16 Hewtone and Young (1985) examined both active (recall) and passive (recognition) knowledge about the Community, and compared this with knowledge of British politics. As expected, recognition-based knowledge was superior, but guessing cannot be ruled out with this measure. The data on British knowledge were certainly illuminating: of 45 British university students, only 44% could name the Industry Secretary and only 55% the Foreign Secretary. Knowledge of the Community is perhaps flattered by the fact that 71% said that agriculture accounted for the biggest share of the Community budget, while only 13% could name the British Minister of Agriculture.

17 ANOVA yielded a significant main effect across countries, $F(3,538) = 9.81, p < 0.001$; the only significant *post hoc* comparisons being those between W. Germany and each of the other countries ($p < 0.001$).

18 See European Parliament written replies to questions 1680/83, 1681/83 and 1683/83 posed by the Revd. I. Paisley (Euro M.P. for Northern Ireland).

19 ANOVA yielded a significant main effect across countries, $F(3,540) = 28.05, p < 0.001$; the only significant *post hoc* comparisons being those between the U.K. and each of the other countries ($p < 0.001$).

20 In the course of influence aimed at change in beliefs, there may also be effects on the evaluation of attributes associated with the primary beliefs; these evaluations may then influence the amount of attitude change obtained (Lutz, 1975).

21 It should, however, be noted that Hewstone and Young (1985) have recently ascertained the content of modal salient beliefs about the Community for British respondents. Eight such beliefs (four positive and four negative) predict overall attitude to some extent (correlations of the order of $+0.40$ for both additive and multiplicative–unipolar beliefs models), but are quite similar in content to some of the beliefs used in the present study.

22 In fact, Eagly and Chaiken (1984) argue that mathematically formulated combinatorial models (including the expectancy-value model) have general explanatory value primarily in relation to the effects of the *content* of the persuasive message.

23 According to Rabier (in press), voting turn-out in the last general elections in W. Germany, France and the U.K. was 89%, 70.4% and 72.7%, respectively. For the last European election, figures were 56.8%, 56.7% and 32.6%, respectively. In Italy, voting is considered obligatory and turn-out is very high indeed.

24 In fact, Hewstone and Wober's (1985; see Wober, 1984) study of attitudes toward the Community also tried to predict intention to vote in the European elections (then three weeks away). Although a multiple regression on the intention measure yielded on R^2 of only 0.06, both overall attitude to the Community ($p < 0.05$) and a four-item measure of utilitarian support ($p < 0.05$) were significant predictors of this criterion.

25 The vast amount of research generated by the attitude–behaviour controversy need not be reviewed in full here. Suffice to say that the topic continues to excite interest in both sociology (e.g., Deutscher, 1973; Schuman & Johnson, 1976) and pyschology (Cooper & Croyle, 1984; Stapf, 1982; Wicker, 1969). Perhaps the major alternative to Fishbein and Ajzen's 'methodological' solution to the problem is a 'mediational' one, whereby 'other variables' (including: other attitudes, competing motives, individual differences, and normative prescriptions of proper behaviour) are taken into account as either moderator or independent variables (see Abelson, 1982; Fazio & Zanna, 1981).

26 In fact Fishbein and Ajzen (1975, 1981) seem to prefer the equation: $B \sim I = f$ $(w_1 A_B + w_2 SN)$. This is, of course, basically identical to equation (4), but fails to specify the components of A_B and SN explicitly. For this reason, Pagel, and Davidson's (1984) version of the equation is preferred here.

27 Interestingly, Fishbein and Ajzen (1981, p. 292) suggest that subjective norms are less important in relation to political issues; on such matters people appear to have low motives to comply with their relevant referents.

References

Abelson, R. P. (1959), 'Modes of resolution of belief dilemmas', *Journal of Conflict Resolution*, **3**, 343–52.

Abelson, R. P. (1968), 'Computers, polls, and public opinion – some puzzles and paradoxes', *Trans-action*, **5**, 20–7.

Abelson, R. P. (1972), 'Are attitudes necessary?' in B. T. King and E. McGinnies (eds.), *Attitudes, Conflict and Social Change*, New York, Academic Press.

Abelson, R. P. (1982). 'Three modes of attitude-behavior consistency', in M. P. Zanna, E. T. Higgins and C. P. Herman (eds.), *Consistency in social behavior: the Ontario Symposium (Vol. 2)*, Hillsdale, N. J., Erlbaum.

Abelson, R. P., Aronson, E., McGuire, W. J., Newcomb, T. M., Rosenberg, M. J. and Tannenbaum, P. H. (eds.) (1968), *Theories of Cognitive consistency: a sourcebook*, Chicago, Rand McNally.

Abelson, R. P., Rosenberg, M. J. (1958), 'Symbolic psycho-logic: a model of attitudinal cognition', *Behavioral Science*, **3**, 1–13.

Achen, C. H. (1982), *Interpreting and Using Regression*, Beverly Hills, Sage.

Adams, J. S. (1963). 'Toward an understanding of inequity', *Journal of Abnormal and Social Psychology*, **67**, 422–36.

Adams, J. S. (1965), 'Inequity in social exchange', in L. Berkowitz (ed.), *Advances in Experimental Social Psychology (Vol. 2)*, New York, Academic Press.

Adams, J. S., and Freedman, S. (1976), 'Equity theory revisited', in L. Berkowitz and E. Walster (eds.), *Advances in Experimental Social Psychology (Vol. 9)*, *Equity Theory: toward a general theory of social interaction*, New York, Academic Press.

Adelson, J. and O'Neil, R. (1966), 'Growth of political ideas in adolescence: the sense of community', *Journal of Personality and Social Psychology*, **4**, 295–306.

Ajzen, I., and Fishbein, M. (1977), 'Attitude-behavior relations: a theoretical analysis and review of empirical research', *Psychological Bulletin*, **84**, 888–918.

Ajzen, I., and Fishbein, M. (1980), *Understanding Attitudes and Predicting Social Behavior*, Englewood Cliffs, N.J., Prentice-Hall.

Allport, G. W. (1935), 'Attitudes' in C. Murchison (ed.), *A Handbook of Social Psychology*, Worcester, Mass., Clark University Press.

Allport, G. W. (1954–79), *The Nature of Prejudice*, Reading, Mass: Addison-Wesley.

Allport, G. W. (1969), 'Attitudes in the history of social psychology', in N. Warren and M. Jahoda (eds.), *Attitudes*, Harmondsworth, Penguin (originally published in G. Lindzey (ed.), *Handbook of Social Psychology*, Addison-Wesley, 1954, Vol. 1).

Almond, G. A. (1960), *The American People and Foreign Policy*, New York, Praeger.

Almond, G. A., and Verba, S. (1963), *The Civic Culture*, Princeton, N.J., Princeton University Press.

Anderson, N. H. (1976), 'Equity judgements as information integration', *Journal of Personality and Social Psychology*, 33, 291–9.

Andrews, F. M., Klem, L., Davidson, T. N., O'Malley, P. M. and Rodgers, W. L. (1974). *A Guide for Selecting Statistical Techniques for Analyzing Social Science Data*, University of Michigan, Survey Research Center, Institute for Social Research.

Aron, R. (1954), *The Century of Total War*, Garden City, N.Y., Doubleday.

Aron, R. (1964), 'Old nations, new Europe' in S. R. Graubard (ed.), *A New Europe?* Boston, Houghton Mifflin.

Asch, S. (1952), *Social Psychology*, New York, Prentice-Hall.

Asher, H. B. (1983), *Causal Modeling*, Beverly Hills, Sage (2nd edn).

Atkin, C. K., Galloway, J., and Nayman, O. (1973), 'Mass communication and political socialization among college students', *Public Opinion Quarterly*, 37, 443–4.

Atkinson, J. W. (ed.) (1958), *Motives in Fantasy, Action, and Society: a method of assessment and study*, Princeton, N.J., Van Nostrand.

Bacot-Décriaud, M., and Plantin, M.-C. (1982), 'Le thème de l'intégration européenne' in P. Bacot and C. Journés (eds.), *Les Nouvelles idéologies*, Lyon, Presses Universitaires de Lyon.

Bagozzi, R. P. (1981), 'Attitudes, intentions, and behaviour: A test of some key hypotheses', *Journal of Personality and Social Psychology*, 41, 606–27.

Bagozzi, R., and Burnkrant, R. (1979), 'Attitude organization and the attitude-behaviour relationship', *Journal of Personality and Social Psychology*, 37, 913–29.

Baker, B. O., Hardyck, C. D. and Petrinovich, L. F. (1966), 'Weak measurements vs. strong statistics: an empirical critique of S. S. Stevens' proscriptions on statistics', *Educational and Psychological Measurement*, XXVI, (2), 291–309.

Barzini, L. (1983), *The Impossible Europeans*, London, Weidenfeld and Nicholson.

Battaglia, F. (1957), 'Introduction' in C. G. Haines (ed.), *European Integration*, Baltimore, Md., Johns Hopkins Press.

Beach, L. R., Townes, B. D., Campbell, F. L., and Keating, G. W. (1976), 'Developing and testing a decision aid for birth planning decisions', *Organizational Behavior and Human Performance*, 15, 99–116.

Becker, G. M., and McClintock, C. G. (1967), 'Value: behavioural decision theory', *Annual Review of Psychology*, 18, 239–86.

Bem, D. (1972), 'Self-perception theory', in L. Berkowitz (ed.), *Advances in Experimental Social Psychology* (Vol. 6), New York, Academic Press.

Benoit, E. (1961), *Europe at Sixes and Sevens*, New York, Columbia University Press.

Bentler, P. M., and Speckart, G. (1979), 'Models of attitude-behavior relations', *Psychological Review*, 86, 452–64.

Berelson, B. (1952), *Content Analysis in Communication Research*, Glencoe, Ill., Free Press.

Berelson, B. R., and Steiner, G. A. (1964), *Human Behavior: an inventory of scientific findings*, New York, Harcourt, Brace and World.

Berger, P. L., and Luckmann, T. (1967), *The Social Construction of Reality*, Harmondsworth, England, Penguin.

Bergius, R., Werbik, H., Winter, G., and Schubring, G. (1970), 'Urteile deutscher Arbeitnehmer über Völker in Relation zur Zahl ihrer ausländischen Bekannten. II: Unterschiede zwischen verschiedenen Kontaktgruppen', *Psychologische Beiträge*, 12, 485–532.

Berkowitz, L., and Walster, E. (1976), *Advances in Experimental Social Psychology (Vol. 9). Equity Theory: toward a general theory of social interaction*, New York, Academic Press.

Bibes, G., Menudier, H., de la Serre, F., and Smouts, M.-C. (1980), *Europe Elects its Parliament*, London, Policy Studies Institute.

Billig, M. (1978). *Fascists: a social psychological view of the National Front*. London, Harcourt Brace Jovanovich.

Bishop, G. (1976), 'The effect of education on ideological consistency', *Public Opinion Quarterly*, **40**, 337–48.

Bissery, J. (1972), 'Comment l'idée de l'Europe vient aux plus jeunes'. *Sondages*, 1–2, 151–9.

Blalock, H. M. (1964), *Causal Inferences in Non-experimental Research*, Chapel Hill, University of North Carolina Press.

Blalock, H. M. (1971), 'Theory building and causal inferences', in H. M. Blalock and A. B. Blalock (eds.), *Methodology in Social Research*, London, McGraw Hill.

Blau, P. M. (1967), *Exchange and Power in Social Life*, New York, Wiley.

Blumler, J. G., and Fox, A. D. (1982), *The European Voter: popular responses to the first Community election*, London, Policy Studies Institute.

Bogardus, E. S. (1931), *Fundamentals of Social Psychology* (2nd edn), New York, Century.

Bogardus, E. S. (1950), 'Stereotypes versus sociotypes', *Sociological and Social Research*, **34**, 286–91.

Bortz, J. (1977), *Lehrbuch der Statistik für Sozialwissenschaftler*, Berlin/Heidelberg, Springer-Verlag.

Boulding, K. E. (1956), *The Image*, Ann Arbor, University of Michigan Press.

Bourdieu, P. (1973), 'L'opinion publique n'existe pas', *Temps Modernes*, **29**, 1292–309.

Brandstädter, J., and Bernitzke, F. (1976), 'Zur Technik der Pfadanalyse: Ein Beitrag zum Problem der nichtexperimentallen Konstruktion von Kausalmodellen', *Psychologische Beiträge*, **18**, 12–34.

Brigham, J. C. (1971), 'Ethnic stereotypes', *Psychological Bulletin*, **76**, 15–38.

Brislin, R. (1980), 'Translation and content analysis of oral and written materials', in H. Triandis, W. Lambert, J. Berry, W. Lonner, A. Heron, R. Brislin, and J. Draguns (eds.), *Handbook of Cross-Cultural Psychology* (6 vols.), Boston, Allyn and Bacon.

Brown, R. (1965), *Social Psychology*, New York, Free Press.

Buchanan, W., and Cantril, H. (1953), *How Nations See Each Other: a study in public opinion*, Urbana, University of Illinois Press.

Budd, R. W., Thorp, R. K., and Donohew, L. (1967), *Content Analysis of Communications*, New York, Macmillan.

Butler, D., and Kitzinger, U. (eds.) (1976), *The 1975 Referendum*, London, St Martin's Press.

Caddick, B. (1980), 'Equity theory, social identity, and intergroup relations' in L. Wheeler (ed.), *Review of Personality and Social Psychology* (Vol. 1), Beverly Hills, Sage.

Campbell, D. T., and Fiske, D. W. (1959), 'Convergent and discriminant validation by the multitrait-multimethod matrix', *Psychological Bulletin*, **56**, 81–105.

Cantril, H. (1944), *Gauging Public Opinion*, Princeton, N.J., Princeton University Press.

Cantril, H. (1965), *The Pattern of Human Concerns*, New Brunswick, N.J., Rutgers University Press.

Carlson, E. R. (1956), 'Attitude change through modification of attitude structure', *Journal of Abnormal and Social Psychology*, 52, 256–61.

Cartwright, D. (1949), 'Some principles of mass persuasion: selected findings of research on the sale of United States War Bonds', *Human Relations*, 2, 253–67.

Cartwright, D., and Harary, F. (1956), 'Structural balance: a generalization of Heider's theory', *Psychological Review*, 63, 277–93.

Chaiken, S., and Baldwin, M. W. (1981), 'Affective-cognitive consistency and the effect of salient behavioural information on the self-perception of attitudes', *Journal of Personality and Social Psychology*, 41, 1–12.

Childs, H. L. (1959), 'By public opinion I mean', *Public Opinion Quarterly*, 3, 327–36.

Childs, H. L. (1965), *Public Opinion: nature, formation and role*, Princeton, N.J., Van Nostrand.

Cialdini, R. B., Petty, R. E., and Cacioppo, J. T. (1981), 'Attitude and attitude change', *Annual Review of Psychology*, 32, 357–404.

Codol, J.-P. (1975), 'On the so-called "superior conformity of the self" behaviour: twenty experimental investigations', *European Journal of Social Psychology*, 5, 457–501.

Cohen-Solal, A., and Bachmann, C. (1983), *L'Angleterre face à la France: Insulaire ou Communautaire?*, Paris, Mimeo. Report for a research grant from the Commission of the European Communities.

Connell, R. W. (1972), 'Political socialization in the American family: the evidence re-examined', *Public Opinion Quarterly*, 36, 323–33.

Converse, P. E. (1964a), 'The nature of belief systems in mass publics', in D. E. Apter (ed.), *Ideology and Discontent*, New York, Free Press.

Converse, P. E. (1964b), 'New dimensions of meaning for cross-section sample surveys in politics', *International Social Science Journal*, XVI, 19–34.

Converse, P. E. (1970), 'Attitudes and non-attitudes: Continuation of a dialogue', in E. R. Tufte (ed.), *The Quantitative Analysis of Social Problems*, Reading, Mass., Addison-Wesley.

Converse, P. E. (1974), 'Comment: The status of non-attitudes', *American Political Science Review*, 68, 650–60.

Converse, P. E., and Dupeux, G. (1962), 'Politicization of the electorate in France and the United States', *Public Opinion Quarterly*, 26, 1–23.

Coombes, D. (1970), *Politics and Bureaucracy in the European Community*, London, George Allen and Unwin.

Cooper, E., and Jahoda, M. (1947), 'The evasion of propaganda: how prejudiced people respond to anti-prejudice propaganda', *Journal of Psychology*, 23, 15–25.

Cooper, J., and Croyle, R. T. (1984), 'Attitudes and attitude change', *Annual Review of Psychology*, 35, 395–426.

Cooper, J., and Fazio, R. H. (1984), 'A new look at dissonance theory', in L. Berkowitz (ed.), *Advances in Experimental Social Psychology* (Vol. 17), New York, Academic Press.

Cowles, M., and Davis, C. (1982), 'On the origins of the .05 level of statistical significance', *American Psychologist*, 37, 553–8.

CRAM (1985), *Exploratory Study into the Motivational Dynamics of the British Relating to Europeanisation*, London, Cooper Research and Marketing Ltd., May Report.

Crockett, W. H. (1982), 'Balance, agreement, and positivity in the cognition of small social structures', in L. Berkowitz (ed.), *Advances in Experimental Social Psychology* (Vol. 15), New York, Academic Press.

Crozier, M. (1964), *The Bureaucratic Phenomenon*, London, Tavistock Publications.

Dalton, R. J. (1980), *The Political Environment and Attitudes towards European Integration: Britain, 1972–1979*, Brussels, Mimeo. Report for a research grant from the Commission of the European Communities.

Dalton, R. J., and Duval, R. (1981), 'The Political Environment and Foreign Policy Opinions: British attitudes towards European integration, 1972–1979', unpublished ms., The Florida State University.

Dankert, P. (1983), 'The European Community – Past, present and future', in L. Tsoukalis (ed.), *The European Community: past, present and future*, Oxford, Basil Blackwell.

Dannenberg, U., and Winter, G. (1975), 'Urteile deutscher Arbeitnehmer über Völker in Relation zur Zahl ihrer ausländischen Bekannten. IV: Unterschiede zwischen verschiedenen Alters- und Schulbildungsgruppen', *Psychologische Beiträge*, 17, 61–83.

Davidson, A. R., & Jaccard, J. J. (1979), 'Variables that moderate the attitude-behaviour relation: results of a longitudinal survey', *Journal of Personality and Social Psychology*, 37, 1364–76.

Davison, W. P. (1968), 'Public opinion', *International Encyclopaedia of the Social Sciences*, Macmillan/Free Press.

Dawes, R. M. (1971), *Fundamentals of Attitude Measurement*, New York, Wiley.

Deheneffe, J.-C. (1983), *Europe as seen by Europeans: ten years of European polling (1973–1979)*, Luxembourg, Office for Official Publications of the European Communities.

Deniau, J.-F. (1958), *Le Marché Commun*, Paris, Presses Universitaires de France.

De Rougemont, D. (1961), *Vingt-huit siècles d'Europe*, Paris, Payot.

Deutsch, K. W. (1952), *Nationalism and Social Communication*, Cambridge, Mass., M.I.T. Press.

Deutsch, K. W. (1961), 'Social mobilization and political development', *American Political Science Review*, LV, 497–502.

Deutsch, K. W. (1967), 'A comparison of French and German elites in the European Political environment', in K. W. Deutsch, L. J. Edinger, R. C. Macridis and R. L. Merritt, *France, Germany and the Western Alliance*, New York, Scribner.

Deutsch, K. W. et al. (1957), *Political Community and the North Atlantic Area*, Princeton, Princeton University Press.

Deutsch, K. W., Edinger, L. J., Macridis, R. C., and Merritt, R. L. (1967), *France, Germany and the Western Alliance*, New York, Scribner.

Deutsch, K. W., and Merritt, R. L. (1965), 'Effects of events on national and international images', in H. C. Kelman (ed.), *International Behavior*, New York, Holt, Rinehart and Winston.

Deutscher, I. (1973), *What we say/What we do: sentiments and acts*, Glenview, Ill., Scott, Foresman.

Dillehay, R. C., Insko, C. A., and Smith, M. B. (1966), 'Logical consistency and attitude change', *Journal of Personality and Social Psychology*, 3, 646–54.

Di Vesta, F. J., and Merwin, J. C. (1960), 'Effects of need oriented communication on attitude change', *Journal of Abnormal and Social Psychology*, 60, 80–5.

Doise, W. (1978), *Groups and Individuals: explanations in social psychology*, Cambridge University Press.

Donovan, P. (1973), 'Who do you think we are?', in J. Barber and B. Reed (eds.), *European Community: vision and reality*, London, Croom Helm.

Duijker, H. C., and Frijda, N. H. (1960), *National Character and National Stereotypes*, Amsterdam, North-Holland Publishing Co.

Duncan, O. D. (1966), 'Path analysis: sociological examples', *American Journal of Sociology*, 72, 1–16.

Durkheim, E. (1898), 'Représentations individuelles et représentations collectives', *Revue de Metaphysique et de Morale*, 6, 273–303 (translated as 'Individual and collective representations' in E. Durkheim, *Sociology and Philosophy*, New York, The Free Press, 1974).

Duroselle, J. B. (1957), 'Europe as a historical concept', in C. G. Haines (ed.), *European Integration*, Baltimore, Md., Johns Hopkins Press.

Eagly, A. H., and Chaiken, S. (1984), 'Cognitive theories of persuasion', in L. Berkowitz (ed.), *Advances in Experimental Social Psychology* (Vol. 17), New York, Academic Press.

Eagly, A. H., and Himmelfarb, S. (1974), 'Current trends in attitude theory and research', in S. Himmelfarb and A. H. Eagly (eds.), *Readings in Attitude Change*, New York, Wiley.

Eagly, A. H., and Himmelfarb, S. (1978), 'Attitudes and opinions', *Annual Review of Psychology*, 29, 517–54.

Easton, D. (1965a), *A Systems Analysis of Political Life*, London, John Wiley and Sons.

Easton, D. (1965b), *A Framework for Political Analysis*, Englewood Cliffs, N. J., Prentice Hall.

Easton, D., and Dennis, J. (1969), *Children in the Political System: origins of political legitimacy*, New York, McGraw-Hill.

Edwards, W. (1954), 'The theory of decision making', *Psychological Bulletin*, 51, 380–417.

Eiser, J. R. (1980), *Cognitive Social Psychology*, Maidenhead, McGraw-Hill.

Eiser, J. R. (1982), 'Attitudes and applied research', in P. Stringer (ed.), *Confronting Social Issues: some applications of social psychology* (Vol. 1), London, Academic Press.

Emerson, R. (1960), *From Empire to Nation*, Cambridge, Mass., Harvard University Press.

Epstein, R., and Kormorita, S. (1966), 'Childhood prejudice as a function of parental ethnocentrism, punitiveness, and outgroup characteristics', *Journal of Personality and Social Psychology*, 3, 259–64.

Erskine, H. G. (1962), 'The polls: the informed public', *Public Opinion Quarterly*, 25, 128–39.

Erskine, H. G. (1963), 'The polls: exposure to international information', *Public Opinion Quarterly*, 27, 658–62.

Etzioni, A. (1965), *Political Unification*, New York, Holt, Rinehart and Winston.

Etzioni, A. (1969), 'Social-psychological aspects of international relations', in G. Lindzey and E. Aronson (eds.), *The Handbook of Social Psychology*, Reading, Mass., Addison-Wesley.

Euro-Baromètres, Nos. 1–21 (1974–84), Brussels, Commission of the European Communities (English language edition).

Eysenck, H. J., and Crown, S. (1947), 'National stereotypes: an experimental and methodological study', *International Journal of Opinion and Attitude Research*, 2, 26–39.

Farquarson, J. E., and Holt, S. C. (1975), *Europe From Below: an assessment of Franco-German popular contacts*, London, George Allen and Unwin Ltd.

Farr, R. M. (1984), 'Social representations: their role in the design and execution of laboratory experiments', in R. M. Farr and S. Moscovici (eds.), *Social Representations*, Cambridge/Paris, Cambridge University Press/Maison des Science de l'Homme.

Farr, R. M., and Moscovici, S. (1984), *Social Representations*, Cambridge/Paris, Cambridge University Press/Maison des Sciences de l'Homme.

Fazio, R. H., and Zanna, M. P. (1978), 'Attitudinal qualities relating to the strength of the attitude-behavior relationship', *Journal of Experimental Social Psychology*, 14, 398–408.

Fazio, R. H., and Zanna, M. P. (1981), 'Direct experience and attitude-behavior consistency', in L. Berkowitz (ed.), *Advances in Experimental Social Psychology* (Vol. 14), New York, Academic Press.

Feather, N. T. (ed.), (1982), *Expectations and Actions: expectancy-value models in psychology*, Hillsdale, N. J., Erlbaum.

Featherstone, K. (1981), 'Socialists and European integration: the attitudes of British Labour Members of Parliament', *European Journal of Political Research*, 9, 407–19.

Feld, W., and Wildgen, J. (1976), *Domestic Political Realities and European Integration*, Boulder Co., Westview Press.

Feld, W. J. (1981), *West Germany and the European Community: changing interests and competing policy objectives*, New York, Praeger.

Festinger, L. (1957), *A Theory of Cognitive Dissonance*, Evanston, Ill., Row, Peterson.

Fischhoff, B., Goitein, B., and Shapira, Z. (1982), 'The experienced utility of expected utility approaches', in N. T. Feather (ed.), *Expectations and Actions: Expectancy-value Models in Psychology*, Hillsdale, N.J., Erlbaum.

Fishbein, M. (1963), 'An investigation of the relationships between beliefs about an object and the attitude toward that object', *Human Relations*, 16, 233–40.

Fishbein, M. (1967), 'A behavior theory approach to the relations between beliefs about an object and the attitude toward the object', in M. Fishbein (ed.), *Readings in Attitude Theory and Measurement*, New York, Wiley.

Fishbein, M. (1980), 'A theory of reasoned action: some applications and implications', in H. E. Howe (ed.), *Nebraska Symposium on Motivation* (Vol. 27), Lincoln, Neb., University of Nebraska Press.

Fishbein, M., and Ajzen, I. (1972), 'Attitudes and opinions', *Annual Review of Psychology*, 23, 487–544.

Fishbein, M., and Ajzen, I. (1974), 'Attitudes toward objects as predictors of single and multiple behavioral criteria', *Psychological Review*, 81, 59–74.

Fishbein, M., and Ajzen, I. (1975), *Belief, Attitude, Intention and Behavior*, Reading, Mass., Addison-Wesley.

Fishbein, M., and Ajzen, I. (1981), 'Attitudes and voting behaviour: an application of the theory of reasoned action', in G. M. Stephenson and J. M. Davis (eds.), *Progress in Applied Social Psychology* (Vol. 1), Chichester, J. Wiley.

Fishbein, M., and Coombs, F. S. (1974), 'Basis for decision: an attitudinal analysis of voting behavior', *Journal of Applied Social Psychology*, 4, 95–124.

Fishman, J. A. (1956), 'An examination of the process and function of social stereotyping', *Journal of Social Psychology*, 43, 27–64.

Flath, E., and Moscovici, S. (1983), 'Social representation', in R. Harré and R. Lamb (eds.), *The Encyclopaedic Dictionary of Psychology*, Oxford, Basil Blackwell.

Fleming, D. (1967), 'Attitude: the history of a concept', in D. Fleming and B. Bailyn (eds.), *Perspectives in American History* (Vol. 1), Cambridge, Mass., Charles Warren Center for Studies in American History.

Florinsky, M. T. (1955), *Integrated Europe?*, New York, The Macmillan Co.

Folsom, J. K. (1931), *Social Psychology*, New York, Harper.

Frane, J. (1981), 'All possible subsets regression', in W. J. Dixon (ed.), *BMDP Statistical Software*, Berkeley, University of California Press.

Friedrich, C. J. (1950), *The New Image of the Common Man*, Boston, The Beacon Press.

Friedrich, C. J. (1969), *Europe: an emergent nation?*, New York, Harper and Row.

Gallup International (1964), *L'opinion publique et l'Europe vue à l'echelle d'une petite ville européenne*, Paris, L'Institut Francais d'Opinion Publique.

Garner, W. R., Hake, H. W., and Eriksen, C. W. (1956), 'Operationism and the concept of perception', *Psychological Review*, 63, 149–59.

Gilbert, G. M. (1951), 'Stereotype persistence and change among college students', *Journal of Abnormal and Social Psychology*, 46, 245–54.

Gorsuch, R. L. (1974), *Factor Analysis*, Philadelphia, Saunders.

Graubard, S. R. (ed.) (1964), *A New Europe?*, Boston, Houghton Mifflin.

Greenstein, F. I. (1965), *Children and Politics*, New Haven, Conn., Yale University Press.

Greenstein, F. I. (1975), 'The benevolent leader revisited: Children's images of political leaders in three democracies', *American Political Science Review*, 69, 1371–99.

Greenstein, F. I. (1976), 'Item wording and other interaction effects on the measurement of political orientations', *American Journal of Political Science*, 20, 773–9.

Greenstein, F. I. and Tarrow, S. (1969), 'The study of French political socialization: toward the revocation of paradox', *World Politics*, 22, 95–137.

Greenwald, A. G. (1968), 'On defining attitude and attitude theory' in A. G. Greenwald, T. C. Brock and T. M. Ostrom (eds.), *Psychological Foundations of Attitudes*, New York, Academic Press.

Guetzkow, H. (1955), *Multiple Loyalties*, Princeton, N.J., Princeton University Press.

Gunter, B. (1985), *Television and the 1984 European Election in Britain: an analysis of content, audiences, knowledge and opinions*, Independent Broadcasting Authority, Research Paper, January.

Guttman, L. (1944), 'A basis for scaling qualitative data', *American Sociological Review*, 9, 139–50.

Guttman, L. (1950), 'The basis for scalogram analysis', in S. A. Stouffer (ed.) *Measurement and Prediction*, Princeton, N.J., Princeton University Press.

Haas, E. B. (1964), *Beyond the Nation State*, Stanford, Calif., Stanford University Press.

Haas, E. B. (1968), *The Uniting of Europe*, Stanford, Stanford University Press.

Hackman, J. R. and Porter, L. W. (1968), 'Expectancy theory predictions of work effectiveness', *Organizational Behavior and Human Performance*, 3, 417–26.

Hallstein, W. (1972), *Europe in the Making*, London, George Allen and Unwin.

Handley, D. (1975), 'Public support for European Integration', unpublished doctoral dissertation, Université de Genève.

Handley, D. H. (1977), 'Support for European Integration as a Political System: a conceptual framework and strategy for comparative analyses', Unpublished manuscript, Departement de science politique, Université de Genève.

Handley, D. H. (1981), 'Public opinion and European integration: the crisis of the 1970s, *European Journal of Political Research*, 9, 335–64.

Harrison, R. J. (1974), *Europe in Question*, London, George Allen & Unwin.

Harrod, D. (1983), *Making Sense of the Economy*. Oxford, Martin Robertson.

Hartley, E. L. (1946), *Problems in prejudice*, New York, King's Crown Press.

Hay, D. (1966), *Europe: the emergence of an idea*, New York, Harper and Row.

Hayakawa, S. I. (1950), 'Recognizing stereotypes as substitutes for thought', *Review of General Semantics*, 7, 208–10.

Hedges, B. (1976), 'The final four years: from opposition to endorsement' in R. Jowell and G. Hoinville (eds.), *Britain into Europe*, London, Croom Helm.

Heider, F. (1946), 'Attitudes and cognitive organization', *Journal of Psychology*, 21, 107–12.

Heider, F. (1958), *The Psychology of Interpersonal Relations*, New York, Wiley.

Heider, F. (1983), *The Life of a Psychologist: an autobiography*, Lawrence, K. S., University Press of Kansas.

Helfant, K. (1967), 'A survey of opinions and beliefs about international relations', in M. E. Shaw and J. M. Wright, *Scales for the measurement of attitudes*, New York, McGraw-Hill.

Henessy, B. C. (1970), *Public Opinion*, Belmont, Calif., Wadsworth.

Herzlich, C. (1972), 'La représentation sociale', in S. Moscovici (ed.), *Introduction à la psychologie sociale*, Paris, Larousse.

Herzlich, C. (1973), *Health and Illness: a social psychological analysis*, London, Academic Press.

Hess, R. D. and Torney, J. V. (1967), *The development of Political Attitudes in children*, Chicago, Aldine.

Hewstone, M. (1983), 'Attribution theory and common-sense explanations: an introductory overview', in M. Hewstone (ed.), *Attribution theory: social and functional extensions*, Oxford, Basil Blackwell.

Hewstone, M. (1984), 'That European feeling', *New Society*, 68, 444.

Hewstone, M. (1985), 'On common sense and social representations: a reply to Potter and Litton', *British Journal of Social Psychology*, 24, 95–7.

Hewstone, M., and Brown, R. J. (eds.) (1986) *Contact and Conflict in Intergroup Encounters*, Oxford, Basil Blackwell.

Hewstone, M., and Wober, M. (1985), 'Public Opinion and the EEC: an analysis of 400 British adults', unpublished manuscript, University of Bristol/I.B.A.

Hewstone, M. and Young, L. (1985), 'British Student's Attitudes to the European Community: a follow-up study', unpublished manuscript, University of Bristol.

Himmelweit, H. T., Humphreys, P., Jaeger, M. and Katz, M. (1981), *How Voters*

Decide: a longitudinal study of political attitudes and voting extending over fifteen years, London, Academic Press.

Hodges, M. (ed.) (1972), *European integration*, Harmondsworth, Penguin.

Holland, S. (1980), *Uncommon Market*, London, Macmillan.

Holmstrom, V. L. and Beach, L. R. (1973), 'Subjective expected utility and career preferences', *Organizational Behavior and Human Performance*, 10, 201–7.

Holsti, O. R. (1969), 'Content analysis', G. Lindsey and E. Aronson (eds.), *The handbook of social psychology*, Reading, Mass., Addison-Wesley.

Holt, L. E. (1970), 'Resistance to persuasion on explicit beliefs as a function of commitment to and desirability of logically related beliefs', *Journal of Personality and Social Psychology*, 16, 583–91.

Holt, L. E. and Watts, W. A. (1969), 'Salience of logical relationships among beliefs as a factor in persuasion', *Journal of Personality and Social Psychology*, II, 193–203.

Holt, S. (1972), 'British attitudes to the political aspects of membership of the European Communities', in G. Ionescu (ed.), *The New Politics of European Integration*, London, Macmillan.

Holt, S. (1973), 'Policy-making in practice – the 1965 crisis', in J. Barber and B. Reed (eds.), *Community: vision and reality*, London, Croom Helm.

Homans, G. (1961), *Social behavior: its elementary forms*, New York, Harcourt, Brace & World.

Homans, G. C. (1976), 'Commentary', in L. Berkowitz and E. Walster (eds.), *Advances in Experimental Social Psychology (Vol. 9). Equity theory: toward a general theory of social interaction*, New York, Academic Press.

Hrbek, R. and Wessels, W. (1984), 'A satisfying balance sheet? Introductory report', in R. Hrbek, J. Jamar and W. Wessels (eds.), *The European Parliament on the Eve of the Second Direct Election: balance sheet and prospects*, Bruges, De Tempel.

Hull, C. L. (1943), *The Principles of Behavior*, New York, Appleton-Century-Crofts.

Hyman, H. H. (1959), *Political Socialization*, Glencoe, Ill., Free Press.

Hyman, H. H. and Sheatsley, P. B. (1947), 'Some reasons why information campaigns fail', *Public Opinion Quarterly*, 11, 412–23.

Hyman, H. H. and Sheatsley, P. B. (1954), 'The current status of American public opinion', in D. Katz, D. Cartwright, S. Eldersveld and A. M. Lee (eds.), *Public Opinion and Propaganda*, New York, Holt, Rinehart and Winston.

Inglehart, R. (1967), 'An end to European integration?' *Americn Political Science Review*, 61, 91–105.

Inglehart, R. (1970a), 'The new Europeans; inward and outward looking?' *International Organization*, 24, 129–39.

Inglehart, R. (1970b), 'Cognitive mobilization and European identity', *Comparative Politics*, 3, 45–71.

Inglehart, R. (1970c), 'Public opinion and regional integration', in L. N. Lindberg and S. A. Scheingold (eds.), *Regional Integration: theory and research*, Cambridge, Mass., Harvard University Press.

Inglehart, R. (1971), 'Changing value priorities and European integration', *Journal of Common Market Studies*, 10, 1–36.

Inglehart, R. (1977), *The Silent Revolution: changing values and political styles among western publics*, Princeton, N.J., Princeton University Press.

Inglehart, R. (1984), *Continuity and Change in Attitudes of the European Community Publics, 1970–1984*, Research Report prepared for the Commission of the European Communities.

Inglehart, R., and Rabier, J.-R. (1978), 'Economic uncertainty and European solidarity: public opinion trends' *Annals of the American Academy of Political and Social Science*, **440**, 66–87.

Inglehart, R., and Rabier, J.-R. (1980), 'Europe elects a parliament: cognitive mobilization, political mobilization, and pro-European attitudes as influences on voter turn-out' in L. Hurwitz (ed.), *Contemporary Perspectives on European Integration*, London, Aldwych Press.

Inglehart, R., and Rabier, J.-R. (1982), *Trust between Nations: primordial ties, societal learning and economic development*, Paper presented at the XIIth World Congress of Political Science (Rio de Janeiro, August 1982).

Inglehart, R., Rabier, J.-R., Gordon, I., and Sørensen, C. L. (1980), 'Broader powers for the European parliament? The attitudes of candidates', *European Journal of Political Research*, **8**, 113–32.

Inkeles, A., and Levinson, D. J. (1969), 'National character: the study of modal personality and sociocultural systems', in G. Lindzey and E. Aronson (eds.), *The Handbook of Social Psychology* (Vol. 4), Reading, Mass., Addison-Wesley.

Insko, C. A. (1967), *Theories of Attitude Change*, New York, Appleton-Century-Crofts.

Insko, C., Blake, R. R., Cialdini, R. B. and Mulaik, S. A. (1970), 'Attitude toward birth control and cognitive consistency: theoretical and practical implications of survey data', *Journal of Personality and Social Psychology*, **16**, 228–37.

Insko, C. A., Nacoste, R. W., and Moe, J. L. (1983), 'Belief congruence and racial discrimination: review of the evidence and critical evaluation', *European Journal of Social Psychology*, **13**, 153–74.

Jaccard, J. (1981), 'Attitudes and behaviour: implications of attitudes toward behavioural alternatives', *Journal of Experimental Social Psychology*, **17**, 286–307.

Jaccard, J. and Davidson, A. R. (1972), 'Toward an understanding of family planning behaviors: an initial investigation', *Journal of Applied Social Psychology*, **2**, 228–35.

Jahoda, G. (1963a), 'The development of children's ideas about country and nationality. I. The conceptual framework'. *British Journal of Educational Psychology*, **33**, 47–60.

Jahoda, G. (1963b), 'The development of children's ideas about country and nationality. II. The National symbols and themes', *British Journal of Educational Psychology*, **33**, 142–53.

Jameson, C. (1981), 'Who needs polls?' *New Statesman*, **101**, 13–15.

Jaspars, J. M. F. (1973), 'The case against attitudes'. Opening Address, Annual Conference of the Social Psychology Section of the British Psychological Society, Bristol, 21–23 September.

Jaspars, J. (1978), 'The nature and measurement of attitudes', in H. Tajfel and C. Fraser (eds.), *Introducing social psychology*, Harmondsworth, Penguin.

Jaspars, J. and Fraser, C. (1984), 'Attitudes and social representations', in R. M. Farr and S. Moscovici (eds.), *Social Representations*, Cambridge/Paris, Cambridge University Press, Maison des Sciences de l'Homme.

Jenkins, R. (1977), *Programme of the Commission of the European Community for 1977*. (Address by Mr. Roy Jenkins, President of the Commission, to the European Parliament). Luxembourg: Office of Official Publications of the EEC.

Jennings, M. K. and Niemi, R. G. (1968), 'The transmission of political values from parent to child', *American Political Science Review*, 62, 169–84.

Jennrich, R. and Sampson, P. (1981), 'Stepwise discriminant analysis', in W. J. Dixon (ed.), *BMDP Statistical Software*, Berkeley, University of California Press.

Jervis, R. (1970), *The Logic of Images in International Relations*. Princeton, N.J., Princeton University Press.

Jodelet, D. (1984), 'Représentation sociale: phénomènes, concept et théorie', in S. Moscovici (ed.), *Psychologie sociale*, Paris, Presses Universitaires de France.

Johnson, N. B., Middleton, M. R. and Tajfel, H. (1970), 'The relationship, between children's preferences for and knowledge about other nations', *British Journal of Social and Clinical Psychology*, 9, 232–40.

Jonas, K. and Hewstone, M. (in press), 'Assessment of national stereotypes: a methodological study', *Journal of Social Psychology*.

Jones, E. E. and Gerard, H. B. (1967), *Foundations of Social Psychology*, New York, Wiley.

Jöreskog, K. and Sörbom, D. (1981), *Lisrel – V.: Analysis of linear structural relationships by maximum likelihood and least squares methods*, Uppsala, Department of Statistics, University of Uppsala.

Journal of Common Market Studies (1963), 'Public opinion and the European Community', 2, 101–26.

Journal of Common Market Studies (1968), 'British attitudes to the EEC', 5, 49–62.

Jowell, R. and Hoinville, G. (eds.) (1976a), *Britain into Europe*, London: Croom Helm.

Jowell, R. and Hoinville, G. (1976b), 'An unconscionable time deciding', in R. Jowell and G. Hoinville (eds.), *Britain into Europe*, London, Croom Helm.

Kaiser, K., Merlini, C., Montbrial, T. de, Wellenstein, E. and Wallace, W. (1983), *The European Community – progress or decline?* London, Royal Institute of International Affairs.

Kaplan, K. J. (1972), 'On the ambivalence–indifference problem in attitude theory and measurement: a suggested modification of the semantic differential technique', *Psychological Bulletin*, 77, 361–72.

Kaplan, K. J. and Fishbein, M. (1969), 'The source of beliefs, their saliency, and prediction of attitude'. *Journal of Social Psychology*, 78, 63–74.

Karlins, M., Coffman, T. L. and Walters, G. (1969), 'On the fading of social stereotypes: Studies in three generations of college students', *Journal of Personality and Social Psychology*, 13, 1–16.

Katona, G. (1975), *Psychological economics*, New York, Elsevier.

Katz, D. (1960), 'The functional approach to the study of attitude'. *Public Opinion Quarterly*, 24, 163–204.

Katz, D. and Braly, K. (1933), 'Racial stereotypes of one hundred college students', *Journal of Abnormal and Social Psychology*, 28, 280–90.

Katz, D. and Stotland, E. (1959), 'A preliminary statement of a theory of attitude structure and change', in S. Koch (ed.), *Psychology: study of a science* (Vol. 3), New York, McGraw-Hill.

Kelley, S. and Mirer, T. W. (1974), 'The simple act of voting', *American Political Science Review*, 68, 572–91.

Kelman, H. C. (1965*a*), 'Social psychological approaches to the study of international relations: definition of scope', in H. C. Kelman (ed.), *International Behavior: a social-psychological analysis*, New York, Holt, Rinehart and Winston.

Kelman, H. C. (ed.) (1965*b*), *International behavior: a social psychological analysis*, New York, Holt, Rinehart & Winston.

Kelman, H. C. (1965*c*), 'Social psychological approaches to the study of international relations: the question of relevance', in H. C. Kelman (ed.), *International Behavior: a social psychological analysis*, New York, Holt, Rinehart and Winston.

Kelman, H. C. (1974), 'Attitudes are alive and well and gainfully employed in the sphere of action', *American Psychologist*, **29**, 310–24.

Kerlinger, F. N. (1973), *Foundations of Behavioral Research*, New York, Holt, Rinehart and Winston.

Kerlinger, F. N. (1984), *Liberalism and Conservatism: the nature and structure of social attitudes*, Hillsdale, N. J., Erlbaum.

Kerlinger, F. N. and Pedhazur, E. J. (1973), *Multiple Regression in Behavioral Research*, New York, Holt, Rinehart and Winston.

Key, V. O. (1961), *Public Opinion and American Democracy*, New York, Knopf.

Kiesler, C. A., Collins, R. E. and Miller, N. (1969), *Attitude Change*, New York, Wiley.

Kim, J.-O. and Kohout, F. J. (1975), 'Multiple regression analysis: Subprogram regression', in N. H. Nie, C. H. Hull, J. G. Jenkins, K. Steinbrenner and D. H. Bent, *SPSS Statistical Package for the Social Sciences*, New York, McGraw Hill (2nd edn).

Kim, J.-O. and Mueller, C. W. (1978*a*), *Introduction to Factor Analysis*, Beverly Hills, Sage.

Kim, J.-O. and Mueller, C. W. (1978*b*), *Factor Analysis* Beverly Hills, Sage.

King, A. (1977), *Britain says Yes*, Washington, American Enterprise Institute.

Kitzinger, U. (1962), *The Challenge of the Common Market*, Oxford, Basil Blackwell.

Kitzinger, U. (1973), *Diplomacy and Persuasion: how Britain joined the Common Market*, London, Thames and Hudson.

Klapper, J. T. (1960), *The effects of Mass Communication*, Glencoe, Ill., Free Press.

Klapper, J. T. (1963), 'The social effects of mass communication' in W. Schramm (ed.), *The science of Human Communication*. New York, Basic Books.

Klecka, W. R. (1980), *Discriminant analysis*, Beverly Hills, Sage.

Klineberg, O. (1964), *The Human Dimension in International Relations*, New York, Holt, Rinehart and Winston.

Knitzer, H. (1978), 'Ideology and American political elites', *Public Opinion Quarterly*, **42**, 484–502.

Kohler, B. (1984), 'The parlementarians and their electorate', in R. Hrbek, J. Jamar and W. Wessels (eds.), *The European Parliament on the Eve of the Second Direct Election: balance sheet and prospects*, Bruges, De Tempel.

Kohn, H. (1957), 'Nationalism and the integration of Europe', in C. G. Haines (ed.), *European Integration*, Baltimore, Md., Johns Hopkins Press.

Kothandapani, V. (1971), 'Validation of feeling, belief and intention to act as three components of attitude and their contribution to prediction of contraceptive behavior', *Journal of Personality and Social Psychology*, **19**, 321–33.

Krech, D., Crutchfield, R. S. and Ballachey, E. L. (1962), *Individual in Society*, New York, McGraw-Hill.

Kriesberg, M. (1949), 'Dark areas of ignorance', in L. Markel (ed.), *Public Opinion and Foreign Policy*, New York, Harper and Bros.

Lakoff, G. and Johnson, M. (1980), *Metaphors we live by*, Chicago, University of Chicago Press.

Lambert, W. E. and Klineberg, O. (1967), *Children's Views of Foreign Peoples*, New York, Appleton-Century-Crofts.

Land, K. C. (1969), 'Principles of path analysis', in E. Borgatta (ed.), *Sociological Methodology*, San Francisco, Jossey-Bass.

Lane, R. E. (1959), *Political life: why people get involved in politics*, Glencoe, Ill., Free Press.

Lane, R. E. (1962), *Political Ideology: why the American common man believes what he does*, New York, Free Press.

Lane, R. E. and Sears, D. O. (1964), *Public Opinion*, Englewood Cliffs, N.J., Prentice-Hall.

Lang, K. and Lang, G. E. (1959), 'The mass media and voting', in E. Burdick and A. J. Brodbeck (eds.), *American Voting Behavior*, Glencoe, Ill., Free Press.

Lazarsfeld, P. F., Berelson, B. and Gaudet, H. (1948), *The People's Choice*, New York, Columbia University Press (2nd edn).

Lerner, D. (1958), *The Passing of Traditional Society: modernizing the Middle East*, New York, Free Press.

Lewin, K. (1938), *The Conceptual Representation and the Measurement of Psychological Forces*, Durham, NC, Duke University Press.

Leyens, J.-P. (1982), *Sommes-nous tous des psychologues?* Brussels, Mardaga.

Lichtenstein, S., Fischhoff, B. and Phillips, L. D. (1977), 'Calibration of probabilities: the state of the art', in H. Jungermann and G. de Zeeuw (eds.) *Decision-making and Change in Human Affairs*, Dordrecht, D. Reidel.

Lieber, R. J. (1970), *British Politics and European Unity; parties, elites, and pressure groups*, Berkeley, Calif., University of California Press.

Lindberg, L. N. (1963), *The Political Dynamics of European Economic Integration*, Stanford, Stanford University Press.

Lindberg, L. N. (1966–67), 'The European Community as a political system', *Journal of Common Market Studies*, 5, 344–87.

Lindberg, L. N. and Scheingold, S. A. (1970), *Europe's Would-be Polity*, New Jersey, Prentice-Hall.

Lindberg, L. N. and Scheingold, S. A. (eds.) (1971), *Regional Integration: theory and research*, Cambridge, Mass., Harvard University Press.

Lippmann, W. (1922), *Public Opinion*, New York, Macmillan.

Lipset, S. M. (1963), *Political Man*, New York, Anchor Books.

Lipsey, D. (1979), 'The reforms people want', *New Society*, 50, 12–14.

Liska, G. (1964), *Europe Ascendant: the international politics of unification*, Baltimore, Md., Johns Hopkins Press.

Lodge, J. (1978), 'Loyalty and the EEC: the limitations of the functionalist approach', *Political Studies*, 26, 232–48.

Lodge, J. and Herman, V. (1980), 'Direct elections to the European Parliament', *European Journal of Political Research*, 8, 45–62.

Lord, F. M. and Novick, M. R. (1968), *Statistical Theories of Mental Test Scores*, Reading, Mass., Addison-Wesley.

Lukes, S. (1975), *Emile Durkheim: his life and work: a historical and critical study*, Harmondsworth, Penguin.

Luttbeg, N. (1968), 'The structure of beliefs among leaders and the public', *Public Opinion Quarterly*, 32, 398–409.

Lutz, R. J. (1975), 'Changing brand attitudes through modification of cognitive structure', *Journal of Consumer Research*, 1, 49–59.

Lutz, R. J. (1977), 'An experimental investigation of causal relations among cognitions, affect, and behavioural intention, *Journal of Consumer Research*, 3, 197–208.

MacCorquordale, K. and Meehl, P. E. (1948), 'On a distinction between hypothetical construct and intervening variable', *Psychological Review*, 55, 95–107.

MacDonald, K. I. (1977), 'Path analysis', in C. A. O'Muircheartaigh and C. Payne (eds.), *The analysis of Survey Data (vol. 2): model fitting*, London, J. Wiley.

Macfarlane, L. J. (1981), *Issues in British Politics since 1945*, London, Longman (second edn).

Machiavelli, N. (1514/1961), *The Prince*, Harmondsworth, Penguin (1961 edn).

Madariaga, S. (1960), *Sciences humaines et intégration européenne*, Leiden, A. W. Sythoff.

Manaster, G. J. & Havighurst, R. J. (1972), *Cross-national research: social psychological methods and problems*, Boston, Houghton Mifflin.

Mandler, G. (1967), 'Verbal learning', in T. M. Newcomb (ed.), *New Directions in Psychology* (vol. 3), New York, Holt.

Maslow, A. H. (1954), *Motivation and Personality*, New York, Harper.

Mathew, D. D. (1980), *Europeanism: a study of public opinion and attitudinal integration in the European Community*, Ottawa, The Norman Patterson School of International Affairs, Carleton University.

McCauley, C. and Stitt, C. L. (1978), 'An individual and quantitative measure of stereotypes, *Journal of Personality and Social Psychology*, 36, 929–40.

McCauley, C., Stitt, C. L. and Segal, M. (1980), 'Stereotyping: from prejudice to prediction,' *Psychological Bulletin*, 87, 195–208.

McClintock, C. G., Kramer, R. M., and Keil, L. J. (1984), 'Equity and social exchange in human relationships,' in L. Berkowitz (ed.), *Advances in Experimental Social Psychology* (vol. 17), New York, Academic Press.

McGuire, W. J. (1960), 'A syllogistic analysis of cognitive relationships', in C. I. Hovland and M. J. Rosenberg (eds.), *Attitude Organization and Change*, New Haven, Conn., Yale University Press.

McGuire, W. J. (1969), 'The nature of attitudes and attitude change', in G. Lindsey and E. Aronson (eds.), *The Handbook of Social Psychology*, Reading, Mass., Addison-Wesley.

McGuire, W. J. (1976), 'The concept of attitudes and their relations to behaviors', in H. W. Sinaiko and L. A. Broedling (eds.), *Perspectives on Attitude Assessment: surveys and their alternatives*, Champaign, Ill, Pendleton.

Merritt, R. L. (1967), 'Interviewing French and West German elites', in K. W. Deutsch, L. J. Edinger, R. C. Macridis, and R. L. Merritt', *France, Germany and the Western Alliance*, New York, Scribner.

Merritt, R. L. (1968), 'The USIA surveys: tools for policy and analysis', in R. L. Merritt and D. J. Puchala (eds.), *Western European Perspectives on International Affairs*, New York, Praeger.

Merritt, R. L. and Puchala, D. J. (eds.) (1968), *Western European Perspectives on International Affairs*, New York, Praeger.

Miller, G. A. (1956), 'The magical number seven: plus or minus two: some limits on our capacity for processing information', *Psychological Review*, 63, 81–97.

Miniard, P. W. and Cohen, H. B. (1981), 'An examination of the Fishbein–Ajzen behavioural-intentions model's concepts and measures', *Journal of Experimental Social Psychology*, 17, 309–39.

Mitchell, A. and Olson, J. (1981), 'Are product attribute beliefs the only mediator of advertising effects on brand attitude?' *Journal of Marketing Research*, 18, 318–32.

Mitchell, T. R. (1974), 'Expectancy models of job satisfaction, occupational preference and effort: a theoretical, methodological, and empirical appraisal', *Psychological Bulletin*, 81, 1053–77.

Mitchell, T. R. and Biglan, A. (1971), 'Instrumentality theories: current uses in psychology', *Psychological Bulletin*, 76, 432–54.

Mitrany, D. (1966). *A Working Peace System*, Chicago, Quadrangle Books.

Moscovici, S. (1961), *La psychanalyse, son image et son public*, Paris, Presses Universitaires de France (2nd edn, 1976).

Moscovici, S. (1973), Preface to C. Herzlich, *Health and illness: a social psychological analysis*, London, Academic Press.

Moscovici, S. (1981), 'On social representations', in J. P. Forgas (ed.), *Social Cognition: perspectives on everyday understanding*, London, Academic Press.

Moscovici, S. (1984), 'The phenomenon of social representations', in R. M. Farr and S. Moscovici (eds.) *Social Representations*, Cambridge/Paris, Cambridge University Press, Maison des Sciences de l'Homme.

Moscovici, S. (1985), 'Comment on Potter and Litton', *British Journal of Social Psychology*, 24, 91–2.

Moscovici, S. and Hewstone, M. (1983), 'Social representations and social explanations: from the "naive" to the "amateur" scientist', in M. Hewstone (ed.), *Attribution Theory: social and functional extensions*, Oxford, Basil Blackwell.

Newcomb, T. M. and Charters, W. W. (1950), *Social Psychology*, New York, Dryden Press.

Nisbett, R. and Ross, L. (1980), *Human Inference. Strategies and shortcomings of social judgment*, Englewood Cliffs, N.J., Prentice-Hall.

Noelle-Neumann, E. (1970), 'Wanted: rules for wording structured questionnaires', *Public Opinion Quarterly*, 34, 191–201.

Noelle-Neumann, E. (1980), 'Phantom Europe: thirty years of survey research on German attitudes toward European integration', in L. Hurwitz (ed.), *Contemporary Perspectives on European Integration*, Westport, Conn., Greenwood Press.

Norman, R. (1975), 'Affective-cognitive consistency, attitudes, conformity, and behavior', *Journal of Personality and Social Psychology*, 32, 83–91.

Nye, J. S. (1971), *Peace in Parts*, Boston, Little, Brown and Co.

Osgood, C. E., Suci, G. J., and Tannenbaum, P. H. (1957), *The measurement of Meaning*, Urbana, Ill., University of Illinois Press.

Osgood, C. E. and Tannenbaum, P. H. (1955), 'The principle of congruity in the prediction of attitude change', *Psychological Review*, 62, 42–55.

Oskamp, S. (1977), *Attitudes and opinions*, Englewood Cliffs, N.J., Prentice Hall.

Ostrom, T. M. (1968), 'The emergence of attitude theory: 1930–1950', in A. G. Greenwald, T. C. Brock, and T. M. Ostrom (eds.), *Psychological foundations of attitudes*, New York, Academic Press.

Pagel, M. D. and Davidson, A. R. (1984), 'A comparison of three social-psychological models of attitude and behavioural plan: prediction of contraceptive behavior', *Journal of Personality and Social Psychology*, 47, 517–33.

Palmerino, M., Langer, E. and McGillis, D. (1983), 'Attitudes and attitude change: mindlessness – mindfulness perspective', in J. R. Eiser (ed.), *Attitudinal Judgment*, New York, Springer.

Peak, H. (1955), 'Attitude and motivation', in M. R. Jones (ed.), *Nebraska Symposium on Motivation* (vol. 3), Lincoln, Neb., University of Nebraska Press.

Pentland, C. (1973), *International theory and European integration*, London, Faber and Faber.

Perry, R. W., Gillespie, D. F. & Lotz, R. E. (1976), 'Attitudinal variables as estimates of behaviour: a theoretical examination of the attitude – action controversy', *European Journal of Social Psychology*, 6, 227–43.

Phillips, J. L. (1967), 'A model for cognitive balance', *Psychological Review*, 74, 481–95.

Piaget, J. (1961), *le Développement chez l'enfant de l'idée de patrie et de relations avec l'étranger*, Bulletin Internationale de Science Sociale, UNESCO.

Pierce, J. C. and Rose, D. D. (1974a), 'Nonattitudes and American public opinion: the examination of a thesis', *American Political Science Review*, 68, 626–49.

Pierce, J. C. and Rose, D. D. (1974b), 'Rejoinder to "Comment" by Philip E. Converse', *American Political Science Review*, 68, 661–6.

Pomazol, R. J. (1983), 'Salient beliefs and attitude change over time: an experimental approach', *Representative Research in Social Psychology*, 13, 11–22.

Potter, J. and Litton, J. (1985), 'Some problems underlying the theory of social representations', *British Journal of Social Psychology*, 24, 81–90.

Prag, D. (1967), 'The treaty of Rome', in J. Calman (ed.), *The Common Market: the Treaty of Rome explained*, London, Anthony Blond.

Puchala, D. J. (1970), 'The Common Market and political federation in Western European public opinion', *International Studies Quarterly*, 14, 32–59.

Puchala, D. (1972), 'Of blind men, elephants and international integration', *Journal of Common Market Studies*, 10, 267–84.

Putnam, R. (1983), 'Comment', in L. Tsoukalis (ed.), *The European Community: past, present and future*, Oxford, Basil Blackwell.

Quinton, A. (1977), 'Common sense'. *Fontana Dictionary of Modern Thought* London, Fontana/Collins.

Rabier, J.-R. (1966), *L'opinion publique et l'Europe: Essai d'inventaire des connaissances et des lacunes*, Brussels, Institut de Sociologie de l'Université Libre de Bruxelles.

Rabier, J.-R. (1972), 'Europeans and the unification of Europe', in G. Ionescu (ed.), *The New Politics of European Integration*, London, Macmillan.

Rabier, J.-R. (1985), *Ou sont donc les citoyens de l'Europe? votants et abstentionnistes lors de l'élection de juin 1984*, Paper presented at the Workshop on the 1984 Direct Elections to the Euro-Parliament, European Consortium for Political Research, Barcelona, 25–30 March.

Rabier, J.-R. (in press), 'Les paradoxes d'un scrutin: Les citoyens de dix pays élisent le parlement européenne', *Révue d'Intégration européenne*.

Reif, K. and Schmitt, H. (1980), 'Nine second-order elections – a conceptual framework for the analysis of European election results', *European Journal of Political Research*, **8**, 3–44.

Renouvin, P. (1949), *L'idée de fédération européenne dans la pensée politique du XIXe siecle*, Oxford, Clarendon Press.

Riffault, H., and Tchernia, J.-F. (1983), *Enquête-pilote: Parlement européen*. Paris Faits et Opinions.

Robertson, A. H. (1959), *European Institutions*, London, Stevens and Sons.

Rogers, W. C., Stuhler, B., and Koenig, D. (1967), 'A comparison of informed and general public opinion of U.S. foreign policy', *Public Opinion Quarterly*, **31**, 242–52.

Roiser, M. (1983), 'The uses and abuses of polls: a social psychologist's view'. *Bulletin of the British Psychological Society*, **36**, 159–61.

Rokkan, S. (ed.) (1960), 'Citizen participation in political life', *International Social Science Journal*, **12**, (Special Issue), 7–99.

Rosenau, J. N. (1961), *Public Opinion and Foreign Policy*, New York, Random House.

Rosenberg, M. J. (1956), 'Cognitive structure and attitudinal affect', *Journal of Abnormal and Social Psychology*, **53**, 367–72.

Rosenberg, M. J. (1960), 'An analysis of affective cognitive consistency', in C. I. Hovland and M. J. Rosenberg (eds.), *Attitude Organization and Change*, New Haven, Yale University Press.

Rosenberg, M. J. (1967), 'Attitude change and foreign policy in the cold war era', in J. N. Rosenau (ed.), *Domestic Sources of Foreign Policy*, New York, Free Press.

Rosenberg, M. J. (1968), 'Hedonism, inauthenticity, and other goads toward expansion of a consistency theory', in R. P. Abelson *et al.* (eds.), *Theories of Cognitive Consistency: a sourcebook*, Chicago, McNally.

Rosenberg, M. J., and Abelson, R. P. (1960), 'An analysis of cognitive balancing', in M. J. Rosenberg *et al.*, *Attitude Organization and Change: an analysis of consistency among attitude components*, New Haven, Conn., Yale University Press.

Rosenberg, M. J., and Hovland, C. I. (1960), 'Cognitive, affective, and behavioral components of attitudes' in C. I. Hovland and M. J. Rosenberg (eds.), *Attitude Organization and Change*, New Haven, Conn., Yale University Press.

Rotter, J. B. (1954), *Social Learning and Clinical Psychology*, Englewood Cliffs, N.J., Prentice-Hall.

Rutherford, M. (1981), *Can we save the Common Market?*, Oxford, Basil Blackwell.

Säarlvik, B., Crewe, I., Alt, J. and Fox, A. (1976), 'Britain's membership in the EEC', *European Journal of Political Research*, **4**, 83–113.

Sampson, A. (1968), *The New Europeans*, London, Hodder and Stoughton.

Schmidt, F. L. (1973), 'Implications of a measurement problem for expectancy theory research', *Organizational Behavior and Human Performance*, **10**, 243–51.

Schönbach, P., Gollwitzer, P., Stiepel, G. and Wagner, U. (1981), *Education and Intergroup Attitudes*, London, Academic Press.

Schuman, H., and Johnson, M. P. (1976), 'Attitudes and behavior', *Annual Review of Sociology*, **2**, 161–207.

Schuman, R. (1976), cited in *The Economist*, 3 April 1976.

Scott, W. A. (1968), 'Attitude measurement', in G. Lindzey and E. Aronson (eds.), *The Handbook of Social Psychology* (2nd edn) (Vol. 2), Reading, Mass., Addison-Wesley.

Seago, D. W. (1947), 'Stereotypes: before Pearl Harbor and after', *Journal of Psychology*, 23, 55–63.

Sears, D. O. (1969), 'Political behavior', in G. Lindzey and E. Aronson (eds.), *The Handbook of Social Psychology*, Reading, Mass., Addison-Wesley.

Sechrest, L., and Yeaton, W. E. (1982), 'Magnitudes of Experimental effects in social science research', *Evaluation Research*, 6, 579–600.

Semin, G. R. (1985), 'The "phenomenon of social representations": a comment on Potter and Litton', *British Journal of Social Psychology*, 24, 93–5.

Seymour-Ure, C. (1976), 'Press' in D. Butler and U. Kitzinger (eds.), *The 1975 Referendum*, London, St. Martin's Press.

Shaw, M. E., and Wright, J. M. (1967), *Scales for the Measurement of Attitudes*, New York, McGraw-Hill.

Shepherd, R. (1975), *Public Opinion and European Integration*, Westmead, Saxon House.

Sinha, A. K. P., and Uphadyay, O. P. (1960), 'Change and persistence in the stereotypes of university students toward different ethnic groups during Sino-Indian border dispute', *Journal of Social Psychology*, 52, 31–9.

Slater, M. (1983), 'Political elites, popular indifference and Community building', in L. Tsoukalis (ed.), *The European Community: past, present and future*, Oxford, Basil Blackwell.

Smetana, J. G., and Adler, N. E. (1981), 'Fishbein's value and expectancy model: an examination of some assumptions', *Personality and Social Psychology Bulletin*, 6, 89–96.

Smith, A. J., and Clark, R. D. (1973), 'The relationship between attitudes and beliefs', *Journal of Personality and Social Psychology*, 26, 321–6.

Smith, M. B. (1947), 'The personal setting of public opinions: a study of attitudes toward Russia', *Public Opinion Quarterly*, 11, 507–23.

Smith, M. B. (1949), 'Personal values as determinants of a political attitude', *Journal of Psychology*, 28, 477–86.

Smith, M. B., Bruner, J. S., and White, R. W. (1956), *Opinions and Personality*, New York, Wiley.

Six, B. (1980), 'Das Konzept der Einstellung und seine Relevanz für die Vorhersage des Verhaltens', in F. Petermann (ed.), *Einstellungsmessung-Einstellungsforschung*, Göttingen, Hogrefe.

Slovic, P. (1974), 'Hypothesis testing in the learning of positive and negative linear functions', *Organizational Behavior and Human Performance*, 11, 368–76.

Spence, J. (1976), 'Movements in the public mood: 1961–75', in R. Jowell and G. Hoinville (eds.), *Britain into Europe*, London, Croom Helm.

Spinelli, A. (1957), 'The growth of the European Movement since World War II', in C. G. Haines (ed.), *European Integration*, Baltimore, Md., Johns Hopkins Press.

Spinelli, A. (1966), *The Eurocrats*, Baltimore, Md., Johns Hopkins Press.

Stapf, K.-H. (1982), 'Einstellungsmessung und Verhaltensprognose. Kritische Eröterung einer aktuellen sozial-wissenschaftlichen Thematik', in H. Stachowiak,

T. Ellwein, T. Herrmann and K. Stapf (eds.), *Bedürfnisse, Werte und Normen im Wandel. Band II: Methoden und Analysen*, München, Fink.

Stapf, K.-H., Stroebe, W. and Jonas, K. (1984), *Das Deutschlandbild Amerikanischer Studenten: Eine empirische Studie*, Berichte aus dem psychologischen Institut der Universität Tübingen, Nr. 15.

Stephan, W. G., and Stephan, C. W. (1984), 'The role of ignorance in intergroup relations', in N. Miller and M. B. Brewer (eds.), *Groups in Contact: the psychology of desegregation*, New York, Academic Press.

Stevens, S. S. (1946), 'On the theory of scales of measurement', *Science*, 103, 677–80.

Stevens, S. S. (1959), 'Measurement, psychophysics and utility', in C. W. Churchman and P. Ratoosh (eds.), *Measurement: definitions and theories*, New York, Wiley.

Stoetzel, J. (1957), 'The evolution of French opinion', in D. Lerner and R. Aron (eds.), *France Defeats EDC*, New York, Praeger.

Strack, F., and Rehm, J. (1984), 'Theorie testen oder Varianz aufklären? Uberlegungen zur Verwendung der Effektgrösse als Gütemass für experimentelle Forschung', *Zeitschrift für Sozialpsychologie*, 15, 81–5.

Streufert, S., and Streufert, S. C. (1978), *Behavior in the Complex Environment*, New York, Winston.

Sumner, G. A. (1906), *Folkways*, New York, Ginn.

Sundstrom, E., De Vault, R., and Peele, E. (1981), 'Acceptance of a nuclear power plant: applications of the expectancy-value model', in A. Baum and J. E. Singer (eds.), *Advances in Environmental Psychology* (Vol. 3), Hillsdale, N.J., Erlbaum.

Swann, D. (1981), *The Economics of the Common Market*, Harmondsworth, Penguin (4th edn.).

Tajfel, H. (1974), 'Social identity and intergroup behaviour', *Social Science Information*, 13, 65–93.

Tajfel, H. (ed.) (1978), *Differentiation between Social Groups*, London, Academic Press.

Tajfel, H. (1981), 'Social stereotypes and social groups', in J. C. Turner and H. Giles (eds.), *Intergroup Behaviour*, Oxford, Basil Blackwell.

Taylor, P. (1972), 'The concept of Community and European integration process', in M. Hodges (ed.), *European Integration*, Harmondsworth, Penguin.

Thomas, W. I., and Znaniecki, F. (1918), *The Polish Peasant in Europe and America* (Vol. 1), Boston, Badger.

Thurstone, L. L. (1931), 'The measurement of attitudes', *Journal of Abnormal and Social Psychology*, 26, 249–69.

Thurstone, L. L. (1946), 'Comment', *American Journal of Sociology*, 52, 39–40.

Thurstone, L. L. (1947), *Multiple-factor Analysis*, Chicago, University of Chicago Press.

Titchenor, P. J., Donohue, G. A., and Olien, C. N. (1970), 'Mass media flow and differential growth in knowledge', *Public Opinion Quarterly*, 34, 159–70.

Tolman, E. C. (1958), *Behavior and Psychological Man: essays in motivation and learning*, Berkeley, Cal., University of California Press.

Triandis, H. C., and Vassiliou, V. (1967), 'Frequency of contact and stereotyping', *Journal of Personality and Social Psychology*, 7, 316–28.

Tsoukalis, L. (1983), 'Looking into the crystal ball', in L. Tsoukalis (ed.), *The European Community: past, present and future*, Oxford, Basil Blackwell.

van der Pligt, J., and Eiser, J. R. (1983), 'Dimensional salience, judgment, and attitudes', in J. R. Eiser (ed.), *Attitudinal Judgment*, New York, Springer Verlag.

van Zeeland, P. (1957), 'Preface', in C. G. Haines (ed.), *European Integration*, Baltimore, Md., Johns Hopkins Press.

Vinacke, W. E. (1949), 'Stereotyping among national-racial groups in Hawaii: a study in ethnocentrism', *Journal of Social Psychology*, 30, 265–91.

Wahba, M. A., and House, R. J. (1974), 'Expectancy theory in work and motivation: some logical and methodological issues', *Human Relations*, 27, 121–47.

Walster, E., Berscheid, E., and Walster, G. W. (1976), 'New directions in equity research', in L. Berkowitz and E. Walster (ed.), *Advances in Experimental Social Psychology (Vol. 9). Equity theory: toward a general theory of social interaction*, New York, Academic Press.

Wegner, D. M., and Vallacher, R. R. (1981), 'Common-sense psychology', in J. P. Forgas (ed.), *Social Cognition: perspectives on everyday understanding*, London, Academic Press.

Weigel, R. H., and Newman, L. S. (1976), 'Increasing attitude–behavior correspondence by broadening the scope of the behavioral measure', *Journal of Personality and Social Psychology*, 33, 793–802.

Wicker, A. (1969), 'Attitudes versus action: the relationship of verbal and overt behavioral responses to attitude objects', *Journal of Social Issues*, 25, 41–78.

Wicker, A. (1971), 'An examination of the "other variables" explanation of attitude–behavior inconsistency', *Journal of Personality and Social Psychology*, 19, 18–30.

Wildgen, J., and Feld, W. (1976), 'Communist publics and activists: Some implications for European integration', *Journal of Common Market Studies*, 15, 77–92.

Wilker, H. R., and Milbrath, L. W. (1970), 'Political belief systems and political behavior', *Social Science Quarterly*, 51, 477–93.

Willis, F. R. (1965), *France, Germany and the New Europe, 1945–63*, Stanford, Stanford University Press.

Wober, J. M. (1981), 'British attitudes towards Europe: an exploration of their inner structure', *British Journal of Social Psychology*, 20, 181–8.

Wober, J. M. (1984), *Voting in Europe: television and viewers' involvement in the 1984 European Parliamentary Election*, Independent Broadcasting Authority, Working Paper, November.

Woodruff, A. D., and Di Vesta, F. (1984), 'The relation between values, concepts and attitudes', *Educational and Psychological Measurement*, 8, 645–59.

Wray, J. (1979), 'Comment on interpretations of early research into belief systems', *Journal of Politics*, 41, 1173–81.

Wundt, W. (1917–26), *Völkerpsychologie* (10 vols.), Leipzig, Kröner.

Wyer, R. S. (1970), 'The prediction of evaluations of social role occupants as a function of the favourableness, relevance and probability associated with attributes of these occupants', *Sociometry*, 33, 79–96.

Zajonc, R. B. (1960), 'The process of cognitive tuning in communication', *Journal of Abnormal and Social Psychology*, 61, 159–67.

Zajonc, R. B., and Burnstein, E. (1965), 'The learning of balanced and unbalanced social structures', *Journal of Personality*, 33, 153–63.

Zawadski, B. (1948), 'Limitations of the scapegoat theory of prejudice', *Journal of Abnormal and Social Psychology*, 43, 127–41.

Subject index

Anglo-French relations, *see* Franco-British relations attitude
ambivalence, 73–4, 92, 124, 154
and behaviour, 59, 214–19
change, 60–2, 64, 74, 87, 203, 209–13
cognitive consistency theories, 61, 62–5, 68, 69
content, *see* public opinion, social representations
definition, 58–60
development of, 204–5
expectancy-value theory, 40, 58, 61, 65, 67–77, 86, 90, 117–24, 150–4, 168–9, 173, 175, 177–80, 183–4, 191, 209–13, 215, 218, 222–4
functions, 60–1, 223
measurement, 59, 71–4
multi-component view, 65–7
structure, 61–77

belief, *see* salient beliefs
bureaucracy, 99, 101–2, 108–9, 114

cognitive mobilisation, 44–6, 184–5, 213
Common Agricultural Policy (C.A.P.), 3, 7, 83, 85, 90, 97, 104–7, 108–14, 138, 146, 157–8, 173, 187–8, 193, 198, 220
common policy, perceptions of, 87, 90, 142–3, 158, 188
Common Transport Policy, 3, 107
Conservative Party, 7, 63, 149, 194
contact, 85–6, 92, 142, 157–8, 184
content-analysis, 95–6, 107, 109, 112, 196–7
credibility gap, 150–3

Dankert, Piet, 146, 158–9, 213
de Gaulle, Charles, 6, 195
discriminant analysis, 181–2, 222

economic policy, perceptions of, 86–7, 142–4
education, 15, 34, 39, 189–90, 203–5
elites, 9, 12–16, 51, 88–9
equity theory, 41, 82–4, 91, 108, 129–37,

155–6, 193, 198, 207–8, 222–4
ethnocentrism, 77–81, 86, 154–5, 199
Euro-baromètre, 22–39, 88, 148, 150, 155–7, 161, 189, 190–1, 195, 198, 202, 204–5, 209, 219, 222
European Community
as scapegoat, 106–7, 197–8
British attitudes, 28–9, 38, 160–2, 177–8, 190–8, 206, 212
budget contributions, 7, 83, 85–6, 110, 138, 157, 162, 193, 198, 207–8
confidence in, 85, 90, 91, 141, 157, 183, 185, 202, 206
French attitudes, 37, 160–1, 176–7, 190
gains–losses, *see* equity theory
interest in, 15, 34, 87, 91, 145, 179, 183–4, 189, 205–6
Italian attitudes, 37, 160–1, 176, 190
knowledge of, 15, 21–2, 34–5, 44–5, 54, 56–7, 59, 92, 102, 145–7, 158–60, 178–9, 184–5, 188, 205
Regional Fund, 83, 85, 173, 207
saliency of, 23, 34–5, 61, 73, 146, 184, 188, 206
Social Fund, 3, 83, 107
solidarity, 31–4, 85, 90, 102, 183, 185, 188, 192, 194–5, 199–202, 206
trust in, 141, 183, 185, 200, 202, 206
West German attitudes, 37–8, 160–1, 175–6, 190
European elections, *see* voting
Europeanism, 39–46
European Movement, 6, 18
European Parliament, 4, 23, 30, 35–7, 42, 159, 205, 213–14; members of, 35–6

factor analysis, 43, 164–6, 188, 222
federalism, 10
FitzGerald, Garrett, 205
Franco–British relations, 32, 101–2, 106, 195–6, 276, n.8
Franco–German relations, 3, 32, 78, 86
functionalism, 11, 33, 41–3, 85, 184, 200

Hallstein, Walter, 3, 18, 23
Heath, Edward, 112, 194

300

Author index

304   *Author index*

For EU product safety concerns, contact us at Calle de José Abascal, 56–1°, 28003 Madrid, Spain or eugpsr@cambridge.org.